COMPARATIVE POLITICS

ENVIRONMENTAL PROTEST IN WESTERN EUROPE

COMPARATIVE POLITICS

Comparative politics is a series for students and teachers of political science that deals with contemporary issues in comparative government and politics. As Comparative European Politics it has produced a series of high quality books since its foundation in 1990, but now takes on a new form and new title for the millennium—Comparative Politics. As the process of globalization proceeds, and as Europe becomes ever more enmeshed in world trends and events, so it is necessary to broaden the scope of the series. The General Editors are Max Kaase, Vice President and Dean of Humanities and Social Sciences, International University, Bremen, and
Kenneth Newton, Professor of Government,
University of Southampton. The series is published in association with the European Consortium for Political Research.

OTHER TITLES IN THIS SERIES

Environmental Protest in Western Europe

edited by

CHRISTOPHER ROOTES

OXFORD

UNIVERSITY PRESS

OXFORD

UNIVERSITY PRESS

Great Clarendon Street, Oxford OX2 6DP

Oxford University Press is a department of the University of Oxford.
It furthers the University's objective of excellence in research, scholarship,
and education by publishing worldwide in

Oxford New York

Auckland Bangkok Buenos Aires Cape Town Chennai
Dar es Salaam Delhi Hong Kong Istanbul Karachi Kolkata
Kuala Lumpur Madrid Melbourne Mexico City Mumbai Nairobi
São Paulo Shanghai Taipei Tokyo Toronto

Oxford is a registered trade mark of Oxford University Press
in the UK and in certain other countries

Published in the United States
by Oxford University Press Inc., New York

British Library Cataloguing in Publication Data

Data available

Library of Congress Cataloging in Publication Data

Data available

ISBN 0–19–925206–8

1 3 5 7 9 10 8 6 4 2

Typeset by Newgen Imaging Systems (P) Ltd., Chennai, India
Printed in Great Britain
on acid-free paper by
Biddles Ltd., King's Lynn, Norfolk

Preface

The environmental movement is perhaps the most important, and certainly the most durable, of the social and political movements that emerged during the last third of the twentieth century. Yet it has been the subject of remarkably little systematic comparative study. Especially surprising is the lack of attention to the development of environmentalism in the great laboratory of social and political experimentation that is the European Union.

The honourable exception is, of course, Russell Dalton's admirable book *The Green Rainbow* (1994), but that book was based upon interviews conducted in the mid-1980s, and it was focused upon a selection of environmental movement organizations (EMOs). As a result, it could not address the issues that arose with the dramatic expansion of such organizations in the late 1980s and early 1990s.

Believing that systematic comparative investigation of environmental movements in western Europe is overdue, we have undertaken an ambitious exploration of the several dimensions of the changing character of environmentalism in eight European countries—the Transformation of Environmental Activism (TEA) project.

There is a need to look afresh at EMOs, but an organization-centred approach would not suffice to illuminate what by the mid-1990s appeared to be the most interesting aspect of the changing character of environmentalism—the rise in several countries of radical environmental protest at best problematically related to any of the established organizations. For that reason, we began our investigation with an analysis of nationally reported environmental protest during the decade in which the transformation of the environmental movement was supposed to have been most fundamental. This book is the result. Subsequent volumes will examine EMOs, and environmental activism at the local level.

The scientific desirability of research does not guarantee that it will be carried out. A major determinant of what gets researched is what can be funded, and the general paucity of broadly comparative research in this area is largely explained by the limited opportunities for funding. We have been extremely fortunate in having obtained almost all of the considerable funds required from a single source—the European Commission. The EC Directorate General for Research (formerly DG XII—Science, Research, and Development) provided funding under the 'Human dimensions of environmental change' programme of Framework IV (EC contract number ENV4-CT97-0514—see Appendix B). Not only did they fund us, but they left us to get on with the task in the way we proposed, without interference of any kind. For that we are extremely grateful.

The EC also contributed to this research by its funding of the ERASMUS network on social movements coordinated by Bert Klandermans. That network laid the basis for collaboration in research, and it was conversations with Maria Kousis, Mario Diani, and Ron Eyerman at the ERASMUS summer school in Crete in 1996 that encouraged me to embark upon this project.

The European Consortium for Political Research (ECPR) also played an indispensable supporting role. The networks upon which this collaboration is based were mostly established and consolidated in a succession of ECPR workshops. Joint Sessions workshops in recent years (Mannheim 1999; Copenhagen 2000; and Grenoble 2001) have provided occasions for the sharing of ideas within and beyond the project.

I am grateful, too, to Taylor and Francis plc (<http://www.tandf.co.uk>) for permission to use in Chapter 1 revised versions of material that first appeared in 'The Transformation of Environmental Activism: Activists, Organisations and Policy-making', *Innovation: The European Journal of Social Sciences*, **12**(2) (1999): 153–73, and to use in Chapters 1 and 2 revised versions of material first published in 'Environmental Protest in Britain, 1988–1997', in Benjamin Seel, Matthew Paterson, and Brian Doherty (eds.), *Direct Action in British Environmentalism* (London and New York: Routledge, 2000), 25–61.

A large-scale crossnationally comparative project of this kind requires uncommon commitment and forbearance of all concerned. Misunderstandings are inevitable, but the cooperation and goodwill of the partners have been exemplary. This collaboration has been a learning process for all of us, but I could scarcely have been more fortunate in my companions. Several deserve special thanks: Dieter Rucht shared his experience of the PRODAT project and played a leading role in the design of the protest event analysis; Manuel Jiménez undertook the network analyses; and Mario Diani listened and gave wise counsel when things became tricky. This project would have been impossible without the efforts of a dedicated band of research assistants, among whom Sandy Miller and Jochen Roose deserve special acknowledgement for the support they gave to other research teams in the project.

In the end, however, my greatest debts are to those nearest and dearest to me. Angela and Zachary have tolerated with remarkable patience my absences, my preoccupation, and the invasive clutter associated with this project for far longer than I or they ever anticipated. To them I am truly, madly, deeply grateful.

CAR

Harbledown, Canterbury
March 2003

Contents

List of Figures

List of Tables

Abbreviations and Acronyms

AEDENAT	Asociación Ecologista para la Defensa de la Naturaleza
AFP	Agence France Presse
ALF	Animal Liberation Front
ANDRA	Agence Nationale pour la Gestion des Déchets Radioactifs
AT	Amis de la Terre/Amigos de la Tierra (Friends of the Earth)
BBU	Bundesverband Bürgerinitiativen Umweltschutz (Federal Alliance of Citizen Initiatives for Environmental Protection)
BUND	Bund für Umwelt und Naturschutz (Association for Environment and Nature Protection)
CAN	Climate Action Network
CDU	Christian Democratic Union (Germany)
CGIL	General Italian Labour Confederation
CISL	Italian Confederation of Labour Unions
CIWF	Compassion in World Farming
CLAC	Comité de Liaison Anti-Canal
CODA	Coordinadora de Organizacíones para la Defensa Ambíental
COGEMA	Compagnie Générale des Matières Nucléaires
DNR	Deutscher Naturschutzring (German Alliance for Nature Protection)
EC	European Commission
EDF	Electricité de France
EEB	European Environmental Bureau
EF!	Earth First!
EMO	environmental movement organization
ENGO	environmental non-governmental organization
EU	European Union
FDP	Free Democratic Party (Germany)
FEA	Federation of Ecological and Alternative Organizations (Greece)
FNE	France Nature Environnement
FoE	Friends of the Earth
FRAPNA	Fédération Rhône-Alpes de Protection de la Nature
GOS	Greek Ornithological Society
HSPN	Hellenic Society for the Protection of Nature
HSPECH	Hellenic Society for the Protection of the Environment and Cultural Heritage
LACS	League Against Cruel Sports

LIPU	Italian League for the Protection of Birds
LPO	Ligue de Protection des Oiseaux
NABU	Naturschutzbund Deutschland (Nature Protection Association Germany)
ND	New Democracy
NGO	non-governmental organization
NIMBY	Not in My Back Yard
PASOK	Pan Hellenic Socialist Party
PEA	protest event analysis
PCI	Italian Communist Party
PPC	Public Power Corporation (Greece)
RSPB	Royal Society for the Protection of Birds
SPD	Social Democratic Party Germany
UIL	Italian Labour Union
WWF	World Wide Fund for Nature

Contributors

Iñaki Barcena is a Senior Lecturer and Researcher in the Department of Political Science and Administration at the University of the Basque Country, Bilbao. His publications include *Nacionalismo y Ecologia: Conflicto e Institucionalización en el Movimiento Ecologista vasco* (with P. Ibarra and M. Zubiaga) (de la Catarata 1995); *Desarrollo Sostenible: Un Concepto Polémico* (UPV 2000); and *Bilbo nora zoaz? ¿Es Sostenible Nuestro Modelo de Ciudad?* (Bakeaz 1999).

Mario Diani is Professor of Sociology at the University of Trento, Visiting Research Professor in the Department of Government of the University of Strathclyde, and European editor of *Mobilization*. Recent publications include *Social Movements* (with D. della Porta) (Blackwell 1999) and *Social Movements and Networks* (ed. with D. McAdam) (Oxford 2003).

Olivier Fillieule is Professor of Political Sociology at the University of Lausanne and member of the Centre de Recherche sur l'Action Politique de l'Université de Lausanne (CRAPUL). His publications include *Lutter Ensemble: Les Théories de l'Action Collective* (with C. Péchu) (1993); *Sociologie de la Protestation: Les Formes Contemporaines de l'Action Collective en France* (ed. 1993); *Stratégies de la Rue: Les Manifestations en France* (1997); *Appel d'Aire: Résistance et Protestation dans les Sociétés Musulmanes* (ed. with M. Bennani-Chraïbi) (2003); and *Logiques du Désengagement* (ed.) (2003).

Francesca Forno is completing a Ph.D. on protest activities in Italy in the 1990s at the University of Strathclyde in Glasgow.

Eunate Guarrotxena is a political sociologist and was a member of the TEA project team at the University of the Basque Country.

Pedro Ibarra is a Professor in the Department of Political Science and Administration at the University of the Basque Country, Bilbao. His publications include *Nacionalismo y Ecologia: Conflicto e Institucionalización en el Movimiento Ecologista Vasco* (with Iñaki Barcena and M. Zubiaga) (1995) and *Social Movements and Democracy* (ed.) (Palgrave 2003).

Andrew Jamison is Professor of Technology and Society at Aalborg University, Denmark. His publications include *The Making of the New Environmental Consciousness* (with R. Eyerman, J. Cramer, and J. Læssoe) (Edinburgh 1990); *Social Movements: A Cognitive Approach* (with R. Eyerman) (Polity 1991); and *The Making of Green Knowledge* (Cambridge 2001).

Manuel Jiménez is a Research Fellow at the Centre for Advanced Study in the Social Sciences, Juan March Institute, Madrid, and an Assistant Professor at the University Carlos III of Madrid. His publications include 'Consolidation through institutionalisation: dilemmas of the Spanish environmental movement in the 1990s', *Environmental Politics*, **8** (1) (1999) and 'Sustainable development and the participation of environmental NGOs in Spanish environmental policy', in K. Eder and M. Kousis (eds.), *Environmental Movements, Discourses and Policies in Southern Europe* (2000).

Maria Kousis is Professor of Sociology at the University of Crete and Resource Editor of *Annals of Tourism Research*. She has edited *The Politics of Sustainable Development* (with S. Baker, D. Richardson, and S. Young) (Routledge 1997) and *Environmental Politics in Southern Europe: Actors, Institutions and Discourses in a Europeanizing Society* (with K. Eder) (Kluwer 2001). She has published articles in *Mobilization, Environmental Politics, Annals of Tourism Research, Humanity and Society*, and *Sociologia Ruralis*.

Magnus Ring is completing a Ph.D. at Lund University.

Jochen Roose is Research Fellow for Sociology of Culture at the University of Leipzig. His publications include 'The German environmental movement at a crossroads' (with D. Rucht), *Environmental Politics*, **8** (1) (1999) and 'The Environmental Movement and Environmental Concern in Contemporary Germany', in A. Goodbody (ed.), *The Culture of German Environmentalism* (Berghahn 2002).

Christopher Rootes is Reader in Political Sociology and Environmental Politics, and Director of the Centre for the Study of Social and Political Movements at the University of Kent at Canterbury, and Joint Editor of *Environmental Politics*. He has previously edited *A New Europe? Social Change and Political Transformation* (with H. Davis) (UCL 1994); *The Green Challenge: The Development of Green Parties in Europe* (with D. Richardson) (Routledge 1995); and *Environmental Movements: Local, National and Global* (Cass 1999).

Dieter Rucht is Professor of Sociology at the Social Science Centre, Berlin. His recent publications include *Protest in der Bundesrepublik* (ed.) (Campus 2001); *Shaping Abortion Discourse: Democracy and the Public Sphere in Germany and the United States* (with Myra Marx Ferree, Jürgen Gerhards, and William Gamson) (Cambridge 2002); and *Women's Movements Facing the Reconfigured State* (ed. with Lee Ann Banaszak and Karen Beckwith) (Cambridge 2003).

Jon Torre is an environmental journalist and was a member of the TEA project team at the University of the Basque Country.

The Transformation of Environmental Activism: An Introduction

Christopher Rootes

The environmental movement is the great survivor among the new social movements that arose in and since the 1960s. Yet if environmentalism has survived, the forms it has taken in western Europe have changed considerably. Whilst there is considerable debate about the extent and significance of some of those changes, others are indisputable.

What is indisputable is that, in one way or another, environmentalism has to a considerable extent become institutionalized. The European Union itself has provided some of the stimuli (Rootes 2002*a*). Environmental issues have been institutionalized in the Directorate General (Environment), have increasingly been taken up by the European Parliament, and have been pressed, with varying degrees of success, upon other Directorates such as those concerned with transport and industry. In the EU member states (as well as in those states that aspire to membership of the European Union), environmental issues have moved up policy agenda, sometimes as a result of pressure from the European Commission (EC), and usually with the aim of raising and harmonizing standards of environmental protection. Environmental protection agencies have been established and have been accorded increasing powers, and national ministries of the environment have been formed and are no longer consigned to the peripheries of government.

Another very visible development is the progress of green parties. Less than three decades since the first was formed, green parties are now represented in the national and/or regional parliaments and local councils of virtually all western European states. Greens have participated in or sustained governments in several European states and, in three of the four most populous EU states, greens have held office as government ministers, most often of the environment.

Scarcely less conspicuous or dramatic has been the rise of environmental non-governmental organizations (NGOs) and environmental movement organizations

I am indebted to Mario Diani, Andy Jamison, Manuel Jiménez, and Dieter Rucht for their comments on earlier versions and for the additional information they provided. They are, of course, absolved from any responsibility for the use I have made of it.

(EMOs). New internationalist EMOs such as Friends of the Earth (FoE) and Greenpeace, which originated in North America as recently as the 1970s, have affiliated organizations or set up branches in almost all EU states and have, since 1980, seen dramatic increases in the numbers of their members and supporters. Older environmental NGOs such as the World Wide Fund for Nature (WWF), national bird protection societies, and nature conservation associations have also experienced great increases in their numbers of supporters. Many EMOs have become substantial organizations with sizeable budgets and numbers of employees. The broad range of environmental NGOs and EMOs has gained considerable exposure in national mass media and enjoys increasing and increasingly regular and institutionalized access to policy-makers and decision-takers, both in government and in the corporate sector.

If the developments so far mentioned are unambiguous and scarcely disputed, others and their significance are the subject of much less agreement. It is generally agreed that there were surges of environmental protest in the 1970s and especially in the late 1980s, and that these fed the rise of EMOs and environmental NGOs. There is much less agreement about whether environmental protest has continued or whether its lower salience in many countries during the 1990s betokened a significant change, perhaps even a terminal decline, in the fortunes of EMOs.

One widely held view is that the environmental movement has been the victim of its own success. As movement intellectuals have become or have been supplanted by professionals and/or experts, EMOs have become more specialized and, increasingly guided by organizational imperatives, have sought to corner particular niches in the market rather than addressing the big picture of political ecology. Thus, it is alleged, the movement has fragmented and has consequently vacated the public space it once occupied (Eyerman and Jamison 1991; Jamison 2001), becoming less a movement than a 'public interest community' (Bosso 2000: 73).

The tale most often told about the existing evolution of the environmental movement in Europe is that it has become so institutionalized that it fails any longer to capture the imagination or command the support of any large part of the public. Because the influence of the environmental movement depends ultimately upon its ability to mobilize citizens to obstruct or embarrass governments and business corporations, any loss of mobilizing capacity tends to diminish it. In this version of events, the institutionalization of the environmental movement has been accompanied by its demobilization, protest is in decline, and the prognosis for the movement is uncertain (van der Heijden 1997; cf. Diani and Donati 1999).

There is, however, another tale, told more frequently in Britain (and the United States) than in continental Europe. This latter tale raises the spectre of 'eco-terrorism' as radical environmental activists abandon a non-violent movement that seems insufficiently effective to meet the increasingly urgent challenges of securing redress of environmental grievances and achieving environmental justice. A less excited version of this story is that, as increasingly established EMOs have vacated the streets in favour of the negotiating table and the boardroom, so protest has been joined by new, more radical groups employing unfamiliar tactics and raising new issues (Rootes 1999*b*; Wall 1999*a, b*).

Each of these tales is told with conviction but the evidence to support one or other of them has, thus far, been largely anecdotal. The purpose of this book is to address these competing claims by assembling and interpreting empirical evidence on the pattern of environmental protest in the years from 1988 to 1997. This decade begins with years that are in most countries presumed to have seen the peak of environmental protest and continues through the years in which the institutionalization of environmentalism is supposed to have had greatest impact upon the environmental movement. How did the incidence of environmental protest vary during those 10 years? How did the claims advanced by environmental protesters change, and how did the forms of environmental protest evolve? Have established EMOs remained prominent in collective action, or have they been eclipsed by other kinds of actors? Has a common western European pattern of environmental activism emerged, or do national patterns remain distinctive?

Before we attempt to answer these questions, it is worth considering why environmental protest is of more than passing interest and why it has wider implications for democratic politics and for policy-making.

THE INSTITUTIONALIZATION OF ENVIRONMENTALISM

One important aspect of the institutionalization of environmentalism has been the increasing involvement of EMOs in policy-making.[1] In all the major states of northern and western Europe, EMOs have been accorded at least some measure of more or less institutionalized access to decision-making arena. Efforts have been made to develop new institutional arrangements and opportunities for communication and debate among EMOs, policy-makers, and established economic actors and interest groups.

In the Netherlands, Germany, and the Nordic countries, such access has become well established. In Britain, EMOs have often felt marginal to the political process, but even there, organizations such as Greenpeace and FoE, once generally regarded as the radical, activist end of the environmental movement, have consolidated their status as unofficial experts in various environmental policy areas and are increasingly consulted by policy-makers. In Sweden and Denmark, the mainstream EMOs (especially the older conservation societies) have, as in Germany, become key actors in a range of activities from ecolabelling to clean production to sustainable transport (Jamison 2001: ch. 5). Many groups, both established and grassroots, have been involved in Agenda 21 activities at the local level. In many cases, relationships of mutual trust and cooperation have developed among EMO leaders and representatives of government and business.

Such developments are testimony to the practical commitment of the EMOs concerned and to the seriousness with which they are now taken by government and business. Nevertheless, they have created tensions within EMOs (Thomson and Robins 1994). What kinds of knowledge and information should they produce and disseminate? With whom should they work? Should they take money from industry and/or development assistance agencies? What kinds of values should EMOs promulgate? EMOs may increasingly be listened to and involved in policy-making, but by those of their activists, more comfortable with the role of critic, this is often seen as a distraction from the tasks of maintaining the commitment and support of EMOs' constituencies.

The institutionalization of environmentalism entails a transformation of the role environmental organizations play, both locally and nationally, in the production and dissemination of knowledge, and in the creation or shaping of the mass 'conscience constituency' of the environmental movement. One consequence of its success is that the environmental movement's virtual monopoly on 'ecological discourse' has been lost. Lost with it have been the unproblematic identities of EMOs themselves (Grove-White 1992; Eder 1996; Jamison 1996). Van der Heijden (1997: 46) speaks for many veterans of the environmental movement when he writes: 'Many environmental organizations have lost their unique movement character and therefore an important part of their strength. It is doubtful whether their stronger position at some negotiating table will compensate for this'.

Observers in Germany and the Netherlands have noted that whilst there has been a continued increase in the numbers of people who are happy to join environmental organizations and, especially, to give money to support environmental campaigns, most of these people cannot be mobilized for direct action of any kind (Blühdorn 1995; van der Heijden 1997). Thus, although there has been a considerable increase in the size of the environmental movement's 'conscience constituency', it is widely believed that there has been a significant decline in the proportion of *active* members and a corresponding decline in the incidence of mass participation in environmental activism since its peak in the late 1980s.

One reading of these developments is that they represent a late stage in the institutionalization of the environmental movement, a stage in which increasing official acceptance of EMOs as partners in environmental policy-making is accompanied by the defusing of environmental contention and the demobilization of the supporters of increasingly formally organized EMOs. This 'institutionalization' of 'the environmental movement' is, however, neither complete nor uncontested. If many EMOs have travelled down the path of professionalization and partnership with governments and/or industrial corporations, others have not.

RESISTANCE?

Even as evidence of the institutionalization of environmentalism was accumulating, there were, in all EU states, recurrent outbursts of environmental protest. Moreover, in some countries, the number of protest mobilizations that were not controlled or coordinated by established EMOs appeared to be increasing. Some such protests were the work of local communities resisting the imposition of developments that threatened their lifestyles or the loss of environmental amenity. But there also appeared in several countries to be an increase in the numbers of less formally organized, even deliberately anarchistic, environmental protests that were the actions of more philosophically committed trans-local environmental activists. Nowhere was this more apparent during the 1990s than in Britain.

The rise or revival of such environmental protest may be, in part at least, a reaction to the institutionalization of environmentalism. Maintaining the expertise necessary to produce informed criticism and constructive alternatives, and to enable EMOs to speak with authority to the powerful, is expensive and requires considerable investment of energy and a steady flow of funds. Successful EMOs such as Greenpeace and, in Britain, FoE, have become substantial 'protest businesses' (Jordan and Maloney 1997) that must balance the conflicting demands of maintaining the support of their swollen 'conscience constituencies' and the allegiance of grassroots supporters with those of their hard-won access to and influence upon governments and corporations. Because large and well-established EMOs are increasingly aware of the extent to which their ability to influence policy—and in some cases a significant part of their funding—is dependent upon their continued access to policy-makers, they are concerned about demonstrating that they are 'responsible'. They are also acutely aware that, as substantial organizations with considerable assets, they, unlike less formal and more *ad hoc* campaigning groups, are vulnerable to threats of litigation.

In Britain, the threat of legal action has increasingly constrained the activities of campaigning EMOs. Thus, FoE was obliged by threatened legal action to withdraw from the battle, beginning in 1992, to prevent the construction of a motorway bypass across Twyford Down.[2] Greenpeace was always careful to avoid exposing itself to the risk of legal liability, and prohibited its local support groups from using the Greenpeace name in autonomous local actions. However, in August 1997, it was sharply reminded of its vulnerability when BP secured a freeze on Greenpeace assets to ensure enforcement of a legal injunction prohibiting Greenpeace from continuing to obstruct BP's oil exploration in the North Sea. Disabled and disconcerted by the threat of litigation, FoE was outflanked in the anti-roads campaigns by more radical *ad hoc* groupings composed of local objectors, national campaigners of various affiliations, and what might loosely be described as 'green anarchists'. FoE was left in the uncomfortable position of having publicly to distance itself from actions of which many of its members and supporters at least privately—and often publicly—approved. The irony is that this rise of 'green direct action' meant that FoE and Greenpeace were put in a compromised position analogous to that in which their own rise had earlier placed older environmental organizations.

The constraints upon established EMOs are not always visible to or well understood by rank and file activists. Frustration at the apparent inaction of established groups was a recurrent theme in activists' explanations of their shift of allegiance to newer and looser groups committed to direct action and relatively uncon-strained by considerations of legality (Fiddes 1997; Seel 1997*b*: 172; Doherty 1999*a, b*; Wall 1999*a, b*). The new environmental protest groups in Britain (Earth First!, Road Alert!, and Reclaim the Streets most prominent among them) were deliberately minimalist in terms of organization. They eschewed formal member-ship and hierarchy, and their boundaries were correspondingly fluid. As one par-ticipant observer put it, 'the protest movement . . . is in a continual process of flux and change; roads protester becomes 'Earth First!er' becomes "The Land Is Ours" urban squatter . . . ' (Plows 1997). Although they were overwhelmingly committed to non-violence, even that could not be taken for granted. Earth First! gatherings debated the continuing efficacy of non-violent direct action, and occasionally spectacular acts of violence were committed against property and sometimes (mostly by animal rights activists) against people as well.

If frustration about the lack of opportunities for direct action presented by the increasingly institutionalized character of established EMOs is one important stimulus to the formation of new groups and to the development of new forms of protest, it is not the only one. EMOs often appear to practice an explicit or implicit division of labour. Radical groups sometimes deliberately draw the fire of hostile forces, and they are sometimes encouraged to do so by more established groups that may then appear more moderate and 'reasonable' by comparison.

Nevertheless, however much established EMOs might succeed in capitalizing upon the openings created by more radical actors, and however much they seek to make common cause with the new radicals, the relationship is inherently tense and complicated. FoE lost face—and attracted much activist criticism—because of the abortive role it played at Twyford Down, and its attempts to make amends by offering support and encouragement to direct activists at subsequent anti-roads protests were by no means universally welcomed or accepted. Declarations of support that remain insufficient for many protesters may nevertheless suffice to threaten the access and standing of established EMOs. Negotiation, whether with public authorities or with corporate actors, requires good faith, and EMOs cannot expect to be accepted as *bona fide* negotiators if they are seen to be keeping a card or two up their sleeves.

As far as their constituents are concerned, different EMOs may appear to operate in different 'market segments'. It is common for EMOs to have substan-tially overlapping memberships. Many committed environmentalists join or lend support to more than one EMO,[3] and many members and supporters of more established EMOs may, recognizing the value of a specialized division of labour, add support for a new group to their personal portfolios of membership and allegiance. Although the dominance of established and moderate groups may stimulate the emergence of new and more radical groups that seek to push envir-onmental issues further than established EMOs appear willing or able to do, there may be natural limits to this process. Recognizing that excessively radical actions may isolate them from the broader populace, newer groups may moderate their actions and adopt more pragmatic strategies.[4]

One reading of the developments we have seen in Britain is that they were simply the kinds of organizational and tactical innovations (Doherty 1999*b*) that were to be expected within a vital and still developing movement as it attracted people who had no previous experience of activism. The new recruits to direct action operated alongside more local, often, at least initially, 'NIMBY'[5] protesters whose actions continued in parallel with, but usually largely independently of, established EMOs. Local protests were often invigorated by the arrival of more radical activists. Local people had, for example, campaigned against the possible extension of the M3 motorway through Twyford Down for 20 years, but it only became a major issue when a small number of non-local activists joined the protest. Because their appearance and their actions appeared to be bizarre, these 'eco-warriors' attracted the attention of mass media with an insatiable appetite for novelty, spectacle, and conflict, and a marked preference for concrete events over abstract principles and complex processes. Twyford Down ended in defeat but, because it generated so much publicity, it attracted emulators and led to the formation of a small army of people committed to direct action who moved on to the sites of other proposed road and infrastructure developments.

This should serve as a reminder that, for all that the larger established EMOs are in many countries unprecedentedly well resourced, in terms of the material resources essential to successful influence upon policy-making and policy implementation, even they remain minnows by comparison with the governments and corporations whose initiatives they challenge. Public opinion remains EMOs' greatest resource, and an often uncomprehending if not overtly hostile mass media is generally the only means by which the public can be addressed.[6]

It is the limitations of the resources at the disposal of even well-established EMOs that best explain their relatively peripheral involvement in most local environmental campaigns and why local campaigners do not rely more heavily upon established EMOs. Local campaigners who do approach a local EMO group for assistance usually discover that the chief resource of such groups is the energies of one or a handful of part-time activists supplemented, on a restricted range of issues, by access to a variably reliable network of information. In the absence of well-resourced local EMOs, local campaigners are obliged to rely largely upon their own resources and, to the extent that they develop effective campaign groups, they may themselves become sources of organizational and tactical innovation within the broader environmental movement (Rootes 1997*c*).

The development of new, more radical environmental networks and local campaign organizations does, however, pose serious problems for hitherto radical campaigning EMOs. Inevitably, they experience difficulties in balancing the need to retain the support of an environmentalist constituency, some elements of which appear increasingly disposed to activism, against their own interests in influencing policy by deepening constructive links with governments and businesses. Such new developments also create uncertainties for environmental policy-makers who fear they can no longer rely on organizations such as FoE and Greenpeace either to act as barometers of activist environmental sentiment or as negotiators on behalf of environmental interests (Rootes 1999*b*, 2002*a*).

These processes may not be universal, but their prominence in Britain leads one to ask whether they are becoming widespread elsewhere in western Europe.[7]

CULTURE, STRUCTURE, AND CONTINGENCY: EXPLAINING CROSSNATIONAL VARIATION

If the resurgence of protest is at least in part a response to the institutionalization of environmental movements, then it is appropriate to consider variations in the extent and the forms of their institutionalization in the various western European states. It is immediately apparent that there are considerable differences among them. France and Belgium have long had much lower levels of EMO membership than the Netherlands, Denmark, Germany, and Britain (van der Heijden, Koopmans, and Giugni 1992). In terms of the aggregate size of membership of national EMOs, the size of their budgets, the numbers of their employees, and their external relationships, the French environmental movement remains markedly less institutionalized than its counterparts in Germany, Switzerland or the Netherlands, (van der Heijden 1997) or Britain (Rootes and Miller 2000).

Such differences may be attributable to long-standing, even primordial, differences in political culture. In comparison with Germany, the Netherlands, the Nordic countries, and Britain, France and (especially) Spain have very low rates of membership of associations of all kinds (Koopmans 1996).[8] It is not then surprising that what appears to be a general feature of national political cultures should be reflected in the particular case of the environmental movement. 'Culture' is one possible line of explanation of these patterns (Jehlicka 1994), and of the coupling of low levels of knowledge about environmental issues with high levels of personal concern and complaint in such countries as Spain, Greece, and Portugal (Hofrichter and Reif 1990). However, what now appears as 'culture' is generally simply the accumulated legacy of historical experience reinforced by institutionalized political arrangements. Another, less contentious, line of explanation is in terms of 'political opportunity structures'.

Political opportunity structures have been invoked to explain anomalies in the patterns of institutionalization of environmental movements and the success of green parties that defy explanation in terms of culture. Thus, whilst environmental movements have been relatively little institutionalized in France and Belgium, these countries have produced more successful green parties than Denmark, Britain, or the Netherlands, countries in which environmental movements have been conspicuously more successfully institutionalized.

However, even if the various strategies adopted by different EMOs in different countries might be explained in terms of differences in national political cultures or national political opportunity structures, consideration of the divergent strategies of EMOs *within* a single country or culture, both at any one time and over time, points to the inadequacy of such interpretations. The conventional wisdom holds that Britain is a country in which, whether for reasons of culture or institutional structures, the 'bureaucratic accommodation' of environmentalism has constrained environmentalists to moderate action and the pursuit of broad political alliances (Rüdig and Lowe 1986; Rootes 1995*a*). This cannot, however, explain the rise of radical environmental protest in Britain during the 1990s at a time when such protests were alleged to have subsided in Germany and the Netherlands.

An explanation that employs the language of political opportunity must reckon with the differences between relatively inert institutional structures and elements of the pattern of political opportunities that are in principle more contingent and conjuncturally variable (Rootes 1997*a*, 1999*c*). To accounts in terms of political institutional structures, consideration of changing balances of political competition must be added. Although the latter may, in part, be contingent effects of structural arrangements, they cannot simply be reduced to the structures that underlie them (Rootes 1995*b*). Moreover, whether or not structural arrangements or conjunctural situations are perceived by political actors as opportunities or constraints varies according to both the culturally conditioned expectations of the actors and to the political ideas, values, and strategies of those actors and the groups to which they belong (Rootes 1997*a*). Although political structures in Britain did not change significantly during the 1990s, the political conjuncture did: the government pressed ahead with road-building, and tactics of direct action protest popularized in the campaign against the poll tax spread to environmental campaigns (Rootes 2003*a*).

CROSSNATIONAL COMPARISONS

The transformation of environmental protest and EMOs has not so far been the subject of systematic social scientific investigation on a crossnationally comparative basis. In the previous sections, the issues and arguments have been laid out mainly in relation to British experience. We shall, in the course of this volume, examine those issues and arguments more closely as we compare and attempt to explain the patterns of development of environmental protest in each of the eight countries covered by our investigation: France, Germany, Greece, Italy, Spain, the Basque Country, and Sweden as well as Britain.[9]

Although limitations of resources obliged us to restrict our investigations to these eight countries, the choice of them was not arbitrary. There are other potentially interesting cases, but the experiences of these eight countries are sufficiently varied that together they encompass the broad range of environmental movement politics in western Europe.

It was observation of events in *Britain*, with its long history of environmentalism, well-institutionalized EMOs, and a recent wave of radical environmental protest that stimulated the development of our research agenda. The peculiarities of its political opportunity structures, and their reputed effects upon the expression of environmentalism, would, however, be sufficient to justify the choice of Britain as one of the countries for comparison.

In *France* the salience of ecology as a political issue has been puzzlingly intermittent (Prendiville 1994). A high incidence and level of public participation in protest in general (Dalton 2002: 62–5) does not appear to have been fully reflected in environmental mobilizations. Between 1975 and 1989, nationally reported ecological protest actions were fewer in number and more dominated by those against nuclear power than in other western European countries. To a much greater extent than in Germany, actions were aimed at the national level rather than the regional or, especially, local levels (van der Heijden 1997: 28–9).[10] They were, moreover, more often characterized by demonstrative, confrontational, and even violent rather than conventional forms of political action (van der Heijden 1997: 43). Ecologism in France has coexisted with what are, by northern European standards, very low levels of EMO membership, particularly of organizations other than traditional nature conservation organizations. Nor are there clear signs of change; four leading EMOs in France doubled their aggregate membership between 1980 and 1995, whereas their counterparts in Germany and in the Netherlands, respectively, experienced twenty- and five-fold increases in membership (van der Heijden 1997: 38–9). After several turbulent years of electoral failure and internal discord, *Les Verts*, thanks to an electoral pact with the Socialists, in 1997 achieved representation in the national parliament and their leader, Dominique Voynet, became Minister for the Environment. This was a matter of contention both within *Les Verts* and among environmental protesters beyond the party. Of more far-reaching significance, however, is the decentralization of a formerly centralized state that appears to have created new opportunities for environmentalists that may encourage them into partnerships with state authorities and away from protest (Hayes 2000, 2002).

Germany witnessed the rise of environmental activism in the 1970s, partly as a continuation of radical youth protest, but in parallel with a steady increase in levels of citizen participation in politics generally (Markovits and Gorski 1993). *Die Grünen* has consolidated its electoral base, has been the junior partner in coalition governments in several *Länder* and, since 1998, at national level, is arguably the most successfully institutionalized Green Party in Europe. Although its origins lay in the new social movements, its claim to be the political representative of all the social movements has become increasingly problematic. Germany has a highly developed, organizationally diverse, and largely successfully institutionalized environmental movement, comparatively well funded and well staffed (van der Heijden 1997: 40–2; Rucht and Roose 2001*a*). It is, according to Blühdorn (1995: 210), a 'mature' environmental movement increasingly based upon a new generation that approaches the 'ecological problem' scientifically and is now concerned not with the defence of nature but with the pursuit of sustainability (cf. Brand 1999). Perhaps it is because German EMOs have become so successfully institutionalized and are now able to act in partnership with corporations that they have experienced the paradox of rising subscriptions from members and supporters but declining numbers of activists. However, the revival of anti-nuclear protest suggests that institutionalization is not the whole or the only story (Rucht and Roose 1999). The scale of the protests stimulated by the transport of nuclear wastes at Gorleben in 1996 and at Ahaus in 1998 demonstrated the continued vitality and preparedness to protest of anti-nuclear and other environmental groups. It also showed how easily latent networks could be activated and thousands, even tens of thousands, of people mobilized for protest even in places relatively remote from the urban centres that house the major concentrations of highly educated supporters of environmental organizations.

In *Italy* a large number of environmental emergencies during the 1970s and 1980s resulted in frequent confrontations between the authorities and local populations supported by EMOs. For this reason, and because the extreme delegitimation of the political system was accompanied by widespread public distrust of established political actors and an unprecedented spread of direct action and protest among the middle classes, there was a high probability of protest wherever a new and environmentally controversial project was sited. Moreover, in a development consistent with the persistent localism of Italian politics, the collapse of the traditional political establishment has had the effect of liberating political energies that have been invested in the construction of new community initiatives against, for example, the effects of traffic upon historic cities. These local actions do not, in general, appear to have much to do with established EMOs (della Porta and Andretta 2002). On the other hand, the participation of Greens in electoral pacts secured their members prominent roles in the local governments of major cities. Despite the Greens' electoral weakness, the left's need of partners in government (1996–2001) gave Greens office in the Environment Ministry and has been credited with a significant institutionalization of environmentalism (Biorcio 2002).

For two decades *Spain* experienced high rates of environmental degradation as the environment was subordinated to the imperatives of the country's headlong dash for economic development. Doubtless as a reflection of levels of associational group membership that are the lowest in western Europe, as well as of persistent localism, Spain has had an extremely fragmented environmental movement and, until recently, relatively low rates of involvement in environmental protest. During the 1990s, however, the membership of EMOs and the incidence of environmental protest grew considerably. It is a matter of contention whether this growth principally reflects a rise in environmental concern or whether it is a more complex product of general politicization, particularly of the young, or, as in Italy, a reaction against the apparent corruption of the political class. Jiménez (1999*a*) suggests that environmental protest has been changing, with an increase in the number of events but a reduced average number of participants. This might be interpreted as evidence that EMOs were opting for symbolic action performed by core activists (acting on behalf of an increasing 'conscience' constituency) whereas high levels of mobilization were mainly produced by NIMBY conflicts that were uniquely capable of mobilizing local populations. As part of a movement at a comparatively early stage of institutionalization, Spanish EMOs grappled with the organizational and strategic dilemmas involved in responding to new opportunities (e.g. by estab-lishing links with public administrations) even whilst their bases of popular support remained underdeveloped. The establishment of new institutionalized links could rarely be reconciled with the generation or maintenance of supporters' involvement, and it increased the risk of EMOs' dependency upon or co-option by the more powerful actors by whom they were increasingly publicly recognized as valid interlocutors. As a result, when EMOs tried to exercise a mediating role in grassroots protests, they risked being bypassed by protesters and losing their ability to act as representatives whilst at the same time, by the very fact of their involvement, they risked compromising their newly won but still precarious stand-ing as interlocutors with the authorities.

A further complication of the Spanish case, and one deserving of special atten-tion, is the extremely high level of protest, including environmental protest, in the *Basque Country*, and the intertwining there of nationalism and ecologism (Barcena, Ibarra, and Zubiaga 1995). The Basque country also provides an opportunity to examine the shifting relationships among localism, nationalism, and environmen-talism in a country that is not itself a state but which straddles the borders of two nation-states.

Greece is another country in which environmentalism is at a relatively early stage of institutionalization. In the first two decades following Greece's emer-gence from dictatorship in 1974, levels of grassroots environmental protest mobilization appear, per capita, to have been even higher than in Spain (Kousis 1998, 1999). Greeks have, however, thus far appeared to exhibit more concern than knowledge about environmental issues, and previous research suggests that protests have tended to remain local, in the sense of defending local amenity values if not always in the spatial scope of the protest actions themselves.[11] In more recent years, however, there has been a considerable growth in the number of national EMOs, and a former director of Greenpeace Greece has become environment minister in a Socialist government.

Sweden stands at the other end of the spectrum. Although Sweden is a country where environmental knowledge and concern have long been at relatively high levels, Swedish environmentalism has, for the most part, been highly institution-alized (Jamison et al. 1990). In an unusually consensus-seeking country, environ-mental campaigners have generally been quickly co-opted into official positions and mainstream parties. Thus, although Sweden experienced a divisive anti-nuclear campaign that produced an electorally successful Green Party, environmental protest has seldom been prominent. However, the rise of animal rights protests and the emergence in 1996 of protests against the building of the bridge over the Öresund between Malmö and Copenhagen, combined with protests against new road developments in Stockholm, appeared to mark the advent of a new, more activist phase in the Swedish environmental movement.

Clearly, the institutionalization of environmentalism takes many forms. Diani and Donati (1999) describe the strategic dilemma of EMOs in terms of the competing demands of resource mobilization on the one hand and political efficacy on the other. Many commentators claim to have observed a general shift of environmentalism away from mass protest and towards public interest lobbies and professionalized protest organizations. Yet, as recent experience shows, there are significant strands of environmental concern and activism that resist institutionalization. It is by no means certain that the radical environmentalist counter-culture that some see as the most significant product of recent environmental protests in Britain[12] will prove durable, but it does appear that a significant level of environmentalist protest may coexist with increasingly institutionalized EMOs.

THE EUROPEANIZATION OF ENVIRONMENTALISM?

The emergence of the European Union as an increasingly important locus of environmental policy-making might be expected to have an increasing impact upon the strategies and tactics of European environmental activists, but it is not a topic that has so far been the subject of extensive research. Most work to date has focused upon the ways in which EMOs have organized in order to address the European Commission (Rucht 1993, 1997).

The relationship between the EC and EMOs is a reciprocal one. EMOs influence EU policy, but, it is suggested, the constraints and opportunities of EU structures increasingly shape and may transform EMOs themselves (Marks and McAdam 1999). The EC for many years provided core funding for the European Environmental Bureau (EEB) in order to encourage the development of a single organization broadly representative of European environmental groups that could serve as a channel of communication between those groups and the EC and vice versa. The EC has also supported environmental NGOs by assisting with specific information and awareness campaigns on environmental issues. EC financial support has mainly been granted to Europe-wide NGOs that focus on the priorities of EC programmes. Thus, for example, the Commission assisted FoE with its Sustainable Europe project. Moreover, contacts between NGOs and the Commission take place on a regular basis and at various levels (Commission of the European Communities 1996: 105–6; Rucht 1997).

Of the 'big four' Brussels-based lobbying organizations—the EEB, CEAT (European Coordination of Friends of the Earth), WWF (for Nature), and

Greenpeace—only Greenpeace did not accept EC funding. EC funding does appear to have entailed some constraint upon the organizations that receive it. As Rucht (1997: 202) observes, it is 'probably not by chance alone' that the EEB, the organization that most depended upon EC funding, was also the one that pursued the most politically moderate course. This did not, however, always save the EEB from accusations from the EC that it was insufficiently 'constructive'. If the existence and support of the EC have acted as a lure to a particular form of institutionalization of EMOs at the European level, it has clearly not produced the kind of untroublesome expert interlocutor that some EC bureaucrats appear to have expected. The EC may well have underestimated the extent to which environmentalists and ecologists were likely to be critical of the EC's modernizing project. Moreover, it underestimated the extent of EMOs' dependence upon their national constituencies and bases of support, and their consequent need to respond to issues raised by new and more radical EMOs as they arose in the several nation states (Rootes 2002*a*).

Insofar as the EC employs EMOs as partners in or agents for its public education and awareness campaigns, their value depends in large part on the extent to which they, rather than national governments or business corporations, are trusted by the public as sources of information on environmental matters.[13] To the extent that they continue to enjoy public confidence, EMOs may be valuable interlocutors and mediators of informed or concerned public opinion on environmental matters. However, that value is diminished when established EMOs are outflanked or undermined by new groupings more reflective of or responsive to mobilized public opinion.[14]

The environmental (and other) policies of the European Union affect the opportunities for EMOs at the national level. Thus, in Britain, during the 1980s, environmental 'campaigners came to see the European Community as an environmental beacon' which provided them with issues, information, and 'authority to challenge domestic practices and procedures' (Lowe and Ward 1998: 21). FoE, for example, was happy to use EC directives to embarrass the UK government and to seek redress of grievances against the UK government by means of complaints to European institutions, despite the fact that FoE's British spokespersons were staunch advocates of decentralization of decision-making and 'subsidiarity', and were generally as unhappy about 'creeping federalism' as any Eurosceptic Conservative politician.

Increasingly, environmental planning in Europe is at the EU level[15] but the implementation of policy remains at the national or local level. Although the EU is, in many countries, seen as a force for higher standards of environmental protection, EU infrastructure projects may conflict with the priorities of local environmentalists. The transport infrastructure developments financed through the Structural Funds, the Cohesion Fund, and the Trans-European Network for Transport (TENs) are perhaps the best example. The Commission and the European Parliament recognized that it was essential that the TENs developments should be consistent with the requirements of sustainable mobility, but there was concern that the major EU funds favoured road construction. The lack of a strategic environmental assessment of TENs may have encouraged local opposition to some projects, but strategic environmental assessments do not automatically guarantee acceptance of proposals by affected populations or by other interested parties whose agenda are different from those of the EC itself.

The TENs project stimulated the formation of Trans-European Networks and NGOs (TENGO) as the coordinating body for EMOs opposed to TENs at the European level, but it also spurred the development of the Amsterdam-based Action for Solidarity, Equality, Environment, and Development (A SEED) as the coordinating body or network of the anti-roads movement at the European level. Whereas TENGO mainly coordinated lobby groups such as WWF, Birdlife International, and CEAT, A SEED served as the coordinating body for action groups at the local level. By organizing meetings, European action days and partnerships between different groups, A SEED sought to make local groups aware that the particular road schemes to which they objected were part of TENs.

As a European network for direct action groups, A SEED marked the emergence of a new form of transnational cooperation of environmental protest[16] and it challenged the assumptions of some observers that transnational EMOs would necessarily be 'quite bureaucratic organizations' (Sklair 1995). It did not, however, signal a lack of awareness of the importance of or opportunities for influencing EU policy by the more orthodox and institutionalized politics of lobbying. A SEED encouraged the formation of TENGO out of recognition of the need for and potential effectiveness of action at different levels. There appears to have been a division of labour between them, TENGO concentrating on lobbying the EU in Brussels while A SEED coordinated the protests of environmental groups in the member states without itself becoming a bureaucratic organization (Radtke 1997) or seeking to be an interlocutor of the EC.

Transport projects are not the only EC-funded infrastructural developments that are or may be controversial. The proposal to build a large EC-financed municipal waste incinerator near Madrid provoked massive opposition from local people and environmentalists. Projects to enhance tourist development, such as the construction of marinas in the Basque Country, have also stimulated protest. Even projects designed to meet EC objectives of sustainable development may provoke local environmental opposition. The development of wind farms has excited protests in west Wales and other parts of Britain, and the proposed construction of dams to provide water for hydroelectric schemes and irrigation has, as in the case of the proposed diversion of the Achelöos River in Greece, given rise to vociferous protest (Close 1998).

Although it appears that infrastructure projects promoted or financed by the EC have become increasingly controversial and have, in many cases, stimulated protests, there has to date been little systematic study of protests at the European level.[17] Claims about the increasing Europeanization of environmentalism are best documented in respect of generalized attitudes, organizational networks, and policies. As far as environmental protest is concerned, the published evidence has, until now, been largely anecdotal.

PRESS REPORTS OF ENVIRONMENTAL PROTEST: PROBLEMS AND POTENTIAL[18]

In order to address these and related questions and to explore similarities and differences from one European country to another, we have examined the public record of environmental protest as revealed in leading newspapers in each of eight nations. Reports carried by mass media provide not only a record of environmental movement activity but much of the material out of which public and elite perceptions of the environmental movement are constructed. But if press reports provide useful data, impressions formed on the basis of a casual reading of them may be misleading. Even knowledgeable observers believed that the incidence of environmental protest in Germany had, in aggregate, declined since the late 1980s. Yet preliminary results from the systematic study of protest events (PRODAT) for the early 1990s suggest that the numbers of protests reported in leading newspapers had actually *increased* (Rucht and Roose 1999). It appears not so much that protest had declined as that, as the novelty of protest waned, so its salience for unsystematic observers declined. What these German findings most clearly demonstrate is the need for systematic collection and analysis of data on the incidence and forms of protest to correct the often false impressions formed by casual empiricism.

Newspaper reports have often been described as 'history's first draft', but this is perhaps a generous way of describing the cumulative account that can be derived from such sources. There is, after all, abundant evidence that media reports of political action are selective and biased in various ways. But that does not mean that media reports have no evidential value at all. By recognizing the limitations, biases, and selectivity of media reports and applying our knowledge of media routines and the sources and consequences of selection and bias, we are able to critically evaluate the picture we can assemble from media reports. We cannot hope, even by the most sophisticated analysis of data derived from media reports, closely to approach an unmediated record of events, but we can reasonably hope to give as comprehensive and balanced an account of events as it is possible to assemble from public sources.

This part of our research employs the methodology of protest event analysis.[19] As a systematic means of documenting protest events, this methodology has considerable virtues, but it also has important limitations. Careful and detailed ethnographies of protest can explore the dynamics of protest and the submerged linkages that are so important to the maintenance and proliferation of campaigns. Such linkages very often go unremarked in even the more scrupulous and thoughtful journalistic accounts and, as a result, they are inaccessible to a protest event analysis of media reports. However, although ethnographic case studies are invaluable to understanding both the particulars and processes of a small number of instances, the extent to which they are representative is always open to question. In their focus on groups and processes of manageably small size, they are often unable to illuminate more than a small part of the bigger picture. Similarly, although it may well be possible to piece together, from their own archives and from extended interviews with their activists, better accounts of the actions of a number of groups than can be garnered from press reports, such sources are notoriously inconsistent both over time and from one group to another. Limited resources mean that any single researcher or project is most unlikely to be able to look at more than a small number of groups in such a detailed way. What we should gain by looking closely at a few groups would have to be balanced against what we should miss, and, adopting such a research strategy, we should miss the whole range of small and evanescent groups and the large number of environmental protests that involve organized groups only peripherally or not at all.[20] Protest event methodology may thus give us a more broadly representative picture of environmental protest as a whole.

Since it is—for reasons of economy—focused upon events, protest event methodology does not encompass the many news reports and feature articles on environmental issues that do not report protest events but that nevertheless have an impact upon public and elite knowledge of and opinion about environmental activists and their concerns. Moreover, because it is limited to reported events, protest event analysis omits the many small and local protests that escape the attention of national newspaper journalists, or that are deemed insufficiently newsworthy by their editors. No less importantly, however, it cannot cover the many activities of environmental organizations and activists that go on behind closed doors and that are, as large parts of the environmental movement become at least semi-institutionalized, an increasingly important means of advancing environmentalist agenda.

However, what people do not see or read about, they do not usually know about, and what they do not know about is unlikely to inform their attitudes. In defence of protest event methodology, it can reasonably be claimed that it is by the employment of these means that we are most likely to get as close as resources permit to a systematic knowledge of those protests that have done most to shape public opinion and to inform elite policy preferences.

Ideally, in order to fully document the media output that has influenced public opinion, elite attitudes, and public policy in relation to environmental activism, we should assemble an account from the whole output of the print and electronic media. In practice, it would be impossibly expensive and labour-intensive to do so, particularly for an extended period such as the 10 years covered here. This, however, is not such a severe limitation as it might at first glance appear. After all, most of the 'research' undertaken to inform even investigative television and radio programmes consists of consulting the clippings or electronic archives of 'quality' newspapers. Moreover, it is the print media to which politicians and their advisors pay most systematic attention, not least because print is less ephemeral and can more easily be consulted as and when required (Anderson 1997: 57–8).

Systematic scrutiny of the whole range of print media would have been desirable, but was beyond our resources. In the absence of comprehensive and easily searchable full text-and-graphics archives of even the 'quality' newspapers, we have had to limit ourselves to analyses of the reports in a single newspaper in each country.[21] It is upon these analyses that the following chapters are based.

NOTES

1. van der Heijden (1997: 31) distinguishes three aspects to the process of institutionalization: organizational growth, internal institutionalization, and external institutionalization. All three are implicated here, but it is principally with the ramifications of the third—external institutionalization—that we are concerned.
2. A site of great scenic value and special scientific interest, near Winchester in southern England.
3. See, for example, Rüdig et al. (1991) for results of a survey of members of the UK Green Party. Only 13% of Green Party members had never joined another conservation or environmental organization; 69% were or had been members of more than one; over half had at some time been members of FoE, a similar proportion having been supporters of Greenpeace.
4. Such considerations appear to have informed recent debates at Earth First! gatherings in Britain (Seel 1997*b*: 175–6). Festing (1997) observes that FoE campaigners 'have noticed an increasing level of debate within the direct action movement about their own limitations ... There was a time when the direct action movement seemed to think itself beyond criticism. That is no longer true'.
5. NIMBY = 'Not In My Back Yard'.
6. The problematic nature of relations between campaigners and the mass media is increasingly well recognized. The best single discussion of the issues involved in movement—media interactions is still probably Gitlin (1980), but specifically on environmental issues, see Hansen (1993) and Anderson (1997).
7. A parallel process of radicalization has occurred in environmentalism in the United States. New groupings such as Earth First! formed in reaction to what had come to be perceived as toothless mainstream EMOs (such as the Sierra Club and the Audubon Society), and local environmental protests uncoordinated by any established EMO have proliferated (Carmin 1999) to culminate in the rise of the 'environmental justice movement' (Schlosberg 1999).
8. Such differences of political culture may, of course, exist within as well as between countries—see, for example, Putnam (1993).
9. A parallel investigation employing the same methodology and protocols is also under way in Ireland (Garavan 2002).

10. van der Heijden's data are based on reports published in the Monday editions of 'national' newspapers (see Kriesi et al. 1995 for an account of the methodology). It is however, problematic to make crossnational comparisons of protest events on this basis. Most obviously, the Monday edition of the French newspaper employed, *Le Monde*, is published on Sundays and so covers a somewhat different time period than do the Monday editions of the other newspapers employed, which were actually published on Mondays. Fillieule (1997) has shown that *Le Monde* systematically underreports protest events outside Paris; the extent of regional selection bias in the reporting of the German, Dutch, and Swiss newspapers is unclear, but it is unlikely to be simply comparable with that of *Le Monde*. Our own investigations suggest that van der Heijden's characterization of environmental protest in France may in part be an artefact of an uncritical reliance upon a single idiosyncratic source—*Le Monde* (see Chapter 3 and Appendix A).

11. Thus Kousis (1997*b*) describes how residents of Thesprotia and Corfu both coordinated their action across their region and carried their protest to Athens in order to prevent the construction of a sewage scheme which would have discharged effluent into a local river (cf. Close 1998).

12. As Faucher (1999) has shown, the counter-culturalism of British Greens finds no echo among the supporters of *Les Verts* in France.

13. There is considerable evidence that they have, in general, been so trusted (e.g. see Milbrath 1984; Christie and Jarvis 2001: 141; Jordan 2001: 358). Perhaps the most spectacular recent confirmation of this occurred in the aftermath of Greenpeace's successful 1995 campaign to prevent Shell from dumping the Brent Spar oil storage buoy at sea. Greenpeace's admission that it had miscalculated the amount of toxic residues remaining in the buoy does not appear to have dented its credibility in the eyes of the public, despite the new fashion among journalists for knocking Greenpeace (Jordan 2001: 346).

14. The institutionalization of the environmental movement is not always seen as a positive thing by EC bureaucrats. As one remarked, 'My problem is that I am not waiting for lobbies, I am waiting for movements. What I hope to have is some kind of... democratic input in my thinking'. He went on to complain that when he meets EMO people at international meetings, 'they don't bring me very much new. I know what they know, what they think, and I cannot use it'. (Ruzza 1996: 217–18).

15. The former UK Environment Secretary, John Gummer, estimated in 1994 that 80% of British environmental legislation had its origins in Brussels (Lowe and Ward 1998: 25). This claim may be exaggerated in the case of Britain, but for smaller EU states, such as Spain and Greece, the proportion is still higher.

16. Rucht (1993) has described the three crossnational forms of cooperation among EMOs as issue-oriented transnational cooperation, stable transnational alliances, and supranational NGOs.

17. For a rare exception, see Imig and Tarrow (1999, 2001).

18. This section draws in part on Rootes (2000: 26–7).

19. See Rucht et al. (1998) for an up-to-date review of the method and its applications.

20. Subsequent stages of the TEA Project complement this research on media reports of environmental protest by examining, by means of surveys, analysis of literature and documents and interviews, EMOs at the national level, and environmental activism at the local level (see Appendix B).

21. For an extended discussion of the methodological issues, see Appendix A.

2

Britain

Christopher Rootes

INTRODUCTION

Although the institutionalization of environmentalism is an almost universal phenomenon in western Europe, uninstitutionalized environmental protest persists, and there are indications that in some countries, during the 1990s, there may have been an increase in the number of protest mobilizations that were not controlled or coordinated by established environmental movement organizations (EMOs). Nowhere was this more apparent than in Britain where campaigns of direct action contributed to the wholesale revision of national transport policy, challenged a number of proposed new commercial developments, stimulated new measures to maintain public order, and inhibited the government's promotion of biotechnology.

Environmental activism has a long history in Britain. The first great wave of formation of organizations campaigning for environmental protection began with the Commons, Open Spaces and Footpaths Preservation Society in 1865. Over the next four decades others followed, including the Royal Society for the Protection of Birds (RSPB) (1889) and the National Trust (NT) (1895). Subsequent waves of organizational innovation produced what was claimed to be 'the oldest, strongest, best-organized and most widely supported environmental lobby in the world' (McCormick 1991: 34). The movement continued to grow into the 1990s.[1] Between 1971 and 1981, the membership of several of the longest established EMOs, including the NT and the RSPB, grew fourfold, and between 1981 and 1991, it doubled again. It went on increasing, albeit more slowly, to the point where, by 2000, the NT had 2.5 million members and the RSPB over one million. By 1998 some 20 per cent of Britons claimed to be members of one or more environmental organizations (Johnston and Jowell 1999: 183).

I am indebted to Ben Seel and Debbie Adams for reading and coding the newspaper reports and for helpful comments on earlier drafts of this chapter, and especially to Alexander Miller who shared the reading and coding of reports and also prepared the tables and graphs. I am also grateful to Brian Doherty and Mat Paterson for their comments on an earlier draft.

Membership of one or another environmental organization is not, of course, the same thing as participation in environmental protest. Although there had been instances of environmental direct action in the nineteenth and early twentieth centuries, the most celebrated involved the assertion, mainly by working class people, of customary rights of access to land. Otherwise, environmentalism in Britain was thoroughly moderate, respectable and reformist, and enjoyed relatively open access to a political establishment itself ambivalent about the impact of industrialization. Conservation campaigners quickly became interlocutors of policy-makers. Local protests against unwanted development that might be seen as harbingers of later protests began to appear in numbers only in the mid-1960s (Rüdig 1995: 222–5).

The development of the modern British environmental movement that began in the 1970s was, however, marked by the formation of new, more activist environmental organizations—notably Friends of the Earth (FoE) (established in 1971) and Greenpeace (1977). FoE and Greenpeace broke with past practice by eschewing charitable status in order to be free to take unambiguously political stances critical of government and industry. They were also distinguished by the breadth of their conception of environmental issues, their unabashed use of mass media to mobilize public opinion in order to exert pressure on government and corporations, and, especially in the case of Greenpeace, their employment of non-violent direct action.

Friends of the Earth launched in Britain with a highly publicized 'bottle drop' of non-returnable plastic bottles on the doorstep of the drinks supplier, Schweppes. But if such publicity stunts were useful in attracting supporters, FoE was committed to influencing policy by engaging government and industry in debate, and to winning arguments by 'getting the science right'. Accordingly, FoE committed itself to arguing the case against the proposed nuclear reprocessing facility at Windscale at the 1976 public inquiry. Some activists saw this as a diversion of energies that defused the potential of the environmental movement to influence policy by direct action. Partly as a result, a UK branch of Greenpeace was established and distinguished itself by spectacular acts of protest to draw attention to Windscale's pollution of the Irish Sea.

Nevertheless, by comparison with its European counterparts, the anti-nuclear campaign confirmed the moderate character of environmental protest in Britain. Anti-nuclear protest was amplified when in 1979 the Thatcher government envisaged the construction of ten pressurized water reactors. Yet, although the campaign did, at various points during 1978–81, employ the forms of non-violent direct action familiar in Britain since the rise in 1958–63 of the Campaign for Nuclear Disarmament, by comparison with events in France or Germany, protests in Britain were notably small and resolutely non-violent. Indeed, the violence of confrontations in France and Germany inhibited British campaigners from enlarging the campaign of direct action (Welsh 2000: 163). The most confrontational actions were locally intense protests designed to obstruct evaluation of/construction at possible reactor/waste repository sites. These were protests mounted by some of the '350 mixed membership groups actively campaigning on the issue throughout the UK' (Welsh 2000: 185) and at best loosely linked to campaigning organizations such as FoE.

The anti-nuclear issue was subsequently deprived of salience when the Conservative government adopted a deliberately low profile approach as it sought to avoid distracting confrontations with environmentalists whilst it concentrated its fire power on the trade unions. The need for additional nuclear capacity evaporated with the arrival of cheap and plentiful North Sea gas, the nuclear power programme was quietly shelved, and so the British environmental movement was deprived of the issue that in continental Europe was the chief stimulus to radical environmentalism.

The revival of the peace movement during the early 1980s largely eclipsed the environmental movement and, despite its lack of direct interest in the environment, probably attracted many who might otherwise have been drawn to environmental protest. By the late 1980s, when the peace movement was in decline, global environmental issues had become matters of widespread public concern. Moreover, they began to enter the political mainstream, and so environmental organizations were encouraged to concentrate their energies on participation in newly receptive national and international arena. Both FoE and Greenpeace were by now committed not only to high-profile critical campaigning but also to carrying out or funding research on environmental issues and, increasingly, to 'solutions campaigning' designed to promote better environmental practice. In this climate, calls for direct action were rare (Rüdig 1995: 230).

If environmental organizations in general prospered, the growth of the newer campaigning organizations was spectacular. Between 1981 and 1991, the numbers of members or supporting donors of FoE grew sixfold and those of Greenpeace grew tenfold. They became substantial operations: in 1995, Greenpeace, with over 200,000 donor supporters, had a staff of 106 and an income of over seven million pounds, and FoE, with over 100,000 members, had a staff of 110 and an income of nearly four million pounds (Rawcliffe 1998: 78–80).

Both FoE and Greenpeace had captured the public mood at a critical moment, and yet, by the mid-1990s, the growth of these organizations had stalled and the numbers of their members and/or supporting donors had stagnated or declined. Moreover, as we shall see, it was discontent with these organizations, as well as with the obduracy of governments, that stimulated the unprecedented rise of radical environmentalism during the 1990s.

However, before we embark on a discussion of the development of environmental protest in Britain during the decade 1988–97, it is important to consider the political context within which that development occurred.

THE POLITICAL CONTEXT

Politically, Britain was dominated for almost two decades by Conservative governments, led first by Margaret Thatcher (1979–90) and later by John Major

(1990–7). Although there were differences between the styles of the Thatcher and Major governments, they were equally strongly committed to economic development. Having diagnosed the causes of Britain's sluggish economic performance as excessive taxation, a bloated public sector, and the irresponsible exercise of power by over-mighty trade unions, the Thatcher government embarked on a neo-liberal programme of deregulation, privatization, tax cuts, and reduction of trade union power. Telecommunications, gas, electricity, and water supplies were all privatized. Bus services were deregulated and/or privatized, and the national rail monopoly was broken up and sold to the private sector. In addition to the piecemeal development of housing and industrial and commercial building, concentrated largely in already crowded parts of southern England and accelerated by the late 1980s boom, the Conservative governments committed themselves to the renovation of Britain's transport infrastructure, principally by building new roads and widening existing ones. By the mid-1990s, the road-building programme—'Roads for Prosperity'—effectively ground to a halt in the face of public opposition, but not before hugely controversial highways had been driven through several areas of recognized scenic and scientific value. The one major rail infrastructure project embarked upon by the Conservatives was the construction of the Channel Tunnel and the associated rail link to London.

Nevertheless, despite their presumptions in favour of economic development, the Thatcher government introduced a succession of measures designed to increase the effectiveness of environmental protection, among them the Wildlife and Countryside Act (1981) and the Food and Environment Protection Act (1986) (Garner 2000: 153). Even the presumption in favour of development has to be seen in the context of Britain's already extremely comprehensive system of landuse planning. The Thatcher government's aversion to regulation delayed but did not prevent the establishment of a unified pollution inspectorate (HMIP) in 1987 and the introduction of integrated pollution control, consolidated by the passing of the Environmental Protection Act in 1990. Building on this, the Major government in 1995 set up the Environment Agency, 'one of the largest organisations of its kind in the world', to unify the pollution control agencies and to implement a single licensing and inspection regime (Connelly and Smith 1999: 259). Yet if this earned the Major government at least grudging respect in some environmental circles, its credibility was soon undermined by a succession of scares over the contamination of food and the hazards of intensive, industrialized agriculture.

The election in May 1997 of a Labour government pledged to 'put the environment at the heart of policy-making' raised expectations, but although by 2002 large-scale road-building had not been resumed, the collision of the government's commitment to economic development with environmentalists' concerns had produced a series of uneasy truces over landuse planning and biotechnology issues.

THE INSTITUTIONALIZATION OF ENVIRONMENTALISM
AND THE RESURGENCE OF RADICALISM

In Britain, EMOs may often have felt marginal to the political process, but even FoE and Greenpeace, long regarded as the radical, activist end of the environmental movement, were by the 1990s frequently consulted by policy-makers and invited to comment upon draft policies. Indeed, the extent of the involvement of EMOs in partnerships with government and/or industry appeared to be restricted more by the limitations of their resources than by any closure of access to the policy-making process.

Such developments have, in Britain as elsewhere, created tensions within EMOs, and it is sometimes claimed that the increasing influence of the environmental movement and the considerable increase in the size of its 'conscience constituency' has been accompanied by a decline in the proportion of *active* members and a corresponding decline of mass participation in environmental activism since its peak in the late 1980s (Jordan and Maloney 1997).

Partly in reaction against the apparent pacification of once radical but latterly increasingly successfully institutionalized EMOs such as Greenpeace and FoE, less formally organized, even deliberately anarchistic, environmental protest has been conducted in the names of networks, quasi-organizations or 'disorganizations' such as Earth First! (EF!), Road Alert!, and Reclaim the Streets.

Their vulnerability to litigation made both Greenpeace and FoE become more cautious about the actions they undertook, but each provided material support and advice to smaller and more directly activist groups. Both, however, found it difficult to continue to do so when the demands of their own campaigns were increasing just as their revenues were stagnating or declining. Their failure to continue support once it had been given was a source of resentment among activists allied to smaller groups, and was claimed by some to have pushed them into the arms of more radical direct action groups.[2]

The rise of new kinds of environmental protest conducted by new kinds of actors, especially in the course of protests against roads and other transport infrastructure projects, made headlines, but at least as remarkable was the frequency with which the new direct action groups and networks made common cause with local environmental protest campaigns that appeared to have little if any connection with established organizations and that were often, at least initially, motivated by 'NIMBY' (Not In My Back Yard) concerns. The emergence of dreadlocked anti-roads protesters as folk heroes in the tabloid press was perhaps the most dramatic demonstration of the changed status of environmental protest in 1990s Britain.[3]

Although protests against the building of new roads and their employment of tactics such as tunnelling, tree-sitting, lock-ons, and tripods captured the imagination of commentators, these were by no means the only environmental protests that took place in Britain during the 1990s. Until now, however, we have had no systematic analysis of such protests or of the balance between them and other less spectacular forms of protest action about these and other, less novel issues.

THE INCIDENCE OF ENVIRONMENTAL PROTEST

The data for our analysis of environmental protest in Britain during the decade 1988–97 is drawn from the printed editions of *The Guardian*.[4] *The Guardian* was chosen in preference to other national 'quality' newspapers because it was published continuously during these years, and enjoyed a relatively high degree of continuity of editorial policy and of journalistic personnel throughout the period.[5] Moreover, from a preliminary comparison of reportage from several sample months spread over the decade, it appeared that *The Guardian*'s reporting of environmental action was, on average, more inclusive.

The discussion that follows is based on an analysis of the results of our examination of all the environmental protests reported in *The Guardian* during the 10 years, 1988–97. For each of these years, all possibly relevant sections of every issue of *The Guardian* were read and every identifiable report of protest involving the explicit expression of environmental concerns was copied. Every protest event[6] contained in those reports was then coded according to a common schedule and entered into an SPSS file.

Altogether we collected data on 2756 such protest events. However, of these, 1433 events were identified from summary reports—reports that give minimal information about a large number of (sometimes geographically dispersed) events often (but not invariably) occurring over an extended period of time.[7] Although the coding rules we employed were designed to yield conservative estimates of events from such reports, their inclusion more than doubles the number of events reported during the 10 years.

Figure 2.1 displays the incidence by year of protest events in which an explicitly environmental claim was articulated, both including and excluding data derived from summary reports.[8] The overall pattern is much as expected. There

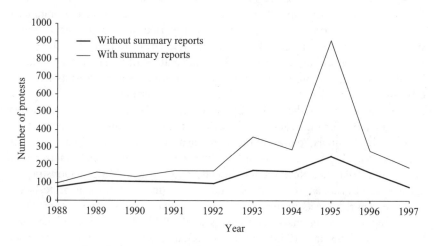

FIG. 2.1. *Environmental protest events in Britain by year*

was a modest increase in the number of reported events from 1988 to 1989, the year which we suppose to mark the peak of the first stage of increased environmental movement activity in Britain: in 1989, at the peak of the development boom encouraged by the Thatcher government's economic development policies, opinion polls placed environmental concerns at the top of the public's agenda, EMOs such as FoE and Greenpeace experienced a surge in the numbers of their supporters, and the Green Party enjoyed unprecedented success in local and European elections.

Although the next 3 years are sometimes regarded as years of demobilization for British environmentalism, at least by comparison with the 1989 peak, the annual number of reported environmental protests remained fairly steady (at around 100 events per year, rather more if summary reports are included) until 1993 when there was a dramatic increase (to 171 events, or 361 if summary reports are included). There followed a modest retrenchment in 1994 before the massive upward spike (to 252 events, or 907 including summary reports) in 1995, after which the number of events fell back sharply. Excluding data from summary reports, the number of reported protests in 1997 was virtually the same as in 1988.[9]

If data derived from summary reports are included, the decline in 1997 is much less pronounced. However, the 1995 peak is very much more striking; including data from summary reports, almost a third of all the environmental protests during the whole 10-year period occurred in 1995. However, if summary reports are excluded, 1995 accounts for a much reduced 19 per cent of all protests. This demonstrates the impact upon our data of a relatively small number of summary reports mentioning but giving minimal detail about a large number of sometimes contemporaneous events.

The number of summary reports of environmental (including animal welfare and anti-hunting) protests varied from year to year. In low single figures up to 1994, it rose to twenty-seven in 1995 before falling back to single figures. In 1995, over 72 per cent of identifiable events were contained in summary reports. The proportion of all protest events reported only in summary reports varied, but it showed a general tendency to rise (from roughly one in four in 1988–90 to over 40 per cent from 1992). This pattern of variation may reflect a long-term change in journalistic practices, but it most probably results from the efforts of journalists to find means adequately to cover the widespread surges of protest associated with the peaks of protest waves.[10] The 1995 peak in particular was remarkable for the near coincidence of a number of campaigns: against the export of live animals, to prevent the dumping at sea of the Brent Spar oil storage buoy, against Shell's operations in the Niger delta, against French nuclear tests in the south Pacific, Reclaim the Streets, and Critical Mass demonstrations against road traffic, as well as various new or continuing anti-roads protests and 'right to roam' protests by the Ramblers' Association (RA). The proportion of events reported in summary reports was markedly higher in each of the three years (1989, 1993, and 1995) that, even excluding summary reports, appear as peaks in the waves of protest than they were in the immediately preceding years. Summary reports thus appear to enhance the salience of what from more detailed reports appear to be the peaks of protest. Nevertheless, they may be considered to give a distorted picture of the incidence of protest and, especially, of the publicly visible volume of protest.

The amount and quality of information we are able to abstract from summary reports is limited,[11] but to disregard them entirely would be to ignore important information about the extent and character of environmental protest. Summary reports amplify the impact of protest by giving the reader the impression that the events reported in greater detail are but the tip of an iceberg. As such they are shafts of light shone upon the large number of protests too small or localized to attract the attention of the national press. Unfortunately, however, it is unlikely that the protests illuminated by summary reports are simply a random sample of all such small or localized protests. It is much more likely that summary reports exaggerate the relative frequency of protests that are part of protracted campaigns, particularly campaigns orchestrated by national organizations.[12] For this reason, data derived exclusively from summary reports must be treated with special caution, and they have been omitted from the analyses that follow.

THE GEOGRAPHICAL DISTRIBUTION OF PROTEST

How much confidence can we have in our data? It should be emphasized that they represent the numbers of events *reported* in one national newspaper, and not the actual numbers of events. In the absence of other information, we simply do not know how many environmental and cognate protests may have gone unreported but we can reasonably surmise that it is a great many and that the extent of under-reporting will not have been constant over time.

Fillieule (1996, 1997) has ably demonstrated the extent of the bias and incompleteness of national newspaper reports of protest in France by comparison with police records and local press reports. Of these sources of data, police records were the most complete, but whilst up to 95 per cent of protest events recorded by the police were also reported in the local press, the percentage reported in the national press was very much lower. Reports in *Le Monde* under-reported events that occurred outside a 'cycle' of protest, but they also under-reported events that occurred outside the Paris region.

It seemed probable that a similar pattern of under-reporting by the London-based national press might also exist in Britain, although the fact that *The Guardian* was historically a Manchester-based paper and is still published in both London and Manchester might make it more likely to be regionally balanced in its coverage than other national newspapers. In fact, the geographical distribution of protests reported in *The Guardian* was wider than we might have expected (see Table 2.1). Just over half (52 per cent) of all environmental protests of which

TABLE 2.1. *The spatial distribution of environmental protests in Britain (1988–97) compared with population*

Region	Percentage of protest events	Percentage of population[a]	Index of representation[b]
London	26.4	11.9	2.21
South East	25.8	18.7	1.38
South West	12.9	8.2	1.57
East Anglia	2.0	3.6	0.55
East Midlands	3.3	7.0	0.47
West Midlands	3.1	9.1	0.34
Yorks and Humberside	5.6	8.6	0.66
North West	8.0	11.0	0.73
North	3.7	5.3	0.70
Wales	3.2	5.0	0.65
Scotland	4.9	8.8	0.56
Northern Ireland	1.0	2.8	0.35
Total N	1,206	58,394,600	

Notes:
[a] Population figures for 1994 from the Office for National Statistics, General Register Office for Scotland, and Northern Ireland Statistics and Research Agency.
[b] 'Index of representation' is a figure obtained by dividing the number of protests by the number of protests expected from the ratio of the total number of events to total population; values above one indicate over-representation of an area in the data set, and values below one an under-representation.

the location was reported occurred in London and the south-east of England, regions that together accounted for just under a third (31 per cent) of the British population.[13] The most over-represented region was London (12 per cent of population but 26 per cent of reported environmental protest). This is scarcely surprising.

In a country as politically and culturally centralized as Britain, a disproportionate share of protest action is likely to take place in the national capital, especially when such action is undertaken or coordinated by national organizations, is allied to lobbying activities, or is designed to put issues on national or international political agenda. London protests were little more than half as likely as the national average to be mobilized on a purely local level (22 per cent compared with 42 per cent), and they were more likely to be part of national mobilizations (58 per cent compared with 42 per cent for the United Kingdom as a whole). Especially striking is the disproportionate share (62 per cent) of London protests involving issues that were international in scope.

London apart, it was the south-west of England that was the most over-represented region: 13 per cent of reported protest was located in the south-west, compared with just over 8 per cent of the population. This over-representation is consistent with a very modest geographical concentration of electoral support for the Green Party and with claims that the south-west is the centre of a 'DIY' counterculture (Jowers et al. 1996) of which environmentalism is a key component.[14]

After allowances are made for the tendency of national protests to be concentrated in the national capital, this pattern of reported protest does not differ radically from the picture of the spatial distribution of membership of EMOs reported in earlier studies. Both Cowell and Jehlicka's (1995) mapping of the spatial distribution of membership of major environmental organizations and Rüdig, Bennie, and Franklin's (1991) survey of members of the Green Party showed that greens were disproportionately concentrated in the south of England *outside* London.

Thus, although the geographical distribution of reported protest was skewed towards London and the south, the extent of that skewing is not so great as to be an implausible representation of the probable pattern of *actual* protest.

THE ISSUES OF PROTEST

The broad pattern of environmental protest revealed in Fig. 2.1 aggregates a number of campaigns about a variety of issues. Four major sets of environmental issues can be identified in reports of protest during the 10 years: transport, including railways, roads, and airports (involved in 28 per cent of environmental protests); animal welfare and hunting (27 per cent); nature conservation (21 per cent); and a broad spectrum of pollution, urban, and industrial issues (20 per cent). Energy, including nuclear energy and nuclear waste (8 per cent), land rights (7 per cent), and issues surrounding alternative production and technology (4 per cent) account for most of the remainder.[15] These and the main components of each of these categories for each year are represented in Table 2.2.

Figure 2.2 shows the trends over time in each of the four leading categories of issues. In each of the 10 years there were at least ten protests concerning nature conservation, with the number rising sharply from 1992 to peak in 1995 before falling back. Pollution, urban, and industrial claims had two peaks—1990 and 1995—and only in 1997 did they fall to single figures. The incidence of protests involving animal welfare issues was more erratic, rising until 1991 then declining sharply before rising strongly to comprise a third of all protests from 1993–5 before falling back again. If anti-hunting protests are disaggregated from other animal welfare issues, there is even less pattern; less numerous overall, anti-hunting protests outnumbered other animal welfare protests in 3 of the 10 years (1988, 1991, and 1997). Protests concerning transport showed a modest 1989 peak associated with the many local protests against the Channel Tunnel and the associated high speed rail link, and began to rise again from 1992 to a sharp peak in 1996 associated mainly with the development of anti-roads protests.

Among other issues, protests concerning energy—over 70 per cent of them involving nuclear power or waste—were raised relatively infrequently and

TABLE 2.2. *Environmental issues raised in protests in Britain by year (percentage of events in which issue is raised by year)*

	1988	1989	1990	1991	1992	1993	1994	1995	1996	1997	Total N
Nature conservation	*18.2*	*10.0*	*15.9*	*9.4*	*37.1*	*25.7*	*21.1*	*29.8*	*13.8*	*19.2*	*279*
Countryside/landscape	11.7	3.6	10.3	4.7	22.7	12.3	11.4	4.8	3.1	10.3	116
Pollution, urban and industrial	*16.9*	*36.4*	*30.8*	*17.9*	*22.7*	*14.0*	*15.1*	*21.0*	*18.2*	*6.4*	*263*
Pollution	10.4	14.5	19.6	4.7	10.3	5.8	6.6	16.3	4.4	3.8	132
Waste (non-nuclear)	0.0	13.6	0.0	4.7	1.0	0.6	0.6	0.0	0.0	1.3	24
Energy	*20.8*	*6.4*	*7.5*	*10.4*	*6.2*	*10.5*	*5.4*	*6.0*	*1.9*	*15.4*	*105*
Nuclear	20.8	2.7	5.6	5.7	3.1	7.6	3.0	2.4	1.3	0.0	60
Animal welfare and hunting	*19.5*	*15.5*	*32.7*	*41.5*	*9.3*	*34.5*	*32.5*	*36.1*	*5.7*	*24.4*	*352*
Animal welfare	9.1	12.7	22.4	17.9	7.2	21.1	25.3	31.3	3.1	6.4	238
Hunting	10.4	2.7	10.3	23.6	2.1	13.5	7.2	4.8	2.5	17.9	114
Transport	*11.7*	*27.3*	*12.1*	*8.5*	*23.7*	*32.7*	*34.9*	*23.0*	*57.2*	*30.8*	*371*
Roads	5.2	9.1	11.2	5.7	19.6	28.1	28.9	15.1	30.2	12.8	243
Traffic	1.3	0.0	0.0	1.9	1.0	3.5	2.4	6.0	25.2	1.3	70
Airports	0.0	0.0	0.0	0.0	2.1	0.6	1.8	2.0	0.6	16.7	25
Rail	3.9	13.6	0.0	0.9	1.0	0.6	0.6	0.0	1.3	0.0	24
Alternative production, etc.	*2.6*	*3.6*	*11.2*	*1.9*	*2.1*	*4.1*	*2.4*	*1.2*	*6.9*	*5.1*	*51*
Land rights	13.0	8.2	9.3	11.3	16.5	0.6	3.0	7.5	6.9	2.6	95
Total N of events	77	110	107	106	97	171	166	252	159	78	

Note: Broad categories of issues in italic; subcategories in roman. Percentages do not sum to 100 as up to 2 issues could be recorded per event.

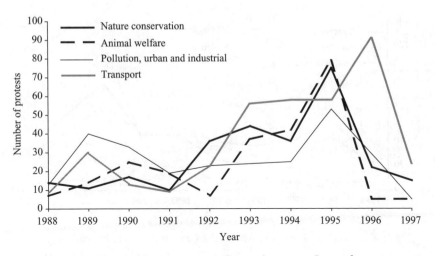

Fig. 2.2. *Four leading environmental issue domains in Britain by year*

showed no clear trend. Land rights was a recurrent issue. Although land rights protests included New Age travelers' demands for access and urban land occupations demanding the construction of affordable housing by The Land is Ours, they were principally concerned with Ramblers' demands for the right to freely roam through privately owned or tenanted land in the countryside. Because land rights protests mainly took the form of RA days of action, they gave rise to relatively few reported protests other than in summary reports. Protests explicitly advocating environmentally friendly activities such as alternative technology or environmentally friendly agriculture were rare and showed no clear trend.

The most strongly emergent issue of contention during this period was transport: the sixth ranking issue in 1988 and 1991, it ranked first or second in every year thereafter; indeed, protests concerned with transport were more numerous than those concerned with all other pollution, urban, industrial, and energy issues combined.

THE FORMS OF PROTEST: TOWARDS MORE CONFRONTATIONAL PROTEST?

For present purposes, we have categorized the forms of protest as: conventional (comprising procedural claims such as demands for judicial review, actions such as collective representations to officials or elected politicians, public meetings, leafleting, and the collection of signatures on petitions); demonstrative actions (including street marches, rallies, and vigils); confrontational actions (including occupations and physical obstruction); minor attacks on property (that stop short of posing a threat to human life, but including theft); and violence (consisting of

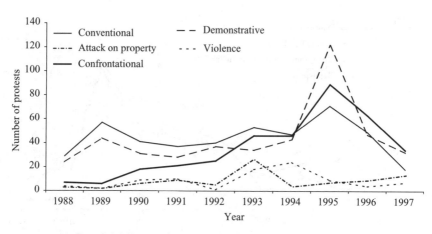

FIG. 2.3. *Forms of environmental protest in Britain by year*

attacks on persons whether or not they cause actual injury, and including attacks on property that might be potentially life threatening).

What is most striking about the picture of environmental protest that emerges from newspaper reports (see Fig. 2.3) is its relative moderation throughout the 10 years. Conventional forms of action and demonstrations were involved in 37 and 31 per cent, respectively, of all reported protests during the 10 years and, apart from the sharp increase in demonstrations (associated disproportionately with animal welfare) in 1995, their incidence varied relatively little over time. In absolute numbers, conventional forms of action peaked in 1989 but then, after falling back in 1990, rose modestly until 1995. However, conventional forms of action, and especially procedural claims, were mentioned in a declining proportion of all reported protests. The pattern of demonstrations more closely followed the trajectory of protests as a whole, peaking first in 1989 and then, more sharply, in 1995 before falling steeply thereafter.

It is frequently claimed by commentators on social movements that the age of mass demonstrations is over. Yet the total number of demonstrations was significantly higher in the second half of our decade than it was in the first (273 compared with 164). Very large demonstrations (involving 500 or more participants) are relatively unlikely to go unreported, so it is worth examining more closely their incidence over time.

The number of such large demonstrations about environmental issues exceeded five in only 3 years—1989 (ten), 1995 (fourteen), and 1996 (seven)—and in 2 years—1990 and 1997—there was only one large demonstration reported. In all, there were twenty-two large demonstrations in the years 1988–92 and twenty-nine in 1993–7. Overall, then, there was a modest increase in the number of large demonstrations.[16] The increase in the numbers of large actions is, however, wholly attributable to the considerable number of demonstrations associated with animal rights, especially those against the export of live animals in 1995. If we consider only protests concerning environmental issues *other than* animal welfare, there was not an increase but a modest *decline* (from twenty in 1988–92 to seventeen in 1993–7) in the number of large demonstrations.

Moreover, the number of large demonstrations needs to be seen in the context of the overall increase in the total number of reported protest events in the second half of our 10 years: over 62 per cent of reported protests occurred after 1992. As a proportion of all protest events, large demonstrations declined modestly during the second half of the decade (from 4.4 to 3.5 per cent), but as a proportion of environmental protests on issues other than animal welfare they declined markedly (from 5.2 to 2.9 per cent).

Estimated numbers of participants were given for only one-third of the events reported, and we might suppose that such estimates will more often be given in the case of large protests. From Fig. 2.4 it is apparent that the total numbers of reported participants in protests involving at least 500 people declined sharply after 1990 and that it rose again only gradually from 1992 to a much more modest peak in 1994 before again falling sharply. Many of these large protests—and all the largest—involved petitions.[17] However, petitions are not only very undemanding of participants but, because they have limited news value except in the context of campaigns that are also pursued by more dramatic means, petitions are also more likely than are large demonstrations to go unreported. If large demonstrations[18] alone are considered, the pattern is somewhat different: the sharp decline occurred after the 1989 peak and was not substantially reversed until the 1995 peak after which they again declined.[19] In both cases, the year in which the number of reported participants in large environmental protests was lowest (by far) was 1997.[20]

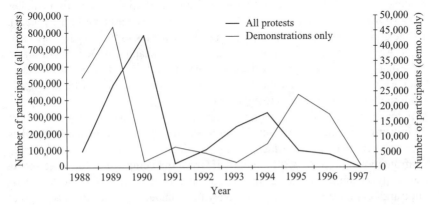

FIG. 2.4. *Number of participants in larger environmental protests in Britain by year (protests with 500 or more participants)*

However we measure it, there was a marked decline in the mean and median numbers of participants in the second as compared with the first half of the decade. Thus, the median number of participants in large demonstrations (demonstrations with at least 500 participants) fell from 2000 in 1988–92 to 825 in 1993–7, and the median number of participants in *all* demonstrations fell from 180 to 105.[21] Clearly, the increased number of demonstrations and other forms of protest was the product of an absolute and relative increase in the number of reported actions involving smaller numbers of people.

Confrontation was present in 19 per cent of protests, but there were considerable changes in its incidence over time. Uncommon at the beginning of the period, confrontation increased almost monotonically from 1992 onwards until by the mid-1990s it was reported as being involved in more than 35 per cent of environmental protests. This, too, is a significant development.

Minor attacks on property amounted to only 6 per cent of all environmental protests. Rare in the first half of our decade, they peaked (at twenty-seven) in 1993 when they were involved in more than one in seven of all reported environmental protests, but otherwise they remained relatively infrequent. Indeed, such attacks on property were present in a smaller proportion of protests in the 4 years since 1993 than in the preceding 4 years (4.1 per cent compared with 5.2 per cent). Given the small numbers and the degree of fluctuation, it would be unwise to purport to detect a trend.

Protests involving violent action—attacks on people or attacks on property that were reckless about potential harm to people—amounted to 6.3 per cent of the total. They peaked in 1993–4 but thereafter fell back to the very low levels of 1988–9. The greater violence of the second half of the decade was concentrated in just 2 years; the number of violent protests in the final 3 years (1995–7) was, in aggregate, precisely the same as that in the first 3 years (1988–90). As a proportion of all protests, those involving violence were, even at their peak, only moderately above the levels of 1990–1 and during 1995–7 they were a smaller proportion of protests than in 1988–92 (3.1 per cent compared with 5.1 per cent). By the end of the decade violent protests had fallen back to the very low levels of 1989. Again, there is no clear trend but, most significantly in view of the alarm bells that have been rung about the rise of eco-terrorism and the need for extraordinary measures to deal with it, there is no evidence at all of a trend towards more violent forms of environmental protest.

A major problem in interpreting the figures on the changing forms of protest derives from the media's perennial interest in novelty and spectacle. This makes it most likely that the most thematically and tactically innovative and the most confrontational protests will be reported. Given the competition for news space, especially when there are novel and or confrontational events to be reported, moderate and less innovative actions are likely to be under-reported. Because a great deal of the activity associated with the environmental movement is local, routine, and seldom confrontational, it is largely unreported in the national press.

The more confrontational actions of animal rights demonstrators are more likely to be considered to have news value, and so the relative importance of them may be exaggerated by the relatively greater frequency with which they are reported. Similarly, to the extent that they were in this period both novel and confrontational, anti-roads protests were especially likely to be reported and their impact amplified by comparison with that of other forms of environmental movement activity.[22]

Journalists themselves testify to the declining news value of routine protest during this period. According to Paul Brown, *The Guardian*'s environment correspondent, by 1992–3 the news desk was suffering enormously from protest fatigue.[23] Whereas previously simply being on a Greenpeace boat was something a journalist could write about, by 1992–3 such a report would only be considered newsworthy if there was a high element of danger (cf. Brown and McDonald 2000). Thus, while the increased incidence of reported events involving confrontation almost certainly reflected a real increase in the frequency of such action, the contemporaneous relative decline in the reported incidence of moderate actions may well reflect a decline in the *reporting* of such actions rather than an actual decline in their frequency.

The increasing volume of environmental news of all kinds also had an impact upon the extent of the reporting of environmental protests. As the number of stories they were offered increased, so environmental journalists were, in the interests of their own survival, forced to be less accessible, and to be more selective in their following up of stories.[24] Paul Brown reported that whereas in 1990 he would never take his phone off the hook, by 1999 he did so most days, relied increasingly upon contacts, and was increasingly fearful of missing an important story. Offered some twenty stories a day, perhaps ten of which might be considered newsworthy, Brown had to whittle these down to three, two or, some days, just one report. By no means all of these stories were of protests, but the implication is that the increasing abundance of environmental news means that the chances of any particular story actually being carried in the press have declined. The likelihood is that the usual principles of news value will select against the moderate and the unspectacular and in favour of the confrontational and, where it occurs, the violent.[25]

This tendency is likely to have been exacerbated by the changes that took place in the character of British 'quality' newspapers during the decade. Increasingly, print media took on the news values of television; pictures and or graphics were increasingly considered essential to a story, many stories appearing only as captions to photographs. Although *The Guardian* was not in the vanguard of these changes, it was not immune from them, and it is likely that the greater news value of stories associated with pictures of confrontation tended further to drive out stories of more moderate and less photogenic action. Another aspect of these changes, and one in which *The Guardian* was no laggard, was the increased requirement of 'colour' even in news stories as 'human interest' became a more important criterion of news value. One consequence of this was the increasing tendency of journalists to personalize stories about protest and even to transform protesters into media celebrities. Thus, to his intense embarrassment, the anti-roads tunneller, 'Swampy', became an icon of the new wave of environmental protest (Paterson 2000).

We should therefore be very cautious in drawing inferences about the changing repertoire of environmental protest from data such as these. Although we are able to show an increase in the number and proportion of *reported* protests that involved confrontation, we cannot say with complete confidence that confrontational protests increased as a proportion of all the environmental protest *that actually occurred* in Britain during these years. What we can infer, however, is that the public visibility of confrontational protest associated with environmental issues increased and that it increased relative to that of moderate protest.

Such is the news value of violence that it is most unlikely that any violent action would, if it occurred, go unreported. For this reason, we can say with some confidence that there was no clear trend towards more frequent resort to violence in environmental protests.

FORMS AND ISSUES

Particular forms of action appear to be associated with different kinds of issues (see Table 2.3). Only 20 per cent of protests regarding pollution, urban, and industrial issues were reported to have involved forms of action more radical than demonstrations, and almost half employed the most moderate and conventional forms of all—appeals and procedural claims; demonstrations (occurring in 34 per cent of protests) were the next most frequently reported forms of action associated with this group of issues. Protests concerning energy issues were scarcely less moderate.

Although land rights protests were distinctive in the extent to which they involved demonstrations (45 per cent), 27 per cent involved more radical actions. The action repertoire associated with nature protection was broader, with 37 per cent involving confrontation or, occasionally, attacks on property. Nevertheless, most protests about nature protection involved forms of action at the moderate end of the spectrum, conventional forms of action and demonstrations being involved in 39 and 34 per cent of protests, respectively.[26]

Transport protests were rather more confrontational; nearly half involved confrontation or attacks on property, and confrontation (39 per cent) was the modal form of action. This, however, conceals a considerable change over time; transport issues were associated especially with conventional appeals in the earlier years and with confrontation from 1992 to 1996. Although the trend towards more confrontation is especially evident in the case of transport-related protests, it is apparent across the broad range of environmental issues.[27]

TABLE 2.3. *Issues and the forms of environmental protest in Britain (% of events involving each issue that involves a form of action)*

	Conventional percentage	Demonstrative percentage	Confrontational percentage	Attack on property percentage	Violence percentage	N
Nature conservation	39.4	33.7	30.1	6.5	0.4	279
Pollution, urban and industrial	47.5	33.5	18.6	1.5	0.0	263
Energy	43.8	26.7	19.0	1.9	0.0	105
Animal welfare	14.3	37.8	14.3	12.6	29.4	238
Hunting	18.4	21.1	44.7	3.5	8.8	114
Transport	30.7	29.9	39.4	5.7	0.5	371
Alternative production, etc.	49.0	29.4	7.8	3.9	0.0	51
Land rights	37.9	45.3	25.3	2.1	0.0	95
N	431	438	348	79	83	

Note: Percentages do not sum to 100 because for each protest up to 2 issues and 4 forms could be recorded.

Nearly half of the minor attacks on property were associated with animal rights protests; one in four was associated with transport-related protests, and most of the remainder were actions such as the symbolic 'theft' of rainforest timbers from DIY stores.

With the exception of animal rights protests, violent action was notable by its absence. Only three protests about a strictly environmental issue during the whole 10 years were reported to have involved violence: in 1989 a McDonald's restaurant was bombed in protest against the destruction of rainforest; in 1996 anti-roads protesters at Newbury fired catapults at construction equipment and injured a security guard; and in 1997 protesters set fire to construction equipment at the site of the Newbury bypass. During the whole decade, in only thirteen protests about a strictly environmental issue were protesters reported to have used force, and on eleven of those occasions (and on fifty-seven other occasions), force was also used by the police. In only seven such protests were protesters reported to have caused injuries, and in five of those protests (and in ten others) injuries were also reported to have been caused by the police.

If attacks on property and, especially, violent actions were exceedingly rare in strictly environmental protests, the same cannot be said about protests concerning animal rights. The distribution of animal welfare protests was bimodal, with demonstrations (38 per cent) and violence (29 per cent) the most common forms of action. This reflects the coexistence of two quite distinct tendencies: an overwhelmingly demonstrative animal welfare campaign, focusing especially on the export of live animals; and an animal rights campaign focused especially upon opposition to fur-farming and experiments on animals, some strands of which were relatively uninhibited about the use of violence. Anti-hunting protests showed a different pattern, with confrontation the modal form of action (45 per cent). A clear majority of both hunting and animal welfare protests involved forms of action more radical than demonstrations, but it is with respect to violence that they were most distinctive (and distinct one from the other). Animal rights protests stand out starkly. Whereas even attacks on property were rare in relation to other issues, they were involved in 13 per cent of animal welfare protests. More extreme forms of violence against property or persons were present in 29 per cent of animal rights protests and 9 per cent of anti-hunting protests.

Data derived from summary reports have been excluded from the foregoing analysis. However, if they are included, the main effects are to emphasize the association of land rights protests with demonstrations, and to reduce the salience of violence in both animal welfare and anti-hunting protests (in favour of demonstrative and confrontational actions respectively). This serves as a useful reminder that, distinctive though animal rights protests were in the extent of their resort to violence, the great majority of the large number of individual protests that were mounted in the course of long-running and geographically dispersed animal welfare campaigns were non-violent.

ORGANIZATIONAL SPECIALIZATION?

The frequency with which reported actions were associated with a particular organization varied over time, but the numbers of groups named in each year corresponded very closely to the number of protests reported. A total of 274 organizations were named in connection with one or more of the 1323 protests, but only a few were mentioned more than a dozen times.

Table 2.4 displays the number of protests involving the eleven organizations most often mentioned in reported environmental protests for each year. The two organizations most mentioned—Greenpeace and FoE—were also the ones most stably represented over time. Remarkably, with the exception of the 1995 surge in which both participated, their reported involvement in protests was relatively unrelated to the total numbers of protest events in a year. The Green Party was most mentioned in the immediate aftermath of its successes in the 1989 local and European elections, and scarcely at all thereafter. The RA was reported to have been involved in protests in every year but 1993, but a marked period of height-ened activity in 1995 appears only if data from summary reports are added.

EF! emerged strongly in 1992–3 but its reported involvement in protest declined both relatively and absolutely after 1995. Since other evidence (Wall, Doherty, and Plows 2002) does not suggest a decline in EF!'s activity, this find-ing may seem surprising. It is perhaps explained by EF!'s very loose form of organization and the consequence that its supporters did not necessarily use EF!'s name but sometimes protested using the names of other similarly structured but more thematically focused organizations such as Road Alert! and Reclaim the Streets, or as part of single-issue campaign coalitions such as the anti-roads group, Alarm UK (McNeish 2000*b*).

The animal welfare groups had their own idiosyncratic patterns of reported activity. The League against Cruel Sports (LACS) was mentioned at a relatively

TABLE 2.4. *Number of environmental protests in Britain involving leading groups by year*

	1988	1989	1990	1991	1992	1993	1994	1995	1996	1997	1988–97
Greenpeace	14	6	11	10	10	10	9	19	6	12	107
FoE	5	9	7	2	10	6	7	26	12	3	87
EF!	0	0	0	1	7	15	6	13	1	1	44
WWF	1	0	3	2	0	3	2	1	2	3	17
RSPB	0	1	4	2	0	1	2	1	2	1	14
Green Party	0	2	9	1	0	1	0	1	0	0	14
RA	3	6	9	7	2	0	3	8	8	1	47
LACS	2	1	1	2	0	4	2	2	0	3	17
CIWF	1	0	4	0	0	0	9	11	0	0	25
ALF	1	0	7	13	1	8	0	2	3	2	37
Justice Department	0	0	0	0	0	14	3	0	0	0	17
Total *N* of events	77	110	107	106	97	171	166	252	159	78	1323

stable, if low level, throughout the 10 years. By contrast, the activities of the Animal Liberation Front (ALF) were concentrated in 1990–1 and 1993, and those of Compassion in World Farming (CIWF) in the campaign against live animal exports in 1994–5. The reported actions of Justice Department were confined to a single bombing campaign in the autumn and winter of 1993–4.

The pattern of their reported involvement in protest appears to confirm the importance of organization and resources to a group's ability to remain publicly visible through media reports. Greenpeace and FoE, in particular, were able to use their resources to offer relatively secure and stable employment to their research and public relations staff who were in turn able to accumulate expertise and to cultivate contacts. By regularly issuing press releases, they were sometimes able to keep issues on the agenda and their names in the news even in the absence of protest, something that was virtually impossible for less well-resourced groups. The temporal pattern of groups' reported involvement in protest also suggests the importance of campaigns as a lens through which media attention is focused on protesting organizations.

If there is evidence that the issues and the forms of protest were quite closely coupled, it is no less clear that there was specialization among groups and organizations with respect to the forms of action with which they were associated (see Table 2.5).

Greenpeace, the organization most frequently mentioned, appears to have had the broadest tactical repertoire, with a fairly even spread across the conventional, demonstrative, and confrontational forms. By comparison, FoE, although it too appears to have employed a broad tactical repertoire, was more firmly anchored in the moderate and non-confrontational: fewer than one in six of FoE's reported actions involved confrontation, and more than half involved no action beyond

TABLE 2.5. *Environmental groups and their forms of protest in Britain (number of events)*

	Conventional	Demonstrative	Confrontational	Attack on property	Violence	Other	Total
Greenpeace	38	33	35	2	0	10	107
FoE	47	31	13	0	0	3	87
EF!	4	13	26	10	0	5	44
WWF	14	1	0	0	0	2	17
RSPB	11	3	0	0	0	0	14
Green Party	3	9	2	0	0	0	14
RA	19	32	0	0	0	0	47
LACS	8	3	3	1	0	4	17
CIWF	6	17	4	1	0	1	25
ALF	0	0	1	16	20	1	37
Justice Department	0	0	0	0	17	0	17
Total N of events	431	438	348	79	83	87	

appeals and procedural claims. If FoE was anxious to repair its links with more radical and grassroots activists, this was not reflected in its own reported repertoire of action.

Not surprisingly, the small number of reported actions involving the World Wide Fund for Nature (WWF) and the RSPB were skewed strongly to the most moderate forms of action. By contrast, EF!'s reported repertoire was concentrated around confrontation, followed by demonstrations and minor attacks on property.[28] The Green Party also appeared tactically specialized: two-thirds of its reported actions were demonstrations. Scarcely less specialized, and also focused on demonstrations, was the RA.

The important distinctions concealed by the broad category 'animal welfare' are apparent when the action repertoires of the most often reported groups are compared. Although the animal welfare group CIWF had a repertoire strongly focused upon demonstrations (and the local groups campaigning against the export of live animals even more so), the ALF was almost exclusively associated with minor attacks on property and more violent forms of action. The still more obscure group, Justice Department, was even more exclusively associated with violence. By contrast, the main anti-hunting group, LACS, appears to have employed a relatively conventional repertoire.

We should be cautious in our interpretations of these figures. These are the *reported* forms of action of the groups listed, and it is possible that journalists sometimes wrongly described actions or wrongly attributed an action to a particular group. It is, however, even more likely that many of these groups' other actions went unreported. The effects of the normal routines and selection biases of mass media are likely to be reflected here. First, the most dramatic, confrontational, and violent actions are those most likely to be reported and, as a result, the groups associated with such actions have a greater likelihood of being mentioned. Second, the larger, better organized and better resourced groups will be better able to mount and to secure publicity for the full range of their activities, and especially for their less disruptive actions. Nevertheless, the picture painted by these figures is likely to be the basis of the image the better-informed members of the public have of the groups comprising the environmental movement.

If there is specialization among environmental groups with respect to the forms of their action, it is greater still when it comes to the issues with which they deal (see Table 2.6). The animal welfare groups (CIWF, ALF, LACS, and Justice Department) were exclusively focused upon animal welfare issues.[29] With the exception of a single event involving the Green Party, none of the more strictly environmental organizations mentioned more than a dozen times was ever reported to have been involved in action on animal welfare issues. The RA was also highly specialized: three-quarters of its reported actions involved land rights, a claim scarcely ever associated with other groups.

If the other environmental organizations appear less specialized, there were nevertheless substantial differences among them. Although WWF and the RSPB

TABLE 2.6. *Environmental groups and their issues of protest in Britain (number of events)*

	Nature conservation	Pollution, urban and industrial	Energy	Animal welfare and hunting	Transport	Alternative production, etc.	Land rights	Other	Total
Greenpeace	17	54	43	0	5	5	0	4	107
FoE	37	23	5	0	35	6	1	4	87
EF!	22	10	1	0	23	1	1	1	44
WWF	11	3	1	0	5	2	0	2	17
RSPB	11	1	0	0	6	0	0	1	14
Green Party	1	9	1	1	3	1	1	1	14
RA	4	1	0	0	0	0	36	8	47
LACS	0	0	0	17	0	0	0	0	17
CIWF	0	0	0	25	0	3	0	0	25
ALF	0	0	0	37	0	0	0	0	37
Justice Department	0	0	0	17	0	0	0	0	17
Total *N* of events	279	263	105	352	371	51	95	53	

were primarily mentioned in reports of protests about nature protection, both were also reported as being involved in a small number of other protests, especially those concerning transport issues. The Green Party was mentioned principally in relation to protests about pollution, urban, and industrial issues. EF! had a broader claims repertoire, and was mentioned most in relation to transport and nature protection protests, with pollution and urban industrial issues a distant third. FoE's claims profile was similar to but rather less specialized than that of EF!. That of Greenpeace, however, was quite distinctive; little involved in transport issues, Greenpeace was strongly focused upon pollution, urban, and industrial issues, these accounting for half the protests in which Greenpeace was named. But it was its involvement in energy issues that most marks Greenpeace out; 40 per cent of its reported action involved energy, and over half of all the protests over energy in which a group was named were protests involving Greenpeace.

Despite the evident fragmentation and specialization of the environmental movement, throughout the decade there were well-documented instances of collaboration between groups whose relationships one might have supposed to be competitive. Thus, in 1990 Greenpeace, FoE, and WWF collaborated in the 'Dirty Man of Europe' campaign to undermine the credibility of the Conservative government's environmental policy (Statham 1997). At various points in the anti-roads campaigns, EF! activists collaborated with FoE. Greenpeace is known to have supported smaller, more specialized groups with pump-priming funds, and FoE was open about its willingness to provide advice and infrastructural support to protesters who took direct action of a kind that FoE, because of its vulnerability to litigation, was itself unable to take (Festing 1997).

There is evidence that activists, ranging from the 'green anarchists' of EF! to the moderate and increasingly professionalized campaigners of FoE, WWF, and other nature protection organizations, regard themselves as belonging to the same broad environmental movement. The Green Direct Action Conference held at Keele University in October 1997 brought together activists from FoE as well as the newer, less institutionalized groups and was notable for its lack of rancour. The FoE spokesman made a forthright presentation of what the movement could and could not expect of FoE, constrained as it was by its vulnerability to legal sanctions, whilst a speaker identified with EF! spoke of a broad movement embracing environmental reformists and radical activists alike. In focus groups we conducted in London in late 1998, representatives of Greenpeace, Transport 2000, the Women's Environmental Network, and an anti-roads protester were happy to regard themselves as all part of the same movement but practising a specialized division of labour.

ONE MOVEMENT OR SEVERAL?

As this research is part of a crossnationally comparative European project, we have adopted a common and inclusive definition of environmental protest.

However, the character and significance of apparently similar issues vary from one European country to another. In most European countries, animal welfare and hunting issues are generally regarded relatively unproblematically as a part, albeit usually a minor one, of the broad agenda of the environmental movement. In Britain, however, anti-hunting and animal welfare protests have quite distinct histories, and although there are some overlaps of personnel and concerns, there are some respects in which they have been at variance with the mainstream of the environmental movement.

Many people who identify themselves as members or supporters of the environmental movement in Britain do not regard that movement as including either campaigners against hunting or animal welfare campaigners. For example, some self-proclaimed conservationists are pro-hunting on the grounds that the preservation of hunting encourages landowners to retain traditional landscape features that on strictly commercial criteria might be removed. Hedges and copses, preserved because they act as refuges for hunted animals, are also sanctuaries for other native wildlife and for many species of endangered flora, and so are considered essential to the preservation of bio-diversity. This is one strand of the pro-hunting Countryside Alliance, the umbrella organization that in 1998 and 2002 organized the biggest street demonstrations London had yet seen.

By failing to distinguish animal welfare and anti-hunting protests from those concerned with more strictly and narrowly environmental issues, we might, in Britain, be conflating two, or even three, quite separate movements. Following Diani (1992), the environmental movement may be defined as a loose, non-institutionalized network that includes, as well as individuals and groups who have no organizational affiliation, organizations of varying degrees of formality and even parties, especially green parties, and that is engaged in collective action motivated by shared environmental concern (Rootes 1997*b*: 326).

The environmental movement milieu in Britain is large and organizationally diverse, and within it there is a variety of groups whose concerns and issue foci are more or less distinct and specialized. The extent to which they share a common identity and are sufficiently networked one to another to constitute a single movement is problematic. Our data permit us to determine the extent to which the various issues and groups that, from a European perspective, might be considered part of the environmental movement do in fact, in Britain, constitute a single network, at least in the limited sense of their being reported as having been present in the same protest events. Of the 321 environmental protests in which two issues were reported to have been involved, in only 17 cases (5 per cent) was animal welfare at issue alongside a more strictly environmental issue.

When we look at the frequency with which each of the dozen most frequently named groups was involved in protests about various issues, a very clear pattern emerges. Of the 329 protests in which one or more of the seven most frequently mentioned environmental groups (other than animal welfare groups) was reported to have been involved, in only one was an animal welfare or hunting issue reported as having been raised. Similarly, of the 110 protests reported to have involved one or more of the five most frequently mentioned animal welfare or anti-hunting groups, only three were reported to have involved any issue other than animal welfare or hunting. Although there was, as we shall see, a degree of specialization in the issue concerns of environmental groups, there is no evidence of the shared concern among EMOs and animal welfare and anti-hunting groups that might justify considering them to be part of a single social movement.

The picture is no less clear if we examine the pattern of interaction among the various groups. In only a relatively small number of cases were two or more groups named as having been involved in the same protest. However, whereas the interactions among the EMOs varied, in not a single case was one of the seven leading environmental groups mentioned as having participated in a protest with one of the five most mentioned animal welfare or anti-hunting groups. If the environmental movement is a network (see Fig. 2.5[30]), then in Britain the animal welfare and anti-hunting groups were at best distant outliers to it, no more closely connected to it than the Labour or Liberal Democrat parties or several charities not primarily concerned with the environment. The impression gained by inspection of the network diagram is confirmed by a formal network analysis employing a dichotomized matrix (see Table 2.7): the animal rights and anti-hunting groups scored much lower on measures of centrality to the network than did the environmental groups.[31]

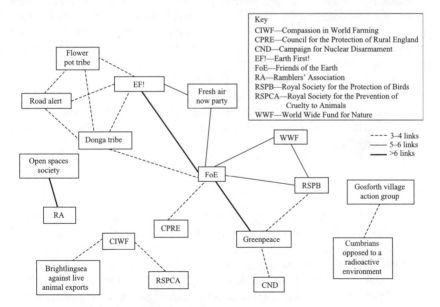

FIG. 2.5. *Networks of groups named in reports of environmental protests in Britain (1988–97) (only links reported 3 or more times are included)*

TABLE 2.7. *The interaction of groups in environmental protest in Britain*

	Acting alone (N)	Acting with others (N)	Freeman's degree
Greenpeace	93	14	12
FoE	56	31	21
EF!	25	19	8
WWF	5	12	11
RSPB	3	11	9
Green Party	10	4	4
RA	35	13	4
LACS	12	5	2
CIWF	19	6	2
ALF	37	0	—
Justice Department	17	0	—

If the network analysis confirms the marginality of the animal welfare and anti-hunting groups in the patterning of reports of action in which two or more groups were named, it also confirms the existence of a network of EMOs.[32] Moreover, it does so despite the fact that some groups—most conspicuously Greenpeace—appeared to show a marked preference for protesting alone.

Anti-hunting and animal rights protests were in Britain quite distinct in incidence and form from those concerned with environmental issues. They were nevertheless part of the political environment within which more strictly environmental organizations operated and it may well be that the actions of hunt saboteurs and animal rights protesters had exemplary value for the environmental movement. They might, however, equally well have had cautionary value, especially insofar as the more extreme forms of action were seen to justify an intrusive and repressive response from the authorities.[33]

However, even in the case of animal rights, the incidence of violence was sporadic and there is no evidence of a trend towards increased violence or attacks upon property.[34]

THE TRANSNATIONALIZATION OF PROTEST?

Tilly (1995) has suggested that the great change that occurred in protest repertoires after the early nineteenth century was the nationalization of protest. Environmental protest might however, be considered to be a special case, since the implications of the injunction to 'think globally, act locally' might be taken to imply a higher priority to local protest or, perhaps, the emergence of transnational, if not yet truly global, protest actions. Table 2.8 shows the distribution of reported protest events by their geographical range for levels of mobilization, scope of the underlying problem, and targets.

TABLE 2.8. *Levels of mobilization, scope of problems, and targets of environmental protest in Britain (percentages)*

	Local/ district	Regional	National	EU	International	*N*
Level of mobilization	38.6	13.6	45.0	0.4	2.4	1132
Scope of underlying problem	40.6	6.0	34.7	6.4	12.3	1311
Level of target	31.5	5.7	61.5	3.2	12.3	1499

Note: *N* for level of target exceeds total number of events and percentages do not sum to 100 because 2 values could be recorded.

Just over half of all environmental protests during the 10 years were mobilized on a sub-national (local, district, or regional) level, and a little under half were mobilized on a national level. Fewer than 3 per cent of protests were organized on a transnational level. The relative prevalence of these levels of mobilization fluctuated over time and, although the proportion of nationally mobilized protests appeared to increase slightly, there was no clear trend.

When the scope of the underlying problem is considered, the proportion of protests attributable to the European Union or international levels is higher, although nearly half were confined to the local, district, or regional levels, and a further third were at the national level. Again, there was no clear trend: national-level problems outnumbered the subnational in only 2 years (1991 and 1997), and the incidence of EU level and international level problems was generally flat except for the sharp increase in both in 1995, mainly attributable to protests against live animal exports and Shell's operations in the North Sea and in Nigeria.

Since a single protest might be aimed at more than one target, up to two levels of target were coded. More than a third of protests were targeted at local, district, or regional levels, nearly two-thirds at national level, and fewer than one in six at a transnational level. There was little temporal variation in the incidence of protests targeted at the EU or international levels, save for an increase in internationally targeted protests in 1995. Protests directed at national-level targets outnumbered those targeted at local, district, or regional levels in every year but 1991, and the relative predominance of nationally targeted protests appeared to increase slightly during the 1990s.

If these data suggest that there was a very slight tendency towards the nationalization of protest, more striking are the complete absence of any trend towards the transnationalization of protest and, especially, the very low proportion of protests that, in terms of their level of mobilization, scope of the underlying issues, or targets, involved the European Union. If an increasing proportion of British environmental policy is made in Brussels or Strasbourg, this has yet to be reflected in the pattern of environmental protest in Britain (Rootes 2002a).[35]

EXPLAINING THE PATTERN

It is clear that over the course of the 10 years from 1988 there was a considerable increase in environmental protest in Britain, at least until 1995. Indeed, because of the declining news value of routine environmental protest, the likelihood is that the magnitude of that increase is considerably understated, especially for the second half of the period.[36] The most economical explanation of the varying incidence of environmental protests over the decade is in terms of the changing balance of opportunities for political action of various kinds, a collection of factors increasingly, if misleadingly, referred to as 'political opportunity structures'.[37]

The wave of environmental protest that crested in 1989 began to rise soon after the re-election in 1987 of the Thatcher government. Renewed economic growth brought with it a substantial increase in the number of motor vehicles on the roads and, especially in southern England, a development boom that markedly increased pressure upon the environment. Development projects such as the high-speed rail link from London to the Channel Tunnel provoked well-publicized protests, and in towns and villages throughout the south there were conflicts between residents concerned to protect the quality of their environment on the one hand, and the proponents of housing, office, and road developments on the other. From August 1988, the popular press highlighted the suspected role of pollution in the deaths of seals on North Sea coasts.

Margaret Thatcher did much to legitimize environmental concerns when, in September 1988, she ended her speech to the annual dinner of the Royal Society with a declaration of commitment to preserving the balance of nature. Conservative leaders were surprised at the response to her speech and taken aback by the number of environmentalist motions presented to the Party conference a month later (Flynn and Lowe 1992: 25–8). The Prime Minister rose to the occasion, telling conference that 'no generation has a freehold' upon the planet but merely 'a life tenancy with a full repairing lease'. Whatever the motive for these speeches,[38] their effect was dramatically to heighten the prominence of environmental issues and to give unprecedented respectability to their articulation.

In the wake of the Prime Minister's pronouncements, media reporting of environmental issues reached a crescendo. The more radical environmental organizations were immediate beneficiaries. In 1988–9 FoE grew from 31,000 to 125,000 paid-up members, and Greenpeace's supporters increased from 150,000 to 281,000 (Frankland 1990: 13). In the 1989 elections to the European Parliament, the Green Party scored almost 15 per cent of the vote. If protest rose only modestly at this time, it is because there was widespread optimism about prospects of progress by other, more conventional means.

The second and more sustained wave of environmental protest began its rise soon after the 1992 general election. Environmental issues did not figure prominently in that election, and the Green Party failed dismally. More importantly, the most closely fought election since the 1970s resulted in the re-election of the Conservative government, no less committed than before to economic development projects, especially road-building.

With the government apparently deaf to criticism of the environmental effects of its policies, and no immediate likelihood of a change of government, the absence of any prospect that conventional politics and reasoned argument might change policy encouraged the adoption of less conventional tactics. A particular stimulus to the adoption of direct action was the vigour of the campaign against the poll tax introduced in Scotland in 1989 and in England in 1990. Although the anti-poll tax campaign was principally coordinated by left-wing activists and had no close connection with the environmental movement, it, the political demise of Mrs Thatcher, and the government's subsequent abandonment of the tax, were represented as evidence of what could be achieved by direct action. The example appealed especially to younger people impressed by the urgency of environmental concerns but dismayed by the apparent quiescence of established environmental groups (Wall 1999a, b).[39] Thus, the closure of political opportunities represented by the re-election of an unresponsive government was conjoined with a proximate example of an apparently successful campaign of direct action (Rootes 2003a).

As in the case of the poll tax, the rise of direct action against roads was paralleled by a significant shift of public opinion against government policy and by increasing conventional opposition from government MPs and local party branches in the constituencies most affected (Robinson 2000). In these circumstances, it is extremely difficult to assess the impact of protest, but it is probable that outbursts of direct action were more the symptom than the cause of widespread public discontent with the government and its policies. Nevertheless, the reporting of direct action served to dramatize and to amplify shifts in public opinion by keeping the roads issue more generally in the news than it would have been had it depended upon the pronouncements of MPs or the more conventional and localized protests of affected residents. The novelty of the alliances forged between local campaigners and eco-activists at Twyford and Newbury and the evident public sympathy for anti-roads protesters encouraged media coverage that accorded unprecedented legitimacy to direct action and may have contributed to its spread.

The greater radicalism of environmental protest after 1992 compared with that of the 1980s is explicable in terms of the changed political conjuncture. In 1988, Margaret Thatcher's speeches had legitimated environmentalists' concerns and raised expectations that the policies of her government failed to meet. In 1989 the political calendar provided the opportunity to large numbers of people to protest by the simple act of voting for a Green candidate in the elections for the European Parliament. In 1992–3 no such opportunity arose, and the environment had in any case slipped from the top of the public agenda. As a result, local campaigners whose concerns were as urgent as ever were pushed into the arms of the direct activists, resulting in the extraordinary sights of middle-class housewives and pensioners carrying tea and biscuits to dreadlocked tree-sitters, tunnellers, and protest campers. Likewise, the wide-ranging campaign against the Criminal Justice Act (1994), a piece of portmanteau legislation that, amongst other things, criminalized trespass, extended the networks of direct activists at the very time that Shell and the French government were providing new reasons to protest, and when animal welfare campaigners were stepping up their action. The Major government's retreat from road-building and its proclaimed commitment to the introduction of more effective measures to protect the environment, and to the tightening of regulations to protect the welfare of transported livestock, contributed to the decline of protest from 1996.

The apparent decline of protest in 1997 may be in part a product of the declining news value of environmental protest in the wake of the 1995 peak, but it may also reflect the changed priorities of news editors in an election year when coverage of conventional politics may have crowded out reports of protest. Certainly, by 1998 reported protest had returned to the levels of 1996 and a 'summer of discontent' witnessed protests on a broad range of issues (Coxall 2001: 119–20). Analysis of reports in *The Guardian* for 1998 reveals that the revival was mainly attributable to protests concerning nature conservation and pollution, urban, and industrial issues, the best publicized of which was a spate of direct action to disrupt field trials of genetically modified crops; transport and animal rights protests remained at 1997 levels.

To the extent that the decline of environmental protest in 1997 was real rather than an artefact of media attention, the anticipation and then the fact of the general election and the change of government are likely to have been at least partly responsible. The Labour Party did not have a history of sympathy for environmentalists but, in its last years in opposition, it is said to have been influenced by personal links between its leading figures and environmentalists (Rawcliffe 1998: 222). Its 1997 election manifesto marked a revolution in Labour rhetoric about the environment. Moreover, manifesto promises to put 'concern for the environment at the heart of policy-making so that it is not an add-on extra but informs the whole of government' were repeated by the new Labour ministers. The Secretary of State for the Environment, Transport and the Regions, John Prescott, presiding over a newly formed department that was claimed to be the most powerful environment ministry in the world,[40] proved to be surprisingly environmentally aware, globally as well as nationally, while the Minister for the Environment, Michael Meacher, won wide respect within the environmental movement.

However, as the debacle over genetically modified (GM) foods showed,[41] the Blair government was very far from being regarded as a panacea by environmental activists; the protests of the summer of 1998 were interpreted as an expression of disillusionment with Labour's failure to put its promises into practice. Nevertheless, although the government's priorities lay elsewhere, it did enough to give few pretexts for sustained large-scale environmental mobilization. Indeed, it showed itself to be adept at defusing environmental issues just as they seemed about to erupt (as they did with hunting, with housing developments on greenfield sites at the beginning of 1998, and with the 'right to roam' and the licensing of genetically modified crops in 1999). It is probably this responsiveness that accounts for the more moderate repertoire of reported protests in 1998; even by comparison with 1997, there was a notable rise in conventional and demonstrative protests while the decline of confrontational protests was sustained.

CONCLUSION

It should be emphasized that what our investigations demonstrate is that there was, during the early to mid-1990s, a considerable increase in the number of reported environmental protest *events*. It is not clear that there was an increase, much less a proportionate increase, in the number of people who directly participated in environmental protests. Thus, although it is clear that tales of the demise of environmental protest are at best premature, it remains possible that the number of protest events increased even as the capacity of the environmental movement to mobilize large numbers of people for direct participation in protest declined.

Whether or not the apparent increase in confrontational protests reflects a real increase in confrontation relative to other forms of protest, it has clearly changed the publicly visible profile of environmental protest. What remains largely invisible, however, is the large number of local, allegedly 'NIMBY' protests. We know from other investigations (Rootes 2001; Rootes et al. 2001) that protests over the siting of waste management facilities such as landfill and incinerators have increased in recent years, but during the 1990s there was scarcely any mention of them in the national press. These and other local planning disputes tend to make it into national news only when they conjoin to spark a political crisis or when they are picked up, usually by feature writers rather than news journalists, for their 'human interest'. Although such protests are by no means novel, it is likely that they have become more common, if only because, as surveys of political participation and social attitudes show, British society has become more directly participatory and less deferential.[42] That, however, is not something we are able to demonstrate from the data analysed in this chapter.

It is possible that in this decade we witnessed the rise of a new generation of environmental protesters with no loyalty to established EMOs. Yet there is little evidence of a sharp generational cleavage within the environmental movement; it may have been younger protesters who took the more physically audacious forms of action, but they did so with the active support of older protesters.[43] Although campaign organizations like Alarm UK brought together members and supporters of a broad range of EMOs, it was younger protesters who made up the numbers of the new, more radical groups (McNeish 2000*b*). Some observers argue that recent anti-roads protests and other local developments betoken the development of an environmental counter-culture on a scale not seen previously (Fiddes 1997). Similarly, whilst some saw the protests against the extension of the M77 motorway across Pollok Park in Glasgow as a continuation of protest by local working-class people first mobilized by opposition to the poll tax, others saw them as the work of radical eco-activists for whom Pollok was simply a battle in the long war against capitalist consumerism.[44]

Although such developments highlight the dilemmas of campaigning EMOs such as Greenpeace and FoE as they attempt simultaneously to develop constructive relationships with government and industry and to maintain their links with grassroots activists, they do not appear to have produced irreconcilable differences within the broad environmental movement. The experience of the 1990s shows that fruitful collaboration can be achieved between protesters and the more institutionalized organizations (Rawcliffe 1998), and that the 'radical flank effect' produced by the existence of direct action has increased the leverage of more institutionalized groups such as FoE. The tactical repertoires of the several parts of the environmental movement may be different but they may be, and often have been, employed in ways that are mutually reinforcing rather than merely competitive, and so may enhance the influence and impact of the environmental movement as a whole.

The pattern of environmental protest in Britain during the decade was quite distinctive in that not only was there a dramatic surge of environmental protest, but, in a striking departure from the longstanding tactical moderation of British environmentalism, there was a clear shift towards more confrontational forms of protest. It appears too that environmental protest in Britain was especially tactically innovative during this period. 'Manufactured vulnerability' (Doherty 1999*b*) may have borrowed rather liberally from the experience of environmental protest in such other countries as Australia and the United States, but the scale of its use and the level of risk taken by the participants does appear to have been qualitatively different from anything previously seen in environmental protests in Britain. These developments, as well as the formation of new groups that seriously attempted to develop new and more flexible forms of organization, the persistence of more established campaigning groups such as Greenpeace and FoE, and the broadening of the agenda and repertoire of the older environmental organizations such as WWF, RSPB, and the Council for the Protection of Rural England, all testify to the vitality of the environmental movement in Britain during the 1990s.

The pattern of protest appears to be best explained in terms of the pattern of opportunities presented by the electoral cycle and the policies and attitudes of governments. Nowhere else in the European Union was a government so determinedly committed to a controversial, large-scale programme of road-building, so resistant to hostile public opinion, or so imaginatively confronted by so heterogeneous an environmental movement.

If the peak of environmental protest mobilization may thus be represented as a distinctive achievement of an obdurate Conservative government as much as of the activists who opposed it, it would be a mistake to suppose that the movement lapsed quietly into repose with the election of a Labour government more sensitive to environmental concerns and to public opinion. The continued ability of environmental groups to mount campaigns, most notably over housing on green-field sites and genetically modified organisms, and the high levels of public support they have attracted, suggest that, even if protest has declined from its peak, the environmental movement is very far from being demobilized. The speed with which the Blair government reacted to a succession of threatened environmental protests suggests that the fear of exciting a new protest wave acts as a constraint upon ministers and officials considering new transport infrastructure projects. In that respect, the unprecedented protest wave of the 1990s lives on.

NOTES

1. Figures for the membership of the major British environmental movement organizations (EMOs) are published annually in the official government publication, *Social Trends*. The numbers are provided by the organizations concerned and 'membership' is, in some cases, construed rather broadly. Figures for Greenpeace, which is not a mass membership organization, refer to the numbers of supporting donors. From 1994 Greenpeace adopted a more restrictive definition of 'supporter' and excluded those who simply purchased merchandise, with the result that its 'membership' shrank; by contrast, World Wide Fund for Nature (WWF) began in 1994 to include donors as well as paid-up members (Rawcliffe 1998: 74).
2. Interview, 'Jeff', 17 December 1999.
3. For a discussion of the 'Swampy' phenomenon, see Paterson (2000).
4. We considered using electronic versions of the paper, but sample comparisons revealed that the versions available on CD-ROM were not full text and did not usually include graphics or reports that were published only as captions to graphics.
5. *The Guardian*'s environment correspondent, Paul Brown, was appointed in 1988 and the environment features editor, John Vidal, in 1989, and both continued in post throughout the decade.
6. A protest event is defined as a collective, public action by non-state actors, involving at least three people, and with the expressed purpose of critique or dissent together with societal and/or political demands.
7. Summary reports are those in which:

   (1) one group is reported to have performed a large number of distinct protests over a considerable time span (e.g. 'every Sunday for the last two years'); or
   (2) a number of groups is reported to have performed a certain number of protests over a considerable time span; or
   (3) a number of groups is reported each to have performed one protest on the same issue or claim on the same day or weekend, usually each group acting in a different location.

8. We also examined the incidence of protest by month and by quarter but found no clear seasonal pattern save for the fact that there was, in most years, least environmental protest in December and November.
9. We should, however, be particularly cautious in our interpretation of the apparent decline of protest in 1997 simply because it is the last year in our series. Whereas the number of

protests recorded for earlier years all include some events which occurred in those years but were not reported until the following year, the events recorded for 1997 include only those actually reported in that year. If events reported in 1998 but occurring in 1997 had been included, the apparent decline of protest in 1997 would have been very much moderated, albeit that the majority of the events in question were reported in a single feature article on animal rights. The 1998 reports are not included here because that year lies outside the scope of the comparative project and because for 1998 we had to rely upon the CD-ROM version of *The Guardian* rather than the microfiche copies we had used for earlier years. Because the CD-ROM version does not include full text and graphics, its coverage is not as complete and is therefore not strictly comparable with that of the microfiche copies of the printed newspaper. Our checks reveal that some 5% of the events we had coded from the microfiche for 1997 were omitted from the CD-ROM version. I am grateful to Alexander Miller for undertaking this work, and to the Faculty of Social Sciences at the University of Kent for providing the funding that made it possible.

10. It is also possible that at the peak of a wave of protest, a journalist, having employed the device of the summary report on several occasions in a short space of time, may become hypersensitive to instances of protest that would not normally be reported and may, by becoming more heavily reliant on the device of the summary report, exaggerate the salience of the peak of the protest wave. In other words, at the peak of the 'media attention cycle' (Downs 1972), a smaller proportion of events may go unreported than at other times. It is noteworthy that reports of RA actions in 1995, almost all of them derived from summary reports, referred to 103 events, more than twice as many as in any previous year.

11. For example, of events derived from summary reports, 45% could not be located even to a region of the United Kingdom; excluding summary reports, only 9% of events were 'location unknown'.

12. Just four campaigns—that against the export of live animals that commenced in 1990 and peaked in 1995, the 1995 RA campaign for the 'right to roam', the 1995 Greenpeace-initiated campaign against the sea-dumping of the Brent Spar oil storage buoy, and the 1997 campaign against deer hunting in the New Forest—account for more than half (780) of all the 1433 protest events derived from summary reports. Excluding summary reports, the same four campaigns yielded just eighty-five protest events. The extreme case was the campaign against deer hunting in the New Forest; although this campaign gave rise to only a single event reported other than in summary reports, when summary reports are included it accounted for a clear majority of all the protest events reported for 1997.

13. The under-representation of Scotland is in part a product of the fact that, because Scotland has its own national press as well as localized editions of several London-based papers, the threshold of salience that must be reached before Scottish events are reported south of the border is almost certainly higher than it is for events occurring in the English regions.

14. If data from summary reports is included, the over-representation of London is reduced and that of the rest of the south-east is markedly increased, but both the impact of a few large campaigns and the high proportion of missing data suggest caution in the interpretation of this data.

15. Because our coding guidelines permitted the coding of up to two issues per protest event, these percentages sum to more than 100.

16. The same is broadly true as well of other forms of action (such as petitions) involving large numbers of people. In only two years—1989 and 1995—did the number of all large protests exceed eighteen and only in 1997 was just one large protest action reported. In all, there were sixty-seven large actions in the years 1988–92 and seventy-four in 1993–7.

17. Because we coded up to four forms of action in connection with each protest event, some forms of action actually taken by small numbers of people will be classified as being involved in a large protest if other forms of action taken as part of the same protest involved, separately or in aggregate, 500 or more people. Thus, an occupation undertaken by a handful of people but following on from a rally or street march with 500 participants will be recorded as a form of action involved in a large protest event. Even so, petitions, which were involved in 37% of large protests, accounted for over 28% of all the forms of action recorded as being involved in large protest events.

18. For these purposes, we have categorized as 'demonstrations' only street marches, public protest assemblies and rallies, and non-verbal protests such as vigils. This categorization of 'demonstrations' is thus more restrictive than the broader category 'demonstrative' used earlier in the broad categorizations of the forms of action and which also includes boycotts, hunger strikes, referendums, press conferences, distributing leaflets/posters, billboarding, graffiti and flyposting, cultural performances, and positive actions.

19. Environmental activists were, however, among the participants in the demonstrations, some of them large, that were mounted against the proposed Criminal Justice Act in 1994–5. However, unless these protests made direct and explicit environmental claims, they have not been included in our data set.

20. Just 750 people were reported as participating in the single large protest in 1997. This compares with 1600 and 2000 in the next two lowest years (1993 and 1990) for large demonstrations, and 22,250 and 76,765 in the next two lowest years (1991 and 1996) for all large protest actions.

21. The same pattern holds if all forms of action involving 500 or more participants are compared: the median for 1988–92 was 3000 compared with 1330 for 1993–7; the median for all protests of whatever size fell from 200 to 100. The declines in the mean number of participants in both protests overall and in demonstrations were even more marked.

22. The strict application of our coding guidelines tends to understate the extent of media coverage of anti-roads protests. A site occupation—the characteristic form of anti-roads protests—may last for many months and be covered by newspapers almost daily and yet give rise to as few as two codeable 'events', one at the start of the protest and another at the point of the protesters' eviction from the site. To mitigate this effect, we coded as a separate protest event every distinct identifiable action—such as a mass trespass or demonstrative gathering—reported as having occurred at such sites.

23. Interview with Paul Brown conducted by Debbie Adams, 2 March 1999.

24. This is partly compensated for by the fact that other journalists are now much more alert to environmental issues and so may include them in their reports.

25. One thing that may work to counter this tendency is environmental journalists' increasing reliance upon contacts and the quality of their contacts with established EMOs such as FoE and Greenpeace, both of which are highly media-aware and very active in producing press releases. When interviewed, Paul Brown asserted that he was

equally accessible to the newer, more radical groups such as EF!, especially since they were adept in the use of new communications technologies. Nevertheless, Brown reported that an average of three press releases a day landed on his desk from Greenpeace alone. It is very likely that, over the decade in which he has been *The Guardian*'s environmental correspondent, a symbiotic relationship has developed between him and Greenpeace and FoE; they feed him stories that he believes he can trust, and so he is more likely to run their stories and has less incentive to seek out other environmental movement sources.

The more spectacular actions of less established groups may be reported, but not necessarily with sympathy or understanding. At the time of the Pollok Park protests in Glasgow, there was much resentment among EF! and allied protesters at what they regarded as the unsympathetic and misleading reporting of their protest by *The Guardian*.

26. One reason for this surprisingly high incidence of confrontation in nature conservation protests—the aspect of environmentalism conventionally considered most conservative—is the frequency with which nature protection issues were raised in the course of anti-roads protests. Our coding procedures allowed for the coding of up to two claims per protest event; in the case of reports of anti-roads protests in particular it was often difficult to decide which was the principal issue of protest and so two claims were often recorded for one event.

27. This is in marked contrast with animal welfare protests which have not become markedly more confrontational but of which a higher proportion were confrontational in the earlier years.

28. Of these ten attacks on property, three involved substantial damage to equipment operated by commercial enterprises against whom EF! was campaigning, but three were the symbolic 'theft' of tropical hardwood from stores.

29. The three protests in which CIWF was reported to have been involved and that involved issues other than animal welfare were all focused on demands for 'environmentally friendly' farming practices.

30. Figure 2.5 is reproduced from Rootes (2000) by permission of Taylor and Francis plc.

31. I am indebted to Manuel Jiménez for providing the network analyses. Higher scores on Freeman's degree are indicative of greater centrality to the network.

32. Protest event methodology, dependent as it is upon media reports, is not well suited to the identification of personal networks or of subterranean or clandestine networks that may exist among groups that do not engage in common public action. The next stage of our research—focused upon surveys, interviews, and more detailed studies of EMOs—sheds more light on these less publicly visible network linkages, but a preliminary analysis of the survey we conducted among over 100 British environmental groups in 1999–2000 does nothing to contradict the picture painted here (Rootes and Miller 2000).

33. Equally, the actions of other groups not included in our survey may have either cautionary or exemplary value for the environmental movement.

34. Minor attacks on property were reported in 13% of animal rights protests. There is no clear pattern to the incidence of such attacks; they were scarcely more frequent in the second half of the decade than in the first, and as a proportion of all animal rights protests, they declined markedly. Thirty per cent of protests involving animal welfare were at least partly violent in form, but of the seventy-two events involving violence, forty occurred in 1993–4; in subsequent years protests involving violence fell back,

both in absolute numbers and as a proportion (13%) of all animal rights protests, to the very low levels of 1988–9.

35. Protests targeted at the EU level include those directed at companies domiciled in other EU states as well as the national governments of other EU states as well as those (very few) addressed to the institutions of the EU itself.

36. Because animal welfare and anti-hunting protests had somewhat different trajectories from those concerning other, more strictly environmental issues, the effect of aggregating them is to moderate the downturns apparent in the trajectory of strictly environmental protest and significantly to exaggerate the 1995 peak.

37. See Rootes (1997a, 1999c) for a discussion and critique of this concept.

38. Some observers regard Mrs Thatcher's speeches as a cynical and opportunistic attempt to leap aboard the already rolling bandwagon of increasing anxiety about the environment that had been detected by opinion pollsters. Insider accounts suggest, however, that they represented a genuine if belated acceptance by the first scientifically educated Prime Minister and her advisers that the balance of scientific evidence about the state of the global environment had tipped in favour of the alarmists.

39. In some cases, the connection between the anti-poll tax and anti-roads protests was quite direct. In the Pollok district of Glasgow, a community that had mobilized to resist the poll tax later did much to sustain the Pollok Free State protest camp in its opposition to the proposal to drive a motorway extension through a neighbouring public park (Seel 1997a; McNeish 2000a).

40. The claim was made by former Conservative Environment Secretary John Gummer (*The Guardian*, 5 July 2001) when the department was dismantled after Labour's re-election.

41. Even when it was clear that public opinion had moved decisively against GM foods, the government seemed more anxious to maintain Britain's position as a major player in the bio-technology industry than to assuage public anxieties or environmentalists' concerns.

42. The British have become steadily more likely to approve of recourse to unconventional protest in response to legislation they consider unjust or harmful even if it means breaking the law. They have also become markedly more likely to say they would themselves take such action in response to an unjust law, the proportion saying they would go on a demonstration rose from 8% in 1983 to 17% in 1994 and 20.5% in 1998 (Jowell et al. 1999: 320). Indeed, in 1994, 8.9% said they had gone on a demonstration in such circumstances (Curtice and Jowell 1995: 154), and by 2000 this had risen to 10% (Bromley, Curtice, and Seyd 2001: 202). In response to a differently worded question in 1996, 31% said they 'definitely' or 'probably' would go on a protest march or demonstration, and 5.5% said they had actually done so in the previous 5 years (Jowell et al. 1997: 320). This latter figure compares with the 5.1% who in 1984–5 said they had gone on a demonstration during the previous 5 years (Parry, Moyser, and Day 1992: 44).

However, the 1993 ISSP survey found that although relatively high proportions of the British said they had in the previous 5 years given money to an environmental group (30% compared with 19% in Germany), or had signed a petition about an environmental issue (37% compared with 31% in Germany), only 3% said they had participated in an environmentalist demonstration, a lower proportion than in Germany (8%), Italy, Spain, or the Netherlands (Dalton and Rohrschneider 1998: 111). It should be noted that this survey predates the peak of the 1990s surge of environmental protest in Britain. The increased number of respondents to the British Social Attitudes surveys since 2000 who report that they have participated in demonstrations may at least in part be a result of that surge.

43. This is well documented in the case of protests against the Newbury bypass ('The Battle of Rickety Bridge', Channel 4 TV, December 1996) and the Pollok anti-roads protests (McNeish 2000*a*), but it was also apparent amongst the substantial audiences at public meetings organized by FoE during 1996–7 (cf. Fiddes 1997: 41).

44. See, for example, Seel (1997*a*). Wall (1999*a, b*) points to the central role played in these protests by activists identifying themselves with EF! (Seel 1997*b*; North 1998; cf. McNeish 2000*a, b*).

3

France

Olivier Fillieule

Research into ecology and environmental movements in France developed as the movements themselves were appearing as a new force in politics at the time of the European and municipal elections of 1989. Yet, although the literature on political ecology is very rich, research dealing with the environmental movement is quite rare. Prevailing French literature bears on the question of the institutionalization of environmentalism within political parties,[1] and on the particular modes of operation of those parties, and little has been written on environmental protest and militancy in environmental associations. This is true both of high-profile international organizations such as Greenpeace or Friends of the Earth (FoE) and of more modest organizations at the local or regional level.[2]

However, knowledge about environmental protest campaigns has greatly increased in recent years due to the general development of protest event analysis in social movement research. Duyvendak's (1994) analysis of the years 1975–89 and Fillieule's (1997) work on the 1980s give us an overview of the rise of environmental protest during the years 1968–80, and its decline after the Socialist Party won the general elections in 1981.

Research on the development of environmental associations at regional level[3] has highlighted three periods of organizational innovation from 1901 onward. The first, at the turn of the century, saw the constitution of learned societies[4] and the first naturalist and conservationist groupings. Then, in the 1960s, associations emerged which sought to oppose planning projects that were in full development (urban and coastal planning, ski resorts, transport projects). It was at the end of this period that branches and subsidiaries of the big international associations were created (FoE, Greenpeace France (GPF), and the World Wide Fund for Nature (WWF)), but it was from 1968 onwards that the rhythm of innovation became firmly sustained. After a dip in the rate of establishment of new associations, doubtless related to the passing euphoria of the left's accession to power in 1981, new associations continued to increase in number, peaking in 1989–90. The

I am indebted to Fabrice Ferrier for his assistance with reading and coding the data derived from *Le Monde*.

latter appears to have been a fruitful period, marked by the development of the subject in the media, and in official and international affairs, as well as by electoral success. These years saw the development especially of associations linked to education and heritage management, and marked a process of institutionalization that continued in the 1990s with the development of eco-civic associations.

This increasing institutionalization leads us to stress a central methodological question that relates to the definition of the object of analysis. With the growing institutionalization of environmental politics (Fillieule and Ferrier 2000), the frontiers between the associational sector, parties, trade unions, and the state are blurring. For that reason, to restrict analysis to a single form of organization would omit consideration of possible alliances of associations with state or para-state agencies, trade unions, or parties. To avoid that, one must begin instead with the observation of protest events themselves if one wants to reconstruct the networks that form around one mobilization or another. To that end, protest event analysis is the most efficient tool.[5]

Until now, apart from the books of Duyvendak (1994) and Fillieule (1997) on protest events in France which cover the period 1975–90, we have had no systematic analysis of environmental protest in France. In this chapter we make an initial contribution to knowledge about the ways in which green protest has developed in the 1990s.

The data on which our analysis is based are drawn from the printed editions of *Le Monde*.[6] Apart from the fact that press data on environmental protest events for the previous decade were drawn from that newspaper (Duyvendak 1994), *Le Monde* was chosen in preference to other national 'quality' newspapers after a preliminary comparison showed that its reporting of environmental events was more inclusive. Moreover, *Le Monde* was published continuously during the decade and has enjoyed relative continuity of editorial policy and of journalistic personnel throughout the period.[7] The discussion that follows is based on analysis of the 259 environmental protest events[8] that were reported by *Le Monde* during the 10 years, 1988–97.

The use of press sources to create a database on protest events is now one of the more established methods in the sociology of social movements. It is also a method that is the subject of a great deal of criticism that for the most part relates to the issue of bias inherent in media sources. Because Appendix A centrally addresses these questions, we shall not deal with them here. Suffice it to say that, in order to understand and reconstruct the rationale governing the selection of news items and the way they are reported in printed media, we have supplemented our data with other statistics (a limited sample of Agence France Presse (AFP) bulletins and data from police archives (Fillieule 1997)) and with qualitative data. In-depth interviews were conducted with six journalists specializing in environmental issues. Taking these two directions to implement protest event analysis, we have tried to refrain from what M. Stephen Weatherford (1992: 151), referring to empirical studies on legitimacy, calls 'measurement driven research', that is, the reiteration of 'conventional measures' which results in their being institutionalized without regard to their pertinence.[9]

In the first two sections of this chapter, we will demonstrate that the French environmental movement is above all characterized by great structural weakness in terms of protest actions. This weakness seems explicable by reference to a number of variables both political (the left's assumption of power and the cycle of alternation of government since 1986) and economic (the persistence of the economic crisis and the resonance of unemployment). In the last two sections, we look at the groups involved in organizing protests to show how, on the one hand, their morphological development has led to a profound process of fragmentation that is unlikely to be propitious for a resurgence of collective action, and how, on the other hand, they have been gradually co-opted by the state and so have been increasingly institutionalized.

THE DECLINE OF ENVIRONMENTAL PROTESTS

The French environmental movement suffers from structural weakness in terms of political importance as well as mobilizing capacity. In quantitative terms, and according to our definition of a protest event, the incidence of reported environmental mobilizations remained quite consistently low throughout the 10 years, 1988–97. On average, only some 22 protest events a year were reported (Fig. 3.1). Whatever the year, ecologists' mobilizations never managed to attract the attention of *Le Monde* more than once a week.

Few campaigns managed to mobilize in a continuous and durable way on an environmental issue, except for Greenpeace International's protest against the resumption of nuclear tests in Mururoa in 1995. The pattern of consistently low levels of protest was disrupted only by a trough in 1993, and by a modest peak in 1997.

It was not, however, only the numbers of protest events that were low. The low number of reported participants per event confirms the impression of general

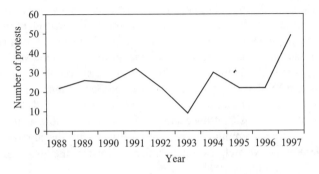

FIG. 3.1. *Environmental protest events in France by year*

weakness.[10] Eighty-three per cent of actions reportedly involved fewer than 2000 people and 40 per cent fewer than 200. One petition against the infamous Superphénix nuclear facility managed to aggregate 200,000 signatures in 1994, but the biggest demonstration of the decade—that against the Rhine-Rhône canal—gathered only 10,000 participants, a very feeble level of participation compared to the 1970s mobilization around nuclear problems. However, such fragmentation is not peculiar to environmental protest and must be considered in light of the overall trend in France towards an increased number of micro-mobilizations (especially of demonstrations of between 201 and 500 people) (Fillieule 1997: 94).

The weakness of the movement can also be observed in the difficulty it has experienced in its efforts to determine a clear political agenda in French politics. Whereas mobilizations of the 1970s were characterized by the prevalence of the anti-nuclear movement (Fessenheim and Bugey in 1971; Creys-Malville in 1977; Golfech and Chooz in 1979; Plogoff in 1980), existing claims are much more fragmented.

Claims related to nuclear power comprised less than 20 per cent of the total for the decade. This result is no surprise since the anti-nuclear movement had already vanished, even if it had not entirely died, by the end of the 1970s (Rucht 1994). As evidence of that, after the Chernobyl disaster of April 1986 only small demonstrations took place in France. Even with this dramatic opportunity to change sentiment in the French population, the movement was unable to mount a significant mobilization. The government and the mass media (including *Le Monde*) succeeded in playing down the accident and made it possible for the French to believe that the effects of the nuclear fall-out stopped at the Franco-German border.

Another important point is that the nature of claims related to nuclear power has changed over time. If, in the 1970s, the struggle was mainly over construction of nuclear plants, in the 1980s and 1990s the focus shifted to the problem of nuclear waste storage, which came to account for about half of all protests concerning nuclear energy.

The growing concern about nuclear waste in France is easily explained. After 1986–7, ANDRA (Agence Nationale pour la Gestion des Déchets Radioactifs)[11] began to look for new sites for nuclear waste depositories. In each of the four sites chosen, local populations proved very reluctant, and violent protests occurred in Gâtine, Bresse, and Aisne. As a result, the Prime Minister (Michel Rocard) decided to cancel the planning process for one year (February 1990). Some months later, ANDRA chose three new sites in Gard, Vienne, and the Haute-Marne districts. No real mobilization followed the beginning of the preliminary investigation of these sites, since ANDRA distributed more than 15 million Francs to the urban communities concerned. Even with the nomination of the Green, Dominique Voynet, as Environment Minister, the problem remained unsolved (Rivasi and Crié 1998).

Another reason for the growing mobilization around nuclear waste storage relates to the changing strategy of the anti-nuclear movement which, after years of useless struggle against the EDF (Electricité de France) or COGEMA (Compagnie Générale des Matières Nucléaires), has more recently tried to mobilize around the more visible and obviously dangerous side-effects of nuclear power. As Rucht (1994: 149) explains:

the anti-nuclear movement could not really overcome its marginal status. As a consequence, rather than fighting against windmills, the focus of the anti-nuclear critique shifted to those problems which cannot even be denied by the pro-nuclear side: that is the issue of nuclear waste, the over-supply of electricity, the disaster of the fast breeder reactor, the rising costs of nuclear reprocessing and the risks of accidents similar to or even worse than Chernobyl.

Figure 3.2 and Table 3.1 also indicate that opposition to infrastructure construction was one of the most salient causes that mobilized protest in the period

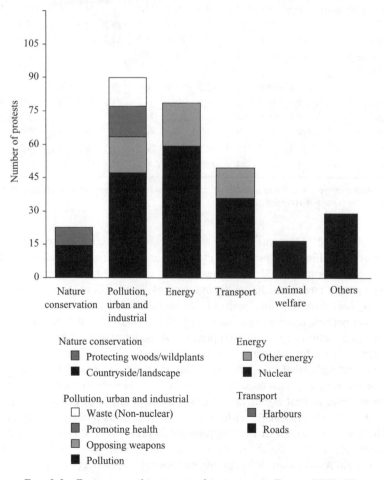

FIG. 3.2. *Environmental issues raised in protests in France (1988–97)*

Fillieule

TABLE 3.1. *Environmental issues raised in protests in France by year (percentage of events in which issue is raised by year)*

	1988	1989	1990	1991	1992	1993	1994	1995	1996	1997	Total N
Nature conservation	*9.1*	*0*	*8.4*	*16*	*4.9*	*33.3*	*20*	*0*	*4.5*	*0*	*23*
Protecting woods, wild flora	0	0	0.4	0.4	0.4	0	16.7	0	0	0	8
Countryside protection	9.1	0	8	15.6	4.5	33.3	3.3	0	4.5	0	15
Pollution, urban and industrial	*31.8*	*7.6*	*52*	*34.4*	*13.5*	*44.4*	*16.6*	*63.6*	*68.2*	*36.7*	*91*
Pollution	22.7	0	36	18.8	9	33.3	13.3	9	22.7	30.6	48
Waste (non-nuclear)	9.1	3.8	8	12.5	4.5	0	0	0	0	4.1	12
Promoting health	0	0	0	3.1	0	0	3.3	0	45.5	2	14
Opposing weapons	0	3.8	8	0	0	11.1	0	54.6	0	0	17
Energy	*22.7*	*57.7*	*28*	*12.5*	*49.9*	*22.2*	*46.7*	*4.5*	*4.5*	*28.6*	*78*
Nuclear	18.2	34.6	20	0	36.3	11.1	46.7	4.5	4.5	18.4	56
Animal welfare and hunting	*13.6*	*11.5*	*20*	*12.5*	*4.5*	*0*	*3.3*	*0*	*0*	*0*	*17*
Hunting	9.1	3.8	20	12.5	4.5	0	0	0	0	0	13
Transport	*9.1*	*15.4*	*4*	*18.7*	*22.7*	*44.4*	*16.7*	*22.7*	*13.6*	*30.6*	*50*
Roads	9.1	15.4	4	15.6	22.7	22.2	16.7	22.7	0	12.2	35
Harbours	0	0	0	3.1	0	22.2	0	0	13.6	18.4	15
Other	4.5	7.7	12	18.8	9.1	22.2	3.3	9.1	9.1	16.3	29
Total N of events	*22*	*26*	*25*	*32*	*22*	*9*	*30*	*22*	*22*	*49*	

Note: Broad categories of issues in italic; subcategories in roman. Percentages do not sum to 100 as up to 2 issues could be recorded per event.

(29.3 per cent). This was mainly due to two campaigns: those around the Somport tunnel in the Aspe valley (Pyrénées) and the Rhine-Rhone canal. These two mobilizations should not, however, be considered as representative of contemporary environmental collective actions. They differed from most struggles in their duration, their capacity to mobilize different sectors of society (political parties, trade unions, local authorities), their use of a broad spectrum of modes of action (legal and disruptive), and the international dimension of the problems (Spain for the former campaign, Germany for the latter).

To disentangle what in our results is due to specific biases of *Le Monde* or of the media in general, we need to understand the rationale of media coverage of environmental protest events and of environmental issues in general. Such contextualization should enable us to understand why certain categories of protest might have been under- or over-represented in press reports. Here two previous analyses are useful: those of Pierre Lascoumes and others (1993) and the Professional Association of Environmental Journalists (JNE) (1998).[12]

From this earlier research, it seems that 'nature' was the environmental topic by far most commonly treated by all the daily newspapers, followed by the questions of water, transportation, waste, and air pollution. This hierarchy was found in the majority of the newspapers. *Le Monde* had good coverage of 'nature' and transportation issues, but it gave a relatively high proportion of space to very diverse subjects (the 'other' category at 18 per cent compares with the 20.5 per cent in our database). By contrast, nuclear energy and water issues were only relatively weakly covered, and articles dealing with the seas were totally absent at a time when AFP dispatches on this topic were numerous. Compared to *Le Monde*, *Libération* was distinguished by its more extensive coverage of nuclear energy, that subject being a personal interest of its leading environmental correspondent.[13] The great number of articles on hunting and fishing in *L'Humanité* undoubtedly reflects the fact that these are primarily leisure pursuits of the paper's predominantly working class readership.

In Lascoumes' research, 'nature' also led the field (34.5 per cent of reports), followed by pollution (26 per cent), environmental policies (18.8 per cent), energy (13.5 per cent), and questions of 'infrastructure' (7.2 per cent).

What conclusions can be drawn from this rapid overflight of the hierarchization of the topics in the French daily press? The extent of *Le Monde*'s focus on 'nature' is striking and raises the possibility that 'naturalist' protest events are over-represented in its reports. By contrast, *Le Monde* is almost mute on the subject of hunting and, in common with other papers, about 'pollution of agricultural origin'. This suggests that certain questions may be 'forgotten' by a press that is more or less influenced by lobbies.[14]

SOME EXPLANATIONS, MORE QUESTIONS

A comparison of the electoral results of green parties with the pattern of environmental protests suggests some explanation of the structural weakness of the environmental movement.

From the symbolic score of René Dumont in the presidential election of 1974 until the European elections of 1979, the ecologists' electoral performances increased continuously, culminating at 5 per cent in 1979. Then, after François Mitterrand's election as President, the progression stopped. In 1986, ecologists were brought together in a new party, *Les Verts*, that scored only 2.5 per cent in the general elections. It was only at the end of the 1980s, as elsewhere in Europe, that the greens began to gain good results, with 10.7 per cent in the 1989 European elections. At the 1992 regional elections, the combined scores of the two ecology parties, *Les Verts* and *Génération écologie*, reached almost 15 per cent, which, compared to the results of greens elsewhere in Europe at that time, was considerable.

However, this success also marked the beginning of the decline, and greens scored only 11 per cent in the general elections of 1993. Considered a poor result by the militants, this caused a serious internal crisis, both between and within the competing green organizations. The European elections of 1994 confirmed the decline, the combined vote of *Les Verts* and *Génération écologie* falling just short of 5 per cent, almost back to the level of 1979. The presidential election of 1995 etched the gloom yet deeper, the Green candidate scoring only 3 per cent.

Several lessons can be drawn from this electoral progress, lessons that may help us understand the weakness of environmental protests.

First, the rise of the environmental movement was contemporary with the political successes of the left. That is why after François Mitterrand's election, and at least provisional and/or symbolic satisfaction of a certain number of ecologists' demands, the movement lost influence and almost disappeared (Duyvendak 1994; Fillieule 1998).

It is, however, more difficult to explain why the movement did not grow again after some years of Socialist administration. The reason is to be found in the fact that, paradoxically, Socialist governments privileged economic questions because they were eager on the one hand to show their competence compared to the right and, on the other hand, because their priority was to reduce the effects of the economic crisis. Environmental problems were relegated to the second rank of the political agenda as well as of public opinion as the French became preoccupied with the erosion of their standard of living and the rise in unemployment.

The rise and fall of environmental protest can be explained in the same terms as the fortunes of political ecology. After Mitterrand's election in 1981, the development of an unfavourable pattern of political opportunities was correlated with a significant decline in the number of mobilizations initiated by new social movements of all kinds. In previous research based on police files dealing with demonstrations during the 1980s (Fillieule 1996, 1998), we have shown that the street was dominated, during the 1980s, by the traditional organizations, especially the trade unions. Nor did the issues of protest have much to do with the supposedly 'post-materialist' agenda of the new social movements; the greatest number of demonstrations revolved around the problem of employment and demands concerning earnings. In the police archives, environmental protests scarcely figured. Moreover, this pattern remained remarkably stable over time.

In the 1990s, the weakness of the new social movements, and particularly that of the ecologist movement, was all the more evident. In the archives of the Paris Police prefecture, from 1987 to 1993 the level of mobilization of the ecologist movement remained extremely low, despite some increase in activity between 1987 and 1991.

Interviews with specialist journalists at *Le Monde* suggest that the increased frequency of environmental coverage after 1989 was primarily due to the development of political ecology. From this point of view, the late 1980s and early 1990s were a kind of golden age. As Roger Cans, environment correspondent of

Le Monde from 1982 to 1995, put it:

The environment only started getting really interesting towards 1988, despite Bhopal (1984), Greenpeace (1985), Chernobyl (1986) and the rest. Because the ecologists scored heavily in the cantonal (1988) and municipal elections (1989), the Politics desk took over ecology politics. The economics supplement commissioned a monthly column at the same time. Everything intensified between 1989 and 1992 (Rio). Since the Rio summit and the disappointing results of 1993 for ecology politics, the environment has receded somewhat from front page coverage.

Perhaps, then, it is less the actual progress of environmental mobilizations that our data describe than the degree of sensitivity of a newspaper like *Le Monde* to the environmental question. When ecology becomes prominent from a political or an institutional point of view, it is likely that the number of protest events covered will increase. When the ecologists accepted a political alliance with the Socialist Party and the Communist Party, in the wake of the left's loss of the presidential elections in 1995, the newspaper began to increase its coverage of environmental affairs. The reason is that the Greens' leaders had announced in their programme a number of reforms such as, for example, the abandonment of the Rhine-Rhône canal. *Le Monde* was thus particularly attentive to mobilizations crystalizing around these conflicts which might have become politically central after a possible victory of the left. After Dominique Voynet was nominated as Minister of the Environment and made decisions concerning the abandonment of the Rhine-Rhône canal and Superphénix, coverage of environmental protests declined, for reasons that Hélène Crié, environmental journalist at *Libération*, explains very clearly:

I think that Voynet's arrival actually contributed to a small decline in the treatment of environmental issues, because Voynet herself does not play up environmental issues... When you have to cover an issue being handled by Voynet, whether it's to do with hunting or Roissy airport, you well understand that in the article you have to talk about her relations with Gayssot (Transport Minister), with Jospin (Prime Minister), in short, political politics rather than the environment... I think it's imperceptible, but there is a rejection/decline in the treatment of the environment and *a fortiori* of the work of the associations. Voynet herself, despite all her speeches, is dismissive of the associations.

MUSHROOMING BY NUMBERS: THE FRAGMENTATION AND DECLINE OF THE ASSOCIATIONS

When we consider the frequency with which reported actions were associated with a particular organization, it appears that the environmental association sector has for years been prey to a double process of fragmentation and institutionalization that contributed to the increasing rarity of opportunities for mobilization.

In order to contextualize the transformation of environmental activism, we first need to consider the morphology of the environmental sector. 'It is estimated that, for the last fifteen years, approximately 40,000 associations, centered on the defence of environment, nature and cultural heritage, were created' (Lascoumes 1994: 227). Among these associations, 1500 were still active and involved 100,000 members, including 5000 activists. This proliferation of organizations is reflected in our data: eighty different environmental associations were reported as being involved in the ninety-five protest events coded in which the presence of an environmental group was mentioned.

This fragmentation of the movement reflects its extreme specialization. This specialization is on two dimensions. On the one hand, associations are specialized along a spatial dimension, from local to transnational: from Parisian neighbourhood level (la Bellevilleuse), to town (Comité de Défense de Vingrau), to district (Association Vivre en Maurienne), to region (FRAPNA, Fédération Rhône-Alpes de Protection de la Nature), as well as from the national level (France Nature Environnement) to a worldwide level (League for the Protection of Birds—LPO, WWF, Greenpeace, FoE). On the other hand, the causes defended are themselves fragmented. One can find, for example, specific organizations against the Rhine-Rhône canal (CLAC—Comité de Liaison Anti Canal), against asbestos (Association Nationale de Défense des Victimes de l'Amiante), against air pollution (Comité de Défense des Victimes de la Pollution de l'Air), against the construction of highways (Collectif de Défense des Régions Traversées par l'Autoroute), against hunting (Rassemblement des Opposants à la Chasse), and in favour of the protection of bears (Ours).

If this diversification is not peculiar to French society, its extreme fragmentation is nevertheless remarkable. This corresponds to what Maresca and Zentay (1997) noticed in their study of environmental associations in the Basse-Normandie region: an ecologist sector characterized by an acceleration in the rate of formation of environmental associations, highly correlated with the increase in the voluntary sector in general; a declining number of participants per association; a shorter life cycle; but a stable global number of adherents. Our results confirm this strong trend towards fragmentation of environmental associations.

This does not, however, imply an absence of structure. The most important federation, France Nature Environnement,[15] is an umbrella organization for many local, district, and regional associations. Nevertheless, its ties with associations are very weak. In fact, environmental networks seem to be more closely tied to prominent regional associations.

Pierre Lascoumes identified four prominent regional networks: FRAPNA (Fédération Rhône-Alpes de Protection de la Nature) for Rhône-Alpes, SEPBN (Société pour l'Étude et la Protection de la Nature en Bretagne) for Brittany, SEPANSO (Fédération des Sociétés pour l'Étude, la Protection et l'Aménagement de la Nature dans le Sud-Ouest) for Aquitaine, and the recent Fare-Sud for the Provence-Alpes-côte-d'Azur (created to campaign against the high speed train—TGV). Each organization was created more than 30 years ago and together they correspond to the so-called 'hard core' of the regional associative networks

(Lascoumes 1994: 242). The distribution of events by regions reflects that structure. Thus, mobilizations should be understood in terms of a previous and strongly tied regional environmental network (Table 3.2).

Excepting the Paris region, which was over-represented, the four most mobilized regions in term of number of protests corresponded exactly to the four most important regional associations in the country as identified by Lascoumes. The geographical distribution of protests reported in *Le Monde* is thus wider than we might have expected. Even if the most important region is Paris (24.1 per cent of reported environmental protest events), the more active regions in the provinces are also over-represented, as much as if not more than the Paris region (Aquitaine contains only 4.8 per cent of the population but accounted for 11.6 per cent of reported protest). Thus, although the geographical distribution of reported protest

TABLE 3.2. *The spatial distribution of environmental protests in France (1988–97) compared with population*

	Percentage of protest events	Percentage of population[a]	Index of representation[b]
Paris region	24.1	18.20	1.32
Rhône-Alpes	12	10.88	1.11
Aquitaine	11.6	4.83	2.40
Provence-Alpes-Côte d'Azur	8.3	7.49	1.11
Bretagne	6.5	4.83	1.34
Languedoc-Roussillon	5.1	3.81	1.34
Midi-Pyrénées	4.6	4.24	1.09
Pays-de-la-Loire	4.2	5.35	0.78
Lorraine	3.2	3.84	0.84
Franche Comté	3.2	1.86	1.75
Auvergne	3.2	2.17	1.49
Basse-Normandie	2.3	2.36	0.98
Poitou-Charentes	1.9	2.72	0.68
Centre	1.9	4.05	0.46
Champagne-Ardennes	1.4	2.23	0.62
Alsace	1.4	2.88	0.48
Picardie	0.9	3.09	0.30
Nord	0.9	6.64	0.14
Limousin	0.9	1.18	0.78
Haute-Normandie	0.9	2.96	0.31
Bourgogne	0.9	2.68	0.35
Corse	0.5	0.43	1.07
Total *N*	216	60,186,184	

Notes:

[a] Population figures for 1999 from the general census (INSEE).

[b] 'Index of representation' is a figure obtained by dividing the number of protests by the number of protests expected from the ratio of the total number of events to total population; values above one indicate over-representation of an area in the data set, and values below one an under-representation.

was certainly biased by the rationale of *Le Monde* (see Appendix A), the extent of that bias is not so great that it fails to offer a good picture of the probable distribution of actual protests.

Apart from the concentration of 52 per cent of the events in the five dominant regions, the spatial distribution of environmental protest events was very fragmented. However, that fragmentation does not mean absence of visibility. Transnational organizations clearly emerge from this environmental landscape: WWF, FoE, and Greenpeace between them account for almost one-quarter of the protests in which groups were mentioned. GPF, despite its weakness in terms of adherents and resources compared to Greenpeace in other European countries, largely dominated the field of nationally reported environmental protest. During the 10 years, Greenpeace was mentioned in every tenth protest covered by *Le Monde*, possibly a reflection of GPF's practice of strategies of 'media saturation' or 'regular drip-feeding' to environment writers in the press.[16] In interpreting our data, particularly when identifying organizing groups, it is thus essential to take into account that the professionalization of environmental groups' media relations is not homogenous across the organizational sector but favours those with sufficient financial resources.[17]

One should also note the relative absence of trade unions. This is striking compared to the historical role of the CFDT (Rucht 1994) in anti-nuclear mobilizations during the 1970s and even after Mitterrand's assumption of power (Table 3.3). A possible explanation of this lies in the high rate of unemployment (constantly more than 10 per cent during the 10 years) which made it difficult to interest trade unionists in environmental affairs.

If trade unions were noticeably absent, political parties were more involved, accounting for 23 per cent of the mentions of groups involved in environmental protests, mostly due to the greens (12.5 per cent) and left parties (mostly the Socialist Party—7.4 per cent). The absence of regionalist parties is also noticeable, whereas they were deeply involved in the movement during the 1970s (mainly with the anti-nuclear groups). This result is not in line with the general

TABLE 3.3. *Types of organizations involved in environmental protest in France (1988–97)*

Types of groups	Frequency	Percentage
Political parties	60	23.3
Unions	9	3.5
Formal associations	141	54.7
Informal associations	7	2.7
Networks	23	8.9
Other	18	7
Total	258	100

Key

PS: Partie socialiste
FRAPNA: Fédération Rhône-Alpes de Protection de la Nature
Robin: Robin des bois
WWF: World Wild Fund
Eau pure: Collectif eau pure

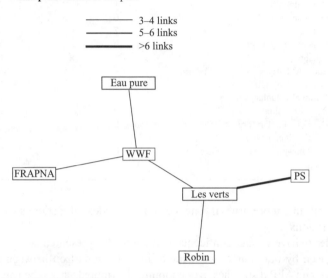

FIG. 3.3. *The network of protests in France: environmental groups and others (1988–97) (only links reported 3 or more times are included)*

withdrawal of political parties from demonstrations that we observed in the 1980s and 1990s (Fillieule 1997). This high degree of collaboration between environmental groups and green parties stresses that in the multi-organizational field of the environmental movement, *Les Verts* assumed a central position.

Network analysis[18] confirmed the centrality of *Les Verts* in the patterning of reports of protest in which groups were mentioned as being involved with others on three or more occasions (Fig. 3.3). Two factors help to explain this.

On the one hand, the commitment of environmental activists to green parties can be explained by the ecological parties' electoral success in the late 1980s. This drained the associational sector of its executive staff, and, as a result, the staffs of green parties are mainly composed of former activists who remain very sensitive to protest politics, for cultural as well as for tactical reasons (such as the need to maintain an image of an alternative conception of politics).

On the other hand, in the absence of direct relationships with elected representatives, environmental association activists are constrained to seek green parties' help since the latter possess most information and the required financial means.

Fillieule

TABLE 3.4. *Groups mentioned in reports of environmental protest in France in* Le Monde *and in AFP reports (January and June 1988, March and September 1994, May and December 1997)*

Group/organization	Le Monde	AFP
Robin des bois	1	1
Greenpeace	0	4
Les Verts	7	4
Génération Ecologie	0	1
Chiche	1	0
Socialist Party	7	0
Gaullist party (RPR)	1	0
National voluntary org.	3	2
Regional voluntary org.	0	2
District voluntary org.	0	5
Local voluntary org.	1	6
Not known	0	7
Total	21	32

That is all the more true if one considers modes of action such as mass demonstrations.

In order to have greater confidence that the results presented here were not too much biased by our source, we made a limited comparison between reports in *Le Monde* and AFP dispatches over 6 months distributed across the whole period: January and June 1988, March and September 1994, May and December 1997.[19]

Table 3.4 suggests that *Le Monde* is marked by an institutional bias. In its reports of protest, *Le Monde* mentioned the presence of political parties fourteen times (seven for the greens and seven for the Socialist party) whereas during the same months the AFP covered only five events that involved political parties. It appears that voluntary groups were less well covered by *Le Monde* than AFP. Our data almost certainly under-represent the actual participation of voluntary organizations, which are less often considered as valuable sources of articles. One reason for that is made clear if one considers the breakdown of events by territorial level of the groups involved. By comparison with the AFP, *Le Monde* had a tendency to neglect local, district, and regional associations.

INSTITUTIONALIZATION

As well as its fragmentation, the voluntary association sector is characterized by a process of relative institutionalization. Associations are increasingly called upon by local and regional authorities to participate in establishing projects, yet they are not offered means to influence the decisions taken. This phenomenon, which must be related to the implementation of decentralization and the transfer of certain responsibilities from central to regional authorities, contributes to curbing the associations' vague attempts at protest and their increasing financial dependence on subsidies from officials and public administrations. It is therefore hardly surprising that legal and lobbying actions have increasingly taken precedence over recourse to protest. The relative pacification of the environmental movement can then be related to its co-optation by the state.

This 'instrumentalization' of the environmental sector by the state takes place not only at local and regional levels, but also at the national level.

The environmental associations in France have much less room to maneuver than their European counterparts... This is so because they are tied to the political powers, whether left or right: The statutes of France-Nature-Environnement reveal that its members do not themselves have the power to modify the association or even its statutes; any such decisions made during a general assembly have to be sent to the relevant Minister and are only valid subject to government approval. Ministerial authorities also vet the code of practice and all the association's official acts (e.g. registers, accounts, annual reports) as well as the way in which certain resources emanating from government administrations are used. These are good examples of statutes imposed upon associations which have received the government seal of approval (associations reconnues d'utilité publique). (Prendiville, quoted in Chibret 1991: 729).

At local level, this phenomenon is all the more strong since local institutions finance more and more expert reports, and try to obtain the associations' agreement to their public policy, the best way of doing so being the creation of *ad hoc* associations totally dependent for their resources upon the local government.

To understand that situation, one must consider the problematic history of the Ministry for the Environment. Historically, it is not possible to disassociate the constitution of the field of environmental associations from the slow and difficult birth of the administration of the Ministry for the Environment. The ministry 'of the impossible' instituted in 1971 never in fact received the administrative and financial means, nor acquired sufficient political legitimacy, to impose truly autonomous action on other ministerial sectors (Charvolin 1993). As a result, in the early 1970s, the state had recourse to associations as a counter-weight in conflicts, and this led to their confrontation with industrialists and locally elected officials. In this context, the Ministry of the Environment needed a powerful and representative associational movement on which to base its own legitimacy, given its iniquitous resources compared to other ministries (Agriculture, Economy and Finances, Industry; Maresca and Zentay 1997). Hence, the implementation of two major kinds of measures intended to ensure greater effectiveness of public policies. The decree of 7 July 1977 instituting an approval procedure to protect natural and urban environments, and the decree of 3 July 1985 dealing with classified installations, both made it possible for the associations to participate in the work of a large number of national, regional, and district consultative organizations (committees for specific sites, for urban issues, district public health and hygiene issues). Moreover, the associations were represented on the management boards of public establishments concerned with the environment, and those for the national parks. The associations thus came to constitute veritable 'external services of a ministry which has none of its own' (Lascoumes 1994: 193).

It is possible to talk of exchanges of service between the state apparatus and the associations. In effect, on the one side associations were given official recognition and institutional legitimacy sustained by the granting of the right to take collective legal action, legal and financial support. On the other, they were expected to provide assistance to the democratic process, a diffusion-promotion of the policy initiated at the time of the creation of the Ministry for the Environment in 1971 as well as a support for the effective implementation of the law. This legally empowered and de facto alliance between the base and the summit was more or less explicitly conceived as a way to stimulate and control intermediary levels, regularly entangled in alliances and local power conflicts. That is why the associations are often perceived by the central authorities as precious auxiliaries to legality. (Joly-Sibuet and Lascoumes 1987: 4).

This policy, aimed at a neo-corporatist integration of the associational sector (Spanou 1991), contributed permanently to determine the strength of the associations. In effect, through the play of conditions for granting the *agrément*[20] and grants, the state encouraged a certain number of large associations in every region, which it legitimized as spokesmen, and required to toe the line as a result of their status, at the expense of a whole set of other groupings, generally more locally oriented and willing to use more contestatory strategies.[21]

All this explains how the current structuring of the associational landscape no longer relates only to a dichotomy between the naturalist associations concerned with protecting the landscape on the one hand, and the more politicized ecological associations more oriented to the protection of quality of life on the other. To this distinction must be added a split between protest associations (much less politically integrated, with little in the way of resources and public audience) and the big representative associations (subsidized and professionalized) associated with state agencies. In this context, the associations that wish to attain their self-defined objectives are faced with a radical choice. Either they accept a gradual integration into decision-making circuits at a local, regional, or national level— which requires professionalization, fund-raising, and the abandonment of direct opposition—or they keep their distance, at the risk of remaining impotent. In effect, in the context of state withdrawal and of decentralization of administrative responsibilities (Fillieule 2000), it becomes extremely dangerous, if not impossible, to resist developing working relations with the local authorities.

In view of all this, one should not be surprised that a central feature of the picture of environmental protest that emerges from newspaper reports (see Fig. 3.4) is its great moderation throughout the 10 years.[22]

If one accepts the well-established stereotype that French social movements, because of the high degree of closedness of the state, adopt confrontational tactics (e.g., see Kitschelt 1986), one might be surprised that contention over environmental issues seems to be very moderate. Violent actions and attacks on property together represented only 6 per cent of the protests reported in the

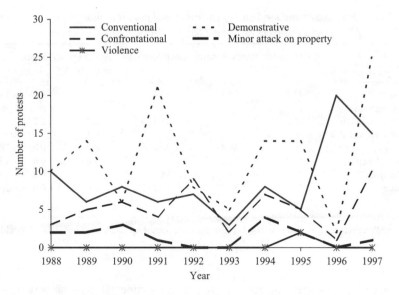

Fɪɢ. 3.4. *Forms of environmental protest in France by year*

decade, a result that is all the more remarkable since the media usually attribute particular newsworthiness to violent events.[23]

The dependence of associations upon the state and local institutions seems not only to limit the use of violence but also to have consequences for the whole repertoire of contention. Actions such as demonstrations, rallies, blockades, and occupations together account for only 50 per cent of the protest events reported during the decade. Demonstrations were only present in a third of the collective actions reported, a striking illustration of the weakness of the movement's mobilization in a country in which demonstrations are exceptionally common (Fillieule 1997).

'Moderate' forms of actions, such as petitions, cultural actions, press conferences, litigation, and procedural complaints account for some 30 per cent of protests. Such a result is all the more important since these forms of actions, because their newsworthiness is very low, do not attract systematic coverage by journalists. These results appear to confirm a deep-seated trend of environmental associations in France towards an 'expert-activist repertoire of contention' (Ollitrault 1996) that needs to be considered in light of both the co-optation and institutionalization of the movement and the transformation of the ecologist identity *vis-à-vis* the critique of their opponents. In response to criticisms of their lack of 'seriousness' and objective information, environmentalists and ecologists tended to change their strategies, writing scientific and expert reports rather than mobilizing public protests.

TABLE 3.5. *Issues and the forms of environmental protest in France (percentage of events involving each issue that involves a form of action)*

	Conventional	Demonstrative	Confrontational	Attack on property	Violence	N
Nature conservation	43.5	26.1	17.4	17.4	0.0	23
Pollution, urban and industrial	36.3	38.5	23.1	2.2	2.2	91
Energy	30.8	47.4	24.4	6.4	0.0	78
Animal welfare	35.3	41.2	11.8	11.8	0.0	17
Transport	28	64	14	6	0.0	50
Other	48.3	37.9	17.2	0.0	0.0	29
N	88	119	52	15	2	

Note: Percentages do not sum to 100 because for each protest up to 2 issues and 4 forms could be recorded.

Since the repertoire of actions used in environmental protests was mainly peaceful, one should not be surprised that there is no strong link between forms of action and kinds of issues (see Table 3.5). However, less than 30 per cent of protests regarding nature conservation issues were reported to have involved demonstrative forms of action, and 17.4 per cent employed confrontational tactics,[24] whereas protests on energy (mainly nuclear waste) and transport issues were rather more confrontational. Almost half of protests concerning energy issues involved demonstrative forms of action, and one-quarter involved confrontational tactics; almost two-thirds of transport protests involved demonstrative actions, but confrontational tactics were involved in only 14 per cent of events.

If we now consider the hypothesis of the impact of the centralization and the power of the state on social movements, our data confirm Duyvendak's results (1994). The 'power of politics' on social movements is confirmed: companies, private persons, and associations were the targets of only around 13 per cent of protests whereas government and public institutions at all levels represented 70 per cent of the targets. Nevertheless, one should read these results carefully since journalists at *Le Monde* usually prefer to focus on mobilizations related to the institutional political arena.

As Table 3.6 shows, the influence of centralization on social movements was confirmed. Although 60 per cent of mobilizations were at the regional, district, or local level, and even though the scope of the problem was in a majority (60 per cent) of cases subnational in that they were construed as local/regional issues by protesters, claims were directed to the national state in more than two-thirds of cases.

Despite the example of the anti-nuclear mobilization with continuing participation of German and Swiss activists, there was little evidence of a

TABLE 3.6. *Levels of mobilization, scope of problems, and targets of environmental protest in France (percentages)*

	Local/district	Regional	National	EU	International	*N*
Level of mobilization	46.9	12.5	23.7	4.0	12.9	224
Scope of underlying problem	44.9	15.1	22.4	5.7	11.8	245
Level of target	23.2	9.4	67.9	1.8	4.9	240

Europeanization of environmental protest. Protests directed at European targets, including the European Union, were rare.

CONCLUSION

The data presented here seem to indicate a decline in the French environmental movement. The low numbers of people mobilized and protest resources mobilizable by the associations, alongside the rarity of protest events, all contribute to a picture of a stricken sector similar to that of most other so-called new social movements in France. It would be premature, given the current state of research, to be categoric about the reasons for such a debacle. We have suggested several here, without being able yet to say with any precision whether the characteristics brought to light should be interpreted as causes or consequences of a decline that has been long established. For the time being, it suffices to underline the points to be taken into account when responding to this question.

First, the decline of the environmental movement should be related to the development of political power relationships in the arena of institutional politics. On the one hand, the left's assumption of power, its continuance in power over several years, and the game of political alternation have contributed to a blurring of traditional political divisions, and have, as it were, snuffed out the dynamic of environmental mobilization, just as they have the ensemble of causes resulting from post-1968 turmoil. On the other hand, the emergence of green parties in the late 1970s and their sudden but ephemeral growth at the end of that decade also had a de-energizing effect on the associational movement. Activists in the associations, having become involved in political parties, left the protest scene for institutional politics which, from the late 1980s, appeared to be a surer means of furthering their aims. From this point of view, the alliance of the greens with the Socialist and Communist left in 1997 marked a climax, with the leader of the greens, Dominique Voynet, assuming the post of Minister of the Environment.

Second, the environmental association sector has for many years suffered both fragmentation and institutionalization, which have contributed to diminishing opportunities for mobilization. Fragmentation took the form of the proliferation of localized associations, consisting of relatively small numbers of people, with insufficient resources to ensure their independence, and focused on demands that were themselves fragmented. Institutionalization took its toll because, whilst associations were increasingly called upon by local and regional authorities to participate in establishing projects, they were not offered the means to influence the decisions taken. This, which must be related to the implementation of decentralization and the transfer of certain responsibilities from central to regional authorities, contributed to curbing the associations' interest in protest, especially given their increasing financial dependence on subsidies from officials and public administrations. It is hardly surprising that, as a result, legal and lobbying actions took precedence over protest.

Third, it seems that in the social world, environmental issues became, paradoxically, victims of their own growing success. The need to protect the environment was unanimously accepted by public authorities, the media, and general opinion, even if there was no agreement over the measures to be implemented. This apparent unanimity was accompanied by a process of dissemination of ecological awareness, very visible in the way in which the media, including *Le Monde*, have come to cover environmental issues from a multiplicity of angles: science, techniques and technologies, political, consumer-oriented, daily life, and so on. Now, in a world where cars, yoghurts, and the mayor of Paris boast green labels, it is difficult for a protest movement to succeed in establishing 'frame alignment processes' to the extent necessary to mobilization.

NOTES

1. See, for example, Pronier and Le Seigneur (1992), Sainteny (1992, 2000), Villalba (1995), Boy, Le Seigneur, and Roche (1995).
2. Apart from Dieter Rucht's research, the main exceptions are Chibre (1991), Lascoumes (1994), and Ollitrault (1996).
3. For a synthetic review of the literature on this subject, see Fillieule and Ferrier (2000).
4. The first being, in 1854, La Société Impériale Zoologique d'Acclimatation, a branch of which, founded in 1912, gave birth to the French League for the Protection of Birds (LPO).
5. See Appendix A for a more elaborated defence of this point.
6. There exists an electronic version of *Le Monde* but sample comparisons revealed that versions available on CD-ROM did not cover all the articles we were interested in; short reports, in particular, were often omitted.
7. Three journalists have covered environmental issues in turn since 1974: Marc-Ambroise Rendu (1974–82), Roger Cans (1982–95), and Sylvia Zappi (1995–9). For more details on the selection of the newspaper and on biases linked to this choice, see Appendix A and Fillieule and Ferrier (1999).
8. See Appendix A for our definition of a protest event.
9. For a similar critique in terms of analysis of electoral behaviour, see Converse (1990).

10. One should be aware, when interpreting the trend, that variations in the total number of protesters are also, if not mainly, due to variations from year to year in the numbers of cases in which data on numbers of participants is missing.

11. Agence Nationale pour la Gestion des Déchets Radioactifs (National Agency for Nuclear Waste).

12. See also Mattout and Metayer (1987), Alazard (1990), Lascoumes (1985) and Joly-Sibuet and Lascoumes (1987). The research of the JNE relates to two periods: October to December 1996 and June to July 1997. Lascoumes' research rests on a corpus of 7235 press articles drawn from more than 150 newspapers. They relate to 8 months of publication, 4 months in each of 1988 and 1989, and include articles of press agencies (27.5%), national daily newspapers (36%), regional newspapers (20%), weekly magazines and monthly magazines (8.5%), and specialized press (8%).

13. Hélène Crié was long-time head of the environmental column in *Libération*. She has written many books on nuclear problems.

14. See Appendix A and Fillieule and Ferrier (1999).

15. Formerly FFSPN, created in 1968.

16. To use the expressions employed by Grégory Derville (1997) in his analysis of Greenpeace's media strategies over the recommencement of French nuclear testing. See also Baisnée (1998) on how the media sector operated during the GPF campaign around the reprocessing plant in La Hague, and Gallet (1999).

17. Compare, for example, Deacon (1996: 173) on the public relations practices of British voluntary sector organizations.

18. I am indebted to Manuel Jiménez for the completion of the network analysis.

19. For the examination of the AFP, we initially retained all the bulletins containing in the heading and/or the text the word 'environment'. Then, we isolated the dispatches treating only events that had taken place in France, to retain finally only those that corresponded to our definition of protest events.

20. An 'Agrément, au titre de l'Environnement or de l'Urbanisme' is an approved accreditation for an association recognized by the Préfet, via an official document which attests to their representativeness at the same time as it gives them the right to go to court (as a civil party, if there has been an illegal breach which threatens the environment) and the possibility of participating in consultative committees.

21. Which Lascoumes (1994: 211) summarizes, defining four types of possible relations between associations and public authorities: an attitude of exclusion (rejection for incompetence, activism, non-representativeness: refusal of official accreditation); an attitude of marginalization; an attitude of instrumentalization (pragmatic use by the state of associational resources); and an attitude of phagocytosis (direct production of rump and/or para-public associations).

22. We have classified the forms of protest as: conventional (comprising procedural claims such as demands for judicial review, actions such as collective representations to officials or elected politicians, public meetings, leafleting, and the collection of signatures on petitions); demonstrative actions (including street marches, rallies, and vigils); confrontational actions (including occupations and physical obstruction); minor attacks on property (that do not pose a threat to human life); and violence (attacks on persons that could cause injury).

23. See Appendix A on the question of biases concerning the forms of protest.

24. The number of minor attacks on property (fifteen cases) is too low to be interpreted here.

4

Germany

Dieter Rucht and Jochen Roose

The German environmental movement may not be the strongest in the world in terms of per capita membership,[1] but there is little doubt that it has been in the front rank if we consider the volume of protest activity. The German movement has also been supposed to be fairly radical by comparison with its counterparts in most Western countries. According to existing accounts, however, this picture has changed. Observers claim that the movement is in decline (Opp 1996: 371), or has virtually ceased to exist (Hellmann and Klein 1994: 2). Others maintain that the movement survives, but has lost its zeal due to a gradual process of institutionalization (Brand 1993, 1999; Wörndl and Fréchet 1994; Eder 1996) and, in particular, the co-optation of the movement's leadership. The extent to which such perceptions are correct can only be judged on the basis of thorough empirical analyses. In the following, we first provide a brief and broad overview of the development of environmentalism in Germany, then we present our data source and, in the main sections, our findings on the pattern and changes of protest. Finally, we summarize and interpret the major results.

THE DEVELOPMENT OF ENVIRONMENTALISM IN GERMANY: A BRIEF OVERVIEW

As in many other countries, modern environmentalism in West Germany did not gain momentum until the early 1970s.[2] However, it would be wrong to assume that environmental questions were put on public and political agenda only by the then newly created environmental groups. Environmental concerns were also expressed and promoted by governments on both the international and national levels, and in West Germany, environmental action programmes were launched in 1970 and 1971, followed by a wave of environmental legislation and first attempts to institutionalize environmental policy (Weidner 1995; Jänicke, Kunig, and Stifzel 1999).[3]

We are grateful to Annika Zorn who thoroughly coded most of the empirical information used for quantitative analysis in this chapter.

Three concurrent developments marked the early phase of the emerging environmental movement. First, local and independent citizen action groups mushroomed and, in part, also united in regional, statewide, and national organizations such as the Bundesverband Bürgerinitiativen Umweltschutz (BBU) (Federal Alliance of Citizen Initiatives for Environmental Protection; founded in 1972). These early groups focused mainly on specific issues such as air pollution, private transport, and nuclear energy. Second, pre-existing organizations for nature conservation became revitalized and, to some extent, politicized. An outstanding example is the Bavarian-based Bund Naturschutz (Alliance for Nature Conservation; founded in 1913) which renewed its programme and leadership in the early 1970s and was instrumental in founding the Bund für Umwelt- und Naturschutz Deutschland (BUND) in 1975.[4] Third, loose networks of individuals and groups adhering to a more general concept of political ecology emerged. They saw an urgent need for a radical change of industrial societies, promoting ideas of decentralization, 'soft' technology, an ascetic and ecologically friendly lifestyle, and sometimes even industrial devolution (Amery 1976). Alongside these new tendencies, some of the traditional organizations for nature conservation, bird protection, and the protection of other animals continued to exist without, at that time, modifying their apolitical ideology and assimilative strategy.

By and large, these different groups represented three ideological strands: old-fashioned *conservationism* aiming to protect particular areas and species by non-conflictual means; modern *environmentalism* that had a broader and more dramatic perception of environmental degradation and did not shy away from political intervention; *political ecologism* whose advocates proposed radical means to save 'planet Earth' and reach a truly ecological society (Rucht 1991).[5] Both old and New Left were initially skeptical about what they perceived as a naive petty-bourgeois movement. Only in the second half of the 1970s, when conflict over nuclear energy was central, did many leftist groups, ranging from Maoists to Trotskyites to anarchists, join the movement and play a role in the 'alternative' and 'green lists' that preceded the formation of the Green Party in January 1980.

During the 1970s, the environmental movement acted mainly as a challenger to established institutions and the dominant policy of economic growth supported by all major parties—the Christian Democrats (CDU), the Social Democrats (SPD), and the significantly smaller Free Democrats (FDP). These forces were not directly opposed to environmentalism, but felt that the movement wanted too much too quickly, and so threatened economic performance and job security. They framed the issue as a matter of 'jobs versus environmental protection'. This conflict was particularly heated in respect of nuclear energy in the second half of the 1970s. Trade unions, backed by employers, organized demonstrations in favour of nuclear energy that attracted up to 40,000 people in 1976, while the anti-nuclear movement staged a large number of protests of various kinds, ranging from collection of signatures to mass demonstrations by up to 120,000 people to disruptive actions including violence. But other issues such as road building, the construction or extension of airports and waste incinerators also mobilized many protesters. Sometimes these were simply NIMBY (Not In My Back Yard) groups opposing a particular local project but, for the most part, they were motivated by broader and deeper worries about the degradation and destruction of the environment which, in their view, was not taken seriously by the established political forces.

During the 1980s, the picture of an outsider movement besieging the political establishment faded away. On the one hand, the establishment gradually became more receptive to environmental concerns and more skeptical about the conventional idea of progress measured in productivity rates and GNP. In any case, growth rates declined and unemployment rose significantly, and certainly not because of too much environmental protection. It also became clear that a significant proportion of the population sympathized with green ideas, as could be seen both by the large numbers of adherents to the movement (Fuchs and Rucht 1994) and green voters (Frankland 1995). Even the CDU, which, together with the FDP, came into power in 1982 (and remained there for the next 16 years), at least rhetorically embraced the need for strong environmental protection and took some concrete measures. On the other hand, parts of the more radical segment of the environmental movement became more pragmatic, focusing on alternative technologies, the technicalities of environmental policy-making, and the parliamentary arena where the greens gained a foothold at all levels, from local councils to the European Parliament. Over time, the groups at the ideological fringes—both left and right—of the environmental movement decreased in numbers and significance, and the environmentalist mainstream became the dominant force. Conflicts between the red–green and the brown–green strands, radicals and moderates, promoters of an extra-parliamentary and a parliamentary strategy, and between the 'fundamentalists' and 'realists' within the Green Party lost much of their importance (Roth and Murphy 1998).[6]

Based on this internal clearing process and the mutual rapprochement between the movement on the one hand and industry and public administrations on the other, the instances of communication, negotiation, and bargaining multiplied (Brand 1999). At the same time, however, direct conflicts continued over issues such as nuclear energy, animal rights, and genetic engineering. Overall, it seems that the movement has become ideologically less diverse and contradictory, but that it has also lost its clear-cut profile and identity due to its specialization and fragmentation among different issue areas, the strengthening of bonds with non-movement organizations, acceptance of funding from industry and public administrations, engagement in joint ventures such as conferences, campaigns, eco-sponsoring, and the like (Bergstedt 1998), and, last but not least, the increasing role of green parliamentary politics.

Some observers praised these more recent developments as signs of maturity, whereas others lamented that the movement has been compromised and sold out. Most of these observations and comments are not, however, based on systematic analysis of the actual changes of the movement but on casual impressions. Investigating the movement's protest activities provides more solid information for assessing whether or not sweeping statements about its decline, crisis, or taming can be substantiated. Such a comprehensive coverage of protest activity also avoids being guided only by the largest or most spectacular protests that often form the basis for dubious generalizations.

THE SOURCE OF THE EMPIRICAL DATA

The data on environmental protest in Germany from 1988 to 1997 is drawn from the daily newspaper *die tageszeitung* (*taz*). This Berlin-based paper is in various ways special when compared to the other four nationwide but larger and more established broadsheets.[7] First, the *taz* is much younger; it was created only in 1978. Second, it has a distinct political leaning which can be characterized as 'left-libertarian'. The paper was initiated by a number of individuals who had a background in New Left and new social movement activities (Flieger 1992) and who believed that a nationwide newspaper supportive of these movements and independent of established interests was needed. In its early phase, the *taz* was close to being a mouthpiece of the new social movements. But in later years, it became a fairly professional paper which, after much internal debate, abandoned its principles of little division of labour, equal (and low!) pay, and collective leadership. In spite of occasional financial crises, sometimes spectacular internal battles, and fairly modest circulation (*c*. 60,000 copies during most of the 1980s and 1990s), the paper is highly regarded and widely read by journalists of the more established press. The paper has largely maintained its unconventional, often provocative and cheeky style. The established press, including flagships such as *Der Spiegel* and *Die Zeit*, acknowledges the *taz* as both a source of inspiration and a pool for the recruitment of young, talented, and creative journalists. The *taz* was even dubbed the best 'school of journalism' in Germany. It publishes six issues per week (Monday through Saturday). Besides its general section, it has only two—and soon three—regional sections, the most important being that for Berlin, where the main editorial department is located.

From its beginnings, the *taz* devoted considerable attention to environmental issues. Since 1986, reporting on environmental problems, including a strong emphasis on nuclear energy issues, has become an elementary and stable part of the newspaper. From the early 1990s onwards, the paper carried a daily section (usually one page) headed 'Economy and the Environment' (previously 'Environment'), currently produced by six full-timers plus a number of freelancers. Reports on environmental matters are concentrated in this and the general section on domestic issues.[8] We have no reason to assume that the *taz* has, for internal reasons (change of personnel, ideological shift), changed the level of attention paid to environmental issues during the period of investigation.

THE INCIDENCE OF ENVIRONMENTAL PROTEST

Following procedures common to the other chapters in this volume, we coded protest events from all relevant sections and every issue of the *taz* from 1988 to (the end of) 1997. Throughout this period we also covered the separate local section on Berlin. This extensive coverage of protests in Berlin allows for comparisons between developments nationally and in Berlin.

Altogether, we have identified and coded 2470 environmental protests[9] of which 865 (35 per cent) were drawn from summary reports (see Chapter 2, note 8). We exclude data derived only from summary reports from our analysis.[10] Of the remaining 1605 events, 1177 (73.3 per cent) were drawn from the general/national sections and another 457 events from the Berlin local section.[11]

Figure 4.1 displays the evolution of protests according to three categories: 'national' protests in East and West Germany combined; national protests in East Germany only; local protests in Berlin.

When looking at all national protests, we see that the number of environmental protests changed significantly but not dramatically over time. It was highest in 1988, the beginning of the period of observation (192 events) and lowest in 1991 (45 events). The 'trough' in the years 1991–3 is likely an effect of two developments that overshadowed German politics in these years: German unification and the influx of asylum seekers and other immigrants. The intense conflict and mobilization around asylum policy and the rise of right-wing extremism probably contributed to a diminution of both the actual level of environmental activity but also of the media attention paid to it.[12] In the last 3 years of the series, the number of events stabilized at a relatively high level.

From these aggregate data we can conclude that the protest activity of the German environmental movement was relatively stable, particularly since

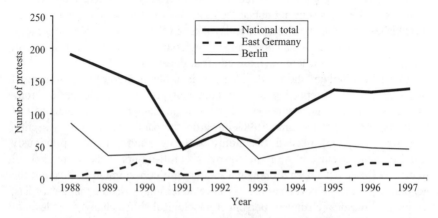

FIG. 4.1. *Environmental protests in Germany (East and West), East Germany, and Berlin by year*

1993–4. We do not assume that this pattern merely reflects idiosyncratic coverage by the newspaper from which these data are derived. Reports of environmental protests drawn from two other nationwide newspapers by a similar coding strategy[13] also reveal a fairly stable development during the late 1970s to 1994, with the exception of a sudden peak in 1986 which was mainly due to anti-nuclear protests in reaction to the Chernobyl disaster (Rucht and Roose 1999: 68). Hence the development of the German environmental movement in recent decades is not characterized by a cycle with a distinct upswing and downswing as exhibited by many other movements (Tarrow 1989; Koopmans 1993; Kriesi et al. 1995: ch. 5).

Given the unequal distribution of environmental problems and density of environmental groups across space, we did not expect protest to be spread evenly across Germany. In particular, before the breakdown of the regime, the more or less ubiquitous repression in East Germany made environmental protest and virtually all other kinds of protest scarcely possible. Environmental groups did exist, but they could hardly protest in public (Rink 2001).

In East Germany (excluding East and West Berlin), the curve of environmental protest remained at a low level throughout the whole period, with a moderate peak in 1990 and a very modest increase towards the end of the period under study.[14] Interestingly, Berlin reflects neither the trend in the East nor that in the West. In the period when protest was infrequent in West Germany, it was relatively frequent in Berlin. This confirms the conclusions of other research that stressed the idiosyncrasy of local protest that often exhibits its own peculiar patterns (Roth 1994; Rucht and Roose 2001b; Hocke 2002), patterns that remain invisible in the aggregate of national protest.

We can further break down regional patterns when looking at the individual states (*Länder*). When we control for population size, levels of environmental protest were clearly below average in the eastern states (Table 4.1). In absolute numbers and relative to the size of the population, Lower Saxony had by far the largest number of protests. This is mainly an effect of the nuclear energy issue which, in this state, accounted for 83 per cent of all environmental protests in the 10 years under study. The conflict around the 'Castor transport', the transport of nuclear waste to an interim, possibly even permanent, disposal site near Gorleben in Lower Saxony was the main focus of the German anti-nuclear movement in the years under investigation. Many protests were directed against these transports, some of them very large. In relative terms, Lower Saxony is followed by Schleswig-Holstein and then the two 'city-states' of Hamburg and Bremen. Berlin, the third city state, occasionally dubbed the 'metropolis of protest', makes a significant but not extraordinary contribution. This, in part, is due to the inclusion of the Eastern section of the city (about one-third of Berlin's total population) where relatively few protests took place. As we know from other checks, our data under-represent rather than over-represent protests in Berlin because most of these are covered by the local section of the newspaper, which is not included here. But even if we were to inflate the figures by a fifth to compensate for this effect, Lower Saxony would still rank ahead of Berlin.

TABLE 4.1. *The spatial distribution of protests compared with population in Germany*

	Percentage of protest events	Percentage of population[a]	Index of representation[b]
Lower Saxony	25.3	9.4	2.69
Schleswig-Holstein	7.2	3.3	2.16
Hamburg	3.3	2.1	1.59
Bremen	1.2	0.8	1.46
Hesse	9.8	7.3	1.33
Bavaria	12.9	14.6	0.89
North Rhine-Westphalia	11.7	21.8	0.54
Rhineland-Palatinate	2.4	4.8	0.51
Baden-Württemberg	6.0	12.6	0.48
Saarland	0.3	1.3	0.26
West German *Länder*[c]	81.7	78.2	1.05
Saxony-Anhalt	3.2	3.4	0.95
Mecklenburg-West Pomerania	2.1	2.3	0.93
Brandenburg	1.5	3.1	0.48
Thüringen	1.5	3.1	0.48
Saxony	1.9	5.6	0.34
East German *Länder*[c]	10.5	17.5	0.60
Berlin[c]	7.8	4.3	1.82
Total *N*	1144	81,422,000	1.00

Notes:
[a] Population figures for 1994 (year average) from the *Statistisches Bundesamt*, 1998: *Statistisches Jahrbuch*, Wiesbaden, p. 46.
[b] 'Index of representation' is a figure obtained by dividing the number of protests by the number of protests expected from the ratio of the total number of events to total population; values above 1 indicate over-representation of an area in the data set, and values below 1 an under-representation.
[c] The East German and West German *Länder* do not include Berlin, as distinguishing protests within Berlin between East and West is mostly not possible.

THE ISSUES OF PROTEST

When considering the six broad categories derived from a more detailed list of environmental issues and ignoring for a moment developments over time, we see a striking feature of the German case (Table 4.2). In the full period under investigation, more than half of all environmental protests (51.5 per cent) can be attributed to the energy issue, almost all of them against nuclear energy. Unlike in many other countries where nuclear energy also played a key role during the 1970s or early 1980s (Flam 1994), the nuclear energy issue has remained the centrepiece of environmental protest in Germany. In 1988 and 1989 protest was mainly directed against the construction and operation of nuclear power stations and especially against the nuclear reprocessing plant in Wackersdorf (Bavaria). In 1989 the industry cancelled the latter project, though some of the construction

TABLE 4.2. *Environmental issues raised in protests by year in Germany (% of events in which issue is raised by year)*

	1988	1989	1990	1991	1992	1993	1994	1995	1996	1997	1988–97	Total *N*
Nature conservation	9.4	12.1	7.9	20.0	10.1	14.8	6.6	10.3	9.0	6.6	9.8	115
Pollution, urban and industrial	24.6	33.9	48.6	28.9	30.4	20.4	17.0	14.0	6.0	7.3	23.0	271
Energy	58.1	43.6	41.4	46.7	26.1	48.1	57.5	57.4	64.7	65.0	52.7	620
Nuclear only	57.1	43.6	37.1	42.2	26.1	48.1	56.6	55.9	64.7	64.2	51.5	606
Animal welfare and hunting	1.6	3.6	0.7	0.0	4.3	1.9	3.8	4.4	0.8	4.4	2.6	31
Transport	6.3	7.9	8.6	22.2	31.9	5.6	11.3	9.6	18.8	12.4	11.8	139
Alternative production, etc.	8.9	10.3	14.3	11.1	7.2	16.7	9.4	16.2	12.8	15.3	12.2	143
Total *N* of events	191	165	140	45	69	54	106	136	133	137		1176

Note: Broad categories of issues in italic; subcategories in roman. Percentages do not sum to 100 as up to 2 issues could be recorded per event.

work was already completed, a decision heavily criticized by the national and Bavarian governments because both had supported the project against strong opposition by the movement. In the following years protest shifted towards the transport and disposal of nuclear waste. The disposal facility near Gorleben was at the centre of conflict, but another disposal site in Ahaus (North Rhine-Westphalia) also attracted increasing attention.

Among the other half of protests, issues of pollution prevailed (23 per cent), followed by considerably lower proportions in the areas of alternative production (mainly protest against genetic engineering), transport, and nature conservation. Unlike in Britain, the issue of animal welfare and hunting was marginal, accounting for only 2.6 per cent (thirty-one events) of all environmental protests.

Looking at the relative weight of these issue domains over time, we can see some significant changes. Pollution, for example, strongly represented between 1989 and 1992, lost much of its significance in the following years, while nuclear energy, uniquely among the countries investigated in this volume, gained in relative weight towards the end of the period under study.

The quantitative evolution of the four most significant protest issue domains can be better seen when absolute numbers are displayed. As Fig. 4.2 shows, the absolute frequency of (almost exclusively anti-nuclear) energy-related protest was highest in 1988, the height of the Wackersdorf conflict, then decreased steeply towards the middle of the period, and increased again to a relatively high point at the end. During the 1990s, anti-nuclear protest shifted from opposition to nuclear reactors and other nuclear facilities to the transport of nuclear waste.

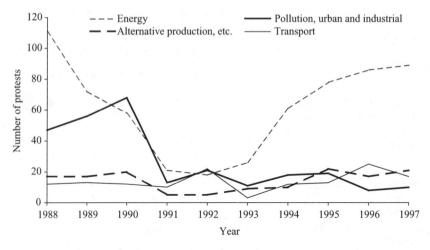

FIG. 4.2. *Four leading environmental issue domains in Germany by year*

Particularly in the area of Gorleben a new wave of protest against nuclear transports started in 1995 (Kolb 1997). In the summer of 1998, after it had leaked that the nuclear containers emitted radioactivity far beyond the legal thresholds, the transports were stopped by the government. When, eventually, a new programme of transport was implemented in March 2001, again it met strong resistance from some 15,000 protesters who faced an even larger police contingent.

Pollution was one of the main issue domains from 1988 onwards, peaking in 1990. Two issues mainly account for this peak: opposition to the export of hazardous waste from West to East Germany and the environmentally damaging behaviour of the Russian Army—an issue of which discussion had not been allowed in the GDR. During the 1990s, protests in this issue domain fell to a fairly low level. The remaining areas of transport and alternative production attracted a modest and relatively stable number of protests throughout the period under investigation.

Though the pattern of anti-nuclear and other environmental protest differs to some extent, they can be considered to comprise a single movement because the organizational basis of these kinds of protest was and still is largely the same. The large environmental organizations mobilized both against nuclear power and other environmental problems. Blühdorn (1995: 172) called resistance against nuclear energy 'the common denominator of all movement organizations and initiatives'. However, this should not obscure the fact that every issue domain also attracted specialized single-issue organizations that sometimes played an important role.

In Berlin, the levels and trends of three out of the four issue domains are significantly different from the national picture. Since no nuclear power facilities exist in and around Berlin, the energy issue was of minor relevance. Only in 1996 and 1997, with the nationwide campaign against nuclear transport, did the weight of this domain increase while that of the other three domains decreased. Throughout most of the 10-year period, transport issues dominated, with a remarkable peak in 1992 when discussion of transport policy in Berlin became prominent; protest culminated against the local government's policy to favour automobile traffic at the expense of public transport. Issues of pollution also ranged high and, in some of these years, even exceeded those of transport. Protests about alternative production remained relatively low and constant.

THE FORMS OF PROTEST

A crude distinction can be made between four types of protest: conventional, demonstrative, confrontational, and attacks on property or violence. Conventional and demonstrative protests together clearly dominated throughout the 10 years, the balance between them fluctuating, but their relative dominance decreased over the last 5 years. Confrontational events accounted on average for about one in four but, apart from becoming slightly more important from 1993 onwards, showed no consistent pattern over time. The proportion of attacks on property and violent acts was considerably higher in the second than in the first five years, with a peak in 1995. These forms of protest were mainly associated with the resistance against the transport of nuclear waste. While minor attacks on property decreased after 1995, forms of protest that consciously accept the risk of injuring people[15] increased in 1996 to account for 13.6 per cent of all protests. In the following year, these violent protests decreased slightly but still were more numerous in that single year than in the whole period 1988–92. These findings clearly contradict statements about an alleged moderation of environmental protests.

Considering the same type of information for Berlin alone, again confrontational events showed no consistent trend. Violent protests were concentrated in a few years (1988, 1992, 1997), with the highest proportion in the last year (Fig. 4.3). Again, this contradicts the common assumption that radical protest has declined.[16]

As a general rule, numbers of participants were low in events including minor attacks on property, let alone violence. This remains true even when we take into account that, in these kinds of protests, numbers of participants were more often reported than in those employing more moderate forms of action.[17]

The pattern of participation in all environmental protests over time (Fig. 4.4a) was erratic. The number of participants was highest in 1988, sharply lower in the next year, and thereafter gradually increased to a remarkable peak in 1994, followed by another sharp decline. Participation in demonstrations did not follow the same pattern (note that a different scale applies to this category) but peaked in 1990, reached a low point in the following year, and gradually

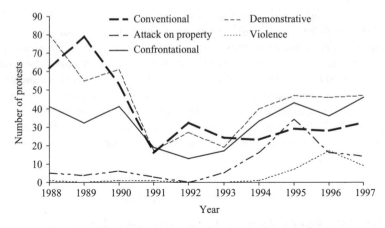

FIG. 4.3. *Forms of environmental protest in Germany by year*

increased thereafter. The striking difference between the two patterns is mainly an effect of the weight of collections of signatures and procedural complaints, often single protests with large numbers of participants that made a major contribution to the peaks.

Of the 610 protests for which we have numbers of participants, 14 involved at least 100,000 people. Among these mass protests, the collections of signatures dominate. In the largest event, 881,000 people objected to plans to build a nuclear reprocessing plant in Bavaria in 1988. Other collections of signatures included a Greenpeace initiative to reduce pesticides in drinking water (755,000 signatures in 1994[18]), an appeal to protect the global climate (650,000 signatures in 1995), and an appeal to stop genetically modified food (550,000 signatures in 1994). The single largest demonstration, attracting 50,000 protesters, was directed against the nuclear reprocessing plant in Wackersdorf, Bavaria in October 1988. This number, however, was dwarfed by various anti-nuclear protests that had taken place in the years before 1988. These included demonstrations of 120,000 and 100,000 people in Hanover in October and March 1979, and a demonstration in Wackersdorf (Bavaria) with 90,000 people in March 1986. Out of the total of 258 demonstrations in the 10 years from 1988–97, 6.2 per cent attracted at least 10,000 people.[19]

The pattern of nationally reported protests is a composite of protests in many areas that may all have their own mobilization dynamics. At least for Berlin, for which we have a comprehensive data set, we can investigate this assumption.

Contrary to findings that emphasize the idiosyncrasies of local protest dynamics (Roth 1994; Hocke 2000) and also the divergent patterns in the evolution of numbers of national and Berlin-based protests (see above), Fig. 4.4(a) and (b) exhibits roughly similar developments both for all environmental protests and for

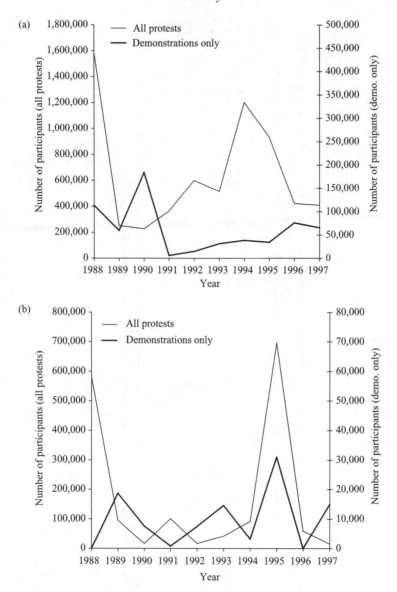

Fig. 4.4. *(a) Participants in larger environmental protests in Germany by year (protests with 500 or more participants). (b) Participants in larger environmental protests in Berlin by year (only protests with 500 or more participants)*

demonstrations only. (Note again the different scales for each line.) With some minor variations, protest participation in Berlin mirrors the national pattern, but in Berlin the low level of environmental mobilization starting in 1989 lasted longer, the peak came one year later, and the decrease in the last 2 years was sharper.

TABLE 4.3. *Issues and the forms of protest in Germany (percentage of events involving each issue that involves a form of action).*

	Conventional (%)	Demonstrative (%)	Confrontational (%)	Attack on property (%)	Violence (%)	N
Nature conservation	33.9	43.5	24.3	1.7	0.9	115
Pollution, urban and industrial	45.4	38.0	20.3	0.7	0.0	271
Energy	25.0	36.3	35.3	11.8	5.6	620
Animal welfare	25.8	51.6	9.7	22.6	3.2	31
Transport	29.5	48.2	17.3	5.0	0.7	139
Alternative production, etc.	47.6	28.7	16.8	12.6	0.0	143
% of all protest events	32.1	37.3	27.3	8.8	3.1	1176
N	378	439	321	103	37	

Note: Percentages do not sum to 100 because for each protest up to 2 issues and 4 forms could be recorded.

ISSUES AND FORMS OF PROTEST

We have already noted that nuclear energy tends to attract more radical protest than all other environmental issues in Germany. Table 4.3 crosstabulates the six issue domains (presented above) with the major types of protest. Among confrontational protests, energy took the lead: 35.3 per cent of the protests in this domain were confrontational. Surprisingly, animal welfare protests did not tend to be confrontational. Considering the category 'minor attack on property', however, it was not nuclear energy but animal welfare that, in proportional terms, took the lead (22.6 per cent), followed by alternative production (mainly protest against genetic engineering) (12.5 per cent), and energy (mostly nuclear energy). It was, however, energy where the highest proportion of protests involved violence (5.6 per cent), with animal welfare next. Violent protest was insignificant or completely absent in the four other issue domains. On the whole, then, protests concerning nuclear energy and animal welfare tended to be more radical than those in all other issue domains, whereas nature conservation and pollution were the most moderate.

Comparing the national results displayed in Table 4.4 with the corresponding figures for environmental protests in Berlin only, major differences are apparent. At the national level, relatively many confrontational protests were concentrated in the domain of energy (35.3 per cent), but not so in Berlin (9.7 per cent). A similar gap can be seen in the minor attacks on property category (11.8 and 3.2 per cent,

TABLE 4.4. *Number of protests in Germany: most active groups by year*

	1988	1989	1990	1991	1992	1993	1994	1995	1996	1997	1988–97
Greenpeace	17	14	23	6	11	9	13	11	8	16	128
B '90/Die Grünen	21	16	15	6	5	6	1	4	8	9	91
BUND	10	16	9	7	12	9	3	5	12	8	91
Robin Wood	12	11	11	6	5	5	1	2	1	5	59
BI Lüchow-Dannenberg	4	11	9	3	0	4	7	4	9	2	53
BBU	4	1	3	2	4	1	1	0	7	2	25
SPD	6	3	2	0	2	2	0	0	3	1	19
Neues Forum	0	1	11	1	0	0	0	0	0	0	13
Bund Naturschutz in Bayern	2	2	0	0	1	1	0	1	3	2	12
Mahnwache Gundremmingen	0	0	1	0	0	2	5	1	2	1	12
BI Schwandorf	2	9	0	0	0	0	0	0	0	0	11
DBV/Naturschutzbund	3	2	0	1	1	1	0	2	1	1	12
Grüne Liga	0	0	3	3	1	0	0	0	3	0	10
DNR	1	1	3	0	3	1	0	0	0	0	9
% of protests involving leading groups	30.9	41.8	43.6	57.8	52.2	57.4	28.3	16.9	33.8	29.2	35.7
Total *N* of events	191	165	140	45	69	54	106	136	133	137	1176

respectively). However, the proportion of violent protest in this domain was higher in Berlin (8.1 per cent) compared to the national level (5.6 per cent). More generally, environmental protests in Berlin tended to be much more confrontational than at the national level (27.3 versus 13.8 per cent), but there were relatively fewer minor attacks on property (3.3 versus 8.8 per cent) and incidents of violence (2.0 versus 3.1 per cent).

ORGANIZATION OF PROTEST

Protest is rarely a spontaneous matter. For the most part, it is planned, prepared, and carried out by groups and organizations which, occasionally, form broad alliances and mobilize for major campaigns (Lofland 1996). Some of these groups are renowned for their spectacular and frequent protest actions while others are no-names and/or very moderate in their activities, probably using protest only as a last resort. Particularly in these latter cases, journalists tend not to report the names of the groups or may provide only vague indications about their identity. Of all the protests considered here, in 657 cases (55.8 per cent) at least one organizational carrier was reported by either mentioning a distinct group name (e.g. BUND) or a more generic label (e.g. Catholic youth groups, trade unions).

Since groups differ considerably in their resources and inclination to stage protest, it is no wonder that a few of them stand out in terms of their reported protest activity. Table 4.4 displays the fourteen groups that were most frequently mentioned as organizing or participating in environmental protest. Taken together, this set of actors was present in about one-third of all protests. The share of these actors did not increase over time—an indication that the big players have not become more important at the expense of the large number of minor protest actors.[20]

Given its preferred strategy and its orientation towards the mass media, it comes as no surprise that Greenpeace ranks first with participation in 128 protest events. The Green Party and the BUND (a major environmental organization with some 240,000 members in the late 1990s) come next, but some groups which are relatively small in terms of membership rank high as protest actors, such as Robin Wood (a split-off from Greenpeace), and the regional citizen initiative (BI Lüchow-Dannenberg) fighting against the nuclear waste disposal and related facilities near Gorleben. Other groups were significantly less often reported as having been involved in protest, among them the Social Democratic Party (SPD), the BBU (a nationwide alliance of environmental groups that was very important in the 1970s and early 1980s), and Neues Forum (an important East German citizen movement created during the breakdown of the Communist regime but that faded away after a few years). The large umbrella group Deutscher Naturschutzring (DNR) which nominally represents more than five million individuals in 108 membership organizations ranked last of this set of groups because its internal heterogeneity does not allow for high-profile protest action. It is worth mentioning that, besides Neues Forum, another East German network, the Grüne

TABLE 4.5. *Most active groups and their forms of protest in Germany by year (number of events)*

	Conventional	Demonstrative	Confrontational	Attack on property	Violence	Other	N
Greenpeace	37	50	53	3	0	9	128
B '90/Die Grünen	38	39	22	2	0	4	91
BUND	55	35	9	0	1	8	91
Robin Wood	16	32	28	0	0	2	59
BI Lüchow-Dannenberg	18	29	17	8	1	2	53
BBU	20	6	0	0	0	3	25
SPD	9	11	0	0	0	0	19
Neues Forum	3	6	5	2	0	1	13
Bund Naturschutz in Bayern	5	6	2	0	0	1	12
Mahnwache Gundremmingen	2	4	6	3	0	0	12
BI Schwandorf	5	6	1	0	0	0	11
DBV/ Naturschutzbund	9	4	0	0	0	0	12
Grüne Liga	2	5	1	0	0	2	9
DNR	8	2	0	0	0	1	9
Total N of events	170	176	120	14	2	23	420

Liga, comprising around 350 local groups, is among the protest leaders in spite of the fact that these groups were created only in 1989 and 1990, respectively. The only major environmental player that is not part of this list of fourteen protest leaders is the World Wide Fund (WWF), known for its moderation and its reluctance to engage in direct conflict.[21]

The extent to which these fourteen groups tended towards either moderate or radical action can be seen in Table 4.5, which, because of the low numbers of cases, provides absolute numbers only. In general, these groups did not engage in violent protests. Some groups, however, participated in protest involving minor attacks on property, though this does not necessarily mean that this was intentional, given the fact that protest sometimes involves very heterogeneous groups and attracts organizationally unaffiliated people whose actions are hard to control. The group that clearly stands out in the category of minor attacks on property is the BI Lüchow-Dannenberg (eight cases), followed by Greenpeace and Mahnwache Gundremmingen, a Bavarian-based anti-nuclear group. In proportional terms, Mahnwache Gundremmingen, Robin Wood, BI Lüchow-Dannenberg, and Neues Forum showed a significant engagement in confrontational action. To a lesser extent, the Green Party too was involved in such activities, but not so the Social Democratic Party. All well-established environmental organizations such as the BUND, BBU, Bund Naturschutz in Bayern, and DNR were overwhelmingly focused on conventional forms of protest. The numbers of cases are too small to make meaningful statements about trends.

For the same set of leading protest actors we can identify the issue domains in which they tended to engage (Table 4.6). By definition, anti-nuclear groups focused exclusively or mainly on energy. But (nuclear) energy was also an important concern for a few other groups such as the Green Party, Greenpeace, and the BBU. Greenpeace's primary protest focus, however, was pollution; the same was true for Robin Wood. With the exception of two Greenpeace actions, animal welfare and hunting was a non-issue for the major protest actors. Otherwise, the BUND, a classic multi-issue environmental organization, as well as the Bund Naturschutz in Bayern and the Grüne Liga, spread relatively evenly across the major domains, while others, as mentioned above, tended to engage in particular issue areas. Interestingly, the Green Party, though rhetorically representing the full range of environmental issues, still exhibited an overriding concern with energy, perhaps as a reflection of the party's roots in the anti-nuclear movement.

LINKS AND NETWORKS

A social movement consists of a broad variety of groups and organizations that not only consider themselves as being part of it but also establish informal and formal links by creating networks, alliances, and firmly organized umbrella groups. This pattern is also reflected in joint protest activity, although journalists hardly provide comprehensive accounts of which groups are actually involved in

TABLE 4.6. *Most active groups and their issues of protest in Germany by year (number of events)*

	Nature conservation	Pollution, urban and industrial	Energy	Animal welfare and hunting	Transport	Alternative production, etc.	Other	N
Greenpeace	13	64	46	2	2	17	6	128
B '90/Die Grünen	7	19	47	0	10	17	4	91
BUND	21	30	20	0	26	20	10	91
Robin Wood	11	28	18	0	9	7	11	59
BI Lüchow-Dannenberg	0	1	53	0	0	1	0	53
BBU	2	7	18	0	0	2	0	25
SPD	1	3	11	0	2	2	1	19
Neues Forum	0	7	6	0	0	0	1	13
Mahnwache Gundremmingen	0	0	12	0	0	1	0	12
Bund Naturschutz in Bayern	2	2	3	0	4	2	0	12
DBV/ Naturschutzbund	6	4	2	0	4	3	0	12
BI Schwandorf	0	0	11	0	0	1	0	11
Grüne Liga	2	2	2	0	3	1	2	9
DNR	2	4	2	0	0	2	0	9
Total N of events	47	133	196	2	44	59	28	420

such cases of joint activity. Nevertheless, we have some information about the extent to which groups tended to collaborate in protest.

While stressing that the number of participating groups is often unreported and, moreover, that the incidence of joint protests may well be underreported, we still find a significant proportion of protests in which more than one group is mentioned. Out of the 197 protests for which the number of participating groups is available, 33 per cent involved more than one group. In some instances the number of groups involved is impressive. In seven protests more than 100 groups participated, including one case with 300 groups. On average, 6.9 groups participated per protest event. The yearly averages fluctuate according to the irregular occurrence of protests in which many groups were present. When comparing the first 5 years with the next 5 years, the average in the second period is slightly below that of the first period (6.7 and 7.0 groups, respectively). Thus, it does not seem that cooperation among groups in protest was increasing over time.

Again, we can focus on the leading protest groups and see to what extent they acted jointly in protest action. A number of groups clearly preferred joint activity (the Green Party, BUND, BBU, Bund Naturschutz in Bayern, DBV/ Naturschutzbund, Grüne Liga), while Neues Forum did so in all its protests (Table 4.7).[22] Other groups, particularly those that focused on a single issue and/or played a dominant role in a distinct region, tended to act alone, as was the case with the BI Lüchow-Dannenberg, Mahnwache Gundremmingen, and BI Schwandorf. All three are regional anti-nuclear groups. Greenpeace and, to a

TABLE 4.7. *Networks of protest among the most active environmental organizations in Germany*

	Acting alone (N)	Acting with others (N)[a]
B '90/Die Grünen	12	70
BUND	28	59
Greenpeace	97	29
Robin Wood	35	24
BBU	5	19
Bürgerinitiative Lüchow-Dannenberg	20	19
SPD	3	15
Neues Forum	0	13
DBV/Naturschutzbund	2	10
Bund Naturschutz in Bayern	1	8
Grüne Liga	2	7
DNR	2	7
BI Schwandorf	6	5
Mahnwache Gundremmingen	10	1

Note:
[a] Sum is not the total of protest events involving this group, because for some events information is missing, whether protest was organized by the group alone or jointly.

lesser extent, Robin Wood are special cases. Greenpeace is known for keeping its trademark distinct and separate and is therefore reluctant to engage in joint protest activity. Moreover, the nature of its activities, which often involve risky and surprising stunts such as climbing chimneys or blocking large ships with rubber dinghies, leads Greenpeace to act alone. This may also be the reason why Robin Wood, though much more cooperative in its approach and non-hierarchical in its structure compared to Greenpeace, still protested alone more often than not.

When investigating who tended to collaborate with whom in protest activity, insofar as this was reported in our source, we find an action network which, in a simplified version, is displayed in Fig. 4.5. To be sure, the actual network is much wider and more complex than displayed in Fig. 4.5. For reasons of simplicity, we have only included the thirteen groups which, according to the available information in the newspaper, each were reported as having been involved on at least three occasions in protest with one or more other groups. This network structure might be considered the core of the larger network.

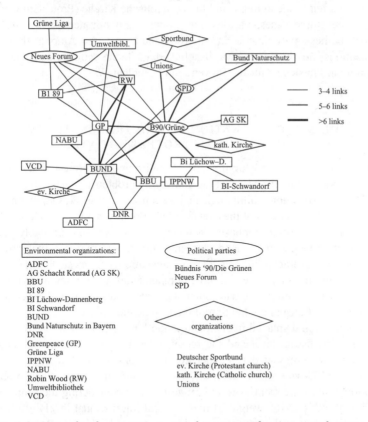

FIG. 4.5. *Networks of organizations named in reports of environmental protests in Germany (1988–97) (Only links reported 3 or more times are included)*

With the exception of NABU and the umbrella organization DNR, all large national organizations (BUND, Greenpeace, Bündnis '90/Die Grünen, BBU) were closely interconnected. Surprisingly, the greens protested most often with at least one other group ($N = 70$). They also had most relations with other groups of the core network ($N = 9$). In addition, Robin Wood, a much smaller national organization but having a strong action component, was part of the network core. Interestingly, two regional groups also belonged to the core. One of them—the BI Lüchow-Dannenberg—was a key actor in the anti-nuclear struggle in the Gorleben area (see above). The second group—the Bund Naturschutz in Bayern—is by far the most powerful state section of the BUND.[23] It existed long before the latter's creation and maintained its distinct profile. We were surprised to see it appear as part of the core four organizations that cannot be said to be environmental organizations: Ärzte für die Verhütung des Atomkriegs (International Physicians for the Prevention of Nuclear War), the Social Democratic Party (SPD) with a particularly strong link to the greens, the Gewerkschaften (trade unions), and the evangelische Kirche (Protestant Church). In the latter three cases, various sub-groups—and not necessarily the main national bodies—participated in environmental protests. Among these four organizations, clearly the SPD was best linked, while the opposite was true for the International Physicians for the Prevention of Nuclear War.

SUB-NATIONAL, NATIONAL, AND TRANSNATIONAL ORIENTATION OF PROTEST ACTIVITY

When we consider the territorial scope of environmental protest in terms of its bases of mobilization, the scope of the underlying problems it raises, and the level of its targets, two countervailing tendencies seem to be at work. On the one hand, the movement's promotion of the slogan 'think globally, act locally' (Rucht 1993) would suggest a strong emphasis on local mobilization, and probably also on local targets. On the other hand, not only are many environmental problems transnational in character but, in addition, transnational actors such as the EU and UN institutions assume more and more competencies in addressing environmental problems and promoting environmental policies. Thus we might expect to find evidence of the transnationalization of environmental protest.

One dimension displayed in Table 4.8 is the level of mobilization. If we combine the local/district level and the regional level, it is clear that sub-national mobilization predominated (53.2 per cent); nationwide mobilization followed (40 per cent); EU-wide mobilization was marginal; and other international mobilization, though more frequent, was still modest. When considering the scope of the underlying problem, the weight of national and international levels was significantly greater. National issues accounted for almost half of protests, but problems relating to other EU countries and to the international dimension beyond the

TABLE 4.8. *Levels of mobilization, scope of problems, and targets in Germany*
(percentages)

	Local/ district	Regional	National	EU	International	N
Level of mobilization	43.9	9.3	40.0	1.7	5.1	665
Scope of underlying problem	28.7	5.3	49.2	8.1	8.8	1140
Level of target	20.2	23.2	50.0	4.0	7.7	742

European Union each accounted for about one protest in twelve. Finally, if we consider the territorial level of the targets of protest, again roughly half were national but targets in foreign countries, both in the European Union and beyond, were, compared to the scope of problems, under-represented. Protests addressing EU institutions were rare. This is in line with other literature which has emphasized environmental groups' recognition of EU-related policies but, at the same time, found relatively little activity directed at EU institutions (Ward and Lowe 1998: 157; Roose 1999).

Looking at these dimensions over time, we cannot identify clear-cut trends. Regarding the level of mobilization, the proportion of EU-wide mobilization was uneven but certainly did not show a trend towards Europeanization. The proportion of other protests with an international mobilization dimension tended to decrease rather than increase in the 10 years under study, as did the number of protests the scope of whose issues was international. Again, the proportion of protests with a scope beyond Germany but within the European Union hardly increased over time. As for the level of targets, no trend was apparent either at the level of the European Union or the wider international dimension beyond the European Union. Instead we find erratic fluctuations which, in the case of target groups related to other EU countries, ranged between zero in 1996 and 10.9 per cent in 1995.

SUMMARY AND INTERPRETATION

While both regular readers of daily newspapers and close observers of the German environmental movement develop their own image of the movement's protest, such a picture is strongly influenced by particular foci of attention and probably by selective memory. Certain events, or aspects of events, are emphasized, while others are neglected. Systematic quantitative content analysis can partly compensate for this selective attention, as it has revealed patterns that run counter to some common assumptions. In this final section we want to highlight three descriptive findings and offer some lines of interpretation.

First, the data show that the environmental movement in Germany cannot be said to be in decline, let alone dead. This is true not only in terms of its protest activity as shown in this chapter but also its organizational infrastructure.[24] One explanation for the overly pessimistic view of the movement's decline could be that the movement of today is no longer perceived as new and exciting as it was in earlier periods. It no longer makes headlines, it is no longer a threat to the established system, its rapid growth is over, and as a result its actual activity and size tend to be underestimated. Looking at the internal discourse of the movement, some observers dramatize the alleged difficulties experienced by the movement in its efforts to raise levels of awareness and activity.

What accounts for this remarkable stability of environmental protest over time? First and foremost, the movement relies on a decentralized and loosely coupled but solid organizational infrastructure comprising a large number of groups and associations. The backbone of the movement does not consist of only one or very few major organizations which, should they be in crisis or disarray, would have strong repercussions for the rest. For example, the BBU, an important national organization in the 1970s and early 1980s, experienced financial problems and internal splits by the mid-1980s and lost much of its previous strength and strategic capacity. However, there were several other organizations to fill the gap, most prominently the BUND, which is probably the single most important player in the environmental movement in Germany. Also, due to its solid infrastructure, the movement remained largely independent from party politics and electoral games that, for example, played a larger role in France (see Chapter 3). Even a poor election result for the Green Party would leave the movement largely unaffected because none of the environmental groups is dependent on the party.

Another important reason for the stability of protest activity is the nature of the political and social context in which the movement operated in the period under study. The political institutions and procedures, including the rules of access to the decision-making process, have not been changed in any significant way in West Germany (for the effect of German unification, see below). Nor were there major environmental policy changes in this period. During the 10 years under study, the same government—a coalition of the CDU and the FDP—was in power. It paid considerable lip service to environmental protection but also, slowly and with some exceptions, strengthened measures and standards for the environment. It also began to consult environmental organizations on a more or less regular basis. However, because there was little or no improvement in the state of the environment, there was no policy outcome that could take the wind out of the movement's sails. Thus, on the whole, there remained enough reasons to continue with protest.

Furthermore, the attitudes of the populace towards environmentalism remained fairly constant in this period (Wissenschaftlicher Beirat 1995: 29; Baukloh and Roose 2002). Environmental protection ranks high among the policy preferences of the German population in spite of problems such as high unemployment rates and the influx of immigrants and asylum seekers that peaked around 1992.

Of course, German unification had repercussions for the environmental movement, though the effects were less dramatic than one might have expected. In aggregate, 'national' environmental protest activity was lowest from 1991 to 1993, the period when the problems resulting from German unification and the large numbers of immigrants were most urgent and tended to overshadow all other domestic political concerns. At the same time, East German environmental groups were just beginning to grow and stabilize but were not ready for powerful protest. After 1993, protest activity increased again in the aggregate, but mainly due to the contribution of West German groups. Given the severity of some environmental problems in a few regions, the East German groups probably have more reasons to protest than their Western counterparts but they remained relatively weak in resources and they lacked experience in the protest business in a totally new institutional context. However, to the extent that the German economy is improving and unemployment rates start to decrease, 'secondary' issues such as environmentalism and women's rights are likely to gain importance, though probably to a greater extent in the East than in the West. We would not be surprised in the near future to witness a stagnation of protest activity in the West but an increase in the East.

A second major finding of this chapter is the absence of remarkable changes of the patterns of environmental protests over time. This complements the picture of relative stability in numbers of protests across the 10-year period. Regarding the distribution of environmental issues, forms, and other variables such as the level of mobilization, we hardly see striking, let alone dramatic, developments in this period. In particular, the data do not support assumptions of a de-radicalization or transnationalization of the movement. A time span of 10 years is probably too short to identify clear-cut trends, but there is a striking discrepancy between the widespread and often strong opinions about allegedly 'obvious' developments and the empirical evidence provided by our data.

The reasons for this stability are essentially those mentioned above to explain the stability in numbers of protests. When it comes to qualitative aspects of protest, additional factors may contribute in accounting for this pattern. First, the relatively large number of groups and protests creates a broad basis of mobilization which, due to its sheer size, is less affected by particular issues or local conflict dynamics. Whereas in, say, Sweden, the aggregate of 'national' protest is strongly influenced by single campaigns or groups which may undergo rapid changes, this is less so in countries such as Britain and Germany where such specifics are more or less absorbed and neutralized in the aggregate picture. Second, notwithstanding national differences, it appears that environmental movements in general, irrespective of their geographical location, tend to exhibit less rapid changes than, for example, peace movements. Whereas the mobilization of peace movements and their choice of tactics may be strongly influenced by a single national policy or even a single decision (such as deploying nuclear missiles, starting an invasion, or entering a war), the aggregate of the environmental movement is a composite of quite different issues and conflicts that each tends to have its own dynamic. Thus, as students of attitude surveys have observed, the result is stability in the aggregate in spite of considerable fluctuations at the level of individual cases.

Consistent with the foregoing is a third significant finding, namely the continuing endurance and vitality of anti-nuclear activism (Kolb 1997; Ehmke 1998). No nuclear reactors have been commissioned since the late 1980s and, though the German and French industries are developing a new reactor prototype, no concrete plans for the construction of new reactors exist. Yet the movement did not fade away as it did in most other countries. During the 10-year period, anti-nuclear protest accounted for slightly more than half of all environmental protest, and actually increased in relative importance in the second half of the period. Our analysis has shown that nuclear protests differed in several respects from other environmental protests. Above all, they tended to be more radical. In addition, they are based on a much more decentralized and informal infrastructure which resembles the SPIN-structure (segmented, polycephalous, integrated networks) described in another context by Gerlach and Hine (1970). Closer inspection of these protests also reveals that the issues of the anti-nuclear struggle have changed. Whereas activism in the 1970s and 1980s was geared to preventing the construction of nuclear facilities (mainly nuclear power stations and a reprocessing plant), the overriding issue in the 1990s was the transport and temporary storage of nuclear waste. On various occasions, this led to massive and partly radical protest, including clashes with police who were mobilized on an unprecedented scale to protect nuclear transports across the country.

How are we to explain this continuity of the nuclear energy issue and, more particularly, the struggle against nuclear transport in Germany? There are several reasons. First, what we observed for the period from 1988 to 1997 is essentially the extension of a previous history of strong opposition against nuclear energy. Between 1975 and 1989, while anti-nuclear energy protests comprised the same proportion of all nationally reported unconventional protests in Germany as in France (12.8 per cent) and was higher than in Switzerland and the Netherlands (7.2 and 5.1 per cent, respectively), the volume of participation, relative to the size of population, was highest in Germany (Kriesi et al. 1995). Moreover, it appears that the largest anti-nuclear demonstrations in the world took place in Germany, attracting up to 120,000 people in one instance. The number of 881,000 people declaring their opposition against the construction of a nuclear reprocessing plant in Wackersdorf (Bavaria) in 1988 is, to our knowledge, not matched by any other anti-nuclear campaign. Furthermore, the German movement demonstrated its strength and viability in the wake of the Chernobyl accident while, for example, its French and Dutch counterparts showed 'virtually no reaction'

(Koopmans and Duyvendak 1995: 248). Hence there is a tradition of strong and relatively continuous anti-nuclear protest in Germany.

As the density and strength of the anti-nuclear network was conducive to keeping the issue on the agenda, so was nuclear policy. Overall, the issue was left in limbo since the mid-1980s. On the one hand, the conservative–liberal coalition in the federal government declared its commitment to nuclear energy, but it did so without daring to strongly promote the construction of new reactors in view of stagnating energy consumption, a majority of the populace skeptical of or hostile to nuclear energy, a strong anti-nuclear movement, and some internal dissent within both parties.[25] On the other hand, the Green Party (since its beginnings) and the Social Democratic Party (since 1986—after Chernobyl) were opting for phasing out nuclear energy, and so were major parts of trade unions since 1986. In addition, the Social Democratic Party was in power in several of the *Länder* where it could delay, if not block, the construction of additional nuclear facilities. The uncertain future of nuclear energy was favourable to anti-nuclear protest because activists felt that, while their cause had become stronger, the final battle was not yet won. This situation contrasts with that in other countries where pronuclear forces had prevailed and finally discouraged the anti-nuclear movement (as in France), where anti-nuclear groups were never particularly strong (Britain and Belgium), or where the anti-nuclear forces had definitely succeeded (Austria, Italy, the Netherlands), or had at least achieved a promise to phase out nuclear energy (Sweden and Switzerland).

Closely related to the stalemate in German nuclear policy was and is the aspect of nuclear reprocessing and waste disposal. Probably more than in any other country, the German anti-nuclear movement considered these two issues as the Achilles' heel of the overall nuclear programme. Consequently, it invested considerable energy in preventing the construction of a reprocessing plant and permanent waste depositories. The results were mixed. After many struggles, plans for a reprocessing plant were eventually abandoned in 1989 while, in consequence of this, contracts with British and French enterprises for the reprocessing of nuclear fuel were expanded. Plans for a permanent waste depository in Gorleben were considerably delayed and their future is still unclear. Partly because of this, however, the pressure to create temporary nuclear waste depositories intensified, because working facilities for nuclear waste had become a legal precondition for the continued operation of existing reactors. In spite of much resistance, two temporary waste depositories—in Gorleben and Ahaus—were built. In consequence, the anti-nuclear movement, which was unable to prevent their construction, tried to block the transport to the depositories of nuclear material from both the British and French reprocessing plants and the domestic reactors.

The campaign against nuclear transports became the overriding concern from 1995 to 1997 and attracted tens of thousands of protesters. Only with the support of a massive police contingent were the transports eventually carried out. The pushing through of these transports was not only met with much criticism far beyond the anti-nuclear movement but eventually resulted in a public outcry in 1998. This happened when information leaked that the radioactive emissions resulting from the transport were far beyond the legal threshold, a fact that the government had tried to keep secret. Overall, the anti-nuclear movement in Germany had good reasons to remain attentive and active.

Even today, with the agreement between the red–green government and the industry to gradually phase out nuclear energy during the next three decades, it is not clear whether these plans will pacify the movement. In March 2001, the transport of nuclear waste again sparked a wave of protest that was widely covered in the mass media. Remarkably, this time leading members of the Green Party (Bündnis '90/Die Grünen), the junior partner since 1998 in the coalition government with the Social Democrats, argued for the need of the transport as a consequence of both international treaties and the national agreement with the industry in the summer of 2000. Nevertheless, resistance reached a similar scale as in 1997 with some 15,000 protesters, many of them practising direct action, and an even larger police contingent. In the medium term, however, anti-nuclear mobilization will become more difficult unless it is spurred by a precipitating incident such as a major nuclear scandal or a terrible accident. The agreement between the 'red–green' government and the industry to phase out nuclear power within 30 years is certainly much less than the core of the movement has wanted. However, in the eyes of many sympathizers in the movement's wider environment, the need to fight nuclear power fiercely is no longer as evident as it was in the past.

NOTES

1. Recent research suggests that the density of environmental group membership is greater in the Netherlands and Britain (Rootes and Miller 2000; Vonkemann 2000).
2. Of course, the modern environmental movement had predecessors. For a brief history of groups and environmental politics in Germany, see Wey (1982).
3. On the state level, the first environmental department was created in Bavaria in 1971. Three years later, the National Environmental Protection Agency was established. However, a Federal State Department on Environmental Protection did not come into existence until 1986.
4. For information on the established and formal environmental organizations, see Leonhard (1986), Cornelsen (1991), Blühdorn (1995), Hengsbach et al. (1996), and Lahusen (1998).
5. The same threefold typology is also applicable to the environmental movement in Italy (Diani 1995).
6. From its beginnings, there were also some minor nationalist, if not right-extremist, groups engaged in or on the fringe of the German environmental movement (see Jahn and Wehling 1991).

7. These are, in the order of the size of their circulation, the *Süddeutsche Zeitung, Frankfurter Allgemeine Zeitung, Die Welt*, and *Frankfurter Rundschau*.

8. Reiner Metzger of the *taz*, interviewed by Jochen Roose, 24 February 1999.

9. An additional forty-four events in the overall data set were explicitly anti-environmental protests which will not be considered in the following analyses.

10. The peak of protests based on summary reports in 1990 is mainly due to a major campaign of cyclists to reduce car traffic in East and West Germany. Under the slogan 'Mobile Without Car', more than 25,000 people in East and West Germany went on cycling tours, walking tours, or blocked streets to demand more support for environmentally friendly transport and a reduction in car traffic. This single initiative accounted for 272 protests in different parts of the country but was reported only in an overview article.

11. Because some events taking place in Berlin are reported in both the local and national sections of the newspaper, the protests drawn from the Berlin section exceeds the remaining 26.7% (corresponding to 428 events). When we refer in the following to Berlin protests, we mean this population of events. Eighteen Berlin protests reported only in the national section are excluded. Among these are five events including violence.

12. We assume that decreasing media attention is mainly reflected in the length of the articles rather than the fact of reporting. A systematic quantitative content analysis can compensate for this bias. Our view is supported by the *taz* journalist Reiner Metzger (see note 8).

13. These data are part of a large collection of protest events from the Prodat-project (Rucht and Ohlemacher 1992; Rucht and Neidhardt 1999). Information is derived from two nationwide quality newspapers (*Süddeutsche Zeitung* (SZ) and *Frankfurter Rundschau* (FR)) spanning the period from 1950 to 1994, and including significantly more variables than the TEA-project. Prodat encompasses all kinds of protests of which environmental protests form only a small proportion. Unlike the German TEA-project, a sampling procedure has been applied, incorporating all Monday issues and the remaining issues (Tuesday through Saturday) of each fourth week. Only the nationwide sections are included in the Prodat study.

It is important to note that the results of the two data sets cannot be compared directly inasmuch as they rely on different sources and a different coverage (sample versus full coverage). Even if we apply the Prodat sample to the TEA-data and exclude the protests derived from the local section of the *taz*, a comparison of the overlapping years (1988 and 1993–4) exhibits, for some variables, significantly different results. These differences are not due to flaws of one or other data set, but result from the fact that the overlap between protests reported by the *taz* on the one hand, and the SZ and FR on the other, is not as great as one might expect. A more detailed analysis of all protests occurring in 1993 shows that out of the 348 protest events reported by the *taz*, only 74 events were also reported by both the SZ and the FR, another 38 events only by the SZ, and another 58 events only by the FR. In other words, 51% of the events reported by the *taz* remained unreported by the SZ and the FR (Eilders 2001).

14. Hence the statement that 'environmental groups and associations in eastern Germany appear to generate hardly any protest' (Rink 2000) underestimates the actual level of protest activity.

15. We labelled this kind of protest as 'violent' irrespective of its result; that is, whether somebody was actually hurt due to the protest. As we concentrate on protest activity, we need to categorize protests according to action rather than to the action's result.

16. Additional information also suggests that national environmental protest did not de-radicalize over time. Taking injunctions by police as an indicator of radical protest, we calculated that injunctions were involved in 1.4% of all protests in the first 5 years and 1.6% in the second 5 years. When considering incidents in which the police used force, the proportion of such cases rose from 0.6% to 0.8%. The absolute numbers are low and police tactics do not necessarily co-vary with protest forms. However, these findings tend to support our interpretation of the results presented above.

17. Out of the total of all 1177 protests derived from the nationwide newspaper section, in 47.3% no numbers of participants were provided.

18. Events with large numbers of participants (for instance collection of signatures) lasting more than one year are split up with one event in every year involved. Thus, half of the participants in the event mentioned above are coded for 1993, when the collection of signatures started, and the other half is attributed to a second event in 1994.

19. The largest confrontational action was a street blockade by 15,000 people to protest against car traffic in 1994. Violent action never included more than 100 participants.

20. For a detailed discussion of this question in relation to organizational resources see Rucht and Roose (2001*a*).

21. By and large this pattern is mirrored by the frequency of mentioning distinct organizations (not only in relation to protest) in the *taz*. Greenpeace led by far with hits in 2272 reports, the BUND followed with less than 1000, Robin Wood with 242, and the other groups ranked according to the order in Table 4.4. However, the importance of the NABU and the WWF can be seen as they were mentioned in 248 and 339 articles, respectively.

22. We produced an analogous table for the groups acting in Berlin (not displayed here). When considering the frequency of protest actions, the BUND was the leader (thirty-six events). Next came Greenpeace (thirty-one), the Greens (twenty-seven), Robin Wood (twenty-five), and a local group (BI Westtangente) that wanted to reduce individual transport (fourteen). Among the groups that tended to join with others in protest, the greens led (seventeen events), followed by the BUND (twelve), the BI Westtangente (eight), the BUND youth organization, and the ADFC (each seven).

23. In the late 1990s more than half of the BUND's members belonged to its Bavarian (Bayern) section.

24. Other data not presented here show that the large national organizations continue to grow, though not at the relatively high rates seen in earlier periods. The medium-sized organizations had more mixed fortunes in terms of membership growth and other resources (Rucht and Roose 2001*a*). As for the plethora of autonomous groups active at the local and regional levels, no recent data are available with the exception of those in Berlin. Scattered information suggests that their number and size are fairly stable (Rucht, Blattert, and Rink 1997). For a detailed analysis of environmental groups and their activities in Berlin, see Rucht and Roose (2001*b*).

25. For example, within the Christian Democratic Party there is an informal group named 'Christdemokraten gegen Kernenergie' (Christian Democrats against Nuclear Power).

5

Greece

Maria Kousis

In the last three decades, Greece has experienced waves of environmental activism initiated by a wide variety of formal and informal groups. Whereas in the 1970s these were mainly products of local environmental groups (Kousis 1999), during the 1980s they were also supported by more than 100 new environmental organizations in various parts of the country, focusing on air, water, and soil pollution as well as quality of life concerns (Kousis and Dimopoulou 2000). Landmarks of the last two decades include the first Pan Hellenic meeting of environmental group representatives in Vayia Aiginis, as well as the formation of political ecology groups or networks such as Oikologiki Kinisi Thessalonikis, Enallaktiki Kinisi Oikologon, and the Pan-Hellenic environmental non-governmental organization (NGO) Conferences, leading in October 1995 to the creation of the Network of Environmental Organizations. During the 1990s, although informal environmental groups remained actively engaged in protest (Kousis 1999), 200 environmental organizations (Tsakiris and Sakellaropoulos 1998) exerted a notable influence on Greek environmental activism.

Existing research has focused on the short-lived Green Party (Karamichas 2001), the political milieu in which environmental organizations surfaced and survived (Botetzagias 2001), and local environmental protest cases between 1974 and 1994 (Kousis 1999). Yet the entire spectrum of environmental protest in Greece has not so far been studied systematically. This chapter aims to address the changes in the character and evolution of the Greek environmental movement by means of the examination of reported environmental protests in Greece during

This study would not have been possible without the dedication and outstanding diligence of Katerina Lenaki (who, as well being the principal coder, also located and coded major environmental issues in *Nea Oikologia* after systematically reading every issue of the monthly periodical for 1988–97); Dora Matta (coder); Vayia Papanikolaou (who read, located, and identified relevant articles); Evangelia Dimopoulou; Katerina Vlasaki (who traced main events covered in annual reviews by *Kathimerini* and *Eleftherotypia*, 1988–97); Katerina Krassanaki (who prepared summaries of annual reviews); and Sandy Miller, who prepared the tables and graphs. The collaboration of staff of *Eleftherotypia*—Sifis Polimilis, Filis Kaitatzis, and Panagiotis Georgoudis—is highly appreciated. Comments by Charles Tilly, Chris Rootes, and Yannis Karamichas are gratefully acknowledged.

the years 1988–97. In doing so it will delineate the variety of actors involved and their repertoires of contention in the context of the socio-political and economic transformations during the decade.

Factors affecting the incidence of environmental protests include the structure of political opportunities and constraints, the forms of organization (informal as well as formal) available to insurgents (McAdam, McCarthy, and Zald 1996),[1] as well as the structure of economic opportunities and constraints (Kousis 1997*a*, 2002; Eder and Kousis 2001).

Changes in the structure of political opportunities impact directly on the emergence and rise of the environmental movement (van der Heijden, Koopmans, and Giugni 1992; Kriesi et al. 1995). Movement mobilization is closely linked to conventional politics in parliamentary and extra-parliamentary national arena, and thus the political opportunity structure is seen as consisting of national cleavage structures, prevailing strategies, and alliance structures. In southern European countries where democracies were consolidated in the 1980s, with socialist governments gaining power, political affiliations with governing parties were an especially important factor (Jiménez 1999*a*; Kousis 1999; Gil Nave 2000; Kousis et al. 2001). Election years, periods of political fluidity, have also influenced the peaks of reported environmental protest waves (Kousis 1999).

Second, the way environmental activists' social space is organized is also crucial for the development of the movement (Gould, Weinberg, and Schnaiberg 1993). Tilly (1994) classifies movements into three types: the professional, the *ad hoc* community-based, and the communitarian. Although it includes professional organizations, the Greek environmental movement is, like those in the other southern European countries that emerged from dictatorial regimes in the early 1970s, strongly marked by the presence of community-based groups (Kousis 1999). Community-based environmental activism, although non-violent, is more radical in its action repertoire and more attentive to local issues. By contrast, the weak organizational base and limited resources of most environmental groups in southern Europe (Ribeiro and Rodriguez 1997) has resulted in Greece in their employment of mostly routine actions such as press conference or petitions.

Leading environmental movement organizations (EMOs) are concerned with the accumulation and administration of funds, the promotion of environmental education and the raising of public awareness about environmental issues, the financing of nature preservation programmes, cooperation with state and non-state organizations, and the publication of material related to their aims. All these are activities characteristic of institutionalized environmentalism (Jamison 1996; Kousis and Dimopoulou 2000). Collaboration between community-based groups and EMOs is rare (Gould, Schnaiberg, and Weinberg 1996; Kousis 1999; Szasz 1994).

The effect of the economic opportunity structure (Kousis 1998; Eder and Kousis 2001) has rarely been considered in the literature on new social movements (Gould, Weinberg, and Schnaiberg 1993; Broadbent 1998). It has been argued that less intensive and later industrialization and urbanization, and greater demand for economic development, did not provide the conditions necessary for the establishment of a strong environmental movement in Greece (Demertzis 1995; Fidelis-Nogueira 1996). In the 1990s, the move towards privatization (Lavdas 1996) shifted mobilization potential from environmental and other new social movement issues to campaigns against privatization. Economic opportunities and constraints may hinder or assist the formation of mobilizations, especially for local groups concerned with local problems. For example, a movement is much less likely to emerge when potential mobilizers depend on the principal polluter (industry or agriculture) for their economic survival. Alternatively, communities dependent on tourism, which rely on a 'clean' environment to sell their product, may be more likely to sustain environmental activism (Kousis 2000).[2]

METHOD

The data for this analysis were derived from *Eleftherotypia*, a major national newspaper with a Sunday edition since the late 1980s. During the 1990s, its circulation was usually second highest in the country, and the mean circulation of its Sunday edition (172,821 in 1993) made it the second ranking national Sunday newspaper (Armenakis et al. 1996). *Eleftherotypia* is a multi-thematic and domestically oriented paper whose first page follows the logic of television news programmes, with time and space being a significant constraint upon news reporting (Acheimastos and Komninou 1998). By contrast with other dailies, *Eleftherotypia* consistently concentrates on domestic political and social issues. It is politically unaffiliated and carries a wide range of political views from a liberal perspective. For the past three decades,[3] it has covered environmental issues and activism more closely than any other national newspaper in Greece (Kousis 1999).

Every issue of the newspaper for the years 1988–97 was read and all articles containing reports of environmental protest were located and photocopied. A 50 per cent sample of these articles was derived and used for the analysis, covering alternate days' newspapers: Monday, Wednesday, and Friday of the first week and Sunday, Tuesday, Thursday, and Saturday of the second week.

The representation of environmental protest was inevitably influenced by changes in the newspaper's editorial policy. Sections labelled 'environment' or 'everyday life' (which carried articles on environmental protest) appeared for 2 or 3 years in the late 1980s or early 1990s but disappeared thereafter. News selection was not determined by rigid editorial policy,[4] but was usually decided on the basis of what issues appeared most important at the time. During the decade, there was a rapid proliferation of mass media and, in an attempt to present different news stories, the newspaper took into consideration what was conventionally reported elsewhere—such as protest events.[5] Simultaneously, the kinds of issues reported appeared to change. More attention was given to economic and political issues and political scandals. Although there were more articles concerning the environment, these were more often matters of information than reports of protest. All these changes appear to have influenced the form of reporting of environmental protest. Especially from the early 1990s, mentions of environmental activism became very brief and gave only limited information.[6]

<h2 style="text-align:center">THE INCIDENCE OF PROTEST</h2>

Figure 5.1 illustrates changes in the incidence of environmental protest events from 1988 to 1997. A clear and steady decrease in the number of contentious events is apparent.

Although *Eleftherotypia* covered environmental issues more steadily than any other Greek newspaper over the last three decades, changes in its structure affected its coverage of environmental issues.[7] Since 1990, parts of the newspaper that previously reported environmental protest, such as a one-page section with small reports covering the entire country except Athens, were discontinued. In part, these changes reflected the changing political climate as the paper focused on political scandals (such as the Koskota scandal between 1989 and 1991), the departure of PASOK in 1989, Prime Minister Papandreou's illness, and the New Democracy government from 1990 to 1993. They also reflected the newspaper's increasing coverage of economic issues, especially given the trends towards privatization, as well as new technologies.[8]

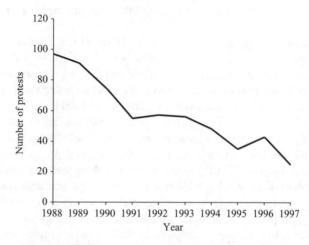

FIG. 5.1. *Environmental protest events in Greece by year*

Changes also appeared in its style of presentation of environmental issues. These reflected a general decline in quantitative, but an increase in qualitative, environmental coverage in the Greek press during the 1990s.[9] The change in the types of articles on environmental issues may in part be a product of the intense competition between all mass media which began in the late 1980s, when non-governmental radio and television increased dramatically (Close 1999). Always concerned with novelty, *Eleftherotypia* appears to have avoided covering routine environmental protests as it did in the past. Instead, aiming to attract more readers, it seems to have preferred qualitative, narrative, and informational coverage that competitors were unlikely to provide. This was especially so in the 1990s, when the newly established large environmental organizations became a major source of environmental news, offering *Eleftherotypia* stories that for the most part were not focused on environmental protest.[10]

Three noticeable peaks punctuate the declining trend evident in Fig. 5.1: 1989, 1993, and 1996, all of which were national election years. Previous research (Kousis 1999) has shown that environmental protesters in Greece, the majority of whom are members of local groups and not of EMOs, are more likely to choose periods prior to national elections to apply pressure on the state. These are times when political candidates tend to succumb to public demands, and are more likely to make promises to which they will be held by their voters. Since pre-election protests did not introduce major changes in the overall pattern of declining reported environmental activism, their effect can only be considered to be secondary.

Public opinion research shows that faith in political parties, whether in government or not, has decreased greatly since the late 1980s (Close 1999). The credibility and legitimacy of the political system were seriously undermined by political scandals, the failure of PASOK to adhere to its programme, and the economic condition of the country (Alexandropoulos and Sertedakis 2000; Kousis, Lenaki, and Vlasaki 2000), and local government appeared to be gaining more independence and power than it had enjoyed in the 1970s and 1980s. In 1989, environmental groups collaborated to create the Federation of Ecological and Alternative Organizations (FEA), which won a single seat in parliament (1989–93), but quickly succumbed to internal divisions exacerbated by external events, notably the parliamentary balance of power and fallout from the war in Yugoslavia (Karamichas 2001).

The political colour of the government does not appear to have had a uniform effect on environmental protest: high in 1988–9 under PASOK, reported numbers of protests decreased steadily under the New Democracy (conservative) government, but fell to the lowest levels of the entire period under the next PASOK government in 1996 and 1997.

Explanations of this pattern might be found in the major changes of the political–economic context in Greece and other southern European countries during the 1990s (Eder and Kousis 2001). Europeanization and economic liberalization pressured the state towards privatization and restricted the subsidization of national industry, an instrument hitherto widely employed in southern Europe (Lavdas 1996). During the 1990s, as environmental and other new social movement protest decreased, waves of anti-privatization protests took place, supported by workers whose jobs were threatened (Kousis, Lenaki, and Vlasaki 2000) and, in 1995–6, farmers in Thessalia mobilized massively against income-reducing measures of the Common Agricultural Policy. In the newspaper itself, finance sections as well as coverage of privatization increased.

Subsequently, increasing economic constraints under neo-liberalism appear to have depressed environmental and other new social movement activism.[11] According to a 1992 poll, environmental concern and awareness were growing faster in Greece than in most other EU countries,[12] but, by the later 1990s, public interest in environmental issues dropped to last place while economic concerns gained primacy.[13]

Another factor probably responsible for the decrease in environmental protest was the increasing institutionalization of environmental activism (Rootes 1999*b*). In the 1990s, the proportion that environmental groups and organizations (formal and informal) comprised of all groups participating in protest changed significantly and steadily from 39 per cent in 1988–90, to 55 per cent in 1991–4, to 70 per cent in 1995–7 (Kousis and Lenaki 1999). Although from the late 1980s to 1996 there was a dramatic increase in the establishment of formal groups, their environmental activism has tended to focus on educational and informational activities, and much less on contentious activism (Kousis and Dimopoulou 2000). In the major Greek environmental NGO database, the more contentious category, 'political ecology', vanished along with the Federation of Ecologists-Alternatives in 1996 (Botetzagias 2001).

SPATIAL DISTRIBUTION

The spatial distribution of reported environmental protests is influenced by the fact that *Eleftherotypia* is an Athens-based newspaper, as well as by the concentration of environmental problems and increased environmental awareness in the country's largest urban centre (Close 1999; Kazakos 1999).

Athens-related events were three times more frequently reported than regional ones. For a short time, the paper provided systematic national coverage of environmental protests outside Athens in a one-page section. Usually, local journalists are connected to the office of the regional correspondent, who acts as an intermediary between them and the editor. After a first filtering and selection of articles by the regional office, the editor decides whether they will be included or not. The editor also determines the extent to which a topic will be covered. It may happen, however, that a local issue gains front-page coverage, which means that it is in the top five news stories of the day.[14] When a local environmental problem is very important, it is usually the Athens-based environmental correspondent who is asked to do the more detailed coverage. This is done in cooperation with the head of the regional correspondents' office. As a result, the decline in mobilizations in Greece reflects the decline of protests in Athens, since the centre greatly appears to influence the periphery.[15]

Recent work using national newspaper reports on the regional distribution of local environmental protest cases in Greece, Spain, and Portugal for the period 1974–94 demonstrates the over-representation of urban environmental protest: more than half occurred in urban areas, more than one-third in rural areas, and less than one-tenth in both (Kousis 1999). The gap between the incidence of rural and urban protest decreased from the late 1980s to the early 1990s (Kousis, Aguilar, and Fidelis-Nogueira 1996). Nevertheless, in Greece more than one-third (37.7 per cent) of environmental protests took place in the Athens metropolitan area.

The pattern shown in Table 5.1 is thus not unexpected. The Athens metropolitan area, which contains about one-third of the Greek population, produced almost half (44.9 per cent) the reported protests in Greece and was the second most over-represented region. Although almost half (44 per cent) of all local protests were based in Athens, two-thirds (69 per cent) of all nationally and one-third (36 per cent) of all internationally mobilized protests occurred there. This striking over-representation in national-level mobilizations reflects the concentration of more resourceful actors, especially the large national EMOs and networks, in an already politically centralized capital.

TABLE 5.1. *The spatial distribution of environmental protests in Greece (1988–97) compared with population*

	Percentage of protest events	Percentage of population[a]	Index of representation[b]
Sterea Ellada and Evia	60.6	42.2	1.44
Athens area	(44.9)	(30.0)	(1.50)
Without Athens	(15.7)	(12.3)	(1.28)
Peloponnisos	5.4	10.6	0.51
Ionian islands	3.1	1.9	1.65
Eperus	4	3.3	1.20
Thessalia	2.8	7.2	0.39
Macedonia	13.6	21.8	0.63
Thessaloniki area	(4.3)	(7.3)	(0.59)
Without Thessaloniki	(9.3)	(14.5)	(0.64)
Thrace	0.3	3.3	0.10
Aegean islands	5.9	4.5	1.32
Crete	4.3	5.3	0.82
Total *N*	579	10,259,900	

[a] Population figures from 1991 Census, *National Statistical Service of Greece.*
[b] 'Index of representation' is a figure obtained by dividing the number of protests by the number of protests expected from the ratio of the total number of events to total population; values above 1 indicate over-representation of an area in the data set, and values below 1 an under-representation.

The Ionian islands were the most over-represented region, mainly due to the mobilizations of the late 1980s concerning the disposal of treated waste into the Kalamas river—which protesters argued would pollute and endanger the local ecosystem of Kerkyra (Corfu)—and to those for the protection of the logger-head turtle, *Caretta-caretta*, in Zakynthos. The Aegean islands were also over-represented. There, protests were more scattered, in terms of environmental issues as well as communities. Protests included those against seed/oil factories in Paros and Rodos, against construction activities in Amorgos, Lindos, Ialissos, Gavrio, Tinos, and Samos, against quarry operations in Siros and Koskino, against waste in Hios, against pollution from the geothermal plant in Milos, and against the expansion of oil tanks in Mitilini. Crete was also well represented.

This pattern suggests an important effect of economic opportunity on reported environmental protest. In these areas highly economically dependent on tourism, protests appear to have stemmed from concern to safeguard economic as well as environmental sustainability. Similar reactions are not as likely in areas dom-inated by agricultural or industrial activities since their negative environmental impacts are not immediately associated with negative economic consequences, as they are in the case of tourism.

The four most under-represented regions were Thrace, Thessalia, Peloponissos, and Macedonia. In less-developed Thrace, only two resident-organized protests occurred, one against bauxite mining, the other against industrial building in the forest. In agriculturally developed Thessalia, the sixteen protests were mostly led by residents, concerned with waste in Volos, construction activities in Trikala, water extraction in Larisa, Volos, and Pouri, industrial activities in Volos, Trikala, and Agria, fish farming in Trikeri, hunting in Trikala, intensive fishing in Alonissos, as well as river diversion in Trikala and Mesohora. In Peloponissos, part of which is industrialized, most of the thirty-one protests were led by residents' groups, while Greenpeace led in two against oil refineries. Protest events led by local groups were concerned with a variety of problems such as construction activities, waste issues, mountain protection, and water extraction.

The under-representation of economically diverse Macedonia, the second most populated region in Greece, reflects the Athenian focus of the paper. Unlike the other regions beyond Greater Athens, many of the eighty-one protests in Macedonia involved local environmental groups protesting about specific com-munities and problems, such as water extraction in Aravissos, energy production related to pollution in Kozani and Ptolemaida, various construction activities and pollution in Thessaloniki, gold mining in Stavros and Olympiada, landfill in Tagarades, as well as road construction and forest destruction in Kavala.

In general, although local groups led most protests in the under-represented regions, they appeared to avoid some of the major environmental problems in their areas, such as those related to intensive agricultural practices in Thessaly, or to chemical agriculture and industrial activities in Peloponissos and Macedonia. With reduced opportunities to connect to resourceful groups and networks, environmental activism in these regions may also have been hindered by economic constraints.

THE ISSUES OF PROTEST

The great majority of environmental protests raised nature conservation, pollution, urban, and industrial issues; alternative production, transport, energy, and animal welfare were raised less often (see Table 5.2).[16] If we examine smaller subdivisions of the claims, nature conservation issues were followed by pollution and health, construction (housing and industrial), alternative production, transport and waste, energy, and animal welfare and hunting, in that order. Because Greece does not have nuclear installations, anti-nuclear actions were almost non-existent. A rare exception was the protest against nuclear weapons and military bases in Athens in 1988.

Examination of changes in environmental claims over the 1988–97 period reveals a variety of patterns. A majority (63 per cent) of nature protection claims referred to countryside and landscape protection, followed by other conservation issues and resource extraction. While the first were strongly present throughout the decade, peaking in 1989 and 1994, other conservation as well as resource extraction claims tended to be more prevalent in the 1990s. Nature conservation claims were favoured by both local protesters and EMOs and were given preferential coverage by *Nea Oikologia*, the oldest environmental periodical in Greece.[17]

Pollution, urban, and industrial claims were prominent throughout the decade, but closer examination shows different patterns among component issues. 'Pollution' (mainly of ocean, lakes, rivers, and air), which includes health claims, was more often raised in the first half of the decade, but then decreased. This was especially true of health claims. Raised in a quarter of protests about pollution, claims concerning health were much more prevalent in the late 1980s, when community-based protests were more prominent. This pattern reflects the institutionalization of environmental protest in Greece. Post-materialist or non-instrumental activism tends to be linked to less contentious and more institutionalized concerns rather than those of local communities.

The second largest category, both in *Eleftherotypia* and in *Nea Oikologia*, was 'housing, industrial, military', mainly consisting of claims against construction (houses and industrial), with anti-military environmental claims accounting for only about one-tenth of the category. The latter were raised only in the first 4 years, chiefly about US military bases in Greece. Anti-construction protests were persistent, reflecting especially the ongoing struggle of urban communities against inadequate regional planning. This confirms the trend in environmental protest cases at the community level in Greece, Spain, and Portugal during 1974–94 (Kousis, Aguilar, and Fidelis-Nogueira 1996).

Protests concerning waste increased. Most concerned domestic waste, but some referred to non-nuclear hazardous waste, and were usually raised by

TABLE 5.2. *Issues raised in environmental protests in Greece by year (percentage of events in which issue is raised by year)*

	1988	1989	1990	1991	1992	1993	1994	1995	1996	1997	Total N
Nature conservation	22.7	65.9	45.3	50.9	33.3	41.1	52.1	34.3	27.9	44.0	246
Pollution, urban and industrial	79.4	49.5	73.3	76.4	70.2	58.9	64.6	54.3	62.8	72.0	387
Pollution	53.6	24.2	26.7	30.9	31.6	23.2	18.8	17.1	25.6	16.0	172
Waste (non-nuclear)	6.2	2.2	16.0	7.3	14.0	12.5	8.3	5.7	30.2	28.0	65
Housing, industrial, and military	19.6	23.1	30.7	38.2	24.6	23.2	37.5	31.4	7.0	28.0	150
Energy	8.2	2.2	8.0	7.3	3.5	8.9	12.5	11.4	9.3	4.0	42
Animal welfare and hunting	2.1	6.6	0.0	1.8	1.8	5.4	14.6	5.7	0.0	4.0	23
Transport	9.3	7.7	10.7	10.9	24.6	8.9	6.3	25.7	4.7	8.0	65
Roads	2.1	4.4	5.3	5.5	12.3	5.4	4.2	2.9	0.0	4.0	27
Alternative production, etc.	21.6	18.7	8.0	12.7	14.0	19.6	4.2	11.4	11.6	8.0	83
Total N of events	97	91	75	55	57	56	48	35	43	25	

Note: Broad categories of issue in italic; subcategories in roman. Percentages do not sum to 100 as up to 2 issues could be recorded per event.

residents' groups. According to a 1990 FEA report, the majority of the 4840 garbage dumps in Greece were unregulated. Progress on this issue was slow, and as late as 1993 Greece was the only country in Europe where urban waste was disposed of untreated in landfills, while in 1995 most hazardous waste ended up in landfills or the sea (Close 1999: 326).

More than a quarter of the protests about 'alternative production' concerned environmentally friendly tourism and recreation while about half referred to environmentally friendly industrial production. Only rarely did protests concern sustainable forestry and natural food. Such claims were more likely to be made by well-resourced international and northern European EMOs, whereas the few, mostly new, Greek EMOs deployed their limited resources elsewhere.

Anti-road protests accounted for 42 per cent of 'transport' protests, and anti-traffic issues for 32 per cent. With peaks in 1992, both were steadily but not strongly present throughout the decade. 'Energy' issues showed no trend over time and were almost exclusively non-nuclear,[18] 40 per cent of them concerning oil. Of the relatively few protests about 'animal welfare and hunting', 60 per cent concerned hunting. Again there was no trend.

If we look at the four leading kinds of issues (see Fig. 5.2), protests about pollution, urban, and industrial issues, as well as nature conservation, declined. Protests about transport and energy issues were broadly stable. Such patterns may best be explained by the institutionalization of environmental activism, which had the effect of toning down the more local concerns voiced in the earlier period.

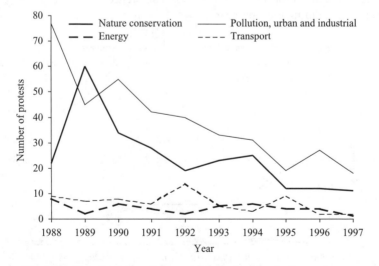

FIG. 5.2. *Four leading environmental issue domains in Greece by year*

THE FORMS OF PROTEST

In general, the forms of protest remained unchanged during the decade. The relative incidence of the less intense forms of action increased modestly, while there were minor decreases in the more intense forms.

Innovations in environmental activism are difficult to trace, but twenty-three apparently 'innovative' protests were identified. Evenly spread throughout the decade and focused on unusual events, most of which were non-violent and symbolic, they included the more spectacular 'hangings' from a waterfall, a bridge, and the energy ministry building, as well as the chaining of activists to a ship carrying toxic material, a pier, and a power plant chimney, abstention from voting, symbolic construction of an illegal building, walking on foot from northern Greece to Athens, carrying a dead bear into the office of the minister of agriculture, the symbolic reconstruction of how a forest is burned and turned into building plots, and offering the prefect (*nomarhi*) small bags containing industrial carbon dust collected from people's homes.

Figure 5.3 displays the incidence of five major types of environmental protest activity during the decade. Conventional protests predominated, followed by confrontational and demonstrative actions. Confrontational protests outnumbered demonstrations, but minor attacks on property (other than theft/burglary) and violence (severe attack on property/arson/bombing) were rare if persistent.

Less than one-third of all conventional protest consisted of signatures, petitions, resolutions, and public letters, but their reported use increased during the second half of the decade. Procedural complaint, litigation, and indoor protest assembly each accounted for about a fifth of conventional protest but none showed any trend. Protests involving press conferences, by contrast, were less often reported during the later years.

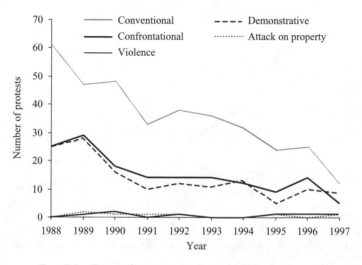

FIG. 5.3. *Forms of environmental protest in Greece by year*

Confrontational protest was dominated by blockades, disruption of events, and occupation, in that order. While the first two showed no trend, occupations declined in the later years. Public protest assemblies accounted for half of demonstrative protests and it was they that were most steadily persistent throughout these years. Even though demonstration marches tended to decline, they still accounted for a quarter of all demonstrative protests. By contrast, non-verbal protests increased from 1993 to 1997.

Although in general there were no great changes in the forms of protest during the decade, the relative 'softening' of actions, in the form of increases in signatures/petitions and in non-verbal protest as well as decreases in demonstrations and occupations, are all consistent with the institutionalization of environmental activism.

Figure 5.4 shows the evolution of the number of participants in larger protests. As expected, although the late 1980s witnessed a larger number of protests (see Fig. 5.1), they had fewer participants than the larger protest campaigns mainly coordinated by EMOs. Thus, it was during 1990–3 that the three largest protests took place, all three involving petitions with thousands of signatures.

In 1990, the environmental organizations 'Friends of the Greek Bear' and 'Nature and Ecology' collected 70,000 signatures protesting the destruction of Valia Kalda by the Public Power Corporation (PPC). In 1991, residents of Drama in northern Greece collected 33,000 signatures against the environmental degradation caused by lignite mining. In 1993, a petition against the diversion of the Akheloos

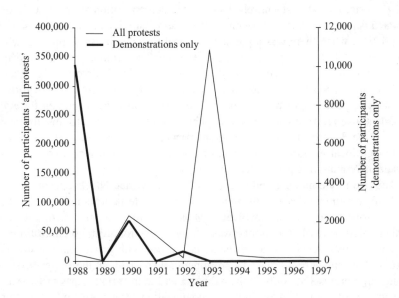

FIG. 5.4. *Number of participants in larger environmental protests in Greece (protests with 500 or more participants)*

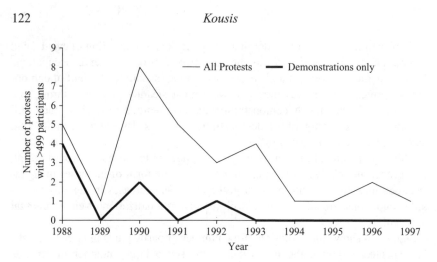

F<small>IG</small>. 5.5. *Larger environmental protests in Greece by year (events with 500 or more participants)*

River collected more than 300,000 signatures from Greece, Germany, and Italy. Part of a campaign by WWF, the Hellenic Society for the Protection of the Environment and Cultural Heritage (HSPECH), the Hellenic Society for the Protection of Nature (HSPN), and the Greek Ornithological Society (GOS), this led to a marked change in the European Commission's stance on the project (Close 1999).

Information on numbers of participants was available for only one-quarter of all protests, and almost entirely lacking for demonstrations, which were only about 5 per cent of all events. Many of these demonstrations took place during the late 1980s, when there was a plethora of local and smaller scale protests which were less likely to be reported in the newspaper. The evolution of protest events with 500 or more participants over the years 1988–97 is depicted in Fig. 5.5.

Over the 10 years, one-third of the forty-five large protests took the form of signatures, petitions, or resolutions. Site or road blockades accounted for eight, and demonstration marches for seven, public protest assemblies for just four. Very few of the 31 protests of 500 or more participants were led by large EMOs. Although local environmental groups/associations participated in some events, residents'/community groups led most of them.

The rise in the number and strength of environmental NGOs appears to have had only a limited impact on the number of large protests. Although in 1993 three of the four large protests involved EMOs collecting signatures, of the large protests during 1994–7, only one was led by an environmental organization; the rest were organized by local residents concerned with waste and construction issues. Residents' groups played a prominent role throughout the 10 years, organizing large protests not only in the Athens area but in various parts of Greece. If the impact of institutionalization and organization have been limited, political opportunities do appear to have influenced the repertoire of environment-related collective action. A clear majority (61 per cent) of large protests occurred during the early 1990s, under the New Democracy government, when PASOK-affiliated activists played a crucial role, collaborating with a variety of environmental groups.

FORMS AND ISSUES

Certain issues were associated with particular forms of protest (see Table 5.3). Conventional protest predominated for all issues, followed by demonstrative and confrontational actions. More violent protest was rare.

Animal welfare and hunting protests were the most conventional of all. The great majority of these were coordinated by environmental organizations or anti-hunting groups. Next most conventional were transport-related protests. These were primarily led by residents' groups, and secondarily by environmental NGOs. Protests concerning nature preservation, of which about 40 per cent involved formal groups or organizations, were also relatively conventional.

Animal welfare and hunting protests were unusually likely to involve demonstrations, but not confrontation. Protests concerning alternative production and nature conservation were also relatively demonstrative, while transport protests were least so. Energy-related protests, led mainly by residents' groups, were the least conventional and the most confrontational. Protests concerning pollution, urban, industrial, and transport issues were all relatively confrontational. Residents' groups led two-thirds of these protests.

Minor attacks on property tended to be associated with particular campaigns, notably the contentious protests by Thesprotians for the protection of the Kalamas

TABLE 5.3. *Issues and the forms of environmental protest in Greece*

	Conventional	Demonstrative	Confrontational	Attack on property	Violence	N
Nature conservation	67.5	24.8	18.3	1.2	2.0	246
Pollution, urban and industrial	60.2	22.5	30.7	1.3	0.8	387
Energy	57.1	26.2	38.1	2.4	0.0	42
Animal welfare and hunting	81.8	31.8	0.0	0.0	0.0	22
Transport	78.5	10.8	23.1	0.0	0.0	65
Alternative production, etc.	63.9	28.9	19.3	1.2	1.2	83
N	356	139	154	7	7	

Note: Percentage of events involving each issue that involves a form of action; percentages do not sum to 100 because for each protest up to 2 issues and 4 forms could be recorded.

river, by residents of communities near the Keratsini oil power plant in the Athens Metropolitan Area, by residents of Olympiada against gold mining in their area, and by groups in Trikala against pollution of the local river. The rare cases of violence appeared in Kato Simi and Aravissos in protests against water extraction, in Olympiada against gold mining, in Heraklion for alternative production, in Athens against construction, tree cutting, and other nature conservation issues, and in Spetses against disposal of hotel waste in the sea.

GROUPS

It is already apparent that two kinds of groups initiated or participated in environmental protests in Greece: environmental organizations and citizens' or community-based groups. Overall, between 1988 and 1997, community-based groups led 63 per cent of environmental protests, while 37 per cent were led by organizations. However, the balance between them changed over time (see Fig. 5.6). The decline of protests led by community-based groups was much more marked than that of organization-led protests, but election periods appeared to influence organization-led protests more than community-led protests.

Organizations include formal environmental organizations, unions, parties, informal environmental groups, networks of groups/organizations, and business/industry. Two hundred and two such groups were identified. Formal environmental organizations active at the international, national, and/or local level were those most frequently reported (47 per cent of all groups). Unions and parties were mentioned less often but steadily throughout the decade. Unions included the Pan Hellenic Union of Foresters, unions of professionals such as physicians

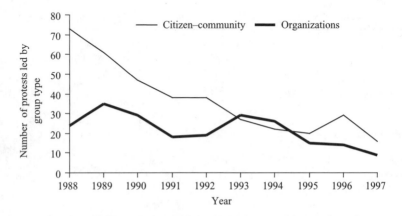

Fig. 5.6. *Environmental protests in Greece by type of initiating or participating group by year*

or lawyers, and labour unions such as GESEE (General Workers Syndicate of Greece). Parties were usually green or leftist, such as Ecologi Enallaktiki (FEA), PASOK, the Communist Party of Greece (KKE), and the Coalition (Synaspismos), but also included New Democracy (ND). Although informal environmental groups such as Keratsini–Perivallon–Politismos (Keratsini–Environment–Culture) or Ecologikes Omades Foititon (Student Ecology Groups) were mentioned less often, they became more prominent from 1994 onwards. A very few networks of groups were reported, but only between 1989 and 1992.

More than a quarter of organization-led protests involved a single group or organization. In only three events, all occurring in 1993, did the number of groups participating exceed eight. In the first of these, nine environmental groups protested against construction activities on a mountain in northern Greece; in the second, twenty-one climbing associations collected signatures in Greece and Europe against the construction of ski resorts in central Greece; and in the third, forty-three environmental organizations in Athens petitioned against the removal of stones from a lake.

The majority of protests were not led by organizations. Usually they were initiated by combinations of community-based groups involving residents, action/struggle committees, cultural associations, parent–student groups, local government representatives, and/or other citizen–worker groups. They were, in effect, 'popular publics' drawing on territorially fixed populations and responding to everyday experiences in urban or rural communities (Kousis and Eder 2001: 11).

Protests initiated by both environmental organizations and community-based groups were rare, accounting for only 4 per cent (twenty-five) of all protests. More or less evenly distributed between 1989 and 1996, 60 per cent of these were outside the Greater Athens area and Thessaloniki and 68 per cent were against the destruction of green areas. Examples of such collaboration concerning cases of serious damage to the local environment included protests against pollution by the Public Power Corporation (PPC) in the prefecture of Kozani, the expansion of oil installations in Elefsina, and the waste landfill in Ano Liossia.

Among the 202 groups reported as initiating or participating in environmental protests, the nine most frequently reported organized groups accounted for the leadership of only one-tenth of all protest events across the decade. The events that these nine groups initiated were more or less evenly spread throughout the decade, with the exception of the last 3 years, which showed lower levels than all previous years. This reflects the institutionalization of the core environmental NGOs during the 1990s, when more typical forms of action have been litigation, lobbying, non-commercial positive action, scientific reports, cultural performances, press conferences, and signatures/petitions/resolutions/public letters (Kousis and Dimopoulou 2000; Botetzagias 2001).

Two of the nine leading organizations are parties: Ecologi Enallaktiki (FEA) and PASOK. Interestingly, six of the eight protests in which PASOK representatives participated occurred either before national elections or while the party was not in government.[19] While the Greek Green Party, Ecologi Enallaktiki, united a wide variety of environmental groups, it was no more prominent than individual ecological organizations such as Enallaktiki Kinisi Ekologon or Fisiolatriki Antikinigetiki Protovoulia (Pro-Nature, Anti-hunting Initiative). Ecologi Enallaktiki had a relatively short life and this is reflected in their lack of protest activities from 1991 onwards.

Among the nine leading organizations appear six of the ten 'core' or most active formal environmental organizations in Greece (Botetzagias 2001): Elliniki Eteria Prostasias Fisis (HSPN), Greenpeace, WWF, Elliniki Eteria Gia Prostasia Perivallodos-Politistikis Klironomias (HSPECH), Elliniki Ornithologiki Eteria (GOS), and Enallaktiki Kinisi Ekologon. In addition to these core groups, the anti-hunting Fisiolatriki Antikinigetiki Protovoulia is among the most prominent twenty, while *Fisi kai Ecologia* is a periodical, and Exoraistikos Syllogos Likavitos is a community-based non-environmental organization.

The organization that initiated most protests during the decade was Greenpeace (either Greenpeace International or its Greek branch founded in 1991)[20] (nine each over the 10 years). It was followed by WWF (eight) and four prominent Greek nature conservation organizations: HSPECH, HSPN, Elliniki Ornithologiki Eteria (GOS), and Fisiolatriki Antikinigetiki Protovoulia (seven each). The last three, which are the oldest national organizations, as well as the environmental journal *Fisi & Oikologia*, appear to have been more active from 1988 to 1994. This may imply a change towards less contentious activism by national-level groups in the late 1990s. The environmental organizations did not make as strong a showing as the parties during national election years, and their primary focus upon competing for resources as well as their inclination towards professionalization imposed strong limits on their potential for contentious mobilization (Kousis and Dimopoulou 2000).

Were differences in the patterns of involvement in protest among organizations and informal community-based groups (shown in Fig. 5.6) accompanied by differences in the issues they raised? Table 5.4 depicts the most frequent primary claims for each of formal organizations and community-based groups. The divergence of their concerns is striking. Organizations were disproportionately involved in protests concerning wildlife and countryside protection, whereas community-based groups were more concerned with a wider set of claims based on everyday life experiences, including countryside protection, but disproportionately focused on pollution and waste issues. Such a sharp divergence in claims-making raises the question of their complementarity. The tendency of most organizations to focus primarily upon wildlife issues contrasts clearly with the intense claims of communities against the deterioration of their local urban and rural environments due to the impact of waste disposal, pollution, and production.

TABLE 5.4. *Community-based and organized/formal groups in environmental protest in Greece by selected primary claims*

Type of primary claim	Type of initiating or participating group		
	Frequency % (protest events)		
	Organized, formal, NGOs	Community-based, informal	Total
Hunted animals, animal welfare	100.0 (19)	—	3.8 (19)
Wildlife, construction (other)	*83.3 (20)*	*16.7 (4)*	*4.8 (24)*
Woods, wild flora	50.0 (24)	50.0 (24)	48 (9.4)
Ocean pollution	52.0 (13)	48.0 (12)	4.9 (25)
Weapons, military installations/activities	46.2 (6)	53.8 (7)	2.5 (13)
Resource extraction	36.0 (9)	64.0 (16)	4.9 (25)
Countryside and landscape protection	26.7 (39)	73.3 (107)	28.6 (146)
Pollution (noise, river/lake, other), traffic, construction (building)	26.1 (37)	73.9(105)	27.8 (142)
Industrial and energy (oil-based) production	24.0 (6)	76.0 (19)	4.9 (25)
Waste (domestic)	2.3 (1)	97.7 (43)	8.6 (44)
Total *N* (% of all protests)	174 (34.1%)	337 (65.9%)	511

The ten leading formal groups' protests were concerned with nature conservation, pollution, urban, and industrial issues. Among leading groups, only PASOK and Greenpeace participated in energy protests. PASOK participated twice in community protests against PPC's expansion of the major lignite-burning power stations of the Kozani region, as well as against pollution by Keratsini's oil-producing plant, and the installation of high-tension power lines in Tinos. Energy-related protests by Greenpeace include those against oil-burning electricity generation in Elefsina (Attiki) and Linoperamata (Crete). Greenpeace and Ecologi Enallaktiki were the only leading groups appearing in transport protests, while PASOK, Greenpeace, and Ecologi Enallaktiki did so regarding alternative production.

Overall, FEA, Greenpeace, PASOK, and Elliniki Eteria Prostasias tis Fisis protested about a wider range of issues than did the anti-hunting group, WWF, HSPECH, Thessaloniki's ecology movement, and GOS. Greenpeace and Alternative Ecologists led on nature conservation protests, followed by the anti-hunting group, HSPN, HSPECH, and GOS. Greenpeace also led on protests concerning pollution, urban, and industrial issues, followed by Alternative Ecologists, WWF, HSPECH, and GOS.

In the majority of the events reported, the initiating or supporting groups did not appear to interact with either formal or informal environmental groups or

TABLE 5.5. *Organized and community-based groups in environmental protest in Greece by form of protest*

Type of action	Frequency (%)		Total (protest events)
	Organized, formal, NGOs	Residents, community-based	
Appeal	43.8	28.1	223
Demonstrative	44.7	37.7	269
Confrontational	10.1	28.5	152
Violent	1.4	3.7	20
Other	—	2.0	9
Total *N*	217	456	673[a]

[a] Includes all four forms of action.

organizations. As Table 5.5 shows, almost three-quarters of these were initiated by community-based groups interacting with one another. Supporting similar earlier findings (Kousis, Aguilar, and Fidelis-Nogueira 1996), the data also indicate that community-based groups tended to opt for more confrontational actions than formal organizations, which showed a preference for demonstrations and appeals. Although rare, violent actions occurred more often in community-led protests. In a minority of protests (see Kousis 1999), members of political parties of all colours, or environmental organizations, participated in resident-led protest.

No leading formal group was reported to have been involved in violent protest. Whereas most formal groups' protest activities were conventional in form, those of Greenpeace and PASOK more often involved demonstrations or confrontations. Greenpeace, for example, occupied an island in northern Greece to protest against pollution caused by oil companies, blockaded a port to protest the expansion of an oil refinery, carried out a sit-in against pollution of the sea by the disposal of oil, and occupied a site to protest against chemical industry pollution. These protests were initiated and run solely by Greenpeace members, in contrast to those led by PASOK which were normally conducted in collaboration with community groups. Alternative Ecologists, PASOK, and Greenpeace employed the broadest repertoire, while those of the large nature conservation societies—WWF, HSPN, HSPECH, and GOS—were the most limited.

These findings reflect the common objectives of core environmental NGOs identified by earlier research (Kousis and Dimopoulou 2000; Botetzagias 2001): the accumulation and administration of funds; the promotion of environmental education and the raising of public awareness on environmental issues (production and use of relevant material, informational campaigns, and cooperation with mass media); the financing, organizing, and administration of nature preservation programmes (scientific research, exchange of scientists and undergraduates, conventions, meetings, discussions); cooperation with state and non-state organizations, authorities or any other suitable agent in order to achieve financial

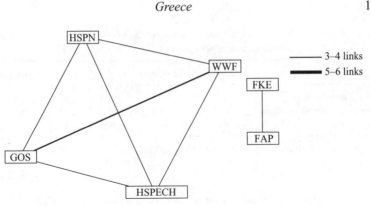

Key

HSPECH	Elliniki Eteria Gia Prostasia Perivallodos-Politistikis Klironomias
HSPN	Elliniki Eteria Prostasias Fisis
GOS	Elliniki Ornithologiki Eteria
FAP	Fisiolatriki Antikinigetiki Protovoulia
FKE	Fisi kai Ecologia
WWF	World Wide Fund for Nature

FIG. 5.7. *Networks of organizations in reports of environmental protests in Greece (1988–97) (only links reported 3 or more times are included)*

and moral support in the preservation of nature; and the publication of journals, books, and other printed matter relevant to their aims.

Greenpeace stood out as the only organization that acted more often alone than with others. At the other end of the spectrum, WWF was notable as the only one of the nine leading groups never reported to have protested alone. Similar tendencies are illustrated in Fig. 5.7, which illustrates inter-group links reported three or more times during the decade. The four organizations tied to the network are all core environmental NGOs, all of which are members of the EEB, and some of which are also members of other non-Greek international environmental groups. The centrality of WWF and GOS may reflect their closer collaboration with the newspaper. Among the two groups on the right, FAP is the anti-hunting group, while FKE is a not very prominent Greek environmental journal promoting NGOs. As a consequence of its tendency to act alone, Greenpeace is missing from the network diagram despite its collaboration with the newspaper.[21]

THE TRANSNATIONALIZATION OF PROTEST?

Table 5.6 depicts five different levels of mobilization, scope of environmental problem, and target of protest. For a large majority of events, protesters were mobilized on a local or district level; in less than 10 per cent were they mobilized

TABLE 5.6. *The levels of mobilization, scope of problems, and targets of environmental protests in Greece (percentages)*

	Local/district	Regional	National	EU	International	N
Level of mobilization	86.8	1.0	9.2	2.7	0.2	577
Scope of underlying problem	87.8	4.1	6.0	2.1	0	582
Level of target	56.5	2.1	49.9	1.8	0.3	570

Note: Percentages for level of target do not sum to 100 because 2 values could be recorded.

on a national level, while protests organized on international, regional or EU levels were extremely rare. Nevertheless, reported environmental protest in 1997 was much less localized than it was in the late 1980s. Environmental activism at the local level, as it appears in the news reports, steadily decreased, while protest at the district/regional, national, and supranational levels remained more or less stable throughout the decade. In general, the level of mobilization varied depending on the types of environmental claims. Mobilizations concerning tourism and industrial activities, environmental education and research, construction, nature protection, and pollution tended to be more local, whereas those opposing military and energy-related activities were markedly less so (Kousis and Lenaki 1999).

The scope of the underlying environmental problem follows a similar pattern. Most problems were identified as local or district in scope, while only a small minority were at the national, regional, or EU levels. Here too there were changes over time (Kousis and Lenaki 1999: figure 2). Whereas in the late 1980s the gap between local and non-local problems was very wide, it decreased steadily through the 1990s. Protests concerning environmental problems that were report-edly local in scope declined, but no such change was noticeable in those whose scope was district/regional, national, or supranational. Even though the types of environmental claims remained more or less the same, they tended to be less local in the 1990s than they were in the late 1980s.

The targets of action are frequently state and economic actors who are, directly or indirectly, involved in the decisions and policies that lead to or intensify ecological marginalization (Kousis 1998). The institutional apparatus of the world economy leads to a continued demand for exploitation of the ecosystem to accompany a greater capitalization of production (Schnaiberg 1994; Broadbent 1998). The most effective environmental offenders come in the form of state, supra-state, or global economic organizations aiming at greater profits and increased competitiveness by externalizing environmental costs (Perrow 1997). In southern European local environmental protest, the major antagonists of the pro-testers were the state (58 per cent), producers (53 per cent), and local government groups (41 per cent) (Kousis 2001). How are these reflected in environmental protests over time?

As Table 5.6 shows, targets were at national level in half the events, and local/ district in more than half. The state and economic actors were the main targets, and very few protests had supranational or regional-level targets. The state was targeted most over waste problems, resource extraction, energy production, military instal- lations, construction projects, and the protection of nature. Although companies were challenged less frequently, they were targeted especially when they did not apply environment-friendly industrial and tourism practices. The proportion of environmental protest directed against the state, high at the end of the 1980s, fell significantly through the 1990s. More moderate and gradual decreases were evident in protests directed at other targets (Kousis and Lenaki 1999).

CONCLUSIONS

The apparent decline of reported environmental protests in Greece between 1988 and 1997 has been uneven. The organization of social space, the structure of polit- ical and economic opportunities and constraints, and the pattern of newspaper coverage itself have all, usually acting in combination, influenced the pattern presented in this chapter.

The effects of changes in the structure of political opportunities and constraints were especially visible in election periods. Although they did not seriously disturb the overall trend in the reported incidence of protest, election years did influence the peaks of waves of protest (cf. Kousis 1999). Yet the political identity of the governing party had little influence on the pattern of protest: the highest as well as the lowest levels of protest took place under Socialist (PASOK) governments while moderate levels occurred under the right-wing (ND) government. If, how- ever, the focus is narrowed to the relatively small number of larger protests, it is interesting that 61 per cent occurred under the right wing government, and that they prominently involved representatives of the PASOK opposition. PASOK, given its easier recourse to and rapport with extra-parliamentary opposition, appeared more inclined to join or stimulate populist protest than did the conser- vative ND. Thus at best partial support is provided for the thesis that protest is stimulated under right-wing governments but depressed under those of the left (Kriesi et al. 1995).

As in other southern European countries that emerged from dictatorial regimes in the early 1970s, environmental protest in Greece was strongly marked by the presence of community-based groups (Kousis 1999). Community-based envir- onmental activism, although mostly employing non-violent forms of action, was more radical in its repertoire than that organized by formal environmental organ- izations, and it was more attentive to local ecosystems and a wider set of envir- onmental issues. In keeping with repertoires expected of more institutionalized actors, most environmental organizations, including leading core groups, favoured more conventional actions privileging appeal and demonstrations over confrontation. Overall, the growth in numbers of environmental organizations and the institutionalization of the related environmental activism occurred simultaneously with a steady decrease in environmental protest activity. However, the steeper decline in reported community-based protest may be the product of changes in the structure and reporting style of the newspaper.

The apparent relative absence of cooperation between community-based activists and organized groups is further testimony to the enormous and enduring obstacles to collaboration among the various wings of the environmental movement (cf. Gould, Schnaiberg, and Weinberg 1996; Kousis 1999). The rare cases of such collaboration show vividly the innate strengths of such a relationship when it comes to confronting major environmental problems.

The consequences of the lack of such cooperation can be seen in the failure, despite favourable media coverage and the support of eminent personalities, of the environmental NGOs' campaign, without citizen group support, against the recent constitutional reform—Article 24. The reform will result in further depletion of renewable natural resources, the curtailment of civic groups' right to appeal against the state, and the restriction of the courts' capacity to scrutinize state-initiated decisions (Botetzagias 2001). As the (admittedly more drastic) SLAPP[22] legislation in the United States demonstrates, such reforms present huge obstacles to challenges by informal and formal environmental activists against responsible authorities at a time when globalization is generating a multitude of intertwined critical environmental, political, and economic issues.

The changing structure of economic opportunities and constraints has been a major factor in the development of environmental protest in Greece. In the 1990s, the moves towards privatization in southern Europe appears to have stimulated a shift of mobilization potential from the issues of environmental and other new social movements to opposition to privatization and economic liberalization. Thus, reported environmental protest appears to have decreased consistently as economic liberalization was introduced. Economic opportunities and constraints may hinder or assist mobilizations, especially for local groups concerned with local problems. Thus, environmental protests against the negative impacts of the still-important agricultural sector remain extremely rare in Greece, especially so in the case of community-based groups given their economic dependence on this sector. On the other hand, communities dependent on tourism, which rely on a 'clean' environment to sell their product, appear more likely to engage in environmental activism. Protests concerning waste, so distinctively an issue of community groups, reflect concerns for the fragile relationship between the quality of limited local natural resources, high dependence on the local economy, and the significance of public health.

Our reliance on one main source of information must be taken into account when evaluating these results. Especially since the early 1990s, the pressure of competition as well as its increasing attention to economic, political, and environmental education appears to have influenced *Eleftherotypia*'s reporting of environmental protest. Nevertheless, despite the likely effects of changes in the pattern of reporting, it appears probable that it is principally the political and economic opportunities and constraints faced by the two major groups of environmental activists that account for the patterns of environmental protest we have identified.

NOTES

1. These are the first two of the three proposed by McAdam, McCarthy, and Zald (1996).
2. Economic opportunities and constraints occurring at the EU or national levels affect professional environmental NGOs, while those at the regional level are more likely to affect community-based environmental movements. This is vividly illustrated in case studies of local environmental mobilizations in six Great Lakes communities in North America (Gould, Schnaiberg, and Weinberg 1996), in eight communities of Oita prefecture in Japan (Broadbent 1998), in the county of Iraklion in Greece (Kousis 1997*a*), in rural communities (Kousis 1998), and in four Swedish communities (Linden 1997; Cf. Kousis 2002).
3. Filis Kaitatzis has been exclusively covering environmental issues for *Eleftherotypia* since the early 1990s; between 1985 and 1993 he covered political, environmental, and international issues.
4. Telephone interview with the editor-in-chief of *Eleftherotypia*, Sifis Polimilis, 15 February 1999.
5. Telephone interview with *Eleftherotypia* staff, 1998.
6. Such 'summary reports' were not coded for the Greek case.
7. Telephone interview with Sifis Polimilis, conducted by Maria Kousis, 15 February 1999.
8. Interview with Vayia Papanikolaou, conducted by Maria Kousis, 23 March 1999.
9. By Peter Diplas in *Kathimerini* (Pridham 2001).
10. According to Polimilis, the environmental organizations improved and assisted environmental issue coverage from their inception in 1990, to the end of the decade. Kaitatzis communicates regularly with environmental organizations in Greece and abroad (e.g. the greens of Germany and Belgium).
11. *Eleftherotypia*'s correspondent in Crete, and a systematic observer of the leftist press, P. Georgoudis, also pointed this out when interviewed.
12. Commission of the European Communities 1992 (cited in Close 1999; Botetzagias 2001). This is understandable given high air and noise pollution in Athens (Kazakos 1999), waste disposal problems all over the country, water scarcity, dependence on tourism, and continuing ties of urban residents with the countryside (Close 1999; Pridham 2001).
13. V-PRC Institute study (1999: 55) as cited in Botetzagias (2001).
14. Interview with Panagiotis Georgoudis conducted by Katerina Lenaki, Iraklion, December 1999.
15. Interview with Filis Kaitatzis conducted by Katerina Lenaki, Athens, 27 November 1999.
16. From an alternative way of viewing as well as coding environmental claims, the environmental problem is seen as being comprised of three parts: *the source/(in)activities* associated with user/s; the environmental *offences* produced (in terms of pollution or

ecosystem disorganization); and the subsequent *impacts* generated, such as aesthetic, economic, health, ecosystem, cultural, and life-endangering (see Kousis 1999).

17. As coded by Katerina Lenaki after systematic reading of every issue of the monthly periodical, *Nea Oikologia* 1988–97 (see Kousis and Lenaki 2000).

18. Anti-nuclear protest events were found in the 1970s and 1980s, mostly relating to the US bases in Greece and the Chernobyl accident (see Kousis 1999). In 1991, NGO concern was also shown by *Nea Oikologia* regarding the Bulgarian nuclear power plant in Kozlodoui (Kousis and Lenaki 2000).

19. 89/9, 90/8, 91/2, 96/1, 92/5, 92/5.

20. Both names are used as found in the reports.

21. If we compare Fig. 5.7 with a network diagram based on a national survey of all Greek environmental NGOs (Botetzagias 2001), a number of discrepancies emerge. The ten core organizations identified by the survey-based network analysis include, as well as the four core organizations apparent from reports of protest: Greenpeace, the Sea Turtle Protection Society, the Society for the Protection and Study of the Mediterranean Seal, Mediterranean SOS, Nea Oikologia, and Arktouros. Furthermore, the anti-hunting group appears from the survey to be linked with GOS. These discrepancies are not surprising when it is remembered that newspapers generally report only (a selection of) public protest events and neglect the many less public kinds of interaction among organizations. For that reason, a network diagram based on protest event data cannot hope to capture all the links, especially the less public links, among groups and organizations. Nevertheless, Fig. 5.7 is valuable as a representation of the coalitions and alliances that exist among organizations engaged in public protest.

22. SLAPP = Strategic Lawsuits against Public Participation.

6

Italy

Mario Diani and Francesca Forno

Prospects looked bright for the environmental movement in Italy in 1988. In the previous year, resounding victories in three anti-nuclear referenda had virtually ruled out nuclear energy as a policy option in the country for the foreseeable future (Diani 1994). Moreover, success in the anti-nuclear campaign had been just the highlight of what had been a remarkably rapid growth in both organizational strength and mobilization capacity. After being involved in anti-nuclear mobilizations and urban struggles in the late 1970s, environmental groups had started to grow in the early 1980s.[1] Legambiente, which was to become the most important environmental organization in the country, had been founded in 1980 as a branch of ARCI, the cultural and leisure time association of the Italian left (although it detached itself from ARCI after its 1986 convention) (Poggio 1996: 78). Membership rates and numbers of local chapters of the most important national organizations were both growing dramatically.[2] The movement's mobilization capacity had increased accordingly, with protest events on environmental issues growing dramatically between 1983 and 1988 (Giugni 1999).

All this encouraged optimism and provided reasons for hope to advocates of a realignment of the Italian political system along green lines. Over a decade later, the picture of both Italian environmentalism and Italian politics as a whole did not quite fit the optimistic expectations of the late 1980s. A new ecological cleavage had not consolidated in the country, nor had one reflecting the broader emergence of 'new politics' and left-libertarian parties (Kitschelt 1989; Kriesi 1993; della Porta 1996). Other new political actors, mostly with a populist, right-wing profile, had stolen the show in the 1990s, from the Northern League to Berlusconi's *Forza Italia*, and the prominence of environmental issues had been

We are grateful to Filippo Legnaioli for his assistance with data collection in Florence and Naples, and to Pietro Iozzelli of *la Repubblica* (Florence), and Luigi Vicinanza of *il Mattino*, for their collaboration. Antonio Cianciullo, environmental national editor for *la Repubblica*, kindly commented on our preliminary findings. Antonio Polito, UK correspondent for *la Repubblica*, also offered valuable assistance. Special thanks to Marco Giugni for sharing with us some unpublished data on protest activities in Italy.

challenged by growing concerns about public order, immigration, public finance, and unemployment.

However, for all the problems encountered by environmentalists in the course of their efforts to influence policy agenda, and for all the electoral disappointments experienced by the Greens, the Italian scenario of the late 1990s was not one of 'doom and gloom' for environmentalists. In the first place, prominent members of the environmental movement achieved considerable political influence. Between 1996 and 1999, the Environment Ministry was led by Green MP Edo Ronchi, and other Green members (including former anti-nuclear leader Gianni Mattioli) served as senior or junior ministers from 1996 to 2001. Legambiente was similarly well placed, with environmental economist Giovanna Melandri occupying another senior ministerial post until the 2001 election, and former president Chicco Testa chairing ENEL (the national agency for electric power). If integration in elite networks and formal inclusion can be regarded as measures of movement success (Gamson 1990; Diani 1997; Giugni, McAdam, and Tilly 1999), then Italian environmentalism certainly achieved some remarkable results.

Although available data on major environmental organizations were not always consistent, there was no sign of decline in membership. Prudent estimates suggested zero growth already in the early 1990s, following the strong rise of the late 1980s (Diani 1995: 36), but other accounts recorded persisting growth throughout the 1990s (Giugni 1999; della Porta and Andretta 2000). Judging by the number of environmental protests reported in newspapers, protest activity was still higher, or at least more visible, in the mid-1990s than in previous periods characterized by intense political mobilization, such as the late 1970s (Giugni 1999). By the mid-1990s, environmental organizations were regarded as representative political actors, to be reckoned with in numerous policy areas (Lewanski 1997).

How can we make sense of a process that is ambiguous, if not contradictory, in its most visible manifestations? Systematic analysis of the intensity and forms of environmental protest in Italy from 1988 to 1997 will help us in this task.[3] Although they are far from the ultimate response to problems of the analysis of collective action (see Chapters 1 and 10), newspapers provide systematic longitudinal data about important features of collective action. We start by looking at the distribution of events across time and space. Does the balance between local and national actions change over time? What is the space for transnational issues? Is there a fall in environmental organizations' mobilizing capacity? We then chart the evolution of the main mobilization issues, documenting in particular the changing relative influence of urban ecology themes on the one hand, and nature conservation and animal rights on the other. Examination of repertoires of collective action enables us better to specify arguments about the institutionalization of environmental politics. We conclude our overview by focusing on the organizational dimensions of environmental action. First, we look at the relative presence of bureaucratic and informal environmental actors along with non-environmental organizations. We then move to a discussion of the role of the major formal environmental organizations, looking in particular at their standing as the 'owners' of specific issues, and even of distinctive forms of action. These elementary pieces of information allow us to discuss several, partially alternative, partially complementary interpretations of the evolution of Italian environmentalism.

THE EVOLUTION OF PROTEST

Environmental protest was at its height in the period 1988–90, with half of the protest events reported in the national sections of *la Repubblica* located in that period. The late 1980s witnessed an attempt by environmental organizations to consolidate their status as major national political actors and to extend the scope of their action and the issues addressed. Campaigners tried to apply the principles and guiding ideas of the anti-nuclear opposition to a far broader range of targets, notably high-risk industrial plants and other dangerous economic activities. Examples include the campaigns against the Acna factory in Piedmont, and Farmoplant in Tuscany, as well as Legambiente's national campaign against the 500 highest-risk firms in the country, and actions against ships cleaning their tanks offshore. Environmentalists also attempted to exploit the momentum generated by the 1987 referendum by promoting two more, one on limitations on pesticides, the other proposing the abolition of hunting.

This was to prove a hazardous choice. In May 1990, referenda were held and, despite overwhelming support for the environmentalists' proposals, the result was not valid because fewer than 50 per cent of eligible voters turned up at the polls. Opponents of the referenda (in particular, agricultural business associations and hunters' associations) had successfully sabotaged the referenda by inviting opponents of the environmental front to abstain from voting. This, combined with the lower salience of the two issues by comparison with nuclear energy, resulted in low turnouts. Failure in the referenda induced a gradual demobilization of the movement, paralleled by modest performances by the Greens in the 1992 and 1994 elections. Environmentalists' capacity to promote visible mobilizations gradually declined. Protests reported in the years 1991–3 amounted to a meager 16 per cent of the total (a reduction of two-thirds over the previous 3 years); only 17 events were reported in 1991 and 1993, and 18 in 1992 (Fig. 6.1).

This was a period in which the crisis of the political system dramatically worsened as the Northern League gained momentum and—from 1992—the Milan judges' investigations exposed massive political corruption (Gundle and Parker 1996). Although protest actions with a clear environmental profile, and capable of having an impact at the national level, increased again from 1993 to 1995, this was mainly due to international developments. French nuclear experiments in Mururoa prompted a wave of protest actions (over half of those that attracted national coverage in 1995), which were not restricted to small professional activist groups like Greenpeace but included much broader coalitions of environmental and other

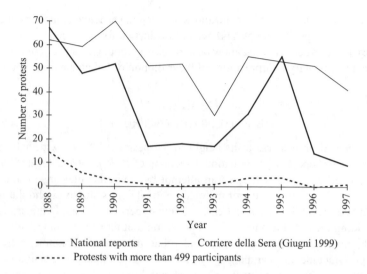

——— National reports   ——— Corriere della Sera (Giugni 1999)
- - - - - Protests with more than 499 participants

FIG. 6.1. *Environmental protest events in Italy by year (national data)*

political and social organizations. In the last two years covered by our analysis, the incidence of reported protest dropped to its lowest level. This period coincided with the victory of the center–left Olive Tree coalition in the 1996 national elections.

There are several possible explanations for such a dramatic fall in reported protest activities in 1996–7. The Greens' position in the executive and the proximity of many environmental leaders to the center–left might have reduced the potential for environmental protest.[4] Media reporting styles might also have played a part. Issue attention-cycle dynamics may have been operating, with other types of protest on hotter issues such as non-white immigration, or law and order problems (prostitution, petty delinquency) displacing environmental conflicts from the top of the media agenda (Forno forthcoming). Nor should the political bias of our source newspaper be overlooked; being close to the center–left coalition, *la Repubblica* might have been more reluctant than other newspapers to report incidents which might cast the new government in an unfavourable light. However, data on environmental and anti-nuclear protest, collected from the Sunday and Monday issues of *Corriere della Sera*, a daily less sympathetic to the center–left than *Repubblica*, show a remarkably similar evolution of protest over time.[5]

The question is therefore whether the apparent fall in environmental protest since the late 1980s was 'real', or whether it might simply have been a reflection of changing political conditions and media orientations. In order to address this question it is advisable to look at local news sections in representative areas of the country (Fig. 6.2). While national reports suggest a clear downward trend, despite the 1995 peak, the picture from local news is more complex. In Florence, there

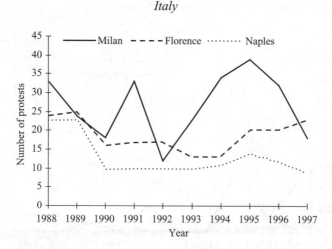

FIG. 6.2. *Environmental protest events in Milan, Florence, and Naples by year*

seemed to be no trend, but rather cyclical fluctuation. Naples experienced a similar pattern, but for a sharper decline of activities in 1990. Oscillations around the average were most substantial in Milan, yet with a trend towards increased rather than declining protest activity. It is tempting to identify a relationship between the evolution of protest and the local administration's political orientation. In Milan, the election in 1993 of an outspokenly anti-environmentalist administration, led by the Northern League, coincided with a massive resumption of environmental protest. In Naples, however, the advent of the Centre–Left administration led by popular mayor Antonio Bassolino apparently had little impact on the overall amount of protest activity; if anything, there was a slight increase during 1993–5.

The greater stability of protest events at the local level suggests that the decrease in protest reported in the national news during the 1990s might have been at least partially due to changes in overall reporting policies, with news about local conflicts increasingly being shifted to the local news sections. It is also worth noting that reduction in protest activities need not imply overall reduction in collective activities. Indeed, voluntary action appears to have spread: from 1993, campaigns such as 'Spiagge Pulite' (Legambiente) and 'Bosco Pulito' (World Wide Fund for Nature, WWF) were launched, and involved tens of thousands of people across the country. In 1995, the transnational campaign 'Clean Up the World' was also coordinated in Italy by Legambiente (Poggio 1996: 107–8). These and similar activities swelled the number of actions dramatically in the second half of the 1990s.[6]

However, the overall trend apparent in Fig. 6.1 does not differ from that of the pattern of protest events mobilizing 500 or more people. The distribution of number of participants in all events, as well as in demonstrations only, points in

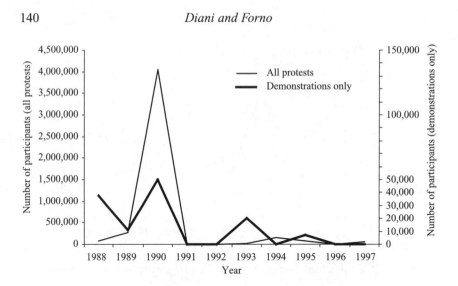

FIG. 6.3. *Numbers of participants in larger environmental protests in Italy (national data) (protests with 500 or more participants)*

the same direction (Fig. 6.3). These findings deserve attention because assessments of the reliability of newspapers as data sources agree that protest activities that attract substantial numbers of participants are very likely to be reported (Hocke 1998; Hug and Wisler 1998; Fillieule 1999). The broad coincidence of the curves tracing the evolution of all events and of larger events suggests that the apparent reduction in protest activity in the 1990s might well be more than a mere reflection of media practices. While overall support for environmental organizations and interest in environmental issues, as well as their capacity to mobilize people in voluntary actions, remained strong throughout the decade (IREF 1998: 158; della Porta and Andretta 2000), environmental activists were less capable of (or less interested in) promoting national protests. At the same time, newspapers were less inclined to report local protests in the national news.

THE TERRITORIAL DIMENSION OF ITALIAN ENVIRONMENTAL PROTEST

In which areas of the country was environmental action most intense in the 1990s? Table 6.1 shows the distribution of events reported in the national news of *la Repubblica* across geographical areas: the north-west, with a strong industrial tradition, the north-east and centre, which has experienced the most dramatic rise in economic activity and wealth since the 1960s, and the south. One-fourth of events occurred in both the north-west and the north-east, with 18 per cent in

TABLE 6.1. *The spatial distribution of environmental protests in Italy (1988–97) compared with population*

	Percentage of protest events (without Rome-based, national events)	Percentage of population[a]	Index of representation[b]
North-east and centre	37.0	28.5	1.30
South	26.0	45.1	0.58
North	37.0	26.4	1.40
N (without Rome-based national events)	205	100	
N (Rome-based national events)	123		
Total *N*	328	56,399,000	

Notes:
[a] Population figures for 1991 from Istat.
[b] 'Index of representation' is a figure obtained by dividing the number of protests by the number of protests expected from the ratio of the total number of events to total population; values above 1 indicate over-representation of an area in the data set, and values below 1 an under-representation.

the south. The remaining third were events of national relevance which happened to take place in Rome but had no specific linkage to that city's problems.[7] The concentration of protest in the north is consistent with available data about the relative strength of the movement in different areas of the country, whether measured in terms of associational memberships or electoral support for the greens (Biorcio 1998; Iref 1998: 153).

While the proportion of events in the north-west and the north-east-centre substantially exceeds what one would expect from the distribution of the general population, the opposite is true, by a substantial margin, of southern Italy. There, protests tended to be concentrated in a few years. In 1988 and 1990, a major conflict developed in Manfredonia about the polluting role of a chemical factory, part of the Enichem group, and the risks associated with ships transporting chemical waste. Water pollution was another major contentious issue, and in 1995 many actions against French nuclear tests took place in the south. This pattern suggests that a more reactive type of protest prevailed in areas with a weaker tradition of participation in environmental associations.

During the decade, over half of all nationally reported environmental protest in Italy was local in its level of mobilization (see Table 6.2). National protests accounted for another third, while mobilizations on an EU or international scale did not exceed 2 per cent of the events. The relative balance between national and local events tended to fluctuate, with more local events being recorded in phases

Diani and Forno

TABLE 6.2. *Levels of mobilization, scope of problems, and targets of environmental
protest in Italy (national data) (percentages)*

	Local/ district	Regional	National	EU	International	N
Level of mobilization	54.8	4.5	38.8	1.3	0.6	312
Scope of underlying problem	43.7	4.0	32.7	0.6	19.0	327
Level of target	22.1	7.8	61.6	0.7	14.4	271

of relatively higher contention (1988–90 and 1995), and national events playing a greater role when overall levels of protest were modest (1992–4 and 1997). Both in 1991 and in 1996, however, local events were relatively numerous despite globally low levels of mobilization.

Protests conducted at the international level were rare but, if we consider the scope of the underlying problem, about one-fifth of events addressed global issues, and the proportion increased, albeit unevenly, in the course of the decade: it peaked in 1995 with the Mururoa nuclear tests, but was still three times higher in 1996–7 than in 1988–90. By contrast, while local problems accounted for almost half of the events, their relative incidence fell considerably despite partial recoveries in 1994 and, particularly, 1996. Although it is more difficult to identify a clear trend for national issues, they were relatively less important in the early years than in the later ones.

Environmental actors mainly targeted political institutions (in about 60 per cent of events) and, albeit on a smaller scale, private companies and business operators (20 per cent). However, they also engaged directly with the general public (17 per cent), with a view to promoting public consciousness through collective action initiatives. The territorial level of target groups also changed over the period. The prominence of local or regional actors drastically declined after 1992, while that of national actors remained broadly stable for most of the decade. The French government's decision to proceed with military nuclear tests accounts for the overwhelming presence of foreign actors among protest targets in 1994–5. Apart from that, however, international actors were rarely targets of protest activities.

Overall, environmental actions moved from local to national and, more impressively, transnational issues, albeit in a context of decreasing visibility of environmental action. Moreover, while concern for global issues grew, it proved difficult to convert into specific action; both coordinated actions on an EU or international scale, and the presence of EU or international actors among protest targets, remained limited. Environmental groups may well be increasingly engaged in transnational cooperation (Dalton and Rohrschneider 1999), but in Italy at least such activities were not among their most prominent.

ENDS AND MEANS

Mobilization Issues

Environmental groups had made serious attempts to encourage environmental lifestyles during the 1990s, through the promotion of specific initiatives and the elaboration of policy proposals in innumerable areas. However, such initiatives only accounted for 4 per cent of the protests reported in the national news section of *la Repubblica*. Despite some attention in the late 1980s, when environmentalism was still perceived as a new phenomenon, coverage was already reduced in 1990, and then remained fairly stable. Even local news did not prove more open to such activities (only 3 per cent of the total). This picture is consistent with accounts of Italian environmentalism in the 1980s that emphasized their political rather than cultural aspects (Diani 1995).[8] Mobilizations on energy issues were similarly modest (3 per cent of national events, 1 per cent local). After some visibility following the 1987 referendum, they disappeared almost completely, reflecting the limited salience of energy as a political issue during the decade.

Animal welfare and hunting accounted for 20 per cent of national events and 12 per cent of locally reported events. They showed a cyclical variation in absolute terms (Figs 6.4 (a) and (b)) and were particularly visible in years of low national contention such as 1993, 1994, and 1996 (although they were more evenly represented in local protests). Nature conservation issues were slightly less conspicuous (10 per cent of national, 15 per cent of local events), yet followed a fairly similar, cyclical path, with national peaks in 1994, and local peaks in 1994 and 1996–7 (again, years of low visibility for environmental action at the national level). Nature protection and animal rights are the classic issues of traditional environmentalism (and in fact are mostly, albeit not exclusively, promoted by conservation organizations such as WWF or various animal rights groups). The limited amount of variation in their presence over time suggests that they represented the backbone of environmental action, which secured a fairly constant level of media attention, and whose relative importance grew when the public visibility of actions on other issues was more limited.

Changes in the public visibility of actions on transport-related issues (including opposition to roads) are instructive, as they highlight differences between local and national coverage, and the importance of taking both into account. On a national basis, their impact seemed negligible—a modest 3 per cent of the total. In Milan, Florence, and Naples, however, transport accounted for 15 per cent of all protests, a figure more consistent with subjective perceptions of the centrality of the issue among Italian citizens. Both local and national data showed a fairly stable distribution of such actions over the decade (Table 6.3 Sections A and B).

Most frequently reported by far were pollution, industrial, and urban issues, which accounted for two-thirds of the total both locally and nationally. When mobilizations were most visible, as in 1988–9 or in 1995, it was because of renewed interest in these issues. When collective action was relatively low, their

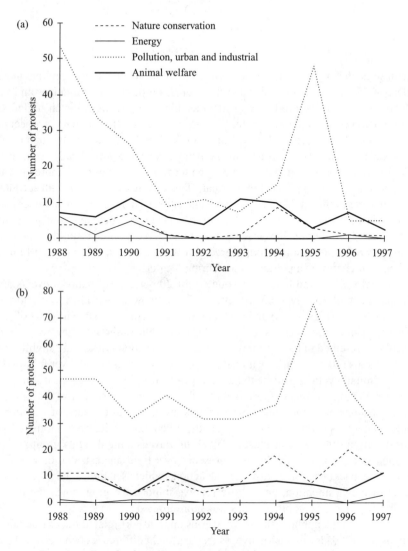

Fig. 6.4. *Four leading environmental issue domains in Italy by year:*
(a) national data and (b) local data

relative presence was more modest. These issues attracted a larger constituency
than the more classical environmental ones, and variation in their relative
incidence over time was more pronounced nationally than locally.

Closer attention to the internal composition of urban and pollution issues
reveals some differences in national trends (Fig. 6.5). Anti-pollution mobilizations
were particularly strong in the first 3 years, and thereafter were regularly below
the average. Conflicts over building construction followed a similar path, while

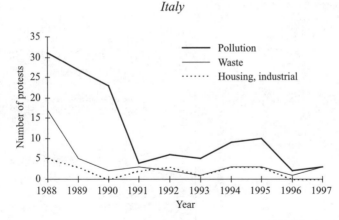

FIG. 6.5. *Protests concerning pollution, waste, and housing-industrial construction in Italy by year (national data)*

conflicts over waste were quite stable but reached new intensity in 1995–7, when the operation and location of waste disposal sites resurfaced as a major issue in many Italian towns, especially in the North. The local importance of waste issues is also illustrated by differences between local and national data. Actions on waste (and also on housing and industrial sites) were twice as frequently reported locally as nationally (25 per cent versus 12 per cent), whereas pollution was by far the most important mobilization issue in the national pages.

In the late 1980s, years characterized by high levels of (interest in) environmental protest, urban issues were clearly dominant. By contrast, in the following period an 'issue mobilization cycle' dynamic seemed to prevail, with different issues taking centre stage in different years. The question is of course whether this was due to an actual reduction in the levels of urban mobilization or, instead, to a reduction of media interest in it. Alternatively, it is possible that, when one set of issues is clearly dominant, mobilization attempts have a stronger profile, which results in better media coverage. However, when this is not the case, then the overall profile of mobilization may be weaker because it lacks a master frame, and different types of issues come in waves.

Forms of Protest

Environmental action was pre-eminently conducted by conventional means (found in 61 per cent of nationally reported protests and 67 per cent of events reported in local sections). National and local data display an even more similar pattern when it comes to demonstrative and confrontational forms (37 per cent and slightly above 10 per cent, respectively). Violence and attacks on property, in contrast, were virtually absent from local reports, but they exceeded 10 per cent of nationally reported events, probably because a local event where violence is used immediately attracts the interest of national media.

TABLE 6.3. *Environmental issues raised in environmental protests in Italy by year (national and local data)*
(percentage of events in which issue is raised by year)

	1988	1989	1990	1991	1992	1993	1994	1995	1996	1997	1988–97	Total N
A. National data												
Nature conservation	6.0	8.3	13.5	5.9	0	11.8	29.0	5.5	7.1	12.5	9.8	32
Pollution, urban and industrial	79.1	72.9	48.1	52.9	64.7	41.2	48.4	87.3	35.7	62.5	65.3	213
Pollution	46.2	56.1	44.3	23.6	35.3	29.4	29.0	18.3	14.2	25.0	36.5	119
Waste (non-nuclear)	25.4	10.5	3.8	17.6	11.8	5.9	9.7	5.4	7.2	37.5	12.3	40
Housing, industrial	7.5	6.3	0	11.7	17.6	5.9	9.7	5.4	0	0	6.1	20
Energy	9.0	2.1	9.6	5.9	0	0	0	0	7.1	0	4.3	14
Animal welfare and hunting	10.4	12.5	21.2	35.3	23.5	64.7	32.3	5.5	50.0	25.0	20.6	67
Animal welfare	4.4	4.2	11.5	29.4	11.8	23.5	12.9	0	42.9	25.0	10.4	34
Hunting	6.0	8.3	9.7	5.9	11.7	41.2	19.4	5.5	7.1	0	10.2	33
Transport	1.5	2.1	9.6	0	5.9	0	3.2	3.6	0	0	3.4	11
Alternative production	9.0	8.3	0	5.9	5.9	0	0	1.8	0	12.5	4.3	14
Total N of events	67	48	52	17	17	17	31	55	14	8	100	

B. Local data

Nature conservation	14.3	15.7	8.5	14.1	9.1	15.7	28.1	8.0	28.2	22.0	*15.5*	*103*
Pollution, urban and industrial	*61.0*	*67.1*	*68.1*	*64.1*	*72.7*	*62.7*	*57.8*	*85.2*	*60.6*	*52.0*	*65.8*	*412*
Pollution	23.3	27.2	23.5	23.3	38.6	33.4	28	37.5	21.1	14.0	27.3	170
Waste (non-nuclear)	19.5	31.4	19.1	25.1	27.3	11.7	22	30.6	35.3	28.0	25.5	160
Housing, industrial	18.2	8.5	25.5	14.1	6.8	17.6	7.8	9	2.8	10.0	11.6	73
Energy	*1.3*	*0*	*2.1*	*1.6*	*0*	*0*	*0*	*2.3*	*0*	*6.0*	*1.3*	*8*
Animal welfare and hunting	*11.7*	*12.9*	*6.4*	*17.2*	*13.6*	*13.7*	*12.5*	*8.0*	*7.0*	*22.0*	*12.1*	*76*
Animal welfare	6.5	5.7	2.1	10.9	9.1	2.0	4.7	2.3	4.2	12.0	5.8	36
Hunting	5.2	7.1	4.3	6.3	4.5	11.8	7.8	5.7	2.8	10.0	6.4	40
Transport	16.9	10.0	21.3	15.6	22.7	17.6	10.9	13.6	14.1	12.0	15.0	94
Alternative production	*3.9*	*4.3*	*6.4*	*1.6*	*0*	*0*	*4.7*	*3.4*	*0*	*2.0*	*2.7*	*17*
Total N of events	77	70	47	64	44	51	64	88	71	50	100	

Note: Broad categories of issue in italic; subcategories in roman. Percentages do not sum to 100 as up to 2 issues could be recorded per event.

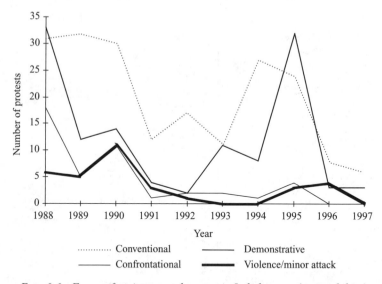

FIG. 6.6. *Forms of environmental protest in Italy by year (national data)*

Figure 6.6 charts the evolution of different forms of protest over time at the national level. With the single exception of a few attacks on property (mainly in protests against the use of animals in scientific experiments) in 1996, confrontational and more radical forms of protest were more frequently employed at the start of the decade than at the end. On the other hand, there are no particular signs of a rise in conventional forms of action since the late 1980s. The years with the highest number of reported events (1988 and 1995) had a relatively low proportion of conventional events. However, in other years where activity was also quite intense, such as 1989 and 1990, the number of conventional protests was very much in line with the average. The same applies to the local level: demonstrative actions oscillated without clear trend, and so did conventional actions (but for two low points—in 1990 and 1996—at times when activity had peaked and was declining). Confrontation varied little, and with no discernible trend, over the decade. Other more radical actions were virtually absent.

Among conventional forms of action, the increasing role of the public presentation of reports, providing new data on specific environmental problems, is worth noting. Legambiente promoted many of those activities, aiming at mobilizing public concerns if not necessarily public action. For example, *Goletta Verde*, a boat specially equipped to collect data about the quality of the Italian seas and shores, started its activities already in 1986, and *Treno Verde*, which visits several Italian cities every year to inform citizens about urban pollution, followed 2 years later. This strategy, intended to attract the public's attention to specific problems, and to back environmentalists' claims by recourse to technical and scientific evidence, became quite important after the collapse of the 1990 referenda. It gained increasing ground at the expense of other types of appeals such as petitions and, in particular, procedural forms such as litigation, which appear to have declined in importance in the late 1990s.

Overall, our data document the overwhelming predominance of pressure over protest in environmentalists' repertoire of action (cf. Dalton 1994). If, however, we were looking for trends 'from protest to pressure', we would only find weak ones. These findings rather support claims that the evolution of the environmental movement in Italy should not be considered in isolation, but as part of the tail of a broader cycle that started in the 1960s (Diani 1995: ch. 7). Since its outset, the environmental movement has been quite moderate, having developed at a time (the early 1980s) in which trends towards the de-radicalization of social movement activity and toward less confrontational repertoires of action were already pronounced. How did mobilizations on different issues differ in their action repertoires? Reflecting the prominence of urban issues overall, the repertoire of mobilizations on urban ecology issues perfectly matched the overall profile both nationally and locally (Table 6.4 Sections A and B). Nor did the repertoires of national and local protest about most other issues exhibit marked differences. Transport issues, for example, displayed a combination of conventional and confrontational techniques (both above the population average).

Actions on other issues differed quite remarkably. The small number of protests concerning energy was largely confrontational both at the national and local level (the legacy of the anti-nuclear movement was still apparent in the 1990s, even though it was much diminished since the 1980s). However, while national initiatives combined confrontation with demonstrative and radical techniques, local actions also included a substantial proportion of conventional actions. Animal rights and anti-hunting initiatives that made the national news were more radical and more demonstrative than those reported in the local news (probably a reflection of the greater accessibility of local news sections, coupled with the modest appeal of those issues to the national media, in the absence of confrontational actions). Nature protection activities were more demonstrative at the local level, possibly reflecting a model of active, participatory local democracy, while they were either more conventional or more confrontational at the national level.

ENVIRONMENTAL ORGANIZATIONS IN PROTEST EVENTS

What was the profile of actors promoting environmental protest? First, reports of a sizable minority of events mentioned no organizations (20 per cent at the national level, 23 per cent at the local level: Table 6.5 Sections A and B). When organizations were reported, four-fifths of those mentioned were formal

TABLE 6.4. *Issues and the forms of environmental protests in Italy (national and local data)*

	Conventional (%)	Demonstrative (%)	Confrontational (%)	Attack on property (%)	Violence (%)	All forms (%)	All forms (N)
A. National data							
Nature conservation	78.1	40.6	12.5	0	0	9.8	32
Pollution, urban and industrial	59.2	38	14.6	2.3	8.5	65.5	213
Energy	21.4	50	28.6	7.1	14.3	4.3	14
Animal welfare and hunting	66.7	31.8	7.6	7.6	3.0	20.3	66
Transport	72.7	9.1	18.2	0	0	3.4	11
Environmentally friendly	71.4	42.9	0	0	0	4.3	14
All issues (%)	60.6	37.2	13.5	3.4	6.8		
N	197	121	44	11	22		325
B. Local data							
Nature conservation	57.3	52.4	2.9	0	0	16.5	103
Pollution, urban and industrial	69.3	35.3	11.9	0.2	0.7	65.9	411
Energy	37.5	12.5	50	0	0	1.3	8
Animal welfare and hunting	58.7	48	8.0	0	0	12.0	75
Transport	78.7	24.5	14.9	1.1	0.9	15.1	94
Environmentally friendly	88.2	17.6	5.9	0	0	2.7	17
All issues (%)	67.3	37.0	11.2	0.3	0.5		
N	420	231	70	2	3		

Note: Percentage of events involving each issue that involves a form of action. Percentages do not sum to 100 because for each protest up to 2 issues and 4 forms could be recorded.

TABLE 6.5. *Organizations involved in environmental protests in Italy by year (national and local data)*

	1988	1989	1990	1991	1992	1993	1994	1995	1996	1997	%	N
A. National data												
Party	17	19	7	4	1	0	4	4	2	0	22.7	59
Union	8	0	0	0	0	0	0	1	0	0	3.5	9
Business/industry	7	0	1	0	0	1	2	0	0	0	4.2	11
Formal environmental group	23	20	32	10	15	14	29	54	12	9	83.8	218
Informal environmental group	2	2	2	2	2	0	0	3	4	0	6.5	17
Network groups	4	6	5	0	0	0	0	0	0	0	5.8	15
Generic environmental	9	6	2	0	0	0	0	2	0	0	7.3	19
Public interest group	3	1	2	0	0	1	0	0	0	0	2.7	7
Other named organizations	2	2	0	2	0	1	4	1	0	0	4.6	12
% of protests involving named organization	19.2	12.3	13.8	5.0	6.5	5.4	11.5	17.3	5.4	3.5		
Total *N* of events	50	32	36	13	17	14	30	45	14	9		
B. Local data												
Party	21	16	4	12	16	8	10	10	4	4	21.3	105
Union	1	4	0	1	0	0	1	0	1	0	1.6	8
Business/industry	1	1	3	1	3	0	2	3	1	3	3.7	18
Formal environmental group	37	42	16	51	33	37	58	58	47	44	86.0	423
Informal environmental group	25	24	23	19	12	6	20	12	4	11	31.7	156
Network groups	3	2	2	1	4	0	2	5	4	2	5.1	25
Generic environmental	2	3	1	0	1	1	3	1	0	1	2.6	13
Public interest group	0	0	1	0	1	0	1	2	0	2	1.4	7
Other named organizations	1	3	1	1	1	1	1	0	0	4	2.6	13
% of protests involving named organization	10.6	12.0	6.3	10.0	8.3	8.3	12.4	14.4	9.8	7.9		
Total *N* of events	52	59	31	49	41	41	61	71	48	39		

environmental organizations. Other environmental groups with a more informal structure played a role in about one-fifth of national events, while non-environmental organizations (parties and, on a much smaller scale, interest groups and other political organizations) were reported in about a third. Locally, the presence of the latter was only slightly smaller, while informal environmental groups (present in about 40 per cent of local protests) were much more prominent than at the national level.

If we take into account that in all likelihood the events for which no organizations were reported were promoted by informal groups with no clear environmental profile, and that in less than 10 per cent of events were both environmental and non-environmental actors reported to be involved, the overall picture changes slightly. A rough estimate suggests that formal environmental organizations were present in a majority (about 60 per cent) of all events, informal environmental groups in about a quarter, unspecified (but presumably informal) groups in another 20 per cent, and traditional political organizations, independently of environmental organizations, in about 15 per cent. While confirming the massive involvement of formal environmental organizations in the campaigns, this evidence also suggests that environmental protest was by no means restricted to specifically environmental actors; other actors also played a far from marginal, and largely autonomous, role.

The involvement of the various actors in protests seems to have changed drastically during the decade. The role of political parties and unions was particularly pronounced in the first two years, when environmental protest was at its highest ever point in the country (Giugni 1999), and in general was higher in the first than in the second part of the decade. Formal environmental groups, already very important in the late 1980s, became dominant by the end of the decade at both the national and local levels. Trends diverged, however, in respect of less formalized environmental actors. Nationally, we register a pronounced reduction in the relevance of both networks of environmental organizations and informal environmental groups. The incidence of the former was above the average in four of the five early years, and correspondingly below the average in four of the remaining years. The presence of informal groups was even more impressively biased towards the early years, when it was regularly above the average. Informal groups also were less active in local protests at the end of the decade, even though their decline there was less pronounced. However, networks of groups were evenly present across the decade.

How are we to account for this shift in the weight of different organizational types? It is tempting to suggest that formal organizations with a clear environmental identity secured the continuity of activities even when the movement's capacity to mobilize on a national scale was reduced, as in the late 1990s. Indeed, our evidence suggests that formal organizations increased their presence in environmental initiatives in the late 1990s. This also applies to local mobilizations, which maintained their intensity as the 1990s progressed. Although one might have expected the role of informal environmental groups and even of 'spontaneous' protests to be highest at the end of the decade, precisely as a consequence of the spread of local action, formal organizations were in fact also massively present in local initiatives.

The decline in the reported presence of non-environmental actors also deserves attention. Again, this cannot be attributed to a global reduction in the intensity of protest activities. However, the consolidation of environmental issues and their 'normalization', also reflected in the relegation of most environmental news to the local pages of newspapers, suggests that there might have been a transition from a situation of relative fluidity to a situation of relative stability in the representation of issues. In the late 1980s to early 1990s, actors with different profiles may have been tempted to engage in competition for control of issues. However, as environmental actors consolidated, and as environmental issues strengthened their profile and became associated with a distinct policy area, other actors may gradually have lost their profile as relevant players in environmental politics.

Was there a Movement? Patterns of Inter-organizational Cooperation

We have movements when sustained networking (alliances, overlapping memberships, etc.) and mutual recognition bind actors promoting collective action on specific issues to one another (Diani 1992). For the purpose of reconstructing the networks, protest event analysis only offers us information about the co-presence of organizations at certain events. It tells us nothing about shared memberships, identities, or those inter-organizational exchanges such as information sharing or informal consultation that do not take a public form. This is also an area where the accuracy of reporting is most essential and may affect results. What follows is therefore a very tentative reconstruction of flows of exchanges based on the limited number of events that attracted media attention.

The large majority of events were promoted by one actor, or at least, it was associated with a single specific actor in media reports. In only one-fifth of events, both locally and nationally, was the presence of more than one organization reported. Our data partially support the expectation that jointly promoted events may be more frequent in years of heightened contention, due to the greater effervescence of the period and the resulting feelings of broader collective solidarity. At the national level, events reportedly involving more than one organization were grossly below the average in two calm periods—1992–3 and 1997. At the local level, by contrast, they were less present in the second half of the period, and were at their lowest in the 1995–6 peak. This might well be revealing of the difference between national and local politics, with the latter more focused on specific issues (Table 6.6 Sections A and B). All in all, however, the frequency of networking—or at least, of reports indicative of networking—showed no clear trends.

This is supported by evidence about specific organizations and their level of involvement in collaborations (Table 6.7 Sections A and B). Notwithstanding

TABLE 6.6. *Interactions among organizations in environmental protests in Italy (national and local data) (percentages)*

	1988	1989	1990	1991	1992	1993	1994	1995	1996	1997	1988–97
A. National data											
Events with more than one organization	17.9	22.9	17.3	23.5	5.6	17.6	22.6	32.7	21.4	11.1	21.0
Formal environmental organizations and non-environmental organizations	9.0	2.1	1.7	5.9	0	5.9	9.7	3.6	21.4	0	6.4
Formal and informal environmental organizations	21.5	0	0	0	0	0	0	1.8	0	0	0.6
Environmental and non-environmental organizations	9.0	10.4	9.6	5.9	0	5.9	9.7	3.6	21.4	0	7.9
Environmental and other movement organizations	1.5	8.3	1.7	5.9	0	0	6.5	1.8	21.4	0	4.9
Total N of events	67	48	52	17	18	17	31	55	14	9	
B. Local data											
Events with more than one organization	22.1	19.2	21.3	25.0	22.7	15.4	23.1	12.5	13.5	29.4	19.9
Formal environmental organizations and non-environmental organizations	6.5	6.8	6.4	9.4	15.9	1.9	8.7	5.7	2.7	9.8	7.0
Formal and informal environmental organizations	5.2	5.5	6.4	7.8	6.8	3.8	1.2	3.4	0	5.9	5.0
Environmental and non-environmental organizations	9.1	9.6	6.4	9.4	15.9	3.8	11.6	5.7	2.7	9.8	8.1
Environmental and other movement organizations	7.8	5.5	2.1	7.8	9.1	3.8	5.8	2.3	1.4	3.9	4.9
Total N of events	77	73	47	64	44	52	69	88	74	51	

Note: 'Environmental organization' without further specification records both specific formal and informal environmental groups, and events in which the generic presence of environmental actors was reported.

TABLE 6.7. *The interaction among groups
named in reports of environmental protests in
Italy (national and local data)*

	Acting alone (N)	Acting with others (N)
A. National data		
Verdi	16	13
Greenpeace	20	17
Italia Nostra	5	3
Lac	0	1
Lav	12	4
Legambiente	41	33
LIPU	7	3
WWF	17	18
B. Local data		
Verdi	25	24
Greenpeace	8	3
Italia Nostra	11	15
Lac	4	3
Lav	10	6
Legambiente	90	71
LIPU	6	12
WWF	68	50

some differences between the national and the local data, the number of events in which the most visible organizations are recorded as the only actor tends to be slightly higher than that of events that they appear to co-promote with other (formal or informal) actors. Interestingly, despite its reputation as an organization reluctant to engage in alliances, the Italian branch of Greenpeace seems to have taken part in joint efforts just as frequently as did the other major players. The only exceptions to this pattern, at least on the national level, are the animal rights groups LAV and LIPU, which in over 70 per cent of protests acted alone, probably due to their greater issue specialization.

If we consider the distribution of the several types of network linkages over time, overall differences between the early and the late years of the decade do not seem very pronounced. Different types of relationship are, however, unevenly present over the period. At the local level, alliances between environmental and non-environmental organizations (8 per cent of events) tended to be above the average in the early years, and below in the later years (particularly in 1995–6). The same applies to linkages between environmentalists and movement organizations in other areas. At the national level, there was no pattern at all, as contacts tended to fluctuate around the average. Altogether, the specificity of the environmental movement as a self-contained sector of collective action seems if anything to have increased over the decade. This impression is also supported by a network diagram, which records only those cases in which two organizations were reported as participating in the same events three or more times (Fig. 6.7). Data show the most visible alliances within the sector to be partially segmented, with multi-issue and pragmatic WWF acting as a bridge between conservation groups such as Italia Nostra and LIPU, while a more tightly integrated political ecology sector included Legambiente, the Verdi (Greens), and Greenpeace. In the late 1980s one can also find significant alliances between the main trade unions, CGIL-CISL-UIL, on the one hand, and left-wing political parties PCI and Democrazia Proletaria (DP) on the other. No actor in either clique, however, appears to have established recurrent collaboration with major environmental groups, at least in the most visible and reported events.

Available newspaper reports trace a picture of the movement network that differs remarkably from the one that emerged from in-depth analysis of the field and direct interviews with environmental groups. While the data presented in Fig. 6.7 portray a movement still largely structured along the conservation versus political ecology dimension, research in the late 1980s in Milan and Rome (Farro 1991;

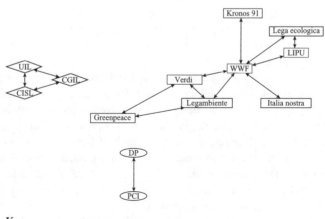

Key

CISL   Italian Confederation of Labour Unions
CGIL   General Italian Labour Confederation
DP   Proletarian Democracy
LIPU   Italian League for the Protection of Birds
PCI   Italian Communist Party
UIL   Italian Labour Union
Verdi Green Party
WWF   World Wide Fund for Nature

FIG. 6.7. *Networks of groups named in reports of environmental protests in Italy (1988–97) (national data)*

Diani 1995: ch. 6) demonstrated a much greater degree of integration and collaboration among the major organizations. One can make sense of this discrepancy by suggesting that newspaper reports are likely to identify multiple organizations in a single event only when all organizations have played a visible public role in its promotion. On the other hand, reporters may not be so reliable in their identification of cases in which one organization supports an initiative originally promoted by another group. This latter type of collaboration is much better captured by fieldwork observation and interviews. While the main movement organizations were strongly integrated in terms of day-to-day consultation and collaboration, they were still perceived as related to more traditional distinctions when it came to the promotion of major public events.

The Major Organizations

Legambiente's widely accepted claim to be the most important Italian environmental organization is supported by press reports, which recorded its presence in about one quarter of events (23 per cent of national and 25 per cent of local actions; see Table 6.8 Sections A and B). WWF's presence was considerable in nationally reported events, but was more pronounced in local events (11 per cent versus 18 per cent). The Greens fluctuated at around 8 per cent. Other prominent groups such as Greenpeace, Italia Nostra, and animal rights groups, LIPU and LAV, received more limited coverage. All in all, the correspondence between national and local data is striking, with the obvious exception of Greenpeace, which does not operate diffusely through local chapters. Differences in this ranking may be partially due to the differential public relations capacity of different organizations. Legambiente, for example, has been very proactive in this respect and has established particularly good links to the publishing group which also owns *la Repubblica*. The weekly *l'Espresso* actually sponsors the *Goletta Verde* initiatives, monitoring the quality of Italian seas and shores every summer. As a result, they might be expected to get particularly good coverage from *la Repubblica*. However, the global visibility of Greenpeace and its notorious focus on media-oriented campaigning do not seem to have secured it overwhelming media coverage.

Differences in the specific issues addressed, and in their perception by media operators, may also have affected degrees of coverage. Groups focusing on educational activities, such as Italia Nostra, or on classic issues such as animal rights (LIPU or LAV), are likely to be disadvantaged in terms of media attention. Sometimes, coverage may be a combination of strong linkages to the media and the capacity or willingness to address marketable, hotly debated public issues. All in all, however, the rankings presented in Table 6.8 are not a simple reflection of public relations strategies or shifting media attention. There is indeed an impressive correlation between these figures and the centrality of environmental

TABLE 6.8. *Environmental protests in Italy involving leading groups by year (national and local data)*

	1988	1989	1990	1991	1992	1993	1994	1995	1996	1997	%	N
A. National data												
Verdi	6	3	6	3	1	0	4	3	3	0	8.8	29
Greenpeace	1	0	2	1	1	4	4	21	3	0	11.3	37
Italia Nostra	2	3	0	1	1	0	1	0	0	0	2.4	8
Lac	0	0	1	0	0	0	0	0	0	0	0.3	1
Lav	2	1	4	1	1	4	2	0	1	0	4.9	16
Legambiente	7	6	6	1	5	3	12	25	4	5	22.6	74
LIPU	2	0	4	0	0	0	2	0	2	1	3.0	10
WWF	4	5	6	3	2	2	5	4	1	2	10.7	35
% of all protests	20.4	14.6	15.9	5.2	5.5	5.2	9.5	16.8	4.3	2.7		
Total N of events	67	48	52	17	18	17	31	55	14	9		
B. Local data												
Verdi	7	4	1	7	5	6	7	9	1	2	7.7	49
Greenpeace	0	0	1	0	0	2	2	4	1	1	1.7	11
Italia Nostra	7	3	0	6	2	2	5	0	1	0	4.1	26
Lac	3	0	0	2	0	0	0	1	1	0	1.1	7
Lav	1	2	0	7	1	1	0	2	1	1	2.5	16
Legambiente	9	12	5	13	17	17	22	32	22	12	25.2	161
LIPU	1	2	1	5	1	1	2	1	0	4	2.8	18
WWF	12	12	7	12	7	8	20	11	15	14	18.5	118
% of all protests	12.1	11.4	7.4	10.0	6.9	8.1	10.8	13.8	11.6	8.0		
Total N of events	77	73	47	64	44	52	69	88	74	51		

organizations in movement networks, according to data collected in Milan (Diani 1995) and at the national level (Farro 1991) in the 1980s. Organizations that were most frequently mentioned by other groups in the movement as regular allies or partners were also mentioned most frequently as promoters of actions in news-paper reports.

Although formal organizations appeared in general to play a greater role in the second part of the decade, the presence of specific organizations in the events varied from year to year. Only WWF had a fairly evenly distributed presence across the whole decade, both nationally and locally. In contrast, Legambiente emerged as the dominant force in Italian environmentalism only since 1992. In earlier years, it was already important, but in the same league as WWF or the Greens. Locally, Legambiente was also stronger at the end of the decade than at the start, but peaked in 1992–5.

The presence of other groups was more uneven. The Greens were more involved in protest activities prior to their assumption of governmental respons-ibilities in 1996, even though this is based on limited evidence and the fall is strik-ing only at the local level. Greenpeace activities were most frequently reported in 1993–5, with a peak in 1995, corresponding to protests spurred by Mururoa. Bird protection group LIPU also received more attention in the media in some years than in others, particularly in 1991 (locally) and 1997. The same applies to anti-vivisection group LAV, whose activities were most visible in 1991 (local) and 1993 (national). All in all, no groups apart from WWF and Legambiente were consistently reported to be involved in campaigning activities. It remains to be seen whether this was due to shifts in media attention, or to these groups' unwill-ingness or inability to conduct more continuous and sustained initiatives (although such an explanation could not account for the similar pattern in reports of Greenpeace actions).

One common trait of movement institutionalization is the deepening of the division of labour among organizations, as well as, more broadly, the consolidation of specific styles of action, commonly associated with specific organizations, and the emergence of distinctive organizational identities and profiles. The repertoire adopted by the major Italian environmental organizations is overwhelmingly based on conventional forms of action (Table 6.9 Sections A and B). In none of the twenty-five events in which violence was used, and in only one of the thirteen events in which property was attacked (both local and national data), was the pres-ence of a major group reported (that one event involving Greenpeace). Overall, most major organizations were disproportionately involved in events where a conventional repertoire of action (lobbying, press conferences, court litigation, public meetings, etc.) was adopted. Groups like Legambiente and WWF were less and less frequently mentioned as repertoires shifted from conventional through demonstrative action to confrontational action. Greenpeace was the only group to be over-represented in demonstrative actions (21 per cent), but not particularly so in confrontational events (unsurprisingly, given its professional and non-participatory

TABLE 6.9. *Groups and the forms of environmental protest in Italy (national and local data)*

	Conventional	Demonstrative	Confrontational	Attacks on property	Violence	%	N
A. National data							
Verdi	22	11	1	0	0	8.8	29
Greenpeace	19	25	1	1	0	11.3	37
Italia Nostra	8	1	0	0	0	2.4	8
Lac	1	0	0	0	0	0.3	1
Lav	12	4	2	0	0	4.9	16
Legambiente	52	30	2	0	0	22.6	74
LIPU	7	3	0	0	0	3.0	10
WWF	29	14	2	0	0	10.2	35
% of all protests	60.6	37.2	13.5	3.4	6.8		
Total N of events	197	121	44	11	22		
B. Local data							
Verdi	33	14	8	0	0	7.7	49
Greenpeace	5	6	1	0	0	1.7	11
Italia Nostra	25	5	2	0	0	4.1	26
Lac	4	4	1	0	0	1.1	7
Lav	9	7	1	0	0	2.5	16
Legambiente	128	45	7	0	0	25.2	161
LIPU	17	2	1	0	0	2.8	18
WWF	92	33	5	0	0	18.5	118
% of all protests	67.3	37.0	11.2	0.3	0.5		
Total N of events	420	231	70	2	3		

nature, and its reliance on symbolic disruption). The Verdi (Greens) were the only group to adopt a balanced repertoire of conventional and confrontational action, especially at the local level—an accurate reflection of both their deep roots in the Italian New Left and their direct involvement in representative roles.

Is it possible to identify any sort of 'problem ownership'? Only partially (see Table 6.10 Sections A and B). On the one hand, certain organizations were more than proportionally involved in the issues to which one would expect them to pay specific attention. Accordingly, the core animal rights groups were the dominant players in their area. The Greens were particularly involved in energy issues, consistently with the presence in their ranks of many former leaders of the Italian anti-nuclear movement. Nature conservation was mainly the preserve of WWF, which was also very active in animal issues. Protests concerning pollution, other urban issues, and transport attracted disproportionate attention from the Verdi (Greens) and Legambiente nationally, and from WWF at the local level (an illustration of how local branches may mobilize on issues that are not so strongly associated with the group at the national level). At the same time, however, the scope of issues covered by each organization was quite broad. With the exception of animal rights groups, all the major organizations showed significant levels of attention for the whole range of issues. In some cases, the involvement was in areas marginal to their conventional profile, as Legambiente's attention to nature conservation and WWF's interest in transport-related issues illustrate. Even LIPU extended its action beyond the animal issue domain. As in the case of repertoires, the Greens showed the most balanced and heterogeneous profile.

The presence of the major environmental organizations taken as a whole also varied considerably across different issues. In particular, while they were crucial promoters in events addressing nature conservation and animal rights issues, their presence in events broadly related to urban ecology themes was far less systematic. Independent organizations, often with an informal structure and loose ties to the major players in environmental politics, substantially contributed to mobilizations on those issues. Their role was particularly conspicuous at the local level, but by no means restricted to it.

CONCLUSIONS

The 1990s undoubtedly saw a reduction in the number of protest events reported in the national news. The fall in demonstrations of some size—those most likely to be reported—also suggests some 'real' decrease in protest. However, it would be excessive to take this as evidence of a decline of environmentalism. On the one hand, the reduced novelty of local environmental actions may partially account for the diminution in national reports (as recorded by local news, protest was still buoyant). On the other hand, the fall in protests reflected not so much a crisis as a shift in environmental activities towards voluntary action campaigns and

TABLE 6.10. *Groups and the issues of environmental protest in Italy (national and local data)*

	Nature conservation	Pollution, urban and industrial	Energy	Animal welfare and hunting	Transport	Alternative production	%	N
A. National data								
Verdi	3	19	3	1	2	1	8.8	29
Greenpeace	2	30	1	4	0	0	11.3	37
Italia Nostra	3	3	1	0	1	0	2.4	8
Lac	0	0	0	1	0	0	0.3	1
Lav	0	0	0	18	0	0	4.9	16
Legambiente	6	66	2	1	4	3	22.6	74
LIPU	2	0	0	9	0	0	3.0	10
WWF	12	15	1	8	1	3	10.7	35
% of all protests	9.8	65.5	4.3	20.3	3.4	4.3		
Total N of events	32	213	14	66	11	14		
B. Local data								
Verdi	8	23	2	9	7	1	7.7	49
Greenpeace	1	7	1	1	1	0	1.7	11
Italia Nostra	10	15	0	1	2	1	4.1	26
Lac	1	0	0	7	0	0	1.1	7
Lav	0	0	0	16	0	0	2.5	16
Legambiente	30	123	0	9	18	8	25.2	161
LIPU	1	0	0	14	1	1	2.8	18
WWF	38	53	1	17	20	2	18.5	118
% of all protests	16.5	65.9	1.3	12.0	15.1	2.7		
Total N of events	103	411	8	75	94	17		

lobbying. The overall presence of environmental organizations in the media showed no signs of decline over the decade; if anything, it seems to have increased by comparison with 1988.[9]

Other signs of institutionalization may be found in the increasing weight in the national news of activities of national scope located in Rome, and in the changes in the composition of the actors promoting the initiatives. At the peak of activity in 1988–9, the issue attracted multiple actors, as a considerable proportion of non-environmental actors, also competing for 'ownership' of the issue, were involved in initiatives. Their presence fell later and thereafter remained at low levels, while the most formal among environmental organizations gradually came to play a dominant role. There seems to be a clear hierarchy among them, with Legambiente leading and WWF coming a close second (especially in local reports). WWF was a constant presence over the decade, whereas other organizations (e.g. Italia Nostra) became less visible, whilst the profiles of others (in particular, Legambiente) grew strongly. Although the initiatives of local groups remained very lively throughout the decade, there seemed to be an overall move from a social movement dynamic towards the consolidation of a specific sector of public interest groups.

On the other hand, division of labour among major organizations was far from complete. Specific groups were strongly associated with distinctive areas of activity (LIPU et al. on animals, WWF on nature protection, Legambiente on urban ecology in general), but overall each organization tended to cover a multiplicity of issues. In general, environmental activism was driven mainly by urban ecology themes. These were not only dominant in general, but tended to be overwhelmingly present at phases of intense contention, while nature and animal rights tended to play a lesser, but more consistent role (also a sign of their greater institutionalization). We may find a similar relationship between the intensity of contention and the visibility of local issues, which was greater at times of high contention. There was also an increase in mobilization issues with a global dimension. Whether this reflects a proper trend towards the globalization of environmental politics remains to be seen, even though the explosion of anti-globalization campaigns since 1999 points towards broader developments in that direction. Political dynamics remained largely within national confines, as the targets of action were overwhelmingly local or national, but that is not surprising and hardly counts as counter-evidence.

The characteristics of protest events are broadly, but not entirely, consistent with the institutionalization argument. On the one hand, activities were overwhelmingly conventional, and major environmental organizations refrained even from confrontation (*pace* the odd example involving Greenpeace), let alone more radical actions. On the other hand, there was no correlation between the intensity of confrontational and/or radical protest and the intensity of activity as recorded in the media. In terms of its repertoire of action, the environmental sector was already institutionalized at the peak of its activity in the late 1980s (see also Diani 1995).

Italian environmental action in 1988–97 only partially evokes the image of a movement engaging in sustained, large-scale collective challenges to authorities. Especially at the national level, environmental action appears instead as something promoted by a set of public interest groups, mostly institutionalized in their forms of action, and whose control over the issues is less and less challenged by other political actors such as parties or unions. It is important to look at movements not as self-contained sets of actors and events but in relation to the broader characteristics of collective action at specific points in time. If considered from the perspective of the major protest cycle that developed between the 1960s and 1970s (Tarrow 1989), or even of the longer term evolution of protest activities on eco-pacifist issues from 1975–95 (Giugni 1999), the evolution of environmental activity in Italy during the 1990s hardly suggests a protest cycle dynamic. Rather, it resembles a series of fluctuations in the profile of an overwhelmingly institutionalized sector of collective action.

NOTES

1. Diani (1990, 1995) and Donati (1996) provide an analytical reconstruction of developments in Italian environmentalism; on a more anecdoctal level, see Poggio (1996).
2. Between 1983 and 1988, in particular, membership in six major organizations— Legambiente, Italia Nostra, World Wide Fund for Nature (WWF), animal rights groups LIPU (birds protection), LAC (anti-hunting), and LAV (anti-vivisection)—had increased by 250% (Diani 1995: 36).
3. Our empirical evidence comes from reports in the national news sections of major Italian daily *la Repubblica*. We sampled 50% of the total issues, evenly distributed across the days of the week. Altogether, we identified 328 events of environmental protest of national relevance. We supplemented this with data from the local news covering the provinces of Milan, Florence, and Naples. Using the same sampling criteria as for the national dataset, we identified 313 events in Milan and 222 in Florence (in both cases from the local sections of *la Repubblica)*, and 168 in Naples (from the local news section of Neapolitan daily *Il Mattino*).
4. Similarly, Kriesi et al. (1995: 61–81) relate the fall in new social movement protest in France in the early 1980s to the Left's accession to power.
5. See Fig. 6.1 and Giugni (1999). The number of events recorded in *Corriere* is actually higher than in *Repubblica*, but this is due to the fact that articles in both the national and the local (Milan and Lombardy) sections of the paper were included, and the latter sections actually seem to report most of the articles. Unfortunately, Giugni's data do not differentiate between reports in the national sections and those in the local sections. However, another analysis of social conflict in Italy, based on a 100% coverage of *Corriere della Sera* but restricted to 1996, identified nine environmental conflicts for that year reported in the national news, and thirty-one events in the local news (Clementi 1997: 405 and personal communication to the authors).
6. These events are usually reported in 'summary reports', that is, reports summarizing in a single article a whole set of related but geographically and possibly temporally

scattered initiatives. Although we exclude them from the analysis due to their distorting effect, such reports are still worth mentioning for the sake of a more complete picture. On environmentalism and voluntary action, see Osti (1998).

7. Events of national relevance in Rome were classified under a separate 'Rome' heading, while local protests in Rome were included in the south category. Our partition reflects a classic model of analysis of Italy's territorial differences (Bagnasco 1977).

8. The Italian media's preference for activities with direct, clear impact upon major political actors and institutions might also account for these modest figures.

9. For example, although in 1997 only 9 protest events were detected from 50% of issues of *la Repubblica*, Legambiente was mentioned in 107 articles out of 38,431 articles available in the paper's electronic archive, while WWF appeared in 81. Ten years earlier, when environmental protest was at its most visible, WWF had secured 61 mentions. In 1994, when Legambiente adopted its current name, the organization was mentioned 103 times, while WWF appeared a record 140 times. (Legambiente used to be called Lega per l'Ambiente. Problems with the search functions in *la Repubblica*'s archive made it impossible for us easily to trace its presence in earlier years.)

7

Spain

Manuel Jiménez

The last decade of the twentieth century was a particularly interesting period for environmental politics in Spain. First, economic growth and higher consumption significantly intensified pressure on the environment, its biodiversity, and the capacity for renewal of natural resources. Second, environmental awareness increased and environmental groups achieved a significant level of organizational consolidation and social and political recognition. Third, during this period, environmental policy evolved from a reactive to a sectoral approach to environmental problems. As a result of the combination of these processes, this decade has seen the incipient configuration of a national environmental policy subsystem within the Spanish political system. The creation of the Ministry of the Environment in 1996 confirmed the increasing political significance of environmental issues.

The rapid transformation of the Spanish landscape that began at least 30 years ago affects almost the entire country. Between 1985 and 1995, the coverage of the highway system quadrupled and is comparable to that of France or Italy and relatively more developed than that of Britain or Japan (Estevan and Sanz 1996).[1] The physical landscape has been transformed by large-scale agricultural change, notably the move away from traditional production methods and crops in favour of intensive production on newly irrigated land (Martín and García 1996). This newly irrigated farmland is often concentrated in the dry south and east of the country where attempts have been made to resolve the shortage of water by diverting rivers and regulating water flows by means of numerous dams.[2] In coastal areas, water deficits and 'desertification' are also the result of tourist developments which were curbed but not halted by the 1988 Coastal Law. Moreover, the tourist industry has evolved towards a model based on residential housing in coastal areas and increasingly in rural areas, equipped with recreational infrastructure such as golf courses and yachting marinas which have enormous environmental impact (Santamarta 1998).

I thank Chris Rootes and Andrew Richards for their comments. I am also grateful to Pilar Lara for her assistance in reading and selecting newspaper reports and to Justin Byrne for revising the text.

The subordination of industrial policy to governments' macroeconomic goals in a context of high unemployment has prevented wholesale clean-up of outdated polluting industries (Castañer 1998), and economic viability has often been achieved at the cost of ignoring even basic environmental measures. The discourse that posits a conflict between environmental protection and employment (through factory closures or the loss of potential foreign investment) has proved more impregnable here than in any other sector.

Environmental demands have run up against the obstacle of a dominant political discourse centred on modernization. In this paradigm, environmental deterioration has been identified as the price to be paid for economic prosperity, for 'catching up' with Europe. This has reduced the opportunities for environmentalists to find allies in the political arena as well as to mobilize resources within society. However, environmental awareness has progressively increased (Gómez and Paniagua 1996: 137–8). Within this broad trend, the environmental problems that Spaniards consider to be most urgent are those that they perceive as affecting them most directly or whose impact is most visible, as in the case of water shortages and forest fires (CIS 1999). At the same time, there has been an expansion in the number and membership of environmental groups, above all at the local level.[3] Both these trends—the growth in environmental awareness and in ecologist groups—have been marked by one of the main features of environmental protest: its localism.

The extent and nature of environmental protest is also related to the opportunities for participation offered by the political context. Many of the constitutional provisions referring to citizens' participation have been progressively developed within the context of democratic consolidation. However, the impact of these democratic reforms has been limited by the prevalence of a conception of political participation as something restricted to voting in elections. Decentralization of political power and responsibility (including the assumption of environmental powers by regional governments) has been one of the main factors contributing to the enhancement of the democratic features of the political system. While the various regional administrations have usually shared and reproduced the restricted conception of citizens' right to participate that is found at the national level, the decentralization process has increased the potential points of access for hitherto excluded actors.

It is at the policy level, however, that we can best analyse the changing political conditions that have shaped environmental protest. Over the course of the last decade, the main features of environmental policy have changed significantly. Spanish integration into the European community since 1986 has been the major stimulus for the institutionalization of environmental policy. The enforcement of European environmental policy has progressed significantly since Maastricht, the reform of the regional structural funds, and the creation of new cohesion funds with an overt environmental dimension (Font 2001). Moreover, the need to put environmental measures into practice has often been the main source of conflicts (as exemplified by the construction of waste facilities).

The slow and partial institutionalization of environmental policy in Spain reflects the strength of the resistance to the introduction of the environment into the state agenda. The impact of historical dependency in the configuration of policies and in policy networks since democratization has been uneven (Lancaster 1989; Subirats and Gomà 1998); certain critical areas for environmental demands have remained closed to new actors and opaque to the general public. Consequently, the integration of the environment into the different policy areas has been uneven, due to the varying degrees of resistance encountered in what is, overall, an adverse political context.

Nevertheless, generally speaking, the formal incorporation of the environment into the national policy agenda (a process in which environmental protests have played an important role) has entailed the creation or upgrading of environmental departments as well as the opening up of formal and informal environmental arena to the participation of diverse sectors involved in the environmental policy process.[4] As the environmental administration gains powers and autonomy within the state structure, it generates its own policy public, including environmental organizations, thereby configuring a policy subsystem.[5] There was, then, in the mid-1990s a more favourable context for environmental demands, coinciding with the first signs of both the constitution of an area of environmental politics and the process of organizational consolidation of the Spanish environmental movement (Jiménez 1999*a*, 2000, 2002).

This chapter analyses environmental protest events reported in *El País* between 1988 and 1997. The following analysis is divided into four parts. The first introduces the protest event data, briefly outlines the characteristics of the source and the problems of selection bias confronted by media event analysis, and comments on the evolution over time of the level of protest and volume of participants. The second section deals with the issues that have proved most conflictual during these 10 years, while the third focuses on the main features of the political repertoire of protesters and the scenarios of conflicts. In the final section, the actors are introduced into the analysis. Here special attention is paid to the main characteristics of the organizational network of protests, and the features of the leading environmental movement organizations (EMOs).

THE EXTENT OF ENVIRONMENTAL PROTEST

El País was chosen as the source of data for this analysis because of its quality, stability over time, and the territorial scope of its coverage.[6] Nonetheless, despite the paper's early interest in the subject, since the 1980s it has not paid particularly great attention to the environment.[7] Although it has been identified as covering demonstrations and protests more comprehensively than its rivals *ABC* or *El Mundo* (Adell 1997: 209), in the case of environmental politics, *El País* is usually more orientated to established politics and institutional sources of information.[8]

Despite this potentially weaker sensitivity towards environmental protests, *El País* is still the best choice for this analysis because the possible alternatives lack the necessary continuity (as in the case of *El Mundo*, published only since 1991), have greater territorial bias (as in the case of *La Vanguardia* which focuses on Cataluña), or were less rigorous (*ABC*).

Nine hundred and thirty-six protest events were identified in the 'Politics' and 'Society' sections of *El País* ('national data'). Another 2309 protest events were coded from the regional editions of Madrid, País Valenciano, and Andalucía, and from the 'Ciudades' section, (altogether, 'regional data').[9] Of the total of 3245 coded protest events, 234 were identified from summary reports—reports that provide succinct information about a large number of related events occurring in a given period of time or (less frequently) in different locations at the same time. As in the other chapters in this volume, the analysis presented here excludes summary reports and focuses on national data. However, regional data is also occasionally included.[10] Unless otherwise specified, the analysis developed here is based on the remaining 738 protest events reported in the national pages of *El País*.[11]

Selection Bias of El País in Environmental Protests Reports

Data on protest events drawn from a national newspaper account for only a small, and potentially unrepresentative, proportion of all environmental protest (Fillieule 1996). The selection bias of *El País* seems to be similar to that of other quality national dailies: its territorial coverage is uneven; it over-represents protests involving public order problems (violent incidents or large and persistent mobilizations); and it varies according to the prevailing national relevance of the issue (either because of its potential politicization, its topicality, or its novelty).[12]

Changes in the structure of a newspaper or in its staff may also modify its selection bias. Our research strategy has been designed to capture such changes and their potential impact on the selection bias of the data. To this end, we have employed interviews with environmental journalists working on *El País* and national–regional data comparisons,[13] and we have considered the influence of these biases when offering explanations of the evolution of protest.[14]

Bias in the reporting of protests is in part a product of the unequal distribution of the newspaper's resources, of local correspondents' variable interest in protests and/or the environment, and the fluidity of their contacts with environmental editors in Madrid. Most protests are local and are covered by local correspondents. To a large extent, the incorporation of local news into the national pages depends on the relationship between the local and the national journalists/sections, a relationship that is not equally fluid among all the various local sections/correspondents.[15]

Table 7.1 shows the distribution of the protest events reported in the national edition across the seventeen Spanish *Comunidades Autónomas* (CA), each CA's percentage of the total national population, and an index of representation calculated from the two previous parameters.

TABLE 7.1. *The territorial distribution of environmental protests in Spain (1988–97) compared with population*

Region	% of protest events	% of population[a]	Index of representation[b]
Navarra	8.2	1.3	6.2
Cantabria	3.9	1.3	2.9
Madrid	24.6	12.8	1.9
Castilla-La Mancha	7.1	4.2	1.7
Baleares	3.2	1.9	1.7
Aragón	3.8	3.1	1.2
Castilla y León	6.4	6.5	1.0
Pais Vasco	5.2	5.3	1.0
Galicia	6.1	6.9	0.9
Andalucía	13.8	17.9	0.8
Asturias	1.8	2.8	0.7
Extremadura	1.5	2.7	0.6
Cataluña	8.8	15.5	0.6
Canarias	1.7	4.2	0.4
Murcia	0.8	2.7	0.3
Comunidad Valenciana	2.9	10.0	0.3
La Rioja	0	0.7	0
Other	3	—	—
N	716	39,433,942	

Notes:
[a] Population figures from the 1991 CENSUS.
[b] Index obtained by dividing the number of protests by the number of expected protests from the ratio of the total number of events to total population; values above 1 indicate over-representation of an area in the data set; values below 1 indicate under-representation.

As expected, the number of recorded protest events is not proportional to population of the different CAs. Two factors contributed, for example, to the over-representation of Navarra: the participation of the terrorist organization ETA in a conflict over the Leizaran motorway in the early 1990s; and the local correspondent's particular interest in environment issues. The unusually active role of the local correspondent in León helps account for the over-representation of Castilla-León, where most reported protests took place in the province of León. The initiative of local correspondents is more decisive in those areas without regional editions. The centre–periphery dynamic of interactions is different in those CAs with a regional edition. In these cases, the national coverage of protests depends more on the initiative of the national editor and the degree of cooperation with regional editors. Regional editions act as filters preventing reports of events from reaching the national pages, since they are usually considered to be mainly of local interest and significance. This explains why all the CAs with their own edition, except Madrid, were under-represented in the national data, and why, in the case of Madrid, 90 per cent of reported protests were the result of its status as the national capital and seldom involved local problems, these latter being reported in the regional pages.[16] This bias should be taken into account when comparing among regions, but such a comparison is beyond the scope of this chapter.

Protest and Protesters over Time

Figure 7.1 shows the annual evolution of all protest events as well as of those reported only in the national edition, distinguishing, in both cases, events coded from summary reports.[17] The overall picture is one of increasing levels of protest over the course of the decade, with two peaks in mobilization: one at the turn of the decade, the other in the last year of the series. These patterns emerge more clearly when regional data are incorporated. Here the positive trend can be seen to be more consistent than it appears from national reports alone. The differences between the two data sets can be attributed to the greater selectivity of the national pages and the greater impact of issue agenda dynamics upon national reports. The concentration of 90 per cent of summary reports in the national edition and during what appears from the inclusive data to be the period of greatest mobilization can be interpreted as a journalistic strategy to report the increasing number of conflicts.[18]

The concentration of most of these protests in a period of just a few years is a potential source of distortion in the longitudinal analysis: the annual proportion of protest events derived from summary reports varied through the years from

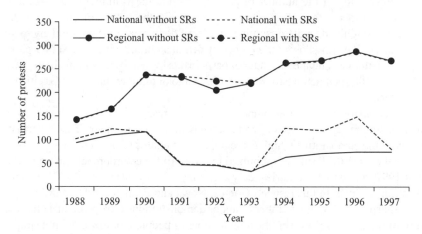

FIG. 7.1. *The evolution of environmental protest events in Spain (national and regional data, with and without summary reports (SRs))*

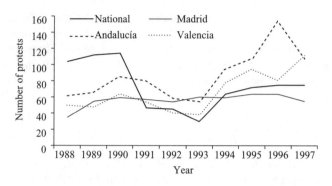

Fig. 7.2. *Environmental protests in Spain: Madrid, Andalucía, and Valencia compared*

zero to 50 per cent of all reported protests. For this reason they have been excluded from the analysis that follows (see note 18). Figure 7.2 compares the evolution of protests reported in the national and in the regional editions.

The comparison of national and regional data sheds further light on the evolution of environmental protests. First, the peaks seem to reflect protest activities of different kinds. While the 1989–90 peak is not perceptible in the regional data, the expansion of protests reflected in the national data for 1995–7 appears to be confirmed by the generalized increase in the three regions. Second, the comparison also moderates the downward trend in the number of events during the early 1990s, part of which can be attributed to the effect of the creation of the section 'Ciudades' (see notes 9 and 14). In all, these data suggest an increase in environmental protests over the course of the decade under consideration.

The evolution of the number of participants and the volume of mobilizations provides further information on basic changes in the nature of environmental protest during the decade. Assuming that large demonstrations are unlikely to go unreported, Fig. 7.3 shows the number of demonstrations with at least 500 participants (columns) and the total sum of participants by year (points in the line).[19] We identified 106 such demonstrations, in which a total of more than 425,000 citizens took part.

By comparison with the other countries represented in this volume, large demonstrations appear to have been relatively numerous in Spain. This is consistent with the comparatively high percentage of Spaniards (6 per cent) who, according to the 1993 ISPP survey, mobilized in favour of the environment between 1988 and 1992; among EU countries, only Germany (9 per cent) and Italy (7 per cent) outstripped Spain in this respect (Gómez, Noya, and Paniagua 1999: 108).

A sharp decline in the number of major demonstrations took place just after the turn of the decade. However, the total number of people mobilized did not simply evolve in line with the number of demonstrations. Although the total volume of protesters began to decrease in the early 1990s, the trend was broken in 1997, which saw a substantial increase. As a result, the two peaks in the number of protest events (1990 and 1997) (see Fig. 7.2) also showed the highest volume of participants in large demonstrations. However, whereas in 1997 there were a few very large demonstrations, the peak in 1990 saw a larger number of relatively smaller demonstrations.

It is possible then to identify some basic trends in the evolution of environmental protests over the course of the decade. First, the level of environmental protests increased between 1988 and 1997. This trend is even more apparent when regional data are taken into account. Second, the decreasing number of large demonstrations suggests a change in the type of protest, or rather, the fact that forms of protest other than demonstrations accounted for the increasing number of reported protests. It appears that large demonstrations decreased not only relatively but also in absolute numbers.[20]

This interpretation is borne out by a comparison of the two peaks in the number of protests (and in the number of participants in large demonstrations). The period 1988–90 saw a series of protests over environmental issues that for different reasons were nationally salient. These included anti-nuclear mobilizations (spurred on by the nuclear accident in Vandellós), the conflict over the Leizaran motorway (in which the participation of ETA resulted in fatalities), a tourist project in the Doñana national park, and the Ministry of Defence's project to establish an airforce testing ground in Anchuras. During the period 1995–7, there were fewer such nationally salient conflicts.

Therefore, as the regional data suggest, in the late 1990s the upwards trend in the number of protests suggests a generalized increase in environmental conflicts of varying intensity across Spain as whole. The extension of the organizational base of the environmental movement at the local level is surely associated with this trend of growing protest activity (Jiménez 2000, 2002). Furthermore, during the first peak, the relatively more centralized structure of *El País* made the national pages more permeable to regional protests. By contrast, the subsequent consolidation of the paper's regional structure has made the national pages less permeable to the same type of protests. This might in fact explain the sharp fall in number of demonstrations in the 1990s as seen in Fig. 7.3.

ISSUES OF CONTENTION

Currently, almost every policy issue has a potential environmental dimension. Many decision-making processes within different policy areas are susceptible to disruption by conflicts framed in environmental terms. In this section, the issues behind environmental protests between 1988 and 1997 are briefly analysed. The trends noted are examined in the evolving contexts of the diverse policy areas in which these demands are inserted, and we consider the extent to which reported protests can be linked to wider debates over the nature of the policy approach.

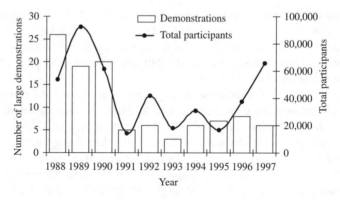

Fɪɢ. 7.3. *Larger demonstrations about environmental issues in Spain (demonstrations with 500 or more participants)*

Table 7.2 shows the distribution of protests and their annual evolution in terms of a series of different kinds of environmental issues.

It is interesting that in Spain, the EU country with the greatest biological diversity, issues related to nature conservation were of relatively little significance (less than 16 per cent of all environmental protests). This might be linked to the relative maturity of conservation policy and the existence of conventional channels that probably serve to limit the potential for conflict. In fact, conservation policy has evolved from an emphasis on urgent measures for the protection of enclaves of the greatest ecological value to a broader strategy of the conservation of biodiversity. By the end of the 1980s, traditional conservation organizations had already redefined their agenda to incorporate this broader perspective. This was not only reflected in demands for the protection of natural areas of interest, but also for the promotion of economic activities and infrastructure development that would be compatible with nature protection in other areas (agriculture, tourism, communication infrastructure, and housing). This explains why the proportion of nature conservation protests increases notably (rising to 38 per cent of all protests) when secondary demands are included, since most of the protests in the categories of water, planning, transport, or animal welfare have a strong conservationist dimension. Similarly, the relative weight of these issues increases if regional data are included (rising to 23 per cent of principal claims, and 42 per cent if multiple demands are considered). This is due to the greater selectivity of national data as well as to the earlier and larger decentralization of conservation policy. The decreasing power of the central state with respect to conservation policy also accounts for the decline in protests about such issues (which is clearest if absolute numbers of protests rather than percentages are considered). The large proportion of such protests in the first years under analysis reflects the high level of coverage of two particular conflicts: the opposition to the development of an

TABLE 7.2. *Environmental issues raised in protests in Spain by year (percentage of events in which issue is raised by year)*

	1988	1989	1990	1991	1992	1993	1994	1995	1996	1997	Total N
Nature conservation	21.2	21.4	22.8	12.8	13.3	23.3	6.3	6.9	13.3	6.7	115
Water	2.9	0.9	1.8	2.1	6.7	30.0	23.4	25.0	18.7	25.3	85
Pollution, urban and industrial	36.5	32.1	40.4	34.0	40.0	16.7	31.3	41.7	41.3	30.7	263
Waste	24.0	15.2	23.7	19.1	22.2	6.7	18.8	15.3	21.3	18.7	143
Pollution	2.9	6.3	6.1	2.1	2.2	10.0	6.3	8.3		8.0	38
Energy	20.2	29.5	13.2	4.3	17.8	10.0	18.8	12.5	14.7	12.0	123
Nuclear	17.3	25.9	12.3	4.3	8.9	3.3	14.1	4.2	5.3	6.7	89
Hunting and animal welfare	3.8	2.7	1.8	4.3			3.1			9.3	20
Transport	3.8	5.4	16.7	36.2	11.1	20.0	9.4	6.9	4.0	6.7	76
Roads	2.9	5.4	15.8	36.2	11.1	16.7	7.8	4.2	4.0	2.7	67
Alternative production		1.8	0.9				3.1	1.4	1.3	2.7	9
Other	11.5	6.3	3.5	6.4	11.1		4.7	5.6	6.7	6.7	48
Total N of events	104	112	114	47	45	30	64	72	75	75	738

Note: Broad categories of issue in italic; sub-categories in roman. Percentages do not sum to 100 as up to 2 issues could be recorded per event.

area just inside the borders of the National Park of Doñana, and the project to establish a military training ground in Anchuras (Castilla-La Mancha).

The main conservation issue reflected in the national press during this decade was forest fires (which were especially prominent in the first half of the decade). Although environmentalists tried to link the problem to the shortcomings of forestry policy, mobilizations rarely reached the national pages of the newspaper. However, campaigning by environmental groups did generate major debates at the regional level, above all in Galicia, Andalucía, Valencia, and Madrid. By different means and with different outcomes, environmentalists' proposals (including a popular legislative initiative in the case of Galicia) were discussed in the parliaments of these CAs.[21]

Nuclear issues, which provided the stimulus for the creation of many ecological organizations in Spain, accounted for just over 12 per cent of all protests in this period. They showed a downward trend from 1989, after the accident in the Vandellós I nuclear plant in Tarragona that led to its eventual closure, and the failure of a state-wide popular legislative initiative in 1991.[22] Subsequently, nuclear protests focused on opposition to the construction of nuclear waste depositories and to French nuclear testing in Mururoa. Together with this decline in anti-nuclear protests, it is interesting that in the 1990s, nuclear issues accounted for a declining proportion of protests about energy, probably due to EMOs' intense campaigning around global climate change and clean energy.[23] However, it seems that only anti-nuclear protests were able to mobilize significant numbers of citizens. Interestingly, while these protests succeeded in delaying the government's plans to build a nuclear waste depository, they seem to have had only limited impact on the policy debate.[24]

The highest levels of protest were registered in the category of territorial planning and environmental quality (urban and industrial pollution). Such protests often incorporated traditional conservation concerns since a road or a housing development might be challenged because of its immediate impact on a natural area, rather than because of the planning models behind it. In the cases of road construction, for example, Spaniards' unquestioned preference for private transport has meant that environmentalists have encountered hostility. The decade was one of enormous expansion of the road network: unprecedented investment in road infrastructure, accounting for a full 23 per cent of total public investment between 1989 and 1991, led to the construction of 3200 km of dual carriageways between 1983 and 1993 (Estevan and Sanz 1996). However, these peaks did not correspond to broader debates over the orientation of road or transport policies but rather to two particular conflicts (the Leizaran motorway in Navarra and the Madrid–Valencia motorway over the Hoces del Cabriel in Castilla-La Mancha) that acquired national significance for different reasons.[25] The more general obstacles not only affected opportunities to mobilize citizens or establish alliances with policy-relevant actors, but also the strategies of the authorities, in the sense of limiting the access of environmentalists to decision-making procedures

(Jiménez 2001). In fact, in 12 per cent of cases, protesters' complaints also made reference to this type of obstacle, and above all to the defective implementation of participation procedures such as those providing for environmental impact assessments and access to information.

Environmentalists have faced an equally adverse context with respect to industrial issues. The high level of unemployment and the administration's habitual support for industrial interests has limited opportunities for protest. Only when industrial activities affected other economic activities, or where the environmental risk was demonstrated by an accident, did protests find a significant echo. Conflicts over waste facilities were the main issue within this broad category, accounting for 20 per cent of all environmental protests. The end of the 1980s coincided with the first attempts by the administration to control waste dumping by promoting waste facilities that faced widespread popular opposition. When the potential or actual environmental damage involved the more diffuse impact of industrial activities or traffic, protests were less frequent: only 5 per cent related to air, water, or soil pollution.

The same factors explain why alternative production figured as the main demand in only a small number of protests, most of which took place towards the end of the period. In 1994, 3.1 per cent of protests (8 per cent if secondary claims are considered) referred to alternative production, usually in the context of discussion of the various national strategies for dealing with industrial pollution (industrial waste, polluted soils, and waters) and the attempt to promote clean production (Jiménez 2001).[26] The occurrence of these demands suggests the (temporary) configuration of an environmental policy subsystem open to public debate and to which EMOs enjoyed access. However, the main and most enduring environmental debate at national level involved the issue of water policy.

For a southern European country such as Spain, water management (leaving aside the issue of water quality and the pollution of rivers) is a particularly interesting environmental issue. In the 1990s, environmental concerns emerged as central considerations in the water policy debate for the first time. In fact, 10 per cent of protests were linked to this issue.[27] The severe drought of the early 1990s led to the so-called guerras del agua (water wars), conflicts that were not always articulated as environmental protests but that definitively contributed to the questioning of the traditional policy approach. This implied the opening of a traditionally closed policy community that had usually disregarded environmental criteria.[28]

As with many other issues, the political opportunities for a pro-environmental coalition first appeared thanks to the introduction of a new legal framework (the Water Law in 1985 replacing nineteenth century legislation in force until then) and in response to the first attempts to established a National Hydrological Plan (NHP) in 1993. Subsequently, they were spurred on by the early 1990s drought and the simultaneous development of opposition to diversions of rivers and to a large number of projects to build dams. As can be seen from Fig. 7.4, the proportion of protests involving water issues increased dramatically after 1993; thereafter they accounted for between 20 and 30 per cent of all protests.

Jiménez

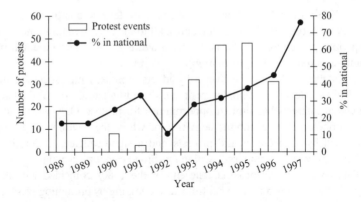

FIG. 7.4. *Protests over water issues in Spain (including regional data (columns) and percentage published in national pages of El País (line))*

The points on the line in Fig. 7.4 represent the total annual number of protests over water (including regional data). Columns represent the annual proportion of these protests that were reported in national pages. The comparison of the evolution of both series suggests the increasing permeability of the national edition of *El País* to protests related to water. The total number of protests increased between 1992 and 1996, when the last Socialist government encountered significant resistance when it attempted to implement the NHP. Although the level of protest dropped again in 1996 and 1997, the proportion of protests in the national pages continued to grow steadily, since the elaboration of the NHP was considered to be one of the priorities of the new Ministry of the Environment. With the national plan paralysed, the new government began to review the 1985 Law and opened a general debate by publishing a white paper on water policy (Libro Blanco del Agua) which helped to keep the issue on the national political agenda. Water policy has become a national issue. It is Spaniards' main environmental concern and occasioned the only reference to the environment in Prime Minister Aznar's investiture speech in May 2000.

Protesters usually (71 per cent) defined the scope of the problem underlying their complaints as local (Table 7.3). Only in 7 and 11 per cent of the events, respectively, did protesters see problems as regional or national in scope. When the underlying problem was considered international (11 per cent), it was seldom related to the European Union (1.4 per cent), not least because many of the problems defined as international involved the Mediterranean area. This extreme localism can be partly attributed to the limited political importance of the environment and the weak institutionalization of regional and national policy arena and national environmental politics.[29] The incipient crystalization of a national environmental policy subsystem in 1994, through the creation of the post of Under-Secretary of State for the Environment, coincided with a clear increase in

TABLE 7.3. *Levels of mobilization, scope of problems, and targets of environmental protest in Spain (percentages)*

	Local/ district	Regional	National	EU	International	N
Level of mobilization	36.6	25.1	35.0	1.9	1.5	738
Scope of underlying problem	71.5	6.7	11.2	1.4	9.2	706
Level of target	18.7	29.8	57.1	5.1	5.4	722

Note: N for level of target exceeds total number of events and percentages do not sum to 100 because 2 values could be recorded.

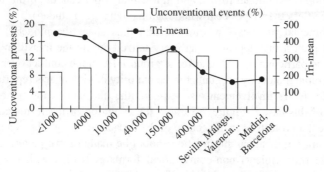

Size of the population

FIG. 7.5. *Distribution of unconventional protests and numbers of participants by size of population of location of protest in Spain*

the number of cases defined as national problems (an average of 15.5 per cent, above all involving water and waste issues). In 1997, the first full year after the creation of the Ministry of the Environment, 32 per cent of protests could be attributed to issues that were national in scope.

Nonetheless, local issues accounted for the majority of participants in environmental protests during the decade (Jiménez 1999b, 2002). This localism of protest corresponds to the numbers of protests occurring in small cities and rural areas. Figure 7.5 shows the distribution of unconventional events and the average number of participants according to the size of the population of the locations in which they took place. In order to increase the size of the sample, regional data were also included. In total, therefore, Fig. 7.5 is based on 811 events that took place in over 280 different locations (including all Spain's provincial capitals).

Half of all unconventional protests took place in village and small towns with under 40,000 inhabitants. The average number of participants (as indicated by the tri-mean[30]) was also higher in rural areas. In fact the larger the place, the smaller was the average number of participants (and the values' dispersion): nearly 500 in village and rural towns, it dropped to 300 in urban areas. This finding coincides with those obtained from analyses of environmental attitudes based on survey data which reveal greater environmental awareness among Spaniards living in small towns with between 10,000 and 100,000 inhabitants (Gómez and Paniagua 1996).

POLITICAL REPERTOIRE

The main feature of the forms of environmental protests in Spain during the decade was their moderation. Although the frequency of large demonstrations and the relatively large numbers of people involved therein is striking, half of all protests took conventional forms, and in less than 3 per cent did protesters resort to violence (less than 1 per cent when regional data are included).[31]

Environmental protests (and movements) thus share the moderation of the culture of protest that appears to have crystalized during the transition to democracy.[32] The participation of the terrorist group ETA in the conflict over the route of the Leizaran motorway accounts for the majority of violent acts reported during the decade; ETA's involvement also explains the unusually wide national press coverage of this case.[33] Figure 7.6 traces the evolution of the forms adopted by environmental protests over the course of the decade. Although the general trends are not immediately apparent, mention should be made of two patterns. First, an increase in (non-violent) non-conventional forms coincided with the peaks of mobilization in 1989–90 and again from 1995 onwards. If regional data is included, the evolution of large demonstrations also follows this pattern, and hence corrects the trend of decreasing numbers of large demonstrations over the decade apparent from the national data in Fig. 7.3.[34] Second, there was a slight increase in the proportion of conventional forms of action. This interpretation, however, relies

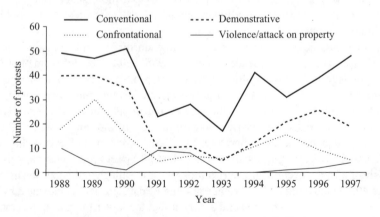

FIG. 7.6. *Forms of environmental protest in Spain*

to a great extent on the trends depicted when regional data are included in the analysis. In the regional data, within a context of increasing numbers of protests over the decade, both demonstrative and conventional forms of protests increased steadily, although the growth of conventional forms was more pronounced. Changes in the political repertoire can be interpreted in the light of transformations in policy, as environmental issues acquired greater public relevance, as the upgrading of the environmental administration was completed, and as a more consensual and open style developed (especially during the years 1994–5). Greater access to the decision-making process through new institutional channels can be interpreted as the state's response to the increasing capacity of the environmental movement to generalize conflicts over specific issues such as industrial waste or water policy; hence the creation at the national level of the Consejo Asesor de Medio Ambiente (Advisory Committee for the Environment —ACE), or the inclusion of environmentalist representatives in similar bodies in the area of water policy. However, data covering such a short period of time do not provide enough evidence to identify a trend towards the integration of environmental protests into the conventional channels. In fact, variations in the types of action over time might well depend on the predominance of certain issues over others in particular years.

Protesters appear to have made limited use of the restricted opportunities for direct democracy[35] but at least eleven popular legislative initiatives have been promoted by the environmental movement in regional parliaments.[36] Reflecting the broadening repertoire of environmental protest, nationwide EMOs have also started to organize consumer boycotts of goods or companies in support of their campaigns. Examples include the successful boycott of firms bottling mineral water in PVC, the promotion of the 'dolphin safe' label on tuna tins and, more recently, the campaign against transgenic food.

In order to examine the hypothesis that the repertoire of protests deployed varies according to the nature of the issue (or the specific configuration of political opportunities offered by each policy subsystem), Table 7.4 shows the distribution of different types of actions within different issue categories.

As expected, protests concerning conservation and hunting were relatively more conventional than those in other issue categories. This is, of course, related to the greater maturity of the policy issue as well as the greater degree of professionalization of conservation groups and their preference for interacting with authorities as lobbyists and experts. In fact, there has been interaction between conservation organizations and the state's nature administration for decades. Those issues related to territorial planning, such as housing, water infrastructure, and road construction (especially if the anomalous case of Leizaran is overlooked) were also relatively more conventional. This is probably due to the numerous instruments and mechanisms for participation provided in the regime governing territorial planning and nature protection, some of which have, despite their limitations, proved quite effective (in particular those referring to the coast, soil, water, and protected natural spaces).

TABLE 7.4. *Issues and the forms of environmental protest in Spain*

	Conventional	Demonstrative	Confrontation	Attack on property	Violence	Total *N*
Nature conservation	64.1	21.4	11.0	3.4	0.7	145
Urban, industrial	46.5	31.3	23.4	1.3	0.3	316
Energy	36.6	43.9	22.0	0.8	0.0	123
Hunting (animal welfare)	70.0	30.0	0.0	0.0	0.0	20
Transport	48.7	19.7	2.6	1.3	23.7	76
Alternative production	55.6	33.3	0.0	0.0	0.0	9
Other	67.3	20.4	10.2	0.0	0.0	49
Percent of all protest events	50.7	29.5	16.8	1.5	2.7	
Total *N* of events	374	218	124	11	20	738

Note: Percentage of events involving each issue that involves a form of action. Percentages do not sum to 100 because for each protest up to 2 issues and 4 forms could be recorded.

Distinct conventional channels are promoted by differences in the legislative and administrative framework regulating each type of issue. Conventional actions, such as, for example, participation in public information procedures in the process of environmental impact studies, largely involve space-related issues, especially the construction of roads and dams. This is not only because provision for citizens' participation exists (norms concerning the establishment of industries also provide for public participation), but also because of the political controversy and public visibility of these administrative procedures. Similarly, the higher proportion of judicial actions regarding industrial issues can be linked to the earlier approval of legislation establishing sanctions for offences involving waste disposal and pollution. However, the greater or lesser resort to judicial means can also be taken as an indicator of the relative level of conflict in each area, and as a preliminary and very rough way of evaluating the efficacy of alternative types of conventional action in these areas. From this perspective, energy, and urban and industrial pollution were the most conflictual issues and recorded high levels of unconventional protest. However, while favouring resort to conflict (in the judicial sphere or through unconventional strategies), the closure of the legal and administrative system, or its inefficacy when dealing with certain types of demands, are not factors that necessarily conduce to violent protest. Consider, for example, the case of anti-nuclear and energy-related protests. While environmental protests on these issues tended to be less conventional, the Spanish anti-nuclear movement was quite moderate by comparison with the more confrontational profile of anti-nuclear protests in other European countries.[37]

A full 30 per cent of the participants in protests were mobilized by anti-nuclear protests, while, in contrast, conservation-focused protests accounted for only 10 per cent of the total volume of participants. In fact waste, water, and nuclear issues were the ones that showed the greatest potential for mass collective action during the decade (Jiménez 1999*b*, 2002).

ORGANIZATIONS AND PROTEST

This section examines the organizational panorama of environmental protests in Spain. A large number of organizations have been involved: some 270 different names were identified, 120 as individual organizers and many others as participants in broader platforms.

It is through this organizational presence that the features of environmental protests (and the changes within them) can be linked to the evolving nature of the Spanish environmental movement. The temporal and spatial continuity of a network of actors is one of the central features defining a social movement.[38] This analysis also modifies the essentially localist profile of environmental protests, since the network of the environmental movement gives insights into the links between local and national levels of contention. At the same time, by examining the organizational structure of the movement it is possible to explore the extent to which these connections make it possible to trace the configuration of an arena of environmental politics or a specialized policy subsystem.

While at first glance the data highlights the wide and highly fragmented organizational spectrum of the Spanish environmental movement, more detailed analysis corrects this picture. In fact, a relatively small number of nationwide organizations participated in 68 per cent of the events in which EMOs were involved (i.e. in 48 per cent of all protests). Regional EMOs (in over half the cases, regional umbrella organizations) participated in 30 per cent of protests, while local EMOs were present in only 26 per cent. Although the proportion of protests involving two or more EMOs was rather modest (just 16 per cent), nationwide EMOs figured in 77 per cent of these cases, while regional or local organizations were involved in only about 30 per cent. Thus, the initial image of organizational fragmentation is complemented by one of a movement network centralized at national level, but with local groups retaining organizational control in their own more limited arena. This section explores the nature of protest organizers, the network of interactions among them, and the features of some of the most prominent organizations.

The Organizational Profile of Environmental Contenders

Table 7.5 shows the total and annual percentage of protests according to the type of organization reportedly involved. Organizations are classified and ranked in descending order according to the overall frequency of their participation in environmental protests. The organizations most frequently mentioned—EMOs—have been divided into two subcategories: discrete organizations and coordinating

TABLE 7.5. *Participation of different types of organizations in environmental protests in Spain by year (percentage of protest events in each year in which each kind of group was involved)*

	1988–97	1988	1989	1990	1991	1992	1993	1994	1995	1996	1997
Environmental organizations											
Discrete groups	52.3	45.7	54.8	42.9	40.4	66.7	56.7	72.2	56.1	59.4	41.2
Coordinating committees	16.6	6.5	10.8	18.4	12.8	20.0	10.0	22.2	12.1	27.5	27.9
Single issue/ad hoc group											
with EMOs	19.8	29.3	17.2	12.2	21.3	15.6	13.3	13.0	13.6	31.9	27.9
without EMOs	6.8	4.3	7.5	17.3	0.0	0.0	6.7	3.7	1.5	1.4	16.2
Political parties	8.8	12.0	16.1	5.1	10.6	6.7	3.3	9.3	9.1	5.8	4.4
Unions	5.6	6.5	6.5	5.1	0.0	4.4	0.0	5.6	16.7	2.9	5.9
Fishermen	2.0	0.0	3.2	0.0	2.1	2.2	6.7	5.6	1.5	1.4	1.5
Neighbourhood associations	1.8	3.3	1.1	1.0	0.0	4.4	3.3	1.9	1.5	1.4	1.5
Other	11.2	10.9	8.6	17.3	31.9	4.4	3.3	7.4	10.6	10.1	4.4
N		*92*	*93*	*98*	*47*	*45*	*30*	*54*	*66*	*69*	*68*
Protests without organization known	9.3	10.3	11.5	17.0	14.0	0.0	0.0	0.0	15.6	8.3	8.0
Percentage of protests with two or more EMOs	14.0	4.8	13.4	9.6	12.8	17.8	10.0	21.9	13.9	25.3	16.0
Percentage of protests involving nationwide organizations	41.9	27	26.7	35	45.3	46.3	42.4	61.5	47.5	49.6	50.5

Note: Percentages and totals based on organizations; 662 valid cases; 76 missing cases.

committees.[39] At least one organization in each category participated in 52 and 17 per cent of protests, respectively (66 per cent if the two categories are aggregated). The positive trend over time suggests that EMOs had an increasing capacity to generate and/or control environmental conflicts. Moreover, the increasing number of coordinating committees as well as protests involving two or more EMOs might suggest an increasing degree of inter-organizational coordination within the movement.[40]

The category of single-issue or *ad hoc* groups refers to those groups emerging in reaction to a specific environmental threat or problem, including so-called NIMBY (=Not In My Back Yard) protests. They are often citizen platforms supported by and composed of a variety of organizations and institutions. *Ad hoc* organizers have also been broken down into two subcategories according to whether they included EMOs, either among the groups supporting the platform or through the presence within their leadership of activists linked to the environmental movement. These citizen platforms can be considered instruments that EMOs (and other protest entrepreneurs) employ to build broader pro-environment coalitions in order to mobilize affected citizens and public opinion. In fact, the category of '*ad hoc* groups' is the one that displays the most unconventional profile of action.[41] It is noteworthy that violence was more often reported in protests where no EMO was reportedly involved. This suggests that EMOs temper unconventional protests and reduce the possibility of resort to violence.

In less than 10 per cent of all protests was a political party reportedly involved, although this figure increases when the participants in *ad hoc* groups are taken into account. Political parties seldom acted alone, and generally their participation was limited to problems defined as local in scope; they were involved in only 4 per cent of protests involving nationwide organizers. Similarly, parties were seldom involved in protests defined as national or international in scope (only eight out of fifty-seven protests). In 90 per cent of cases, it was only the local branch of the party that was involved. While these data may under-represent the participation of political parties in protest, their role as organizers of protests appears strictly secondary and essentially confined to the local level, which plays little role in generating nationwide debates on environmental issues. This is especially striking in a political system such as that of Spain, where participation is almost exclusively focused on the electoral game, and where politics is publicly constructed around the party leaderships. Although the main political parties have gradually included environmental issues in prominent positions in their electoral agenda, their proposals have rarely been objects of political debate at the national level.[42] The most consolidated approach to ecology is that developed by the United Left (Izquierda Unida, IU), a party which has taken up the green flag and has been involved in frequent interaction with part of the environmental movement.[43] The weakness of the Greens, Los Verdes, is reflected in their limited presence in environmental protests, their territorial fragmentation having denied them visibility at national level.[44]

The presence of trade unions was also very limited (6 per cent), although substantially less localist than that of political parties; 32 per cent of protests involving trade unions were defined as national or international in scope. In contrast to the political parties, the greater environmental activism of trade unions was at the level of the national federations. Higher percentages in 1989–90 reflected the trade unions' participation in the anti-nuclear campaign in Catalunya against the Vandellós nuclear plant, and in 1994–5, their participation in the advisory committee, ACE. The main trade unions have incorporated the green issue recently, and more credibly in the case of the leftist Comisiones Obreras, CCOO (AAVV 1995: 92).[45] Other unions also participated in protest, including those related to the fishing industry, as exemplified by the protests of Spanish fishermen against the use of illegal fishing methods in the Mediterranean or in the Bay of Biscay (Tarrow 1995).[46]

Neighbourhood associations took part in fewer than 2 per cent of protests (7.5 per cent if regional data is included). However, local residents were the main social group in non-conventional protests. Environmental activists usually find themselves alone when facing issues or contexts that do not facilitate the mobilization of ordinary people, such as when the issues concern diffuse environmental impacts (as in cases involving alternative industrial technologies, reduction of emission levels), or when they involve global or distant problems (rainforests, depletion of the ozone layer), or when they concern overall lifestyles (the use of the car, consumption behaviour) (Jiménez 1999*b*).

The Organizational Network of Environmental Protests

Social network analysis provides information on the nature of interactions among different organizations, as well as making it possible to identify the most important actors of collectively organized protests. The localist nature of environmental protests has increasingly been tempered by the presence of national EMOs (either acting alone or with others) and the linkages between local EMOs and *ad hoc* organizational forms and these nationwide actors. Supra-local EMOs provide environmental protests with territorial and temporal continuity, as well as ensuring the incorporation of otherwise isolated events into the environmental movement's field of contention. Thus, the geographical and temporal continuity produced by (or reflected in) the interaction among a variety of protest organizers has implications for the identification and definition of social movements as a political phenomenon.

Figure 7.7 represents the structure of the most frequent links among organizations within the network of environmental protests in Spain. The diagram is built upon those ties among pairs of organizations that were reported at least three times in the national pages of *El País* during the decade.[47] The outcome is a network of ties containing twelve groups: seven nationwide EMOs (effectively all the national-level organizations), the three main Spanish political parties, and the

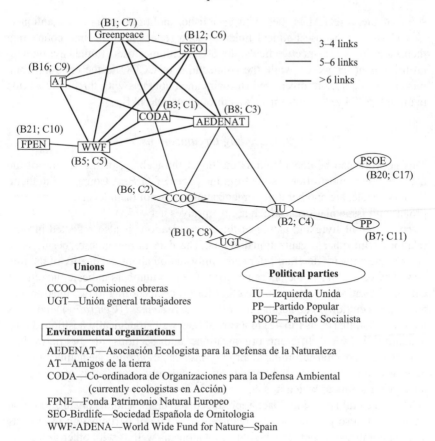

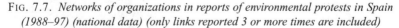

Fig. 7.7. *Networks of organizations in reports of environmental protests in Spain (1988–97) (national data) (only links reported 3 or more times are included)*

two peak unions. The relatively broad presence of parties and unions does not contradict the previous emphasis on their limited role as pro-environmental actors. They appear in the diagram because they have usually joined the same organizations (on many occasions the same type of organizations), and these ties link them, directly or indirectly, to the core EMOs. Furthermore, media bias favours established political actors.[48]

The diagram groups the three different types of actors: EMOs (in boxes), parties (in ellipses), and trade unions (in diamonds). It identifies the organizational core of the Spanish environmental movement at the national level. All EMOs but one are adjacent to one another. The high level of internal interaction may indicate the existence of a cohesive identity among groups or at least of pragmatic alliances for achieving common goals.[49] At the same time, the diagram highlights some of the core EMOs' ties with established political actors. As mentioned, CCOO and IU (whose political links are also reflected in the line connecting them) are, in their respective fields, the organizations closest to the environmental movement. However, while the connections of CCOO to the environmental movement seem more diversified (it maintained contacts with three EMOs), the main link of IU to the movement was through AEDENAT.

The Leading Organizations

This network can be considered as the tip of the iceberg, or the section of the network that is most often visible from the pages of *El País*. Connected to them, but less visible, are another thirty organizations (most of them local environmental groups and issue platforms which are themselves networks).[50]

The different style and nature of these organizations is also reflected in their relations with other organizational actors. The data in parentheses beside each actor in the network diagram offer some information about the quality of the role played by each actor in the entire network. The two numbers indicate the rank of each organization in relation to the other forty-one according to two measures of the actors' centrality. The number after B (for *Betweenness (Centrality)*) indicates the actor ranking (from 1 to 42) in terms of how well strategically positioned it is, mediating between different organizations and sections of the network.[51] Similarly, the position according to the *(Eigenvector) Centrality*, the number after C, indicates how well connected an actor is, considering the richness of the ties of those other actors to which it is connected.[52]

These centrality rankings are reproduced for eight leading organizations in Table 7.6. It also gives for each organization its rate of participation in protests and the number of events in which it acted alone as well as with other groups.

TABLE 7.6. *Networks of protest among the most active environmental organizations in Spain*

	Percentage of protests	Acting alone (N)	Acting with others (N)	Position in the network (ranking)	
				Betweenness	Centrality (Bonachivs)
CODA	9.4	24	38	3	1
AEDENAT	9.4	19	43	8	3
WWF/ADENA	5.4	10	26	5	5
Greenpeace	15.5	69	34	1	7
CCOO	3.2	3	18	6	2
IU	4.5	7	23	2	4
SEO/Birdlife	3.9	11	15	12	6
Amigos de la Tierra	2.6	4	13	16	9

The outlying case is that of Greenpeace, which carried out almost 70 per cent of its actions alone, compared, for instance, with 30 per cent in the case of AEDE-NAT. This of course is largely a reflection of the different protest styles of the two organizations. Greenpeace, above all in the 1990s, developed an extensive network of interaction both within the environmental movement and with other social movements, and this is reflected in their centrality scores. Greenpeace is the actor with the greatest *betweenness*; this means that it maintained relations with different sections of the networks and so potentially had rapid access to or control over mobilization resources. By contrast, AEDENAT ranks somewhat behind in terms of *betweenness* but its *centrality* is higher. These differences underline arguments advanced earlier; AEDENAT was better connected to a higher number of powerful actors in the network (including IU and CCOO) than was Greenpeace, but was probably less well connected to certain (less radical) sections of the movement.

The most central organization is, however, CODA, due to its nature as a Coordinating Committee of Environmental Organizations. The centrality measures also help to qualify the role played by *Amigos de la Tierra* and SEO/Birdlife in the protest network. Not only did they participate substantially less often than the other four EMOs in Table 7.6 (3.9 and 2.6 per cent, respectively), but they are also placed at the margins of this network (as their ranks in terms of *betweenness* indicate). Their marginality was a product of their conventional character and, in the case of SEO/Birdlife, specialization on conservation issues.

By contrast, although IU and CCOO also participated in protest only relatively seldom (4.5 and 3.2 per cent, respectively), they tended to participate with EMOs rather than acting alone, which gives them a central position in the network. Less green parties, such as the Socialist Party (PSOE) or the centre–right Popular Party (PP), occupy more marginal positions in the network.[53]

The evolving participation of these leading organizations sheds some light on the changing organizational features of environmental protests during the decade. The annual number of protest events involving the participation of these most central organizations is shown in Table 7.7.

The EMOs most active in protest—Greenpeace, CODA, and AEDENAT (the latter two unified in *Ecologistas en Acción* in 1999)—appear to have become more active over time.[54] The increasing level of participation by nationwide organizations, as well as the increasing number of protests involving two or more EMOs, can be related to, among other factors, the creation of ACE. During its first year of existence (1994–5), ACE prompted intense coordination, not only among EMOs, but also with other members of this advisory committee. This period coincides with higher levels of conventional protest as well as with the proportion of events defined as national in scope. These changes—greater network cohesion and relevance of nationwide EMOS and (consequently) conventionalization of forms and globalization of demands—are undoubtedly influenced by ACE.

TABLE 7.7. *Number of environmental protests in Spain involving leading organizations by year*

	1988	1989	1990	1991	1992	1993	1994	1995	1996	1997	1988–97
Greenpeace	8	10	8	7	9	6	11	15	19	10	103
AEDENAT	4	2	5	1	7	1	13	10	11	8	62
CODA	2	6	4	3	8	3	11	4	11	10	62
WWF/ADENA	3	4	5	2	3	2	4	3	7	3	36
IU	3	8	1	1	1	0	4	5	4	3	30
SEO/Birdlife	3	1	3	1	2	1	4	0	4	7	26
CCOO	2	3	3	0	2	0	3	6	0	2	21
Amigos de la Tierra	2	1	1	2	1	0	4	0	1	5	17
Total N of events	94	110	116	46	45	33	63	71	74	74	726

ACE both called the attention of the media to EMOs participating as well as stimulating greater interaction among EMOs.

The variation in the number of protests attributed to each organization is influenced by the nature of its activities and by the media selection bias. This bias favours professionalized EMOs whose greater expertise and information enables them to obtain coverage. This bias is less apparent if regional data is included: then the most active nationwide EMO was AEDENAT (9.2 per cent compared with Greenpeace 6.1 per cent).

Table 7.8 shows the distribution of protests in which the leading organizations took part according to the main issues of the protest. The leading actors clearly have broad agenda. This is especially true of AEDENAT and CODA, which participated in protests in all issue categories. The agenda of ADENA/WWF or Amigos de la Tierra appears less broad (due probably to the conservationist bias of the former and to the reduced protest activity of the latter). At the same time, Table 7.8 also reflects each organization's issue specialization. AEDENAT's protests were concentrated on energy issues (the field in which it was the leading organization, above all on nuclear issues) and pollution. Greenpeace dominated protests concerning industrial and environmental quality issues, a reflection of the importance of the creation of Greenpeace—Spain in 1984 in promoting the Spanish environmental movement's incorporation of environmental quality issues into its agenda. Overlaps usually imply collaboration and a division of labour by specific cases or themes (Jiménez 2000). CODA and WWF had similar agenda, although CODA's was more varied. CODA was most visible in the areas of hunting and water policy.

The different organizations' specialization influenced their repertoire of action. This is partially confirmed by the analysis of the more usual forms of action of the big four organizations. However, as the data also indicate, the type of organization, or its ideology, also influences the selection of the form of protest chosen to advance its demands. Table 7.9 compares the extent to which each of the leading organizations resorted to different types of protest.

TABLE 7.8. *Leading environmental organizations and their issues of protest in Spain*

	Nature conservation	Urban, industrial	Energy	Hunting	Transport	Alternative production	Water	Other	Total
Greenpeace	12	59	11	0	1	3	10	7	103
AEDENAT	2	16	21	1	7	1	5	9	62
CODA	16	9	1	1	6	1	17	11	62
WWF/ADENA	17	2	0	0	6	0	5	6	36
IU	3	6	13	0	2	2	1	3	30
SEO/Birdlife	8	0	3	1	2	0	3	9	26
CCOO	2	10	4	0	1	0	2	2	21
Amigos de la Tierra	1	3	0	0	2	0	5	6	17
Total N of events	105	228	107	18	75	9	77	44	663

TABLE 7.9. *The protest repertoire of leading environmental organizations in Spain*

	Conventional	Demonstrative	Confrontational	Minor attack	Violence	Other	Total
Greenpeace	53	22	27	2	0	2	103
AEDENAT	43	14	5	1	0	2	62
CODA	57	4	1	0	0	1	62
WWF/ADENA	33	2	0	0	0	3	36
IU	14	13	2	0	0	3	30
SEO/Birdlife	23	2	0	0	0	1	26
CCOO	12	7	1	0	0	1	21
Amigos de la Tierra	16	2	0	0	0	0	17
Total N of events	335	85	106	6	18	35	663

There is no record of violent protests involving any of these EMOs. As might be expected, given their more radical approach to ecological issues, AEDENAT and Greenpeace employed more unconventional and radical repertoires, while ADENA/WWF, SEO/Birdlife, and Amigos de la Tierra focused almost exclusively on conventional channels of participation.

However, AEDENAT (which is a more or less typical social movement organization) and Greenpeace also differed from each other, Greenpeace making less use of political types of protest, including lobbying, but more of unconventional actions, typically media-directed 'theatrical' confrontations performed by professionalized activists. The median number of participants in Greenpeace's actions was lower than that of events involving AEDENAT, an organization more committed to mass participation.[55] The fact that activists were arrested in 35 per cent of the unconventional protests performed by Greenpeace, even though the use of force was uncommon, is probably a reflection of the more spectacular character of its activities.[56]

The profiles of CODA and WWF are closer to those of conventional organizations that concentrate their efforts on established channels. Again, however, the two organizations have distinct profiles. While WWF is a professionalized international EMO (a public interest lobby), CODA is an umbrella organization that very loosely coordinates and supports a wide variety of local, regional, and national groups (including AEDENAT) which differ in the degree of their radicalism. These factors help to account for certain similarities between them, such as the conventional character of their action (in the case of CODA, unconventional protests are actually carried out by its member organizations), as well as differences (for instance, the media orientation of WWF, and the greater level of conflict introduced by CODA in conventional protests by its recourse to formal complaints and legal actions, and the importance of the local autonomy of CODA's members).

Paradoxically, the organization with proportionally the most unconventional profile was IU. This in part reflects IU's preference for joining environmental protests when they adopt visible forms, usually mobilizations. Furthermore, in its capacity as a parliamentary party, IU has often channelled the demands of the environmental movement towards the political sphere through press conferences and parliamentary procedures, activities that fall outside the definition of protest events employed here.

The organizations also differ with respect to the targets of their actions. Although generally speaking the largest proportions of criticism and demands were directed at the administration and the government, CODA and ADENA relatively more often addressed their demands to the members of the government than did AEDENAT or Greenpeace.[57]

In sum, the analysis of the organizational panorama of environmental protests indicates that most protests were local, but it also suggests that such protests were increasingly connected to a set of EMOs that comprise a cohesive group and whose activities cover all type of issues. As the protest analysis focuses upon this core set of actors, the nature of the protests changes, claims are established more often in global terms and the repertoire becomes more conventional, and more sensitive to the political opportunities offered by the environmental policy arena.

CONCLUSIONS

By analysing environmental protest events reported in *El País* between 1988 and 1997, this chapter has portrayed a general picture of increasing protest, largely as a consequence of the spread of local conflicts across the country. Environmental problems were mostly restricted to local politics. Established political actors rarely participated in protests when problems moved up to the national decision-making arena where the general parameters of environmental policies are defined. Furthermore, mass mobilizations occurred more often in rural areas and small cities. It is those problems with a clearer impact at the local level, and that are more visible to local residents, that have generated wider mobilizations.

Conflicts over waste facilities, water policy, and nuclear plants showed the greatest potential for mass collective action. On other, less locally salient issues, on which, because their impact was diffuse or because they involved remote, global, or lifestyle issues, people were more difficult to mobilize, and environmentalists were left alone in the defence of the environment.

The political repertoire of protests, and the extent to which it changed over time, varied according to the nature of the policy issue or the specific configuration of political opportunities framing the decision-making process in each policy area. Distinct levels of conflict and of institutionalization of protest were associated with differences in the legislative and administrative framework. In those fields, such as nature conservation, in which policy was more mature and environmentalist participation was more established, conventional forms of action were more frequent than in policy areas closed to environmentalist demands, such as industrial and energy issues.

Fluctuations in the level of protest and in political repertories have also been linked to issue policy cycles. The number of protests concerning both conservation and nuclear issues declined over the decade, in the former case probably due to progress in conservation policy and in the latter because there were few new stimuli to protest. By contrast, waste and water issues increased as, in both cases, the adoption of a sectoral approach by the state in an attempt to control and rationalize the management of resources, and the adoption of new legislation and national plans triggered numerous local conflicts. These protests gave environmentalists an opportunity to open traditionally closed policy communities. In both cases, protests can be linked to wider debates over the nature of policy.

With both waste and water, the presence of a network of environmental organizations at the local and national level, in institutional spheres of participation as well as in the streets, enables us to establish the links between local conflicts and policy definition, and between contentious and conventional politics. The localist nature of environmental protests has increasingly been tempered by the presence of nationwide EMOs and the linkages between them and local EMOs and *ad hoc* organizations. Supra-local EMOs provide environmental protests with territorial and temporal continuity, as well as incorporating otherwise isolated events into the environmental movement's field of contention. By the mid-1990s, signs of network centralization were associated with the incipient emergence of an environmental policy subsystem at the national level.

In general, the observed trends—increasingly conventional forms of protest and increasing frequency of claims defining environmental problems globally—can be interpreted in light of transformations taking place in the environmental policy domain. Subsequent developments have, however, cast doubt on the real prospects for the consolidation of the environment as a policy subsystem. The Ministry of the Environment created in 1996, during the first conservative government (1996–2000), has been responsible for hardly any progress in Spanish environmental policy.

NOTES

1. Although (especially in the 1990s) most road projects in theory took environmental impact into account, in practice very few were substantially modified or rejected on environmental grounds. (For discussion of the application of the Environmental Impact Assessment directive, see Escobar 1994.)
2. In the early 1990s, the National Hydrological Plan (NHP) envisaged the construction of 270 new dams (Martínez 1997).
3. The growth of the environmental movement has been based mainly on the increase in the numbers of volunteers and with strictly limited economic resources. According to various surveys conducted during the 1990s, the membership of environmental movement organizations (EMOs) rose from just 1% to 2.5% of the adult population (Chulia 1995; ENRESA 1998).
4. Environmental policy achieved greater relevance during the last Socialist government (1993–6) as reflected by the elaboration for the first time of a national strategy for the environment and the creation of a parliamentary commission devoted specifically to environmental issues. As part of this process, environmental groups were recognized, at least formally, as legitimate interlocutors. A new set of environmental laws strengthened environmentalists' capacity to take part in decision-making processes, related for instance to environmental impact assessment, access to environmental information, and participation in advisory committees (Jiménez 2001).
5. A policy subsystem is defined by the 'interaction of actors from different institutions who follow and seek to influence governmental decisions in a policy area' (Jenkins-Smith and Sabatier 1993: 16).
6. According to the Oficina de la Justificación de la Difusión and the Estudio General de Medios (see *El País* 25 May 1997), *El País* is both the largest selling newspaper in the country and the one with the largest readership. It currently has eleven different editions.

7. At least in quantitative terms, the coverage of environmental information in *El País* seems to be slightly below the 2.3% average coverage in Spanish newspapers (CEIA 1999). With a liberal, centre–left orientation, *El País* first appeared in 1976. It was, imitating *Le Monde*, probably the first newspaper in Spain to include the heading 'Ecology' within its 'Society' section (Fernández 1995: 114). The newspaper's early interest in the environment can be attributed to the journalist B. Varillas, himself an environmental activist and a pioneer of environmental journalism in Spain, as well as to the favourable context during the transition and while the Socialists were in opposition. However, the paper's affinities with environmentally unfriendly Socialist governments (1982–96) probably accounts for its subsequently more limited interest in controversial environmental issues. (On the political profile of the Spanish media, see Gunther, Montero, and Wert 1999.)

8. Data on environmental demonstrations in Madrid collected by Adell for the period 1991–6 show that *El País* covered fifty-two demonstrations, while *El Mundo* and *ABC* each reported seventy. I am grateful to Adell for this data.

9. The section 'Ciudades' was published between summer 1990 and December 1994.

10. Regional data is included either to increase the size of the sample, thereby enabling more detailed analysis of certain features of protest events, or to explore the nature and changes in the selection bias of our data, since by comparing events reported in the national and the local pages it is possible to identify certain dimensions of the selectivity of the data.

11. If the regional data were included, the total number of events would increase to 3047.

12. These three sources of bias can easily be considered in terms of the four usually mentioned in the literature: the size of the event; the occurrence of violence (and/or police intervention); the proximity of the event to where the newspaper is published; and its placement in the media cycle (Hug and Wisler 1998: 143). Hocke has stressed the importance of the participation of established actors as the most significant news value in national newspapers (Hocke 1998). The relation between national relevance and reported protest is far from clear-cut. When, for any reason, an environmental problem acquires national public relevance—such as a forest fire, a drought, and the NHP in early 1995—it does not necessarily mean that related protests will be covered more extensively, since, for instance, pro-environment actors/actions or environmental journalists may be marginalized in favour of institutional actors and sources of information.

13. Two environmental editors, R. Ruíz and I. Mardones, and one local correspondent, F. Moreno, were interviewed.

14. Problems related to the systematicity of the data selection bias are discussed in greater detail in Chapter 10. In the particular case of *El País*, two considerations have been taken into account. First, the period of publication of the local section 'Ciudades' (1990–4) coincided with a substantial decrease in the number of protests registered in the national section. It seems likely (and environmental journalists agreed) that the decrease in reported events in the national pages was in part because such events were covered in the 'Ciudades' section. Second, the concentration of summary reports in the national pages during a period of a few years can be linked to the appointment of a new environmental editor, Ruiz, whose different journalistic style might have led to an over-representation of this sort of long-standing conflict in relation to similar conflicts that had taken place in previous years.

15. Ruíz highlighted the difficulties involved in covering regional/local information from Madrid (given the regional/local character of environmental issues). The precarious and unstable employment conditions of local correspondents might have a greater impact at the level of local correspondents, reducing the fluidity of the relationship between local and national editions/journalists.

16. This also explains the limited (less than 10%) overlap between the protest events covered in the national and the regional edition.

17. The increasing resort to summary reports might indicate a change in the character of communication of environmental issues among both journalists and environmentalists—away from negative and catastrophic accounts in favour of more informed reports and more positive reporting that pays more attention to the causes than the effects of environmental degradation and focuses upon solutions.

18. In this analysis, the national data include ten protest events from two summary reports concerning events taking place simultaneously in different locations. Similarly, twenty-four events coded from five summary reports have also been included in the regional data.

19. Estimates of numbers of participants were missing from only 20% of reports of demonstrations, but the fact that during the 1990s *El País* developed local sections may have gradually reduced the news value of the size even of large demonstrations. As a result, these data have to be interpreted cautiously: focusing on large demonstrations may help to cope with problems associated with missing data, but it does not ameliorate the bias of the data. On the influence of news values in the coverage of protests in national newspapers, see Hocke (1998).

20. As mentioned, this might indicate, however, a change in the selection bias of *El País* with respect to the size of demonstrations prompted by the declining news values of local environmental conflicts during the 1990s.

21. The main policy initiatives concerning conservation in the 1990s were those related to the elaboration of a national biodiversity strategy (Estrategia Española para la Conservación y Uso Sostenible de la Biodiversidad) as a consequence of Spain's adhesion to the Biodiversity Convention in 1993.

22. On the popular legislative initiative, see AAVV (1991). Although they are little reported in the national pages, in some cases (e.g. that of Domeño in Valencia) protests against the construction of buildings for the storage of radioactive fuel rods were quite intense in the late 1980s.

23. New debates are developing in this area, some of which, such as the controversy over the location of wind turbines, cause internal tensions within the environmental movement.

24. However, the possibility of bringing forward the calendar for closing Spain's nuclear plants was one of the few environmental issues discussed during the 2000 general election campaign. The new National Energy Plan approved in 1992 maintained the existing policy of a moratorium on the building of new reactors and extending the planned life of existing reactors, while also reinforcing the reliance on large coal-burning power stations and so increasing CO_2 emissions in the production of electricity.

25. The bloody intervention of ETA in the first case, and the public dispute between the Socialist Minister of Public Works and his fellow party member holding the presidency of Castilla-La Mancha in the second. The Plan for Infrastructure Development (1993–2006) was centred on the development of high speed trains; it introduced environmental criteria as a priority at the time of choosing between different project options but failed to develop a broader perspective on the issue (Vega 1993).

26. Discussion of the health impact of pollutants such as the dioxins produced by waste incinerators reflects the greater attention given to health risks in everyday life. Sometimes, these are as subtle as the risk represented by the continual exposure to electromagnetic fields created by high voltage lines, the carcinogenic substances found in PVC water bottles, the risks of babies' teats and dummies made of this material, or the effects of transgenic food, to mention the main new concerns that show a diversification of the issues and policy arenas, at least, according to the reported protests. Apart from this trend towards new issues and the diversification of demands, it has proved impossible to identify any other clear trend in the evolution of environmental protests in terms of distinct issues. Local Agenda 21, which in other EU countries has defined a favourable framework for increasing activities by EMOs and other social actors, has scarcely been developed in Spain (Lafferty 1999).

27. This category falls midway between those of conservation and infrastructure issues.

28. Despite the construction of some highly contested infrastructure projects (notably the Itoiz dam in Navarra), the mid-1990s saw a questioning of the previously dominant policy orientation, centred on trying to satisfy increasing demand for water (from new irrigated land and massive housing developments in critical areas such as the Mediterranean coast). Environmental groups played a decisive role, not only in opposing particular projects but also by mobilizing support for alternative policies for the sustainable use of limited water resources.

29. The scant significance of the environment in national politics may be emphasized by the selection bias of the media: the anonymous character of the voices that speak for the environment (the low visibility of green parties and limited interest of parties and public elected officials) and the frequent prevalence of personalities (the who) rather than the issue (the what) in the media's political coverage (Fernández 1995).

30. Tri-mean = $(q1 + 2*\text{median} + q3)/4$. Where q = quarter/quartile.

31. Most of the daily or routine activities of EMOs are conventional and are rarely reported in newspapers due to their limited news value. Lobbying, participation in advisory committees, and other similar activities that have a limited protest component were excluded from the definition of protest event used in this investigation. Media bias could explain the scant representation of protests adopting the form of administrative action, despite the comparatively great importance of administrative procedures in state–citizen interaction in Spain. Similarly, media selection would also account for the low percentage of complaints, such as watchdog activities of groups in interaction with police or competent authorities, compared to judicial actions which are more costly but more noticeable (Jiménez 1999*b*).

32. Little research has explored this issue (but see Aguilar 1996).

33. The violence of protests depends not only on the type of action but also on the actual course of events. In fact, almost 10% of the unconventional events, those classified as violent aside, involved violent incidents, usually implicating the intervention of police.

34. This reinforces the hypothesis of the decreasing news value of local protests (as far as size is concerned) in the national edition of *El País* (see note 20).

35. Regional data do not provide either sufficient information about the direct participation of environmental organizations in local councils, where referendums and direct participation in sessions were probably more frequent than the data suggests. Local council sessions provide recurrent opportunities for local protests, which often disrupt business, but, as in the case of neighbourhood associations, EMOs have also started to

participate formally in local activities through the presentation of motions, often with the support of political parties.

36. Initiatives from EMOs have also been introduced by opposition parties on the left, (essentially the coalition Izquierda Unida and various left-wing nationalist parties). Legislation providing for popular legislative initiatives (PLI) was passed at the national level in 1984, and during the second half of the 1980s in most autonomous communities. In every case, the legislation comprises a restrictive regulation of this mechanism for direct participation. The eleven PLIs advanced by EMOs account for some 25% of all PLIs presented so far (Camps 1997).

37. According to Duyvendak (1995: 173), in France 20% of anti-nuclear protests involved violence compared to 7% of protests on other ecology issues.

38. According to the conceptualization proposed by Diani (1992), a social movement is a 'network of informal interactions between a plurality of groups and/or organizations engaged in political or cultural conflicts, on the basis of shared collective identities'.

39. The main criterion behind this classification is the presence of the environmental movement in the organizational base of protest in Spain. In the Spanish context of local environmental protests and limited institutionalization of EMOs, this dimension would appear better to capture the main features and trends in this area of contention than the formal–informal distinction applied in accounts of other countries covered in this volume, where the main, ongoing organizational novelty described is the emergence of radical/informal groups in a context of established and highly institutionalized EMOs. Most in the EMOs category could be considered formal organizations, whereas there is greater organizational fluidity among the coordinating committees. In contrast, the level of organizational formalization among *ad hoc* groups is often low.

40. The expansion in the number of EMOs and the movement's agenda represented the main organizational change in the 1980s and early 1990s, while in the late 1990s the main developments have included processes of inter-organizational coordination and unification (Jiménez 2000).

41. The mere act of creating such a platform, when made public, may itself constitute a protest event.

42. Water and nuclear issues are the two partial exceptions in this respect, and have become particularly prominent at the CA level. The most striking case is that of the Balearic Islands, where environmental issues are at the centre of political debate and led to a left–green–nationalist coalition government in 1999, the first time greens had participated in a regional government.

43. IU's electoral programme in the mid-1990s was similar to that of any Green Party in the European Union, and IU even applied for membership of the Europeans greens as part of its overt strategy of occupying the green electoral space. Electoral alliances with green parties at the CA level were also frequent in the 1990s. In other CAs, some nationalist parties have also been greening their profiles: for example, the Unión del Pueblo Valenciano, as well as other regionalist or nationalist forces such as Chunta Aragonesista or Iniciativa per Catalunya which have recently joined the National Confederation of green parties.

44. Founded in 1984, Los Verdes initially lacked the support of the Spanish environmental movement or other social movements and limited their activities to electoral campaigns. Prone to constant splits over the territorial model of organization and electoral strategy, Los Verdes were not a significant political force during the decade. It was

only in 1993 when they achieved, in coalition with IU, their first representatives in some regional parliaments and major city councils.

45. Environment movement interaction with the minority, anarcho-syndicalist union federation, CGT, has been very intense in some areas.

46. Similarly, agricultural organizations have been very active in certain local conflicts. Most recently, they have collaborated with EMOs over transgenic crops.

47. This is an undirected graph in that affiliations are established by the coincidences of actors as organizers of protest events. Network analysis has been carried out using UCINET V (see Borgatti, Everett, and Freeman 1999).

48. In the case of political parties, we have mentioned that with the exception of IU, the involvement of the main political parties in environmental protests is confined to the local level and opportunistic in terms of electoral benefits. In fact, PSOE and PP would not be in the diagram if their regional branches had been identified separately.

49. Elements that are also definitional of social movements (see note 38).

50. Other non-governmental organizations (NGOs) (such as the National Organization of Consumers or the National Confederation of Neighbours' Associations) are also present. The criteria used to define the boundaries of the network was that it would include all organizations appearing at least twice in a sub-sample of 150 protests with two or more organizations codified in the national data.

51. The betweenness value reflects the extent to which each organization stands on central nodes of the network; it measures how often an organization is on the geodesic or shorter path between each pair of actors in the network. A high level of betweenness gives an actor a mediatory position between different organizations and clusters of organizations; usually it is interpreted as a position that gives control over information or resources (Freeman 1979).

52. The underlining idea of the Eigenvector Centrality, is that an actor's power (e.g. in the form of mobilizational resources) is conferred by the importance (centrality) of the actors to which is connected. The measure is considered to be robust (ratio $1 > 2$, see Bonacich 1972).

53. The PP's higher level of betweenness (variety of interactions) makes its position in the network more similar to that of IU, as until the PP's 1996 electoral victory, both were opposition parties.

54. In fact, a longitudinal network analysis would show a trend towards greater cohesion in the network: as indicated by the reduction of the number of components and increasing density in the main component, and centralization around national organizations (see also Jiménez 1999*b*).

55. However, Greenpeace changed its strategies in the 1990s, incorporating lobbying and other regular forms of protest in its repertoire.

56. There is no evidence that the police followed a different policy when other organizations resorted to the more confrontational forms of protest of the type favoured by Greenpeace.

57. However, the real difference here is the greater attention that Greenpeace gives to companies: whereas other organizations seldom target firms, they were the object of 30% of Greenpeace's protests.

8

The Basque Country

Iñaki Barcena, Pedro Ibarra, Eunate Guarrotxena, and Jon Torre

Environmental protest in the Basque Country has been distinguished by its intensity and its frequency as well as by its association with the cause of Basque nationalism (Barcena, Ibarra, and Zubiaga 1995, 1997, 1998). In this chapter we analyse the transformation of environmental protest in the Basque Country during a decade in the course of which environmental concerns became increasingly autonomous of the national question and instead became more embedded in the struggles of local communities to preserve their quality of life.

The data is drawn from reports published in the newspaper *EGIN* during the 10 years, 1988–97. We chose this newspaper rather than others because it has paid greater attention and given more precise and extensive treatment to environmental protest than have other print media. Because *EGIN* has a special affinity with Basque nationalism, and because this has influenced its treatment of environmental protest, it might be thought to be an unreasonably biased source. However, it is clear from the long-established study of the validity for the study of collective action and social movements of data obtained from newspapers (Dantzger 1975; Franzosi 1987; Rucht and Ohlemacher 1992; Fillieule 1995; Barranco and Wisler 1999) that no publication is entirely free of bias. Indeed, 'given the fact that newspapers are always biased, it is futile to spend too much energy on trying to eliminate bias. Given the fact that trends and differences are usually more interesting than precise levels, one should rather try to make the bias as systematic as possible.' (Kriesi et al. 1995: 271).

Although *EGIN* is sympathetic to radical Basque nationalism and to environmental protest, we encountered no special problems when coding the information obtained from its reports. Indeed, *EGIN*'s extensive coverage and frequent use of photographs, graphics, and other reports gave us a better understanding of many protests than would have been possible had we relied upon a more conventional source.[1]

THE INCIDENCE OF PROTEST

During the 10-year period of 1988–97, *EGIN* reported a total of 887 protest events that raised issues concerning the environment.

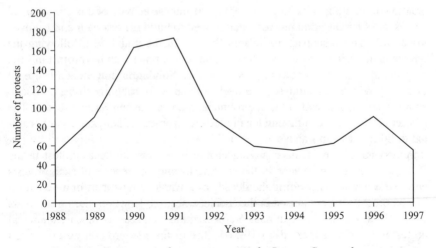

F<small>IG</small>. 8.1. *Environmental protest events in the Basque Country by year*

As can be deduced from Fig. 8.1, only in two years—1990 and 1991—was the average annual number of protests exceeded. This peak reflects the conflict over the Leizaran motorway. At the end of the 1980s, the Government of Navarra and the Diputación of Gipuzkoa (Institutions of the Basque Country) undertook the construction of a motorway between Irurzun in Navarra and Andoain in Gipuzkoa with the aim of improving the system of communications between the two provinces. Opposition to the evident environmental impact that the motorway would have on the valley of Leizaran was articulated around Lurraldea, an organization which proposed a highly innovative and active campaign strategy. Following a phase of broad social mobilization, the Basque nationalist armed organization—ETA—decided to participate, putting pressure on the companies and provincial governments involved. In the end, in 1992, an agreement was reached in which the administrations and Lurraldea agreed on a route for the motorway different from that previously proposed.

Other increasingly acute problems, such as the rubbish tip at Aranguren, the quarries of Atxarte, and the Sakana motorway project, also contributed to the 1990–1 peak. Following a period in which protest gradually declined, in 1996 there was a modest revival due to conflicts such as that over toxic waste (lindane) at Barakaldo and that over the Bizkaia waste incinerator, but especially to the increase in opposition to the Itoiz reservoir.

The Itoiz reservoir, framed within the so-called Canal of Aragón, is a project of the Government of Navarra that aims to take waters from the mountainous zone of the province towards areas requiring irrigation or to the larger urban nuclei situated further to the south. The flooding by the waters of the reservoir of a rural population nucleus and of an important landscape enclave led to the creation of the Itoiz Coordinator in 1986. The intense activity of this group ran up against a Navarrese administration determined to build the reservoir and involved in several cases of corruption related thereto. In the mid-1990s, following the government's reiteration of its determination to continue with the project in spite of judicial decisions decreeing its illegality, Solidarios con Itoiz (Those in Solidarity with Itoiz) paralysed the work with an act of sabotage that gave rise to an important debate within the environmental movement and Basque society. The project has continued, although legally the Government of Navarra is not permitted to fill the reservoir above a specified level.

A first indication of the changing character of environmental protest in the Basque Country can be seen in the shifting location of reports of such protests within the newspaper. During the decade as a whole, almost half of all environmental protests were reported in the 'Society' section. However, during the years 1988–91, it was in the 'National News' section that reports of environmental protest most often appeared; in 1990–1, 221 of the 336 protests were reported there, but thereafter, except in 1997, most reports of environmental protest appeared in the 'Society' and, to a much lesser extent, 'Local News' sections.

The principal reason for this pattern was the newspaper's special treatment of the issues surrounding the Leizaran motorway. The discursive and strategic connections of that conflict with Basque nationalism dictated that, as a nationalist newspaper, *EGIN* was obliged to include it in the section dealing with problems affecting the Basque nation. Subsequently, when environmental conflicts lost that nationalist dimension, the percentage of protests appearing in 'National News' declined rapidly, while their presence in the 'Society' section increased.

The salience of the Leizaran conflict was also reflected in the spatial distribution of protests. More than a third of reported protests took place in Navarra, which experienced two peaks of protest: the first, between 1988 and 1991, reflecting a series of campaigns about specific problems including many actions in places directly affected by the Leizaran motorway; and a second in 1992, principally centred around the Itoiz reservoir conflict. The capital of Navarra, Irunea (Pamplona), was particularly important, accounting for almost half of all the environmental protests reported in Navarra.

Bizkaia was the province with the second largest number of protests (282). Here protests peaked between 1990 and 1992, with disputes over the construction of the superport of Bilbao, the Artxarte quarries, and the toxic wastes of the Asua steelworks. A subsequent peak in 1996–7 was principally due to two conflicts: the lindane dispute in Barrakaldo and that of the incinerator in Erandio–Bilbao.

Gipuzkoa ranked third in the incidence of protests (195), the peak period 1989–92 again reflecting the struggle against the Leizaran motorway. Other localities were the sites of protests against projected recreational harbours or the high speed train. The fourth province, Araba, was the site of only fifty-six protests, of which fifty took place in the provincial capital, Vitoria–Gasteiz, the majority related to the Garoña nuclear power station.

TABLE 8.1. *Levels of mobilization, scope of problems, and targets of environmental protest in the Basque Country (percentages)*

	Level of mobilization	Scope of underlying problem	Level of target
Local	50.6	41.2	19.3
Regional/provincial	29.1	51.7	59.1
Basque Country	17.8	3.3	8.0
Spanish state	2.3	0.5	11.3
EU-countries	0.1	0.7	0.9
International	0.1	2.7	1.3
Total *N*	887	882	858

LEVELS OF MOBILIZATION, PROBLEMS, AND TARGETS

One of the striking things about Basque environmental protest during the decade was its localism (see Table 8.1). Approximately half of all reported protests (449) were local in their level of mobilization, and only in 1989 were local protests outnumbered by protests at other levels. The importance of the local was especially notable in years such as 1990 and 1991, when the Basque national ecologist organizations were better structured and, above all, were well spread over the territory. The presence of local sections of Basque national organizations in many localities, as well as the emergence of many strictly local groups from the early 1990s onwards, ensured that mobilization was predominantly local.

However, the issues around which people and groups mobilized, and the institutions to which their protest was directed, were predominantly provincial. In over half the cases, the issue that gave rise to the mobilization had consequences for the province (a provincial highway, an incinerator collecting provincial waste) with the predominance of protests against provincial problems greatest in 1990–2. Clearly, localism had not reached the point where local groups only mobilized around problems generated by their local institutions; rather, they mobilized around the local consequences of supra-local decisions.

The Basque country ranked third as a level of mobilization (158 protests), but what is not apparent from the aggregate figures is the protracted decline in the numbers of such protests from 1989 to 1996. This is of some significance, as it indicates the gradual destructuring of the Basque environmental movement or, at least, its growing inability to develop protests at this level. Protests mobilized at the level of the Spanish state occupied an almost residual position (twenty protests), and protests mobilized at European Union or international levels were exceedingly rare.

The local character of Basque environmental protest is further underlined if we compare the relation between organizations and level (Fig. 8.2). It was not only

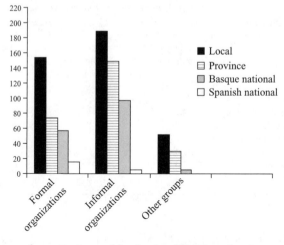

FIG. 8.2. *Forms of organization and levels of mobilization of environmental protest in the Basque Country*

the informal local coordinations that gave priority to local mobilizations; so too did the stable formal ecologist organizations that operate throughout the whole territory.

CLAIMS AND ISSUES

Amongst the issues of protest, transport loomed large until 1992, especially with the conflict over the Leizaran motorway. Subsequently, protests concerning transport declined as fewer such projects were proposed by the various public authorities. The second great issue was opposition to other construction projects, including marinas, commercial ports, and reservoirs, the peak years (1995–6) being those of greatest tension in the Itoiz conflict (Table 8.2).

Anti-nuclear protest was principally centred on the nuclear power station proposed for Lemoiz[2] and the one actually built, outside the borders of the Basque Country, at Garoña.[3] Protests declined as the Lemoiz conflict lost its central position within the Basque environmental movement. However, protests concerning waste of all kinds (steel dust in Asua, lindane on the left bank of the Nervión river, the Erandio–Bilbao incinerator) grew in importance, especially in Greater Bilbao during the most recent period (1995–7).

It appears, then, that there was a significant anti-developmentalist component within Basque ecologist protest, and this was especially marked in a decade in which a relatively large number of substantial infrastructural projects were constructed or proposed.

TABLE 8.2. *Environmental issues raised in environmental protest in the Basque Country by year (percentage of events in which type of issue was raised by year)*

	1988	1989	1990	1991	1992	1993	1994	1995	1996	1997	N
Nature conservation	1.9	1.1	5.5	7.5	5.7	10.2	12.7	6.5	3.3	5.5	52
Pollution, urban and industrial	36.5	38.6	25.8	31.2	44.3	50.8	50.9	71	78.9	72.7	390
Energy	15.4	11.4	4.9	4	9.1	10.2	9.1	11.8	4.4	7.3	67
Animal welfare and hunting	1.9	1.1	0	0	5.7	1.7	1.8	1.6	0	1.8	11
Transport	32.7	39.8	61.3	52.6	30.7	20.3	23.6	8.1	11.1	27.3	325
Alternative production	0	2.3	2.5	3.5	1.1	3.4	0	0	0	0	15
Other	11.5	5.7	0	1.2	3.4	3.4	1.8	1.6	2.2	5.5	25
Total N of events	52	88	163	173	88	59	55	62	90	55	

THE FORMS OF PROTEST

Environmental protest in the Basque Country during the decade was much more demonstrative than confrontational or violent. Rallies and demonstrations featured in 186 and 176 protests, respectively. In parallel with the overall incidence of protest, they reached a high point in 1990–1, subsequently declined, and rose again in 1996.

Conventional forms of action were next most frequently reported, with press conferences (109 events) and formal procedures such as gathering signatures, petitions, resolutions, or letters (eight-two) most frequent among them. Again, both evolved in parallel with the overall ebb and flow of protests.

Next most frequent were confrontational protests with forty-five public sit-down protests or blockades of roads, and twenty-two occupations. Almost as frequent (fifty-two) were serious attacks on property (classified as 'violent' because of their potentially damaging impact on people), the majority of them ocurring in a single year—1990—at the height of the wave of sabotage carried out against companies working on the construction of the Leizaran motorway.

Interestingly, in view of ETA's continuing campaign of violence against the Spanish state, violent protests of whatever degree virtually disappeared during the later years (1994–7). On the other hand, there was an increase during those years in other forms of protest that were generally demonstrative, peaceful and, on some occasions, involved civil disobedience. Such protests mostly involved innovative actions such as suspension from bridges, climbing buildings, and descent of rivers.

We classified as 'innovative' those protests that took forms differing from those employed in earlier years. In total, 105 such 'innovative' protests were counted. Two main periods of innovation were apparent: one in 1990 (seventeen actions) and another in 1995–6 (thirty-nine).

In the first of these, members of the Anti-motorway Coordinator (Leizaran), later known as Lurraldea, climbed public buildings in Donostia and Irunea. Also in 1990, there were several protest-related ascents of the cliffs of Atxarte threatened by quarrying. Other actions during that year included the blocking of polluting sewers in Gernika by environmental groups from the area, and the invitation to dine upon waste extended by members of Eki to the managers of the Durango paper mill.

In the second period (1995–6), pride of place was taken by the intense activity generated by Solidarios con Itoiz. Exclusively dedicated to this type of innovative action, they carried out a broad and varied range of protest actions that generally mixed elements of denunciation, imagination, spectacle, and civil disobedience: on three occasions they paralysed work on the reservoir, they climbed public buildings, trees or the reservoir infrastructure, chained themselves, and blocked the entrance to a company.

For 505 protests (57 per cent), *EGIN* provided information about the number of people participating. Small protests of under 100 persons accounted for just over half of those where information on numbers of participants was reported, such actions including press conferences, rallies, and innovative demonstrative protests. Just over one in four were medium-sized protests (between 100 and 1000 persons), generally involving marches or small demonstrations.

Large protests that brought together more than 1000 persons were reported on 89 occasions. Some of these were very important, such as the demonstrations of up to 40,000 people related to Lurraldea's opposition to the Leizaran motorway in 1990–1. Nonetheless, large-scale mobilization was exceptional; among large protests, demonstrations of up to 5000 people predominated, and over the course of the decade the number of large-scale mobilizations gradually declined whereas the reported incidence of small protests was relatively constant and that of medium-sized protests gradually increased.

Only 15 per cent (134) of environmental protests were not part of a campaign. The intense campaign around Leizaran accounted for a full third of the 753 campaign-related protest events, concentrated in the period 1988–92. The second most important campaign (131 protests)—that surrounding Itoiz—rose over the course of the decade until it reached a ceiling in 1995–6. Other significant campaigns concerned the Erandio–Bilbao incinerator (thirty-seven protests), the Aranguren rubbish tip (thirty-one), the Atxarte quarries (twenty-six), and pollution of rivers (twenty-six). Over the decade, except for the cases of Itoiz and the high speed train, the importance of national campaigns decreased, local campaigns disappeared, but the frequency of regional and provincial campaigns was maintained.

TABLE 8.3. *Issues and the forms of environmental protest in the Basque Country (percentage of protests about an issue involving action of various kinds)*

	Conventional	Demonstrative	Confrontational	Attacks on property	Violence	Other	N
Nature conservation	36.5	28.8	7.7	1.9	0	25.0	52
Pollution, urban and industrial	22.8	46.2	11.3	0.3	2.3	17.2	390
Energy	20.9	59.7	6.0	0	1.5	11.9	67
Animal welfare and hunting	45.5	54.5	0	0	0	0	11
Transport	27.1	44.9	5.2	4.0	12.9	5.8	325
Alternative production	46.7	33.3	20.0	0	0	0	15
Other	28.8	44.0	0	0	0	28.0	25
Total *N* of events	229	403	72	15	52	114	

If we compare the issues with the forms of action employed in protests concerning them (Table 8.3), only a modest degree of specialization is apparent. Nature conservation stimulated unusually conventional protests, and those concerning energy were exceptionally demonstrative. However, in protests concerning the most emblematic issues—the Lemoiz antinuclear conflict ('Energy'), the Leizaran motorway ('Transport'), and the Itoiz reservoir ('Industrial')—demonstrative forms of action predominated over more conventional ones.

Nor were there great differences amongst the organizations in their use of the different forms of protest (see Table 8.4). Violence and attacks on property were seldom associated with any group, and demonstrative forms of action predominated. Interestingly, only Greenpeace was reported to have employed mainly conventional forms of action.

ORGANIZATIONS

As might be expected in a place where environmenal protest was so marked by localism, the number of organizations mentioned in dispatches was very large. In the course of the decade, as many as eighty-seven organizations of the most varied political and social composition took part in some form of environmental protest. One or more of these eighty-seven organizations played a role in one or more of 814 protests. Only in 8 per cent (seventy-three protests), was no group mentioned, the majority of these being anonymous or clandestine actions.

TABLE 8.4. *Groups and their forms of protest in the Basque Country (number of events)*

	Conventional	Demonstrative	Confrontational	Attacks on property	Violence	Other	N
Eguzki	46	104	9	1	0	34	194
Coordinadora Lurraldea	53	95	8	0	0	8	164
Coordinadora de Itoiz	19	49	3	0	0	13	84
HB	11	24	4	0	0	1	40
Coordinadora Aranguren	7	19	9	0	0	0	35
EKI	28	30	8	0	0	9	75
Solidarios con Itoiz	2	7	6	0	1	13	29
UAB	3	8	3	0	0	11	25
Asamblea anti-TAV	2	6	2	0	0	4	14
Greenpeace	9	1	1	0	0	1	12
ERREKA	6	10	1	0	0	3	20
Total *N* of events	229	403	72	15	52	114	

The outstanding role played by the informal organizations must be emphasized, most of them represented by the 'big coordinators' (Lurraldea/Leizaran and Itoiz). In the early 1990s, Lurraldea played a particularly important role. The more formal organizations were quite constantly involved, Eguzki being especially important (present in 194 protests).[4]

The evolution of the activity of the groups and coordinators as a whole was linked to the periods of greater or lesser effervescence in those conflicts in which they were involved (see Table 8.5). This parallelism is clearly evident in the case of the coordinators, with some of them disappearing once the project was completed. Similarly, the visibility of the traditional ecologist groups tended to parallel that of the causes they espoused as, for example, in the cases of Eguzki with the Eibar–Gasteiz motorway, Eki with the lindane waste in Barrakaldo, and Erreka with the Bizkaia waste incinerator.

The most important groups and the issues with which they were concerned are indicated in Table 8.6.

It is instructive that one leading organization of some importance—HB—is not an ecologist group but the political organization of the Basque nationalist left.

If we analyse where, and in which issues, these groups played a leading role, then Table 8.6 comes as no surprise. The coordinators were focused upon 'their' particular demands whereas the stable formal organizations addressed a broader

TABLE 8.5. *Number of environmental protests in the Basque Country involving leading groups by year*

	1988	1989	1990	1991	1992	1993	1994	1995	1996	1997	1988–97
Eguzki	26	32	15	23	17	14	20	11	19	17	194
Coordinadora Lurraldea	11	23	54	59	17	0	0	0	0	0	164
Coordinadora de Itoiz	1	3	4	14	11	16	9	13	12	1	84
HB	1	7	5	9	5	2	2	3	3	3	40
Coordinadora Aranguren	0	1	15	13	4	2	0	0	0	0	35
EKI	0	8	11	13	9	7	6	3	14	4	75
Solidarios con Itoiz	0	0	0	0	0	0	0	13	13	3	29
UAB	0	0	7	9	0	1	2	3	2	1	25
Asamblea anti-TAV	0	0	0	0	0	0	4	1	4	5	14
Greenpeace	0	0	0	3	2	4	0	2	0	1	12
ERREKA	0	0	0	0	5	0	1	3	10	1	20
Total *N* of events	52	88	163	173	88	59	55	62	90	55	

TABLE 8.6. *Groups and the issues of environmental protest in the Basque Country (number of events)*

	Nature conservation	Pollution, urban and industrial	Energy	Animal welfare and hunting	Transport	Alternative production	Other	Total
Eguzki	11	92	42	6	22	10	10	193
Coordinadora Lurraldea	0	2	0	0	162	0	0	164
Coordinadora de Itoiz	0	78	0	0	4	0	2	84
HB	2	23	1	0	12	2	0	40
Coordinadora Aranguren	0	32	0	0	3	0	0	35
EKI	5	42	12	4	3	6	2	74
Solidarios con Itoiz	0	29	0	0	0	0	0	29
UAB	24	1	0	0	0	0	0	25
Asamblea anti-TAV	0	0	0	0	14	0	0	14
Greenpeace	1	10	1	0	0	0	0	12
ERREKA	0	13	1	0	1	0	5	20
Total *N* of events	52	390	67	11	325	15	25	

range of issues. Of the latter only Greenpeace was relatively specialized—upon pollution and urban industrial issues—but it was a relatively minor player in Basque environmental politics.

INNOVATION?

As we have indicated, the classic demonstrative forms of protest were sustained, ebbing and flowing in line with the Leizaran and Itoiz conflicts. However, starting with Itoiz, there was an increase in the frequency of forms of protest that implied a call to action and, especially, of press conferences. There was an evident change of orientation as communication through the media appeared to be much more effective than direct mobilization.

Violent actions also declined. In the Leizaran conflict, a conflict still framed within radical Basque nationalist culture, ETA was very much present. The many acts of anonymous sabotage, although not claimed by ETA, were probably the work of groups close to ETA. The 'violent' acts at Itoiz were of a quite different kind. At Leizaran, a clandestine armed organization, or its support groups, destroyed machinery. At Itoiz, in broad daylight, with witnesses and fully accepting the risk of being arrested, a group carried out spectacular actions. Political terrorism had been replaced by civil disobedience (Casado da Rocha and Perez 1996). In the Basque context, such actions were innovative, their innovation consisting in their search for spectacle, for a new communicative strategy that demanded attention from the mass media and from the public in general.

In collective action, increased reliance on communication via mass media has usually been seen as a response to the weakening of actors' ability to mobilize confrontation and protest (Diani 1997). However, in the Basque case it perhaps bore more relation to the search for alternative channels of pressure at a time when the agenda of national political conflict had changed, and when the administration was still unable to resolve environmental issues. Protest actions of this type served to take debate, and the Basque ecologists, onto the street and to encourage people to carry out principled actions such as the eco-sabotage at Itoiz.

These spectacular actions were a mimetic reflection of the international 'Greenpeace model', but at the same time they adapted a tradition of radical activism that is peculiar to the Basque Country. This tradition was heir to a myth of violence, inherited from ETA's armed confrontation but, in reaction against the sinister terror that ETA's violence had become, it was transformed into more spectacular and less morally compromised forms of action.

This trend had begun in 1990 when protesters climbed public buildings in Donostia and Iruñea, and the Atxarte quarries, in the latter case paralysing industrial activity. However, the most important such actions were those generated in 1995–6 by Solidarios con Itoiz, a group almost exclusively dedicated to this type of action. On three occasions they brought work on the reservoir to a halt, and scaled buildings or the reservoir structure as well as chaining themselves and blockading the head office of a company. Their repertoire included a broad and varied range of forms of protest which mixed denunciation, imagination, spectacle, and civil disobedience. Their intention was at all times to act meticulously in order to avoid physical harm to people, in the presence of the mass media, and with video recordings to serve as a faithful witness to the purity of their action.

TOWARDS LOCALISM

From an examination of the level and scope of mobilization, the numbers of participants in mobilizations, and the character of campaigns, a tendency towards increasing localism is apparent. In the course of the decade, the number of large environmentalist mobilizations promoted by 'general' organizations established throughout the territory declined.

Conflicts such as that of Leizaran (and, earlier, that of Lemoiz) framed environmental conflict in a nationalist 'package'. Nonetheless, although some analysts maintain that nationalism made use of the ecological discourse, in those years it was ecologism that used nationalism as a discursive tool. Increasingly the main strategy has been one of a localism that has used environmental frames for its purposes.

Thus, the number of mobilizations whose scope was national declined. At the same time, protests by small groups remained frequent, while big mobilizations decreased. The more important campaigns were those that had a clearly local origin but a national resonance; mobilization was initiated by means of a problem promoted by local activists (not always environmental activists) and then extended throughout the territory.

This localist dimension was strengthened by the stable organizations themselves. Mainly present in local-level mobilizations and dealing with problems whose scope was local, the fundamental role of these national (Basque), stable, and general organizations has been to support local mobilizations promoted by informal organizations.

At least quantitatively, just two conflicts—Leizaran (1990–1) and Itoiz (which peaked in 1996)—dominated environmental protest during the decade. Comparison of the two is instructive for although it had highly original features, Leizaran reiterated existing forms whereas Itoiz inaugurated a new way of carrying out and interpreting environmental conflict.

Leizaran

Leizaran was probably the last ecologist conflict directly connected with radical nationalism. The Basque environmental movement had emerged at Lemoiz and, until Leizaran, it developed in close relationship with both the radical Basque nationalist movement and the culture of Basque nationalism.[5]

Thus, at Leizaran, the movement sought the support of radical nationalism. The processes of absorption of the environmental movement and, on occasion, the not very peaceful cooperation between nationalists and ecologists (above all when ETA made its appearance[6]) did not prevent the alliance with the radical nationalists from appreciably increasing the mobilizing capacity of the environmental movement. In the first few years, the ensemble of political élites upheld a common line of confrontation with the ecologists/nationalists, but in the case of Leizaran divisions appeared among the élites and these facilitated mobilization.

At first the Anti-motorway Coordinator, Lurraldea, attempted to oppose its own model of transport, more consonant with the defence of the land and its people, to the 'Pharaonic and despoiling' public works policy of the administration. However, this frame later shifted towards another with more possibilities for transformation—the democratic frame—even to the extent of abandoning specifically environmental claims (Ibarra and Rivas 1996).

Thus, it was argued that the lack of dialogue and negotiation was the great problem of Basque society and that this lack also affected ecological demands. For Lurraldea, the important thing was not to prevent the project (in fact the route agreed upon did not differ much from the original route) but rather to obtain a dialogue with the institutions in order to show that dialogue and political negotiation were adequate means for resolving the problems of the Basque Country. It was a way of demonstrating the value of the strategy of radical Basque nationalism—the principal ally of the Coordinator—of promoting negotiation aimed at achieving greater sovereignty for the Basque Country in exchange for an end to ETA's violence. The struggle for negotiation over an environmental issue thus had favourable repercussions upon the democratic frame of radical nationalism, which had as its central strategy the demand for national political negotiation.

Itoiz

From 1992 onwards, once the Leizaran conflict had finished, a new conjuncture opened. The Basque environmental movement no longer appeared interested in giving priority to alliances with radical nationalism, either because the latter was on occasion too powerful an ally (one that ended up absorbing the original claims), or because as an ally it was a handicap when it came to attempting to open a dialogue with the institutions, or because of ETA's growing loss of legitimacy. As a consequence, the discourse of the Basque environmental movement changed and was no longer framed within the Basque national conflict.

The Itoiz conflict was above all an expression of localism.[7] Defence of the local is the central axis around which the causes and consequences of the new environmental movements come together. Local movements signify the resistance of a community to what are perceived as attempts at the invasion of, or aggression against, their territory by external institutions or élites. Rather than actually existing with its frontiers and characteristics clearly predefined, the local space that is defended must first be constructed. The local is what is culturally local (Preston 1997), and defence of the local is an expression of the need of individuals to build themselves a space of their own, to feel themselves linked to a shared and shareable territory in which they can be recognized. That need generates the construction and corresponding sublimation of the space, and invasion from outside is perceived as something directed against interests that the inhabitants themselves define as vital, as something directed against the very life-world of those individuals.

Defence of the local does not necessarily involve an exclusively ecological vision. Indeed, what is considered to be under attack is not so much nature in the abstract as a specific nature, shaped around, used by and linked to a specific human community (Kamieniecki and Koleman 1995). Two main currents have appeared within the radical ecologist movements: post-materialists and 'communitarians' (Doherty 1999*b*; Rootes 1999*d*). The former are not necessarily linked to the natural space they have decided to defend; it is their orientation towards values and social post-material criteria for planning which leads them to identify themselves with nature. For the communitarians, however, the natural space is the territory in which they live, to which they feel themselves to be morally and emotionally linked, and which they defend because they perceive that their survival as a human community depends upon the preservation of that specific territory.[8]

Itoiz represents this return to the local, the return to an ecologism that is midway between the 'neighbourhood' and environmentalism, to an ecologism that keeps its distance from the big ecologist organizations (although it accepts their help[9]) and from the political parties (which it distrusts). It is an ecologism that believes it can recover (and wants to recover) the original authenticity of the social movements.

The Itoiz conflict also exemplifies localism from an institutionalist perspective. The environmental movement is not only influenced by a localist philosophy; its strategy is also shaped by the local political context or, more exactly, by local policy-making. The rules of play and political styles of the different institutions and other political actors involved in each conflict delimit the possibilities of environmentalist actors. Thus, subjective localism is emphasized by the salience of an objective local political context.

CONCLUSIONS

Many students of environmentalism have commented on the institutionalization of a movement that was, when it emerged in the 1970s, radical and protest-oriented. For many, institutionalization is a process that ensures its continuity but transforms its activity, with the result that environmental movements do not survive as movements of mass mobilization (Eder 1996: 214). Moreover, environmentalist discourse has been adopted by political institutions and is no longer a monopoly of the environmental movement. Institutionalization has generated greater resources, cooperative relationships with institutions and companies, and access to experts, but it has also produced declining mobilizations, as the environmental movement has ceased to be the opposition and has come to play a more symbolic role (Donati 1996).

In the Basque case, it would be premature to reach such conclusions. On the one hand, by comparison with previous periods and with some specific groups, there has been greater cooperation with the political institutions. On the other hand, however, the majority of the ecologist organizations, including the *ad hoc* coordinators, while they appear to have distanced themselves from the protest-oriented and anti-institutional scenario and discursive frame of radical Basque nationalism, have not embarked on a determined process of institutionalization. Instead, they seem to have found a new ecological space, 'eco-localism', from which to continue their work. In this respect, it would seem that the movement is following the famous slogan 'Think globally, act locally'.

NOTES

1. *EGIN* is the only newspaper that publishes a weekly supplement dedicated to environmental questions. This supplement is an important medium for the diffusion of dossiers and information about campaigns, conferences, and meetings of the Basque and foreign ecologist movements, but it is essentially dedicated to subjects that deal with environmental consciousness-raising (environmental education, dossiers, reports, book reviews, conferences). The kinds of events with which our study is principally concerned are mainly covered in other sections of the newspaper: principally in 'Society', 'National News', and 'Local News'. Indeed, only 27 of the 887 protest events we identified in the 10 years were reported in the 'Environment' supplement, but it was nevertheless a useful source of contextual information.

   EGIN was closed down in July 1999 by order of the special tribunal, the Audienca Nacional of Madrid.

2. The project to build a nuclear power station at Lemoiz, a village on the coast of Bizkaia, gave rise at the end of the 1970s to an important anti-nuclear protest movement across the Basque Country. The struggle led by the Anti-nuclear Committees coincided with a period of strong social mobilizations and was the first step towards the construction of a broader Basque environmental movement.

   During the period that the conflict lasted, confrontation escalated between protesters and the economic and political interests that supported the nuclear power station. The kidnapping and assassination of a nuclear engineer by ETA in 1981 paralysed the project. Subsequently, the Basque environmental movement has every year continued to demand the dismantling of the plant.

3. Unlike the Lemoiz conflict, that of Garoña has a more symbolic dimension. The Garoña nuclear power station, which is located very close to the Basque Country, continues to operate and on a regular basis Basque activists demonstrate in the Basque Country to demand its closure.

4. There are two main, general, and stable environmental organizations (organizations that raise demands against all environmental grievances on principle throughout the Basque Country)—Eki and Eguzki. The latter was over-represented in *EGIN*, inasmuch as it forms part of the organizational network of radical Basque nationalism. It was probably more active in the decade than Eki (which has a more 'leftist' ideological orientation, although it is not in confrontation with Basque nationalism) as it was better implanted in villages and small towns, but the difference is most certainly exaggerated.

5. For the relations between ecologism and nationalism in general, see Barcena, Ibarra, and Zubiaga (1997).

6. The presence of ETA was decisive in the Lemoiz case, and the nationalist/ecologist conglomerate (rather than alliance in that period) was virtually unaffected by ETA's violent actions. At Leizaran, ETA's actions were marginal, hardly influenced the process and, nevertheless, created dissension within the alliance between nationalists and ecologists.

7. On the phenomenon of localism, see Rootes (1999*d*), Smyth (1998), and Kousis (1999).

8. According to their spokesperson, Patxi Gorraiz, the Itoiz Coordinator was not so much an ecologist group as, above all, a neighbourhood movement of single and exclusive opposition to the Itoiz reservoir; their aim was 'to beat the reservoir and nothing else. When we have defeated it, we will disappear.' (Quoted in Casada da Rocha and Perez 1996: 136. See also Beaumont et al. 1997.)

9. The relationship between Greenpeace Spain and the Itoiz Coordinator is significant in this respect. The collaboration between the two did not prevent mutual criticisms over the 'hardest' action of the Solidarios, a support group of the Coordinator (the cutting of an essential cable to the reservoir works). The Solidarios received the support of the Coordinator and were criticized by Greenpeace, which considered that the actions of the partners of the Coordinator were too radical.

9

Sweden

Andrew Jamison and Magnus Ring

Over the past 15 years, in Sweden as in most of the other industrialized countries of western Europe and North America, there have been changes both in the form and the content of environmental activism. Most fundamentally, a relatively autonomous and coherent environmental 'movement' has given way to a more variegated and diffuse array of actors and groups promoting quite different types of environmental agenda, often in the name of sustainable development and focusing primarily on global issues (see Lash et al. 1996; Jamison 2001).

At the same time, new cadres of usually younger activists have come to take part in looser, smaller, and often more radical forms of activist networks, practising types of action that are quite different from the previously characteristic forms of environmental political activity. Environmental protest has thus come, in Sweden as elsewhere, to represent highly divergent social and political interests.

These transformations have differed in important ways from country to country, particularly in terms of the relations that have developed between the 'formal' and 'informal' types of environmental protest. If we are to understand the transformations of environmental activism that have taken place in Sweden in recent years, it is therefore necessary at the outset to attempt to place these developments in a somewhat broader contextual framework.

As in other countries, the environmental political agenda has changed dramatically in Sweden in the course of the 1990s. From being a relatively specialized and delimited area of policy-making and political activity, environmental concern has become a part of the more general quest for so-called sustainable paths to socio-economic development. This new agenda has provided a range of opportunities for environmentalists at the same time as other, usually younger, activists have risen up in protest. In Sweden, there has been a split between those activists and organizations interested in cooperating with governmental authorities and businesses, and those who are 'reinventing' direct action forms of protest, often in the name of an extreme version of animal liberation and/or militant environmentalism (Linton 2000).

There are both short-term and long-term historical reasons for this bifurcation, or polarization, of environmental politics. One important factor is the 'comparative advantage' that Swedish authorities and companies have been able to derive from their uniquely early efforts to respond to the environmental 'crisis' in the 1960s. Sweden was the first country in the world to establish an environmental protection agency (in 1967) and to adopt a comprehensive law on environmental protection (in 1970). Sweden has also, since the 1960s, tried to play an active, even pioneering, role in international policy negotiations and in international environmental politics more generally (Lundqvist 1996).

This comparatively early institutionalization of environmental politics meant that Sweden was quite successful in dealing with many of the first generation of environmental issues: industrial pollution, chemical regulation, and infrastructural expansion. Moreover, Swedish activists have been able to take a leading role—and occupy international opportunity 'niches'—in relation to the new kinds of 'global' environmental issues that have emerged in the 1990s. A former energy activist has played a leading role in the global climate deliberations, while others have come to occupy key positions in international environmental networks.[1]

In the formative period of environmental activism in the 1970s, however, the strong hand of the state made it difficult for an autonomous 'movement' to come into being (Jamison et al. 1990). Pressures for the incorporation of environmentalism were substantial, both from the state and especially from the parliamentary Centre Party, which played a dominant role in the opposition to nuclear energy in the 1970s. Atomic energy had been a priority of the post-war social democratic government and so the nuclear debate struck particularly deep chords in the national mentality and political economy. It was not merely intense and divisive but also somewhat more official and widespread than in most other countries. An important legacy of the 1970s was a polarized political culture, with strong and influential pro- and anti-nuclear sentiments spread deeply, and more or less evenly, through the body politic, both sides claiming allegiance to one or another form of environmentalism. In many ways, the entire society is an environmental 'movement'—at least in terms of rhetoric—and it is thus difficult to distinguish explicit activism and particular protest events from other forms of environmental politics (Lidskog and Elander 2000).

Seen in a longer historical perspective, the country's geography, and the relations to the natural environment that have been formed through the centuries, have strongly affected the ways in which environmental politics have come to be articulated in Sweden. The large and largely unpopulated tracts of forest land, as well as the country's peripheral location at the northern end of Europe, are especially significant, as is the mechanical and chemical bias of Swedish industry. In the land of Linneaus, nature has taken on a particular kind of dual meaning in the Swedish mentality. For the dominant culture, it has been seen primarily as a resource base that has been mined and exploited comparatively effectively and resolutely. Sweden's economic development has been based through the centuries on resource-extraction and, in the nineteenth century, on technologically advanced engineering firms such as Ericsson, Alfa Laval, ASEA, Nobel, and Volvo (Jamison and Baark 1999).

For a vocal minority, however, nature in Sweden has been a much more spiritual and emotive realm, a second home. Throughout Swedish history, a kind of primitive, or anti-modern, naturalism has periodically manifested itself, and in the twentieth century, the Nobel prize-winning poet Harry Martinson and the filmmaker Ingmar Bergman, among many other cultural figures, have given this position particularly eloquent expression (Elzinga et al. 1998). By comparison with many other European countries, and somewhat similarly to Norway and Finland, there is a strong polarization in the Swedish mentality in relation to the natural landscape, and this has had a noticeable influence on environmental activism. In all three countries, there have been two very different forms in which environmentalism has developed. Some environmental activists have been given a prominent role to play in the official corporatist regime of decision-making and policy deliberation, while others have been explicitly extremist and anti-modernist and generally intransigent in their demands.[2]

Another important contextual factor is the long bureaucratic tradition, with a comparatively active and interventionist state apparatus. Already in the eighteenth century, scientists like Linneaus were employed by the state to conduct investigative surveys of the country's natural resources, and in the twentieth century, Sweden has been both comparatively early and comparatively ambitious in subjecting environmental issues to the full bureaucratic treatment.

In the 1990s, new forms of professional activity have largely supplanted direct protest organizations as the main actor coalitions or clusters on the environmental political scene. Professionalized environmental organizations take part in policy deliberations and political lobbying, and have played a central role in constructing programmes of sustainable development or green business, including efforts in technology and product innovation, environmental consumption and labelling projects, environmental management and assessment activities. In these activities, environmentalists often cooperate with business firms and governmental authorities at national, local, and European levels. Several types of non-governmental organizations (NGOs) operate in Sweden, ranging from imported transnational organizations, such as Greenpeace, World Wildlife Fund, and Friends of the Earth (FoE), to more home-grown variants such as The Natural Step (which has, over the past 10 years, exported its consultant management activism to several other countries).

There has also been a noticeable increase in membership and activity on the part of Sweden's traditional conservation organization, the Swedish Association for the Protection of Nature (Svenska Naturskyddsföreningen, or SNF), established in 1909. As the Swedish government has cut its expenditure and transferred to the private sector primary responsibility in many areas of environmental policy and research, the need has arisen for a new kind of national body to take on some of the tasks previously handled by the state environmental protection agency. Not without some difficulty and a good deal of soul-searching, SNF has taken on a new consultative role, coordinating local Agenda 21 and stimulating environmentally conscious consumption, for example, while also seeking to maintain its traditional 'people's movement' character, with local groups organizing nature excursions as well as representing environmental concern in local politics.

Interestingly, even though SNF and the parliamentary Green Party have represented the environmental cause effectively and have exercised a great deal of influence over state policy-making in the 1990s, a certain number of what Mark Dowie (1995) has termed 'fourth wave' environmental activists have nonetheless emerged in Sweden, concerned in particular with animal rights. The primitivist, anti-modern tradition has been mobilized in dramatic fashion, perhaps in part because the country's economic difficulties in the early 1990s made it difficult to give sustainable development much more than rhetorical meaning. In Umeå, a small university town in the north, as well as in Linköping, a university town south of Stockholm, an animal rights sub-culture has developed, and its actions have increasingly received a good deal of attention. Sweden has one of the strongest animal rights movements in Europe, and many activists combine their animal rights interest with veganism in a new kind of radical environmental 'sub-political' identity. There is also a sizable 'new age' constituency, with numerous spiritual bookshops and a range of diverse cultural manifestations marking a visible presence in Swedish urban life. More than in many other European countries, there is also a noticeable anti-new-age academic backlash, with critical treatments of 'anti-science' receiving notable attention in the media.

ANALYSING PROTEST EVENTS

We have analysed the coverage of environmental protests over the 10 years 1988–97 in one of the main national newspapers, *Dagens Nyheter* (*DN*).[3] In the 559 articles that we located in the course of examining alternate days' newspapers, we identified 263 protest events that met all the common criteria. In the pages that follow, we report some of our findings. But before doing that, some words of methodological reflection are in order.

One significant point is that the liberal newspaper *DN*, the journalistic flagship of the powerful Bonnier media empire, changed quite fundamentally during the 10 years. The paper has seen its circulation diminish, and it is no longer the main national daily that it once was, although it remains the largest morning newspaper. A rival Stockholm paper, the conservative *Svenska Dagbladet*, has approached *DN* in circulation, and competes for much of the professional and cultural readership, while a business daily, *Dagens Industri*, a kind of Swedish version of the *Financial Times*, has taken much of the business readership. *DN* has also been subjected to somewhat more active steering and control by its owners.

In relation to environmentalism, the paper has also gone through some significant changes. Yet, for many reasons, *DN* is still probably the best source for data on protest events. In the 1970s, *DN* was one of the main channels through which the new environmental and anti-nuclear movement groups transmitted their message. Especially during the second half of the 1970s, when the nuclear debate was the main political topic in the country, the paper was filled with articles on various aspects of the nuclear controversy, and most of its journalists were visibly on the side of the *nej* (no) sayers. It was a heady time in Sweden, and *DN* was a central 'actor' in the debate.

Throughout the 1980s, *DN* continued to give environmental activism a good deal of attention, but, as we have been informed by a journalist working on the paper, its interest in environmental issues diminished during the 1990s. For one thing, the newspaper has shrunk in size, with fewer pages and less room given to all issues, but there has also been what might be termed an identity shift on the part of the newspaper in general, and its environmental journalists in particular. The journalist also informed us that, whereas there were ten journalists on *DN* working on environmental issues in the late 1980s, now there is only one, and that one only on a half-time basis. Even so, while the quantity of absolute coverage might have declined, there can be little question that the paper continues to take environmental issues seriously.

It appears, however, that explicit environmental protests are somewhat less interesting than they once were. More interesting to the environmental journalist on *DN* to whom we spoke are the new approaches to environmental management and production taking place in businesses, and the new, more 'responsible' activities of environmental organizations. The data reported here probably underrepresent the absolute numbers of protest events, but they provide as good a picture of the overall patterns of transformation of environmental protest in Sweden as it is possible to obtain from any one source.

ENVIRONMENTAL PROTEST EVENTS IN SWEDEN

There are, at the outset, some difficulties in using the term 'protest event' in relation to Swedish environmental activism. Well over half the articles we identified as being concerned with environmentalism could not be characterized as dealing with protest events, since the events they described were both more 'constructive' in character and more conciliatory in form. As other evidence amply suggests, there is a strong tendency in Swedish environmental politics towards peaceful, constructive political activity of a kind that barely qualifies as protest by any meaning of the term (Lundqvist 1996).

Nevertheless, at the beginning of the period there were a number of rather large protests against the so-called Scandinavian Link (the major infrastructural project connecting Oslo to Copenhagen, which includes the bridge between Malmö and Copenhagen, and the building of highways along the western coast of Sweden). These protests, which were in many respects the most significant protest events in our period, included the tree-hugging protest actions along the west coast that blocked highway construction, as well as several large demonstrations

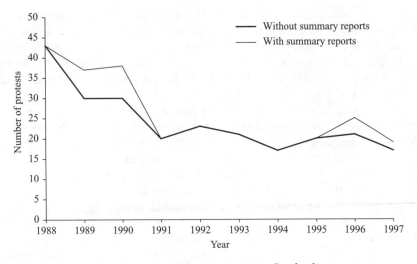

FIG. 9.1. *Environmental protest events in Sweden by year*

and other political manifestations against the bridge between Sweden and Denmark. At the end of the period, animal rights activists started to make an impact.

As we can see from Fig. 9.1, there was a significant shift in the level of reported protest events between the years 1988 and 1989 and between 1990 and 1991. There are several possible explanations. In addition to the changes in the reporting policy at the newspaper, there was also a change in the climate of public debate in the media in general in these years. The fall of the Soviet Union and the emergence of democracy in eastern and central Europe took on special importance in Sweden due to their geographical proximity, but also to strong historical and cultural ties with Poland and Russia, eastern Germany, and the Baltic countries. The fall of the Soviet empire thus had major repercussions on political culture in Sweden.

Another factor of importance is that 1991 was an election year in Sweden. This was an election campaign that did not focus much attention on environmental issues as had been the case in 1988, when, after the nuclear accident at Chernobyl, the Green Party had entered the parliament for the first time. Due in part to the developments in eastern Europe, but also to the decline in economic fortunes that had struck Sweden in the late 1980s, there was an overwhelming emphasis upon economic issues in the campaign leading up to the election which brought to power a non-socialist coalition, led by the conservative Carl Bildt.

The Swedish government had responded promptly to the new doctrine of sustainable development when it was presented in 1987 in the report of the World Commission on Environment and Development, *Our Common Future*. The

government had taken an active part in the first round of climate change negotiations, and, in general, the late 1980s had been marked by rising environmental
concern and continuing rising memberships in the large organizations, particularly SNF and Greenpeace. By 1991, however, the tide had turned, much as in the
early 1980s, and membership rates started to decline, which they continued to do
throughout the 1990s (Boström 2001).

In a newspaper in which most space is devoted to features and entertainment,
the reporting of environmental protest appears to have been strongly influenced
by the presence or absence of other newsworthy issues. Thus, in the period from
October 1994 to February 1995, there were no reports of environmental protest at
all because almost all media, including *DN*, devoted single-minded coverage to
the sinking of the ferryboat Estonia and its aftermath.

A majority (51 per cent) of reported protests took place in Stockholm. Sweden
is in many ways a state with a dominant centre and Stockholm is, of course, the
national capital. Most major media—television channels, newspapers, magazines,
and so on—are located in Stockholm, and the Stockholm area has one-sixth of the
total population of Sweden. Since *DN* is a Stockholm newspaper, it is not
surprising that the capital city dominates, but Gothenburg was also well represented (10.5 per cent of protests), followed by Malmö (4.7 per cent). Protests were
also reported in other major cities and in some smaller towns where major environmental conflicts occurred during the period, in Kungälv over the Scan Link and
in Vilhelmina over conflicts about the rights of the native population in Lappland.
All cities were represented more or less according to the size of their population,
with the exception of Stockholm. Interestingly, the numbers of reported protests
in Stockholm held up during the whole period while protests in Malmö and
Gothenburg were more often reported during the first years. In the case of
Gothenburg this can be explained by the Scan Link protests, but one can also
assume that if a newspaper's interest in covering protest activities diminishes, the
reporting of more remote areas (from the newspaper's perspective) is first to go.

CHANGES IN ISSUE PROFILE

There were three notable aspects of the issue profile of Swedish environmental
protest over the 10 years. First, a number of issue areas (particularly animal rights
and conservation) grew in importance. Second, a number of issue areas, particularly the 'classical' environmental concerns of the 1970s (industrial pollution and
nuclear energy) declined in importance. Third, issues such as opposition to roads
and traffic and the infrastructure projects of 'modernism' remained important
throughout the entire period.

As Fig. 9.2 suggests, the issue area that grew most significantly was animal
welfare and protests against hunting. Protests concerning pollution almost
vanished, and other issue areas also tended to decline. Either the issue areas that
previously characterized environmental protest have become less interesting to the

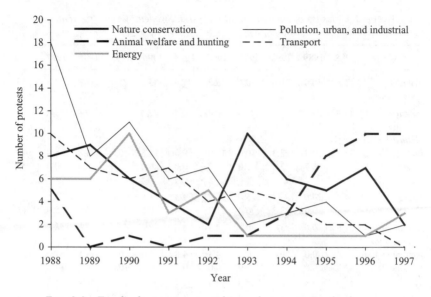

FIG. 9.2. *Five leading environmental issue domains in Sweden by year*

media, or there has been an actual decrease of protest mobilization around these issues. A combination of both of these explanations is perhaps most plausible.

Table 9.1 provides information about how the proportions have changed among the subcategories of protest. For instance, waste was an issue area of significance in the first half of our period and then completely vanished from the data. This reinforces the hypothesis that the kinds of issues that were debated in the 1970s and 1980s had been dealt with sufficiently by the authorities, and that they had largely disappeared into the realm of 'routine' politics and administration. By 1987, Swedish environmental authorities had become quite experienced in regulating industrial pollution and managing and treating waste; as a result, explicit protests about these matters subsided. The strong bureaucratic tradition and the comparatively early creation of national and local environmental author-ities had, in effect, taken the classical environmental issues off the protest agenda.

The numbers of reported protests concerning energy, comprising both nuclear and other energy issues, also declined noticeably. The nuclear issue, still visible at the beginning of our period, faded from view. Here again, the strong arm of the state was effective in removing an issue from the arena of explicit protest. Protests concerning transport have mostly been about roads, with protests focused around the west coast highway expansion in the early part of our period and the Stockholm motorway development, or so-called Dennis project (named for its main promoter, Bengt Dennis), at the end. In general, protests against planned or ongoing road construction have taken precedence over protests against other

TABLE 9.1. *Issues of environmental protest in Sweden by year (percentage of events in which issue is raised by year)*

	1988	1989	1990	1991	1992	1993	1994	1995	1996	1997	Total N
Nature conservation	18.6	30.0	20.0	20.0	8.7	47.6	35.3	25.0	33.3	11.8	59
Pollution, urban and industrial	41.9	26.7	36.7	30.0	30.4	9.5	17.6	20.0	4.8	11.8	62
Pollution	37.2	13.3	23.3	10.0	13.0	9.5	11.8	10.0	4.8	5.9	40
Waste (non-nuclear)	4.7	6.7	3.3	5.0	8.7	0.0	0.0	0.0	0.0	0.0	8
Energy	14.0	20.0	33.3	15.0	21.7	4.8	5.9	5.0	4.8	17.6	37
Nuclear	9.3	0.0	23.3	0.0	21.7	0.0	0.0	5.0	0.0	5.9	18
Animal welfare and hunting	11.6	0.0	3.3	0.0	4.3	4.8	17.6	40.0	47.6	58.8	39
Animal welfare	9.3	0.0	0.0	0.0	4.3	4.8	17.6	30.0	38.1	41.2	30
Hunting	2.3	0.0	3.3	0.0	0.0	0.0	0.0	10.0	9.5	17.6	9
Transport	23.3	23.3	20.0	35.0	17.4	23.8	23.5	10.0	9.5	0.0	47
Roads	23.3	16.7	3.3	15.0	8.7	14.3	23.5	0.0	9.5	0.0	30
Traffic	0.0	0.0	10.0	20.0	8.7	4.8	0.0	5.0	0.0	0.0	11
Alternative production, etc.	11.6	13.3	26.7	25.0	8.7	14.3	29.4	30.0	0.0	11.8	40
Total N of events	43	30	30	20	23	21	17	20	21	17	

Note: Broad categories are in italic; sub-categories are in roman.

infrastructure projects; the early mobilization against the bridge to Denmark disappeared by the end of our period. Animal welfare was the only issue area in which there was an increase during the period, largely because of the new, more militant forms of protest that emerged in the 1990s. Indeed, by the end of the 10-year period, animal rights had become the dominant issue in reports of protest.

The striking rise of animal rights protests in the 1990s is based on a relatively small number of dramatic actions, such as the release of mink from captivity, attacks on animal experimentation laboratories, and demonstrations and sabotage at shops selling animal products. These protests were almost entirely the work of young people who identify themselves with a vegan sub-culture, and coverage of the activities has also included feature articles on the backgrounds of particular activists. There was thus a conspicuously high news value in these protests, and this raises questions about how significant or representative they really were.

Let us now consider the range of issues that were in decline, namely the classical environmental protest issues of the 1970s: industrial pollution and energy.

In Sweden, opposition to hydroelectric dams in the northern rivers was one of the first environmental issues of importance, and in the 1970s it combined with nuclear energy to pit an anti-modernist coalition against the forces of modernization, represented by the energy and electricity industry. During the 1990s, there was a very sharp decline in protest events about energy issues, the only significant new protest concerning a hydroelectric project in the north in 1997. In 1992, four public demonstrations provided a last hurrah for anti-nuclear opposition.

Some issues remained important throughout the 10-year period. Roads and infrastructure projects have been a recurrent protest theme. Consistent with the observation that it is primarily in the period of decision-making and planning that there is an 'opportunity' for broader public debate and protest actions, such protests seem to have faded away as the projects were implemented. When the decision was made, the protests disappeared.

CHANGES IN THE FORMS OF ACTIVISM

In addition to the changing profile of the issues raised in protests, our material also provides information about the forms and organization of environmental activism.

From Fig. 9.3 the predominantly conventional and peaceful character of environmental protest in Sweden is apparent. Signatures and public letters were the most common forms of action, accounting for about one in four of all reported protests. But public protests, demonstrations and blockades were also well represented. Most rallies (eight) were in 1988, and most blockades (six) in 1990, most of them associated with the protests against the Scan Link project.

Thus, conventional and demonstrative forms of protest action were the most common reported strategies. Violence and attacks on properties were relatively

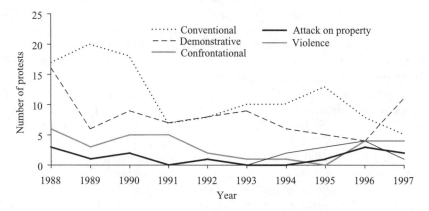

FIG. 9.3. *Forms of environmental protest in Sweden by year*

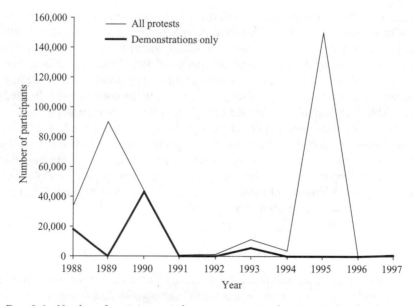

FIG. 9.4. *Number of participants in larger environmental protests in Sweden (protests with 500 or more participants)*

rare but, towards the end of the period, more disruptive actions were reported, most of them associated with animal rights issues. Severe attacks started in 1994 and thereafter there were two, three, or four such cases per year.

Very few protests involved more than 500 participants, and most of those that did were conventional in form. Especially after 1990, large demonstrations were rare and involved relatively few people (see Fig. 9.4).

Few protests resulted in injuries. Injuries were only reported at the beginning and the end of the period. Not surprisingly, in light of the predominantly conventional character of protest, policing appears to have been restrained. Arrests were quite rare, occurring in only thirteen cases (5 per cent). The use of force by police against protesters was still less common, occurring in 4.2 per cent of cases. Injunctions were used in only 6.8 per cent of protests.

It appears from the newspaper reports that the more conventional forms of environmental protest decreased in frequency as did protests overall, but that more confrontational forms of action tended to increase both in absolute terms and, especially, relatively. In light of the comments of the journalist we interviewed, it is likely that this pattern—and especially the decline of the more conventional forms of protest—reflects changes in media attention at least as much as any actual change in the pattern of environmentalists' actions.

It is clear from Table 9.2 that the Conservation Society (SNF) was the leading group in reported protest during the decade. Its primacy is even greater if one

TABLE 9.2. *Number of environmental protests in Sweden involving leading groups by year*

	1988	1989	1990	1991	1992	1993	1994	1995	1996	1997	1998–97
Fältbiologerna (Field Biologists)	3	1	0	1	1	3	1	0	1	1	12
Folkkampanjen mot kärnkraft och kärnvapen (Anti-nuclear campaign)	0	1	4	0	0	0	0	0	0	1	6
Greenpeace	6	3	3	2	6	1	0	1	2	0	24
Jordens Vänner (Friends of the Earth)	0	2	0	0	0	2	0	0	0	0	4
Miljöförbundet (Environmental Union)	2	3	1	2	2	2	0	0	0	0	12
Conservation Society (SNF)	2	5	7	5	4	4	1	1	3	1	33
WWF	0	1	1	0	1	5	0	2	0	1	11
Trädkramarna (Tree-huggers)	3	2	0	1	0	0	0	0	0	0	6
Nordiska samfundet mot plågsamma djurförsök (Nordic society against animal experiments)	2	0	0	0	0	0	1	0	1	3	7
Total *N* of events	43	30	30	20	23	21	17	20	21	17	239

considers that the Field Biologists (Fältbiologerna) are the (independent) youth group of SNF, receiving funds from the mother organization but having their own elected leadership. Aside from Greenpeace, the next most reported group after SNF, many of the other groups mentioned in the newspaper articles are particular campaign organizations that are temporary and more of the nature of 'front' organizations. One of the most significant groups in the late 1980s, Trädkramarna ('Tree-huggers'), was organized to protest against the motorway construction associated with the Scan Link project along the Swedish west coast. The tree-huggers took their name from the Chipko movement in northern India, which had been active in the 1970s and 1980s in protesting against so-called social forestry projects. The action group against the Öresund bridge (Aktion stoppa bron!) was also an *ad hoc*, campaign organization, modelled after the People's Campaign Against Nuclear Energy that had been a large popular front in the 1970s. In these campaigns, many of the leading activists were also members of SNF or its youth organization.

Only a relatively small amount of protest activity was linked to Jordens Vänner (the Swedish branch of the international organization, FoE), which had been one of the central groups of the anti-nuclear campaign. Not even the fact that during this period they joined forces with the Environmental Union (Miljöförbundet— an umbrella organization of primarily local groups) seems to have had much impact as far as reported protest activity is concerned. Rather, the opposite seems to have been the case. It is worth noting, however, that one of the founders of FoE, Lennart Daleus, became the leader of the parliamentary Centre Party, which in the 1970s was the dominant member of the People's Campaign. In this context, it should be remembered that the anti-nuclear movement in Sweden had an unusu- ally strong parliamentary representation. Both the Centre Party and the former Communist, now Left, Party were official members of the People's Campaign, along with some twenty other environmental and non-environmental groups (Jamison et al. 1990).

Violent protest activity was almost exclusively associated with animal welfare (rights) protests (see Table 9.3). Given that these protesters were often young, this suggests a picture of a radical youth issue that was to some extent organized. However, one should remember that most violent protests were also 'anonymous'. No established group wants to be recognized as taking part in such protests even though it is well known that many of the protesters involved were members of the Field Biologists (Fältbiologerna) or, more commonly, an animal rights organiza- tion. By and large, the evidence underlines the impression that environmental protest activity was a rather peaceful and conventional affair in Sweden. This was true even of protests concerning animal welfare.

TABLE 9.3. *Issues and the forms of environmental protest in Sweden (percentages)*

	Conventional	Demonstrative	Confrontational	Attacks on property	Violence	Total N
Nature conservation	39	16	2	2	0	59
Pollution, urban and industrial	29	21	11	4	0	62
Energy	22	10	3	3	1	37
Animal welfare and hunting	12	15	5	4	9	39
Transport	19	15	12	1	0	47
Alternative production, etc.	27	16	1	0	0	40
N	116	81	31	13	10	

Note: Percentage of events involving each issue that involves a form of action. Percentages do not sum to 100 because for each protest up to 2 issues and 4 forms could be recorded.

ORGANIZATIONS AND PROTEST EVENTS

There was a significant change over the decade in respect of the types of organizations that have been involved in environmental protest events.

As Table 9.4 illustrates, some groups, such as Nordiska Samfundet mot Plågsamma Djurförsök (Nordic Society against Painful Animal Experiments) and Trädkramarna, were more or less completely devoted to one issue, whereas others, such as Greenpeace and SNF, addressed very diverse portfolios of issues. It is noteworthy that just as the two largest issue areas—nature and pollution—were the ones that showed the clearest decline, so the organizations, such as Jordens Vänner (FoE), that focus upon such issues were not at all represented in the latter half of the period studied. Others, such as World Wide Fund for Nature (WWF) have never been prominently involved in protest.

About one-fifth of the protest events coded were parts of a campaign. More than half of these (twenty-five) were national campaigns, seven were crossnational with two or more EU countries, and thirteen were other crossnational campaigns. Well over half of all reported protest events involved identifiable interest groups. Greenpeace and SNF were by far the most active, although smaller organizations, such as the Animal Liberation Front, rose in importance during the later years. The numbers of protest events involving formal organizations declined markedly in 1994 and 1995. Informal organizations more or less vanished from the data in 1990 and only reappeared in 1996. The significant

TABLE 9.4. *Environmental groups and their issues of protest in Sweden*
(number of events)

	Nature conservation	Pollution, urban and industrial	Energy	Animal welfare and hunting	Transport	Alternative production, etc.	Other	Total
Fältbiologerna	2	2	0	1	5	1	3	12
Folkkampanjen mot kärnkraft och kärnvapen	0	0	5	0	0	1	1	6
Greenpeace	0	13	5	1	2	4	5	24
Jordens Vänner	4	0	0	0	0	0	0	4
Miljöförbundet	0	4	0	0	5	1	3	12
SNF	10	8	4	2	3	14	6	33
WWF	6	3	0	2	0	3	0	11
Trädkramarna	0	0	0	0	6	0	1	6
Nordiska samfundet mot plågsamma djurförsök	0	0	0	7	0	0	0	7

finding here is the decline in the frequency of protests involving formal organizations, which is not, as might be expected, matched by a rise in informally
organized activities.

Significantly, in the most recent years, organizations appeared with names such
as Animal Alliance, the Saviours of the Rivers, Animal Liberation Front, Animal
Avengers, Eliminate the Fur Industry, Friends Against Dennis, Earth's Future,
Action, Stop the Bridge, and the List of Justice. Each was reported only once and
all are non-established, most of them small organizations relatively unknown to the
general public. Most, by choosing provocative names, indicate a more direct
action-oriented stance or position. Many are also obviously oriented towards animal rights issues. They are loosely connected and tend to be divided between those
that combine environmental protest with protest against other issues and those that
are oriented towards only one single campaign or specific aspect of an issue.

As Table 9.5 indicates, clearly the activities of environmental movement organizations are overwhelmingly peaceful. The most conventional forms of protest
predominate. If any group marks itself out it is Greenpeace, the most confrontational of the groups identified here. The actions of SNF, by contrast, were overwhelmingly conventional. This is not surprising. SNF is a more established NGO,
which does not usually take part in militant protest activity, but is focused on
lobbying or in other ways seeking to influence elected officials, both at the local
and national levels. Its rare forays into more confrontational activities are typically carried out by the youth organization.

Half the environmental protests in Sweden during the decade were mobilized at
a sub-national level (see Table 9.6). The scope of the problems they addressed was

TABLE 9.5. *Environmental groups and their forms of protest in Sweden*
(number of events)

	Conventional	Demonstrative	Confrontational	Attacks on property	Violence	Other	Total
Fältbiologerna	3	5	4	0	0	3	12
Folkkampanjen mot kärnkraft och kärnvapen	3	3	0	0	0	0	6
Greenpeace	7	6	8	3	0	5	24
Jordens Vänner	2	2	0	0	0	0	4
Miljöförbundet	6	4	1	0	0	2	12
SNF	22	5	0	0	0	9	33
WWF	7	2	0	0	0	4	11
Trädkramarna	2	2	2	0	0	1	6
Nordiska samfundet mot plågsamma djurförsök	2	4	1	0	0	1	7

TABLE 9.6. *Levels of mobilization, scope of problems, and targets of environmental protests in Sweden (percentages)*

	Local/district	Regional	National	EU	International	N
Level of mobilization	45.7	4.3	42.9	1.4	5.7	210
Scope of underlying problem	30.5	5.0	39.7	0.8	23.8	239
Level of target	28.8	0.4	69.1	2.5	8.9	259

distributed among the national, sub-national, and international levels, but a tribute perhaps to the long history of central government action to protect the environment, the targets addressed were primarily at the national level. The European Union, Swedish membership of which had been so controversial among environmentalists and non-environmentalists alike, was scarcely implicated in environmental protests at all.

CONCLUSIONS

On 1 July 2000, the bridge between Sweden and Denmark opened to great fanfare and high expectations. In several respects, the bridge provides a symbol of the transformation of the patterns of environmental protest that has taken place between 1987 and 1997. From being one of the main targets of organized political opposition at the beginning of the period while the negotiations for its construction were being conducted, the bridge has become a part of a new process of economic expansion which has contributed to a decline in environmental protest activity. The decision to build the bridge led to the departure in 1994 of Olof Johansson, Environment Minister in the conservative government that came to office in 1991, who opposed the project. As leader of the Centre Party, he had been in the forefront of the anti-nuclear movement in the 1970s.

As work on the bridge began in 1995, the previously widespread opposition was transformed, with the help of public relations and corporate sponsorship, into a remarkable tide of support and enthusiasm. When the project was completed, opposition had, according to opinion polls, declined from a high point of 50 per cent at the beginning of the 1990s to less than 10 per cent. The project had become an important part of an ambitious plan for an economic and cultural resurgence for southern Sweden, while the organized environmental opposition had been more or less marginalized.

In the country at large, the dominant environmental topics of the 1970s—industrial pollution and nuclear energy—have largely disappeared from the political agenda, while a new cluster of global issues has received increasing attention, particularly from the professional environmental organizations, businesses, and political parties. It is in the nature of these issues that it is more difficult to act directly against them. Their emergence has been one of the factors contributing to the more general institutionalization of environmental organizations, or to a shift from protest groups to pressure groups (cf. Diani and Donati 1999). But, as our protest event analysis has clearly indicated, there has also emerged a new range of issues, from animal rights to ecological consumption. Moreover, as in other countries, environmental issues have been combined with, or more accurately subsumed under, other political issues, such as women's rights, welfare reform, and human rights.

A noticeable feature of the Swedish environmental political landscape and of the patterns of protest that we have been analysing, is the strong continuity, over our 10-year period, of certain issues, such as those connected to infrastructural projects—highways, bridges, and traffic more generally—and nature protection and conservation. These issues have been central to Swedish environmentalism throughout the twentieth century. In many respects, environmental activism in Sweden is more continuous than in many other countries, and there is a less ideological or left-wing bias than in other northern European countries, such as Germany, Denmark, and the Netherlands. The Green Party, which was formed in the early 1980s, is also, unlike its counterparts in other European countries, a rather traditional political force in Sweden, and has appealed to voters from across the political spectrum.

The protest event analysis supports the contention that Swedish environmental politics are best seen in terms of a heterogeneous cluster of different actors acting in diverse ways. The key dividing line appears to be between an institutionalized 'mainstream' environmentalism and a more specific and radical form of animal rights activism. While many of the leading environmental organizations in Sweden have been undergoing a process of institutionalization and taking on new tasks, often in alliance with actors in business and government, a new wave of activism has emerged. Among animal rights protesters, militant forms of direct action have been practised—both against animal experimentation and hunting—that have been closely connected to an emergent vegan and more general vegetarian life style.

There has also emerged, in relation to local Agenda 21 projects in many municipalities, a form of local project-making that has ranged from recycling facilities and new collective gardens to workshops for ecological design and renewable energy (Bovin and Magnusson 1997). These new forms of entrepreneurship are somewhat like the consulting activities that have been carried out by new organizations, such as The Natural Step, trying to spread an environmental consciousness into business, government, and other political groups. This is a form of environmental politics that is seldom reflected in protest events, however. While environmental organizations and activists are developing new roles and competencies, the dominant focus of environmental activism in Sweden seems to have moved beyond explicit protest into a new phase integrating environmental concern into social and cultural life more generally (Jamison 2001).

It is important for academic observers of environmental politics to keep up with these changing patterns of activism, and to develop new concepts and theories for understanding the new social roles and cultural activities that are taking place. Some of these changes can be detected in the protest events and explicit political actions that are conducted and covered in the media, but many of them are carried out in a more hidden and less publicly accessible realm of sub-politics or cultural politics. The analysis of protest events reported in a national newspaper can provide only a limited understanding of the transformation of environmental activism. It needs to be supplemented by other types of interpretation if those transformations are to be properly understood.

NOTES

1. The Swedish contribution to international environmental politics is quite noticeable: Hans Blix headed the International Atomic Energy Agency; Thomas Johansson was deputy director of UNDP and a key participant in the climate change deliberations; Björn Stigson was executive director of the World Business Council for Sustainable Development; and Margot Wahlström is EU environmental commissioner.
2. It is no accident that Norway is the country that produced both the early formulations of 'deep ecology' in the writings of the philosopher Arne Naess, as well as a unique brand of cco-populism (Rothenberg 1995). In Finland, the radical animal liberation 'wing' of environmentalism is similar to its Swedish counterpart in its rejection of much of the 'modernist' project, as well as of the reformist and technocratic focus of mainstream environmentalism (Kontinen et al. 1999).
3. The reading was undertaken by Emily Jamison Gromark, and the coding by Magnus Ring.

10

Conclusion: Environmental Protest Transformed?

Christopher Rootes

Although it has antecedents stretching well back into the nineteenth century, the modern environmental movement emerged only during the late 1960s. The environment was only one—and by no means the most prominent—of the many concerns of the New Left and the student movements that emerged during that decade and that so firmly re-established protest as a part of the politics of liberal democratic states. Nevertheless, the public expressions of environmentalism were profoundly influenced by the repertoires of contention of the time. From the beginning of the 1970s, street demonstrations, non-violent direct action, and boycotts were employed, especially by the members and supporters of new environmental movement organizations (EMOs) such as Friends of the Earth (FoE), to draw attention to environmental ills and to put pressure on governments and corporations to change their policies and practices. During the 1970s, Greenpeace emerged, refined the tactics of symbolic protest, and, by skilfully attracting and managing media attention, mobilized public opinion to bring pressure to bear on the perpetrators of environmental degradation. By so elevating the profile of environmental protest, these new, campaigning organizations caught the public imagination and, during the 1980s, they were the fastest growing organizations within a burgeoning environmental movement.

The public's concern with the environment reached a crescendo towards the end of the 1980s, and by the early 1990s, environmentalism was to varying degrees and in various ways institutionalized in most western European states. Environmental protection agencies were set up or, where they already existed, were given increased powers. Ministries of the environment were established within national governments, and political parties that had during the previous decade treated the appearance of the greens as a temporary nuisance began to green their own agenda. However, almost as rapidly as it had risen, public alarm about the environment subsided into routinized concern, and the environment ceased to be front page news.

I am indebted to Dieter Rucht for his comments on an earlier draft and for supplying preliminary versions of the graphs, to Mario Diani for comments, and to Jeffrey Roberts for his assistance with the graphs.

But what did this imply for the environmental movement and, especially, for the environmental protest with which it was so publicly identified? While it was generally acknowledged that the institutionalization of environmentalism in western Europe was well advanced, the implications of that institutionalization for environmental protest and for the character of the environmental movement were much less clear. In keeping with a long tradition of social movement studies, it was widely assumed that the institutionalization of environmentalism entailed the demobilization of the environmental movement and the progressive displacement of protest by less public and more conventional forms of action. The successes of the movement had turned many environmental groups into substantial and relatively well-funded organizations that came increasingly to resemble large formal organizations in other spheres of human activity. As they gained better access to newly receptive governments, officials and corporations, such organizations were supposed to be less and less inclined, or indeed able, to mobilize their increasingly numerous but overwhelmingly passive supporters in any activity more demanding than signing a cheque or a credit card debit authorization.

This picture of a movement so demobilized as to be on the brink of extinction was, however, contradicted in some places by spectacular new eruptions of environmental protest, by the rise of new, more radical environmental groups, and by the responses of older, more established EMOs to the rise of those new groups. The legend of the terminal decline of environmental protest began to appear less credible. Indeed, had environmental protest ever really gone into decline in the 1990s, or had observers simply become so used to it that they had ceased to remark its occurrence? Had the forms of environmental protest and the issues raised by them changed, and how did they vary from one country to another? Were the new outbreaks of protest, so evident in Britain and Germany, paralleled elsewhere in western Europe? Was there evidence of the emergence of a new wave of environmental activists dissatisfied with the efforts and the impact of the more established environmental organizations, and, if so, how did they relate to those older groups? Has the increased centrality of the European Union to the formation of environmental policy been reflected in a diversion of environmental protest away from national targets and to actors and institutions at the European level?

In previous chapters, we have attempted to answer these questions for each of eight countries in turn. In this chapter, we attempt to bring the threads together, to compare developments across the seven nation states for which we have data, and to come to some general conclusions.

THE INCIDENCE OF PROTEST

It might have been expected that three decades of the building of European institutions and of their increasing centrality to environmental policy would, by the mid-1990s, have produced some convergence among the public manifestations of environmentalism. However, if we compare the incidence of reported environmental protests during the course of the decade across all seven states, it is immediately apparent that there was no consistent pattern. The graphs of the incidence of protest presented in the country chapters represent the absolute numbers of protests in each year but, to assist comparison, in Figs 10.1 and 10.2, we present the data in the form of the percentages that protests in each year comprise of the total number of environmental protests reported in each country during the whole decade.

In four countries—Germany, Italy, Greece, and Sweden—the number of reported protests was highest in the first year of the decade, but whereas it declined more or less steadily thereafter in Greece and, to a lesser extent, in Sweden, in 1995 it rebounded in both Italy and Germany to levels close to the 1988 peaks. However, whereas the number of reported protests declined sharply thereafter in Italy, in Germany it was sustained and was higher in 1997 than in 1995. The pattern of environmental protest in Spain is quite similar to that in Germany, although the early peak came later, in 1991, in Spain and the rise of protest from 1994 was sustained through 1997. In France, however, the number of reported environmental protests was highest in 1997, at the end of the period, and markedly higher then than in 1988. In Britain, reported protest rose from 1988 and then plateaued before rising sharply from 1993, peaking dramatically in 1995 and subsiding markedly in 1997. In none of the countries was the evolution of protest during the decade a simple linear trend; fluctuations appeared from year to year, apparently as a result of locally or nationally peculiar issues and events. There was in all countries a

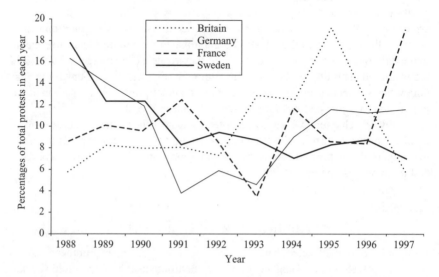

FIG. 10.1. *Environmental protests in Britain, Germany, France, and Sweden*

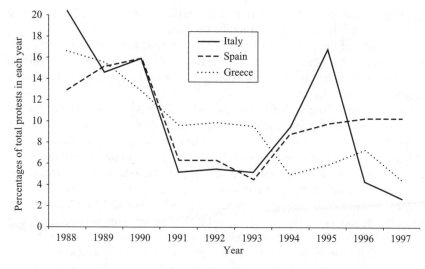

FIG. 10.2. *Environmental protests in Italy, Spain, and Greece*

decline in reported protest during the years 1991–3, but the decline came later in France and it was only very modest in Britain. Otherwise, there is nothing approaching a uniform pattern across all seven countries.

This was the decade in which the institutionalization of environmentalism was supposed to have been accompanied by its demobilization, yet there is no clear and unambiguous evidence that environmental protest actually declined during those 10 years. Newspapers generally report only a small proportion of environmental protests, and from our interviews with journalists, we know that, despite the growing number of environmental stories brought to their attention during the decade, they experienced increasing difficulty in getting reports of environmental protests into print. As the novelty of protest has diminished, and as environmental issues have been assimilated into the political and, increasingly, the economic mainstream, newspapers are very probably reporting a declining proportion of all the environmental protests that actually take place.[1]

There are, however, periods in which the concatenation of protest at the peak of protest waves revives media interest for a time. By comparing newspaper reports with police records of protests, Fillieule (1997) demonstrated that, in France, individual protest events were more likely to be reported if they occurred during rather than outside protest waves. This helps to explain the surge in the number of reported protests in Britain in 1995, and, especially, the extraordinary increase in the number of summary reports of protest in that year (see Chapter 2: Fig. 2.1). The effects of media attention cycles and protest cycles may, then, interact so as to magnify the apparent incidence of protest at the peaks of protest and to reduce it at other times. Thus, given what we know about the pattern of media reporting of protest events, environmental protest may actually have become more rather than less frequent during the decade.

It is clear that the patterns of reported environmental protest vary from country to country, but what does our data enable us to say about the crossnational variation in the aggregate numbers of protests? Were there *more* protests in some countries than in others?

We are dealing here with countries of widely differing sizes, population densities, and degrees of centralization, and our data is drawn from newspapers that, simply as a consequence of the variations in the size and geographical distribution of the populations they cover, very likely report varying proportions of the events that occur within the states concerned. It is improbable that the same proportions of the protests that actually occur will be reported in even the most inclusive national newspaper in Germany or Britain, with 82 million and 59 million people, respectively, and where the local press is highly developed, as in Greece, with its 10 million people and negligible local press. It would be heroic to assume that the space available for reports of protest is constant regardless of population, but it is likely that the amount of newspaper space available for reports of protest varies independently of the size of the population served. For that reason, it is not especially useful to calculate the incidence of protest per capita of population.[2]

On the face of it, even among those countries for which we coded reports from each day's newspapers, there are quite striking crossnational differences in the numbers of nationally reported environmental protests, ranging from 1323 in Britain and 1177 in Germany to 259 in France. The fact that there were roughly five times as many nationally reported environmental protests in Britain or Germany as in France certainly tells us something about the relative salience of environmental protests to the editors and readers of national newspapers in each country, but it is not unambiguous evidence that there were actually more protests in Britain or Germany than in France.

Previous research has concluded that the number of environmental protests was much lower in France than in Germany, the Netherlands, or Switzerland (Kriesi et al. 1995; van der Heijden 1997). Our own research gives us reason to be skeptical about such claims. In the first place, it needs to be remembered that that earlier research, like ours, enumerated not actual protests but *reports* of protest in a single national newspaper in each country—*Le Monde*, in the case of France.

However, nationally reported environmental protest is only a part—and clearly a variable part—of all the protests that take place in a given country. Newspapers are selective in what they report, and the patterns of selectivity in reporting differ even among apparently similar 'quality' newspapers. As we have discovered, the criteria of news relevance of *Le Monde* were more focused upon the national state and formal political institutions than were those of any other newspaper we employed as a source. This suggests an unusual indifference on the part of *Le Monde* to those protests that were not addressed to the state and/or did not involve formal, national-level political actors.

There are, however, other, more substantive reasons why the national media may more seriously under-report environmental protests in France than elsewhere. In contrast to the entrenched image of France as a peculiarly centralized state, the French environmental movement is unusually decentralized, and it is probable that, concomitantly, environmental protest there is also relatively decentralized. In part this may reflect the long-standing importance of communal politics, itself partly a reflection of the diversity of traditions and affiliations in a territorially extensive state, and a counterweight to what was until the 1980s a highly centralized state. It may also be a consequence of the unresponsiveness of the national authorities to environmental protest during the 1970s, the decade in which the modern environmental movement began to emerge. The apparently increasing decentralization of environmental activism may reflect the increasing decentralization of the French state, and the increased opportunities this has created for environmental activists at the regional and local levels (see Chapter 3 and Hayes 2002).

ISSUES

If the incidence of environmental protest varied from country to country, so too did the nature of the issues about which protests were raised (see Fig. 10.3).

The most striking singularity in this respect was the prominence of the nuclear issue in Germany. Although nuclear issues were sometimes capable of mobilizing large numbers of people in demonstrations (as they did in Spain), in no country other than Germany did nuclear energy lead in terms of the proportion of protest events it stimulated. In Germany, however, nuclear issues were raised in a majority

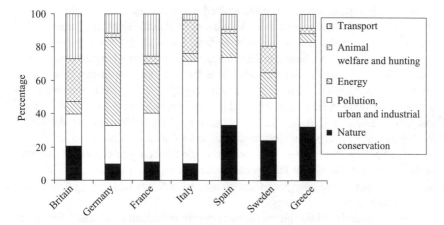

FIG. 10.3. *Issues of environmental protest in seven western European states, 1988–97 (percentage of cases involving each category of issue)*

of environmental protests. Although it was surges of anti-nuclear protest that accounted disproportionately for the peaks of the protest waves in Germany, in only one year (1993) were nuclear issues raised in less than a third of protests. Even in the quietest years, nuclear issues remained more prominent there than anywhere else in western Europe. In France, where anti-nuclear protests had been so salient in the late 1970s, nuclear issues were raised in only a little over 20 per cent of protests, and even fewer after 1994. In Britain, nuclear issues were raised in fewer than 5 per cent of protests. Another difference is that in Germany, a number of national EMOs as well as more local campaign networks raised nuclear issues, whereas in Britain, anti-nuclear protests were mostly the preserve of a single organization—Greenpeace—whose actions were more oriented towards putting pressure on governments and corporations by attracting the attention of mass media than towards stimulating mass protest. Thus, at the very time that Germany was experiencing a great wave of protests against the transportation of nuclear wastes, anti-nuclear protests elsewhere in western Europe had all but disappeared.

In other countries, too, the issue profiles of environmental protest were idiosyncratic. Thus, in Spain, water, including the construction of dams and the diversion of rivers, was a major issue. It was in Britain, France, and Sweden that transport projects, principally concerning road-building and the construction of high-speed railways, comprised the highest proportion of reported protests. Britain, Sweden, and Italy were the only countries where animal welfare issues, including protests against hunting, stimulated a significant proportion of protests.

Pollution issues were raised everywhere but they comprised a relatively declining proportion of nationally reported environmental protests in Italy and Britain, and a more sharply declining one in Germany, Greece, and Sweden. The most general explanation for the decline of pollution-related protests is that, as governments across the European Union have recognized the seriousness of pollution, and as even the most reluctant among them have increasingly effectively implemented EU environmental regulations, so the most obvious forms of industrial pollution have declined in severity and, hence, in their frequency as subjects of urgent citizen complaint. The ecology of issues may also be a factor as the rise of new issues both diverts media attention and refocuses the efforts of protesters. Just as the issues surrounding unification are commonly credited with diminishing the salience of environmental issues in Germany at the beginning of the 1990s, so the decline of pollution-related protests in Germany from 1994 onwards mirrors the increase in reports of anti-nuclear protest. It is likely that the frequency of reports of the latter reduced the space available for reports of the former, but it is also possible that a substantial part of the energies of environmental activists was during those years diverted to anti-nuclear protests.

Survey researchers have characterized environmentalism in southern Europe as being more often than in northern Europe concerned with threats to immediate well-being rather than with global environmental issues (Hofrichter and Reif 1990).

As our data demonstrates, the former are, however, clearly no less capable than the latter of stimulating collective protest. The pattern of reported environmental protests during 1988–97 is consistent with the picture painted by survey research: Italy, Greece, and Spain stood out as the countries in which the highest proportions of environmental protests concerned urban, pollution, and health issues. The likely explanation is that in countries where the impact of urbanization and/or industrialization has been greatest relatively recently, and where effective regimes of environmental protection have been only belatedly introduced, the threats implied by environmental degradation appeared relatively immediate, and concerns about their impact upon human health and well-being were heightened. By contrast, in those countries that had earlier experience of urban or industrial pollution, and effective regimes of planning, control, and remediation, relatively fewer stimuli to protest were presented by urban, pollution, and health issues.

In the course of the 1990s, however, the distinctiveness of the southern European countries became more muted. Health, in particular, was less often raised as an issue in environmental protests. There are two possible explanations for this. First, the trends towards reductions in the levels of the more obvious forms of pollution may be especially noticeable in those southern European countries where levels of concern about pollution were greatest at the beginning of the decade. Second, as the reported incidence of protests about pollution issues in the local sections of newspapers in Italy was relatively stable, their decline in national reports may reflect a decline of media attention rather than simply a decline in public concern with the issues. In Italy it appears that the kinds of pollution issues that concern citizens have changed over time, away from spectacular and nationally reported industrial pollution and toward the pollution caused by motor vehicles, an issue that may excite many local protests but few national reports of protest events. It is unlikely that this is a peculiarly Italian phenomenon.

THE CHANGING FORMS OF PROTEST

Despite the mass media's fascination with the spectacles of violence and confrontation, the great majority of environmental protests reported during the decade were moderate or conventional in form. The predominance of conventional forms of action in reported protests in Italy, Spain, Greece, and, less surprisingly, Sweden, is particularly striking. In each case, over 40 per cent of reported protests employed conventional tactics, including procedural complaints such as appeals for judicial review, collective representations to officials or elected politicians, public meetings, leafleting, and/or the collection of signatures on petitions. In no country did the proportion of reported protests that employed a strictly conventional repertoire fall below 25 per cent of the total for the decade (see Fig. 10.4).

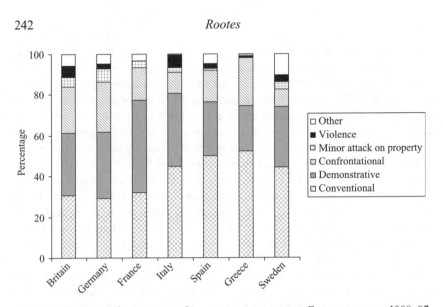

Fɪɢ. 10.4. *Forms of environmental protest in seven western European states, 1988–97 (percentage of protests involving each form of action—principal form only)*

In general, the relative frequency of conventional protests varied in parallel with the frequency of protest overall, but in Italy and Spain there was a modest tendency for conventional action to become more frequent relative to other forms, particularly in periods of relative demobilization. Conversely, with the resurgence of protest in Britain and Germany, there was a fall in the proportion of conventional actions reported. It is possible that these patterns of reported protest reflect short-term tactical shifts in the repertoire of environmental protesters, but they also suggest the impact of the ecology of news coverage, with reports of more spectacular forms of action tending, when they occur, to crowd out reports of the more conventional.

Italy presents perhaps the clearest case of a thoroughly domesticated environmental movement. Especially at the national level, environmental action was promoted by a set of public interest groups, mostly institutionalized in their forms of action, and whose control over the issues was less and less challenged by other political actors such as parties or economic interest groups. This was not, however, the product of a recent process of institutionalization. Since its outset, the Italian environmental movement has been mostly quite moderate, having developed in the early 1980s at a time when there were already pronounced trends in Italian politics generally towards the de-radicalization of social movement activity and towards less confrontational repertoires of action.

We noted earlier that our data does not support claims that environmental protest has systematically and permanently declined since the 1988–9 peak. Nevertheless, there might appear to be some support for the demobilization thesis in the fact that the number of larger protest actions (involving 500 or more people)—and the aggregate numbers of participants therein—have in a majority of the countries markedly declined relative to the overall numbers of protests.[3] Both the numbers of such protests and the numbers of participants in them declined substantially in Italy and Greece, although in Spain the decline in numbers of participants was not as great as that in the numbers of large demonstrations. In Britain, the decline in numbers of larger demonstrations was only relative—the absolute number increased—but the numbers of participants fell substantially. In Germany, the numbers of large demonstrations and people mobilized therein broadly paralleled the overall incidence of protest. Only in France, in the last years of the decade, was an absolute as well as relative increase in the numbers of large demonstrations, as well as numbers of participants, reported.

If there has indeed been a trend toward the demobilization of the supporters of the environmental movement it is at best a modest and inconsistent one. Certainly there is no clear universal and linear trend, and for that reason it would be folly to invest much in the interpretation of the evidence. Nevertheless, one possible explanation of the decline in the numbers of large protests in the latter part of the decade in Spain, Italy, and Greece is the relative absence there of nationally salient environmental issues. By contrast, the national salience of the nuclear issue in Germany meant that the numbers of large demonstrations and participants therein revived more or less in line with the revival of anti-nuclear protests. The issues that generated most protest in southern Europe, and those that, in the latter half of the decade, sustained the rise of protest in Britain—especially those concerning roads and airport construction as well as animal rights—generally gave rise to a relatively large number of very localized, and usually smaller, actions rather than mass mobilizations.

Another possibility is that as mass demonstrations and petitions lost novelty and hence news value, so they were less likely to be reliably reported by newspapers. This is especially likely in the case of petitions. In most countries, the willingness of citizens to sign petitions has increased to the point where it is questionable whether petitioning should any longer be considered as a form of unconventional political activity (Dalton 2002: 62–3). Certainly, petitions about environmental issues are no longer novel and nor are they ordinarily newsworthy. Peaceful street demonstrations and rallies have also become more routine and so may also have lost their capacity to attract media attention.

If the news value of mass demonstrations has been declining as they ceased to be novel, it should not be surprising if the organizers of protests have increasingly deployed their limited resources more strategically, especially by staging symbolic protests designed to attract media attention rather than by attempting directly to mobilize large numbers of their supporters (cf. Jiménez 1999: 161–2). Thus, the declining aggregate numbers of people mobilized in large protests might better be interpreted not as evidence of the declining capacity of an increasingly institutionalized environmental movement to mobilize large numbers of people, but as a reflection of the deliberate strategic choice of the organizers of protest to deploy their energies in more cost-effective ways. Increasingly institutionalized EMOs employ a broad range of tactics and they are less dependent upon highly public mass demonstrations to impress observers and to gain access to policy-makers or publicity for their campaigns. It is perhaps not so much that they *cannot* mobilize their supporters for mass demonstrations as that they see no tactical advantage in doing so.

This is not, however, necessarily a permanent state of affairs. Greenpeace UK, as part of its concern to 'get solutions into actions', to respond to its supporters' desires to be more involved, and to exploit the recently developed resource of its active supporters' network, has increasingly shifted the balance of its protest activity away from elite actions and towards forms of protest such as mass trespass.[4] Moreover, as the German case and the sharp revival of the numbers of protesters at the end of the decade in Spain and France show, even movements that have come to rely primarily upon other means of action are capable of mobilizing large numbers of people should the issue and the occasion demand. There does not, then, appear to have been any general abandonment of large demonstrations and rallies as tactics.

Another factor in the relative decline of large protests has been the rise of new radical groups that do not make a fetish of large numbers and do not mount protests solely or mainly in order to attract media attention. Earth First! and kindred networks and 'disorganizations' deliberately avoid formal organization, and are committed to direct action as a declaration of commitment and/or a direct disruption of the activities of those they target rather than as a means of attracting publicity. Their rise tends to encourage the proliferation of small-scale protests at the expense of large set-piece demonstrations and rallies. The fact that such groups were, during the decade, more evident in Britain than in any of the other countries considered here helps to explain why only in Britain was there an increase in the overall number of protests unaccompanied by a proportional increase in the numbers of large demonstrations or numbers of participants therein.

THE PERSISTENCE OF DISRUPTIVE PROTEST

Overall, disruptive protests comprised around one-third of nationally reported protests in Germany and Britain, nearly 25 per cent in Greece, and less than 20 per cent in France, Italy, Spain, and Sweden. In Italy, disruptive protest was increasingly uncommon, and the relatively high proportion of disruptive protests that involved violence was entirely a phenomenon of the early years of the decade. With the partial exceptions of Germany and Britain, there was no clear evidence of any trend towards more extreme tactics over time.

Perhaps surprisingly, in view of what has been written about the institutionalization and domestication of environmentalism in Germany (Blühdorn 1995;

Brand 1999), environmental protest in Germany was, in aggregate, more disruptive, even violent, than in any of the other countries we studied. Moreover, it became more violently disruptive towards the end of the decade. In Britain, although the incidence of confrontational protests rose dramatically during the 1990s, violent actions were rare and largely confined to animal rights protests that were at best marginal to the environmental movement. In Germany, by contrast, confrontational forms of protest were present throughout the decade and, broadly speaking, rose and fell with the general waves of environmental protest. Attacks on property, and (less commonly) on people, increased sharply both relatively and in absolute numbers from 1994.

What explains the patterns of protest repertoires? France was the country where demonstrations comprised the highest proportion of all nationally reported protests, but otherwise the patterns revealed do not conform particularly well with the usual stereotypes of national political cultures. The relatively high proportions of violent protest in Britain and Sweden are counter-intuitive, as are the relatively low proportions involving violence in France, Greece, and Spain. However, these anomalies largely disappear if animal rights protests are distinguished from more strictly environmental protests. Indeed, it appears that repertoires are less a matter of national cultures than of movement cultures, the culture of environmentalism being overwhelmingly non-violent whereas those of the anti-nuclear and, especially, the animal rights movements have, in most countries, significant (minority) strains of violence.[5]

Yet the issue that dominated both the late 1980s and the mid-1990s peaks of protest in Germany was the same—nuclear energy. In 1988–9, protests focused upon and culminated in the abandonment of a nuclear processing facility under construction at Wackersdorf in Bavaria, whereas from the mid-1990s they were focused upon the transportation of nuclear wastes to repositories at Gorleben and Ahaus in northern Germany. The explanation for the much more confrontational and sometimes violent character of the latter wave of protest lies less in the character of the issues than in the dynamics of the anti-nuclear movement and its interaction with the authorities. After years of uncertainty during which the future of the nuclear energy industry remained unresolved and during which the movement had been frustratingly unable to prevent the construction of temporary waste depositories, the campaign to prevent the transportation of nuclear waste had the character of a last ditch battle to prevent nuclear energy being accepted as a permanent part of Germany's industrial establishment.

Clearly, movement cultures do not exist in a social and political vacuum. Thus, the instances of violent environmental protest in Italy and Spain are best seen as carry-overs into the environmental arena from other, wider political ructions—in Italy, the tail end of the widespread political violence of the 1970s and 1980s, and in Spain, the temporary association of militant Basque nationalism with environmentalist struggles. Similarly, the dramatic rise of confrontational environmental protest in Britain in the 1990s was the crest of a wave of more general confrontational protest that rose with the campaign against the poll tax. National political cultures, then, appear to explain little by comparison with the interaction between movement cultures and the impacts of political conjunctures.

ORGANIZATIONS

In all countries, it was evident that there were within the environmental movement two coexisting strands: one consisting of formal EMOs most of whose activities do not revolve around protest; the other consisting of local campaigns, more informal groups and *ad hoc* coalitions.

In Germany, the major EMOs were reportedly involved in a majority of protests only in those years (1991–3) that marked a trough between the waves of protest. Die Grünen, Robin Wood, Greenpeace, BUND, and DNR were all relatively more prominent in reported protests in the years 1988–91 than in 1994–7. Newer, smaller, more specialized, and more local organizations became more prominent towards the end of the period. A similar, if more muted, pattern appeared in Britain. Greenpeace, FoE, WWF, the Royal Society for the Protection of Birds, the Green Party, and the Ramblers Association were reportedly involved in 27 per cent of protests in the first half of the decade, but in only 18 per cent in the second; only once in the latter 5 years did the number of protests in which they were named exceed the low point of the previous half decade. A much sharper decline in the relative salience of the major groups occurred in Sweden; named in almost half the protests reported in 1988–93, they were reportedly involved in only 20 per cent of those thereafter.

Such findings are consistent with the thesis that the institutionalization of EMOs, which has induced them increasingly to focus upon 'constructive engagement' with government and industry, has led to their demobilization, or, more precisely, to the decline of their inclination or ability to mobilize people for protest. It is also testimony to the impact of the formation of new, smaller groups and the revival of local protests to which established national EMOs are usually marginal where they are involved at all.

These trends were not, however, universal. In Italy, nationally reported environmental protest became increasingly dominated by the leading formal environmental organizations, chiefly at the expense of political parties, trade unions, network groups, and other environmental organizations. Even at the local level, formal environmental organizations increasingly displaced informal environmental groups from reports of protest during the later years of the decade. In Spain, the increased prominence of the seven leading environmental organizations was even more striking; mentioned in fewer than a third of reports of protests in the first half of the decade, they were involved in more than half of nationally reported protests in the latter 5 years. In Greece, although community groups led a majority of all environmental protests, there was during the decade a marked trend towards the greater prominence of leading national environmental organizations.

It appears, then, that in the southern European countries, unlike those of northern Europe, nationally reported environmental protest was increasingly dominated by formal EMOs at the expense of more informal groups. This pattern is consistent with the relatively belated consolidation and institutionalization of national EMOs in southern Europe, and with the increasing differentiation of the environment as a specialized issue domain within national politics. It is, in short, an earlier stage of the process of institutionalization, occurring against political and institutional backgrounds quite different from those of northern Europe, that has marked the changing pattern of environmental protest in southern Europe.

NETWORKS

The existence of large numbers of environmental groups, the occurrence of protest, or even the clustering of a large number of protests over a given period of time, is not proof of the existence or vitality of a social movement (Diani 1995, 2003). If social movements are networks of organizations and individuals engaged in collective action and sharing a common identity, then it is important, if we are to answer questions about the character of the environmental movement at this stage of its development, that we should examine reports of protest for evidence of networks linking the participants in them. Protest may be only part of the action repertoire of EMOs and of the environmental movement generally, but it is at least evidence of collective action without which the continued existence of a movement would be problematic (Rootes 2003*b*).

However, in attempting to study the networks that constitute the environmental movement by means of protest event analysis we face two main difficulties. The first is that most of the interaction among established EMOs does not take the form of public protest and so is unlikely to be reported in newspapers, let alone reflected in our coding of newspaper reports of protest events. The second is that, even where EMOs are involved in their planning or organization, many protests are not mounted in the names of established EMOs, both because established organizations are cautious about exposing themselves to legal liability, and because it is often considered tactically advantageous to form *ad hoc* campaign groups better able to effect broad-based mobilization in particular campaigns.

Our network analyses are based on only that minority of protests in each country in which at least two organizations were reported to have been involved. Although the number of such links examined is, as a result, relatively small in relation to the total number of protests, by examining such co-occurrences of reported involvement we have been able to represent the most publicly visible links in the collective action of the environmental movement, and we are also able to shed light on the extent of segmentation of protest networks. Thus, for example, we have been able to demonstrate that animal rights protests in Britain were quite unconnected to the mainstream of the environmental movement, and that the revived anti-nuclear protests in Germany were relatively well-integrated into the network of established EMOs. This latter finding is especially significant because it demonstrates graphically that even substantially institutionalized movement organizations may, should the issues so require, return to the streets and make common cause with more radical activists.

Not surprisingly, the forms of the environmental networks revealed by reports of protest vary from country to country. In Britain, a country with a large, well-established, organizationally and thematically diverse national EMO sector (Rootes and Miller 2000), the network of groups interacting in environmental protest appears less tight than it does in Germany, where the structure of the movement is more decentralized and where protest has been so dominated by a single issue—nuclear energy. The British network structure is less tight, too, than in Spain, where the movement consisted of a smaller number of weakly institutionalized groups that were, by their lack of resources, constrained to greater interdependence.

Network analysis also reveals differences from country to country in the extent to which environmental protest is a specialized activity distinct from other spheres of political and social life. In Britain and in Greece, no non-environmental organization was reported to have been linked in protest with any environmental group on three or more occasions. By contrast, in France and Germany, political parties were relatively prominent in networks of protesting organizations, whereas parties (and trade unions) were more peripherally involved in Spain. In Italy, political parties and trade unions appear in the networks of environmental protest only because they were linked with other parties or trade unions respectively, and not because they had been linked in reports of protest to environmental organizations. Germany was distinctive in that only there did churches appear in the network. The distinctiveness of these patterns reflects the peculiarities of national politics as well as the configurations of alliances about particular issues.

LOCALISM

The extent to which protests were mobilized on a national or sub-national level, addressed issues whose underlying scope was national or sub-national, or were targeted at national or sub-national actors varied considerably. In both Germany and Britain, just over half of all protests were mobilized at a local or regional level and had national-level targets. In Sweden, however, although 50 per cent of environmental protests were mobilized at a sub-national level, more than two-thirds had national-level targets, a tribute perhaps to the persistence of the habits of political claims-making appropriate to a relatively centralized state.

In Italy, and especially in Spain and Greece, the characteristic localism of political culture has been fully reflected in the character of environmental protest. In Greece, 90 per cent of protests were local mobilizations around local issues, although half of them were targeted at national authorities. However, in each of these countries, during the course of the decade, national EMOs became relatively more important, not least as organizers of protest. There appears, then, to be evidence that the traditional localism of environmental politics in southern Europe has begun to yield to a pattern of protest increasingly mobilized at the national level and addressing national-level problems and targets. However, particularly in Greece, where these tendencies appear to be strongest, the trend may have been exaggerated by the changing character of newspapers' coverage of environmental issues. The integration of environmental issues into mainstream policy agenda and political debates, and more sophisticated reporting of environmental issues, may, paradoxically, have reduced media coverage of local environmental protests because, in the competition for newspaper space, the environment may be considered already to be covered by regular political news, feature articles, and scientific reports. It is possible, too, that local environmental conflicts, having become endemic, progressively lost their news value.

The formation of national environmental organizations may itself lead to a decline in media coverage of local, single-issue campaigns. The new organizations are interesting to journalists simply because they are new, and also because they might possibly be harbingers of more widespread change. Moreover, they offer increasingly hard-pressed journalists a lifeline, because it is much simpler and more economical to use the news feeds from formal organizations, particularly those that are relatively sophisticated in public and media relations, than to follow the narratives of a diversity of geographically dispersed local protests. Thus, news generated by the press releases of formal national environmental organizations may tend to eclipse reports of informal local protests. For all these reasons, the decline of local environmental protest in southern Europe may be more apparent than real.

However, if in southern Europe there has been a *real* trend away from the historical localism of environmental contention and towards national levels of organization and trans-local, even global, environmental concerns, it is not difficult to explain. In Greece and Spain, the stabilization of national democratic politics has been one factor, and this has been reflected even in the increasing disconnection of environmentalism from nationalism in the Basque Country. Another factor has been the impact of the European Union and the increasing connectedness of environmentalists in these countries, not least through their involvement in organizations developed to lobby EU institutions (including the European Environmental Bureau), with those countries of northern Europe where EMOs and environmental consciousness were already highly developed. The predominance of local environmental protests appears to have declined because knowledge of environmental issues has become more sophisticated, and because awareness has increased that the structures of political opportunity have changed. Paradoxically, the relative prominence of French environmental activism at the local or regional levels has increased for the same reason. What is peculiar about France, formerly so centralized administratively, is that, at least insofar as environmental matters are concerned, the structures of political opportunity have been transformed so markedly in the direction of decentralization (Hayes 2002).

EUROPEANIZATION?

In view of the progressive consolidation of the European Union and given the development and implementation of an increasingly large common corpus of EU environmental regulation, it might be expected that there would by now be clear evidence of trends towards the Europeanization of environmental protest. Yet, as we have already seen, there was surprisingly little similarity between the patterns of incidence of protest during the decade from one country to another.

Nor did we find evidence that protests were, to any great extent, mobilized on a European level, addressed issues whose underlying scope was European, or were targeted at European-level actors. In all countries, the great majority of protests were focused on the national and sub-national levels, with relatively small proportions mobilized on, targeted at, or even addressing problems whose underlying scope was identified as being at an EU level (see Table 10.1).

Nowhere did we find clear evidence of a trend towards the Europeanization of environmental protest in terms of the level of mobilization of protesters, the scope of the problems underlying the protests, or the targets of protest. It is understandable, given the logistical difficulties that confront it, that mobilization at the EU level should be so rare. More surprising is the evidence that other EU countries, companies domiciled in other EU states, or the European Union itself were relatively rarely mentioned as either the targets of protest or as the sources of the underlying problems against which protests were ranged.[6]

The institutions of the EU itself were especially infrequently mentioned in these respects. This is not difficult to explain. For most of the 1990s, the European Union tended to be seen by most environmentalists in most of the countries covered here as an ally rather than an object of complaint. Moreover, the structure of EU institutions has tended to encourage lobbying rather than public protest. In any case,

TABLE 10.1. *EU-related protests as percentages of all protests (1988–97)*

	Britain	France	Germany	Greece	Italy	Spain	Sweden
Level of mobilization	0.4	4.0	1.7	2.7	1.3	1.9	1.4
Scope of underlying issue	6.4	5.7	8.1	2.1	0.6	1.4	0.8
Level of target	3.2	1.8	4.0	1.8	0.7	5.1	2.5
N	1311	245	1140	582	327	706	239

Note: *N*s vary; those given are for scope of the underlying issue. The figures are based on 100% coverage of reports, except for Greece, Italy, and Sweden, where they are based on a 50% sample.

public protest is less likely to be directed at the European Union because there is as yet no European public sphere and no EU-wide mass media. As a result, even when environmentalists do protest in Brussels or Strasbourg, it is national news media and national governments that tend to be targeted. Probably the most important reason why protest remains resolutely at the national or local level is that, however much policy and regulation is made at the EU level, it is at the national or the local level that policy is implemented, and it is the implementation of policy rather than its formulation that leads to most protest. Because environmental protest is mobilized or targeted mainly at the local or national levels, it is shaped primarily by the habits and dynamics of local and national politics, and for that reason it is not surprising that there appears to have been at best a very limited Europeanization of tactical repertoires (Rootes 2002*a*, 2004).

THE NATIONAL CONTEXTS OF ENVIRONMENTAL PROTEST

Nowhere does environmentalism exist in a vacuum remote from the impact of other political issues and wider political contexts. In most of the countries encompassed by our research, the 1990s were years in which environmentalism consolidated its position, and they followed years of political turbulence, sometimes punctuated by political violence, associated with the rise of the 'new social movements'.

In Britain, however, the great political battles of the early 1980s were not associated with new social movements so much as with classic industrial disputes. Even the peace movement, so important a constituent of the new social movement sectors in countries such as Germany and the Netherlands, was in Britain semi-institutionalized by its domination by a single organization (the Campaign for Nuclear Disarmament) and its self-conscious orientation towards the Labour Party. Thus, in Britain, as phenomena distinct from and outside conventional politics, the new social movements were scarcely developed by comparison with those of several continental European states (Rootes 1992). However, at the beginning of the 1990s, just as Italy, Germany, and Spain were becoming markedly less contentious societies and as environmental movements were becoming semi-institutionalized, Britain, for reasons that had little directly to do with the environmental movement, was entering a new phase of contention that was to have a dramatic impact upon the character of environmental protest. The mobilization against the poll tax had effects that flowed on to the environmental movement via anti-roads protests and that made the movement more confrontational even as leading EMOs were becoming increasingly institutionalized (Rootes 2003*a*).

The only other country in which there was a substantial radicalization of protest was, a little later in the decade, Germany. There, however, it was not so much that other political events and movements contributed to the radicalization of environmental protest as that the old iconic issue of German environmental protest—nuclear energy—was highlighted by the German government's belated attempts to deal on German soil with the wastes produced by German nuclear power stations. Germans who had remained silent for years as German nuclear waste was shipped by train and boat to reprocessing facilities in Britain and France were suddenly agitated by the prospect that such reprocessed waste might be transported back to Germany for long-term storage. This excited diffuse fears about the possible effects of radiation, and the fact that it implied permanence for the nuclear industry was one factor stimulating protest. Another was the increasing exasperation with the re-elected but ailing conservative government of Helmut Kohl. The radicalization of tactics in the revived German anti-nuclear protests also occurred in the aftermath of the well-publicized tactical innovations of the British anti-roads movement, and there is more than merely circumstantial evidence that the latter was at least part of the inspiration for the former.

Transnational influences upon tactics may have become more important in an increasingly inter-communicating world, but the incidence of environmental protest seems to have more closely reflected the dynamics of national politics and to have resisted any pressures to Europeanization.

Thus, in Britain both the electoral cycle and more general cycles of protest appear to have had effects upon the incidence of environmental protest. The levels of reported environmental protest were lower in both the election years (1992 and 1997) than in the immediately preceding years. Similarly, in Sweden, the number of environmental protests fell in the election years of 1991, 1994, and 1997. They fell particularly sharply in 1991, an election year in which environmental issues did not figure prominently as they had during the preceding election in 1988 when environmental protests were at their peak. In Greece, however, protests increased during election years, although local protesters' customary tendency to attempt to apply pressure on the state by mounting protests during elections appears to have had only a modest impact. In Germany, reported environmental protests rose sharply in 1994, an election year in which the Kohl government was re-elected. In France, the investment of environmentalists' energies in the campaigns of green parties, the disappointment of their hopes in the general election of 1993, and their accession to government in 1997 are all credited with depressing the incidence of environmental protest (see Chapter 3), yet 1997 was actually the peak year for reported environmental protest in France.

Clearly, it is not merely the fact of a general election that influences the number of environmental protests in a particular year so much as whether or not environmental issues are important issues of contention in those elections. Where major political parties do not highlight the environment during election campaigns, their mobilization of opinion on other issues appears to overwhelm the widespread but diffuse public concern about environmental issues and so to contribute to the demobilization of protest. However, it is also possible that in such circumstances the press itself, focused as it is during elections upon the agenda of political parties, reports a smaller proportion of environmental protests than it does at other times.

Environmental protests may also be influenced by more general cycles of protest. As we have seen, in Britain the cycle of protest that began with the campaign against the poll tax in 1990 prepared the ground for the anti-roads protests of the mid-1990s. In the Basque Country, environmental protest was for a time subsumed by the larger nationalist movement and struggled to assert its separate identity.

In some cases, declines in protest appear to have been responses to tactical errors by environmentalists themselves. Thus, in Italy, the defeat in 1990 of referendum proposals to limit the use of pesticides and to restrict hunting appears to have contributed to the demobilization of protest, but there too it was probably the wider political context that was decisive. The rise of the Northern League, the exposure of massive political corruption, and the consequent collapse of the political establishment so transformed national political agenda as to marginalize environmental concerns.

Developments at national level were in various ways mirrored at local level, reflecting the impact of similar but locally idiosyncratic mixes of political institutional, cultural, contextual, and contingent factors. The Swedish picture, for example, was one of a process of institutionalization in a stable polity so actively inclusive that it was impossible to sustain protest waves for long. Italy, by contrast, presented a picture of local innovation in a polity in which the traditional modes and institutions of interest mediation had very recently collapsed, and where a new wave of environmentalism arose, characterized by new forms of 'participation from below'.

Attempts have been made to explain the development of social movements in terms of 'political opportunity structures' (Kitschelt 1986; Kriesi et al. 1995). Unfortunately, this useful concept has been overburdened by being stretched to include all manner of the factors that bear upon the outcomes of political contention, so that genuinely structural factors are confounded with others that are merely contingent or conjunctural (Gamson and Meyer 1996, Rootes 1997a, 1999c). Strictly structural factors, political institutional arrangements foremost among them, explain little if any of the variation in the patterns of environmental protest among the seven states we have considered.

Nor do refinements that characterize states in terms of their strategies towards the environmental movement fare much better (Dryzek et al. 2002, 2003). States that were, at least with respect to particular environmental issues, strong during the decade and at least passively exclusive, experienced both relatively high (Britain and Germany) and relatively low (France) numbers of nationally reported protests. Italy, whose state was weak and, for most of the decade, passively exclusive with respect to environmental issues, does not, once allowances are made for the size of their respective populations, appear to have experienced markedly more or less environmental protest than Sweden, whose state was strong and actively inclusive. Moreover, contrary to what these theories propose, disruptive protest was no more common in exclusive Italy than in inclusive Sweden.

The focus upon state strategies entails the recognition that they may both change over time and vary as between different environmental issues, and it serves to emphasize that structural factors are incapable of explaining the considerable temporal variation of protest within each of the several states. It is the contingent and conjunctural dimensions of political opportunities rather than the truly structural ones that best explain the patterns we have observed (cf. Tarrow 1994).

It does appear that the failure of governments to respond to issues of widespread public concern is a common precondition of substantial mobilizations of protest. The most striking cases considered here are those of the British anti-roads protests and those in Germany against the transportation of nuclear waste. But such mobilizations are not simply autonomic responses to the actively or passively exclusionary strategies of governments. They occur against a backdrop of other political issues and, in particular, they derive many of the interpretive frames, strategies, and organizational forms they adopt from previous manifestations of environmentalism and from other mobilizations of protest. This 'path dependency' of environmental protest is too easily missed by those who would insist upon a classificatory approach to the explanation of the events we discuss. What we find are not tidy examples of types that can be comfortably pressed into the boxes of classificatory schemes, but a series of nationally idiosyncratic narratives that reflect the realities of politics as the interplay of human agency and the opportunities presented, and the constraints imposed, by a wide variety of structures and contingent events.

CONCLUSION

Increasingly many claims have been made about the character and incidence of environmental protest and their implications for environmental movements and those with whom they interact. However, such claims have mostly been little more than assertions based upon casual observation and anecdote. We have in this volume been concerned to remedy that by employing the methodology of protest event analysis in order to explore the development of environmental protest in seven of the major states of western Europe. In particular, we have been concerned systematically to confront the hypothesis that the institutionalization of environmentalism has entailed the demobilization of the environmental movement. This we have done by examining the public record of environmental protest during the 10 years during which that institutionalization and demobilization are supposed to have occurred.

As Charles Tilly (2002) has reminded us, empirical research simultaneously embodies both theories explaining the phenomena under investigation and theories about the evidence concerning those phenomena. We have in this investigation employed protest event analysis of newspaper reports because it is the only reasonably practical and economical way of studying publicly visible protest activity across whole countries and over extended periods of time. However, we have not uncritically appropriated newspaper reports as evidence. Conscious of the implications of selectivity and bias in reporting, we have used other contextual information and interviews with journalists and editors to inform our interpretations of the reports of protest events that constitute our principal sources of data. We believe that, as a result, we have more grounds for confidence in our conclusions than those of previous practitioners of protest event methodology who have been less conscious of, and candid about, its limitations.

We have demonstrated that, although the character of environmental protest has varied from one country to another and within countries over time, reported environmental protest has not consistently declined. Nor has it universally changed in ways that are consistent with a linear process of institutionalization and domestication. The incidence of environmental protest fluctuates according to the supply of mobilizing issues, and the reporting of protest depends upon the vagaries of competition from other events and issues as well as the interest and attention of journalists and editors.

Given what we now know about the ways in which the media's reporting of environmental issues changed during the course of the decade, it is probable that in several countries the actual (as distinct from the reported) incidence of environmental protest increased rather than declined. Certainly, there is no clear evidence to support claims that the institutionalization of environmentalism has entailed the demobilization of protest. In western Europe, as in most industrialized countries elsewhere, environmental protest is not merely tolerated but increasingly widely publicly approved, but because it is no longer novel, it is no longer assured of media coverage. As a result, its salience has declined even if its incidence has not. The consolidation of national-level EMOs has, especially in northern Europe, been paralleled by the persistence or proliferation of less formally organized local protests, but we have shown by means of network analyses that neither this nor the rise of new, more radical environmental groups has entailed the disintegration of environmental movements.[7]

The considerable variation in the incidence of environmental protest from country to country and over time clearly reflects the continuing impacts of the contingencies of national politics and the idiosyncrasies of national political institutions and cultures. The impact of the increased competence of the European Union in environmental matters upon the pattern of protest has been surprisingly muted everywhere. We found no evidence of any trend towards the displacement of national targets in favour of EU institutions in any of the seven states. Moreover, there was at best a very modest trend towards the Europeanization of the issues raised by environmental protests and the forms they have taken. More striking was the extent to which both issues and forms of protest reflected the distinctive concerns and idiosyncratic dynamics of politics within each of the several states.

It would be simplistic to represent the repertoire of environmentalist action as a straightforward reflection of the patterns of opportunities and constraints with which it is confronted, not least because the forms of action are shaped by activists' political philosophies as well as by instrumental considerations. Nevertheless, the increased centrality of environmental issues on public agenda has created greater opportunities for effective action by more conventional means, and it provides fewer provocations to more confrontational (and more newsworthy) forms of action. Organizations such as Greenpeace that did so much to raise the profile of environmental protest during the 1980s have not simply abandoned protest but, as their opportunities for advancing their causes by other means have grown, so has the range of their activities. The environmental movement is an increasingly mature one, but it continues to embrace a considerable diversity of national, regional, and local groups. Protest remains part of the repertoire of environmentalism, but it is only one part of an increasingly diverse repertoire. Protest has not been supplanted but supplemented.

The evidence suggests that in this critical decade the institutionalization of environmentalism has not been accompanied by an unambiguous decline of environmental protest. Indeed, it appears that the institutionalization of environmentalism may be a self-limiting process, as the expectations raised by increasingly established groups stimulate new demands and the formation of new groups to articulate them, and as these new demands and groups in turn influence the agenda and actions of older groups. It is inevitable that the incidence, concerns, targets, and forms of environmental protest will change. However, given the inherent conflicts between the requirements of economic development and human interests in the protection of the environment, it is difficult to imagine a future in which there is neither reason nor will to protest.

NOTES

1. In particular, it is questionable whether the apparent declines of reported protests in Greece and Sweden reflect real declines in the number of events so much as our source newspapers' declining interest in local environmental protests.
2. The per capita incidence of reported protests varied significantly from one country to another. Employing a standardized sample (based on alternate days' newspapers) for each country, the number of nationally reported protests per capita ranged from 2.7 per million inhabitants in France, through 5.7 in Italy, 7.5 in Germany, 10.4 in Spain, 11.9 in Britain, to 27.5 in Sweden, and a remarkable 55.4 in Greece. (The standardized samples comprise rather more than 50 per cent of the protests identified from the coding of every day's newspapers, principally because some protests are the subject of reports on more than one day but do not give rise to more than a single reported protest event.) The per capita incidence of reported environmental protest in the Basque Country was still higher (*c.* 175 per million), but the pattern and degree of selectivity of reporting in a newspaper serving 2.6 million people in what is juridically a sub-state region is more comparable with that of regional newspapers elsewhere than it is with the national newspapers that are our sources in all the other cases considered here.
3. We have assumed that newspapers were more likely reliably to report large protest actions than smaller ones. Although we set the threshold for 'large' demonstrations at 500, it is possible that over the years what is regarded as a large demonstration has

changed. A number of recent demonstrations of over 500 hundred people in Britain have gone unreported in the national press. For example, a protest in November 2002 against government plans to increase the number of airport runways in south-east England was estimated by the BBC to have attracted 3000 demonstrators, but was reported by only one of the four general national quality newspapers (*The Times*).

4. Greenpeace UK spokesman interviewed by Ben Seel, May 2000.

5. There are exceptions to even this modest generalization. In Greece and in Spain, animal rights and anti-hunting protests were the most conventional in form of all environmental protests. However, it is noteworthy that in both countries the numbers of such protests were small. It is perhaps the case that, in countries where animal welfare issues do not command wide public support or concern, protesters are less likely to compound the unpopularity of their cause by employing more contentious forms of action.

6. This finding may appear to contradict that of Imig and Tarrow (1999, 2001), who found that, although the number and proportion of EU-related protests was very low, it rose significantly between 1983 and 1997. In fact, their data appears to show a pattern of trendless fluctuation until about 1995, with only 1997 showing a very marked increase. However, their data and ours are not comparable because their data, aggregated for ten or twelve EU states, cover all protests whereas ours are restricted to those about environmental issues. (In their data, only 88 out of 490 protests involved non-occupational groups, of which environmental groups were only some.) Moreover, their data is derived from Reuters reports, probably selected for their national/international importance and their interest to the business community, whereas ours are drawn from all environmental protests reported in one national newspaper in each country. Not only, on Imig and Tarrow's own account, is it likely that the Reuters data is biased towards the 'more important' and higher level protests, but it is likely that as the business community has become increasingly persuaded of the importance of the European Union, so Reuters, as a news service selling its services primarily to business, will have become more assiduous in its coverage of EU-related protests. However, if Imig and Tarrow's data possibly exaggerate the relative incidence of EU-related protest in more recent years by comparison with earlier years, our own, because it is limited to protests occurring on the territory of just seven states, might tend to underestimate it for the whole period. Unfortunately, we have no systematic evidence for the incidence of EU-related environmental protests in Brussels. Nevertheless, since there was no increase in reported overall EU-related protest in Belgium in the years 1980–95 (Reising 1999; Rucht 2001: 141, n. 20), it appears unlikely that it has been sufficiently frequent to contradict our conclusions.

7. We shall provide further evidence of the extent and linkage of local environmental protests to national EMOs in a subsequent volume.

Appendix A

The Methodology of Protest Event Analysis and the Media Politics of Reporting Environmental Protest Events

Olivier Fillieule and Manuel Jiménez

Protest event analysis (PEA) has become increasingly popular since the early 1980s. Indeed, it has almost become a sub-field within the sociology of social movements, with its own theoretical debates, epistemological issues, methods, and even vocabulary.[1] The positive effects of this situation are several.

First, PEA has reinforced the tendency that began at a theoretical level in the 1980s to integrate different approaches. This integration has been consolidated by a degree of harmonization of methods and trends in empirical research. At the same time, because it enables the construction of a diachronic relationship between the development of movements and social contexts, PEA has contributed to the testing of key hypotheses. Especially significant improvements have been those related to the identification and functioning of action repertoires, cycles of mobilization, and the political opportunity structure. More precisely, by taking account of the temporal dimension, PEA highlights the facts that social movements cannot be reduced to the organizations involved in them and that movements do not exist in isolation from other contemporaneous movements at either the national or international levels. Hence, one must logically develop an analysis in terms of process, rather than thinking in terms of structural determinants. Discontinuities in the temporal series allow a reading of the impact of any particular factor on levels of mobilization and help to avoid the danger of a retrospectivity that would lead to the analysis of only the most visible mobilizations or, worse, only those that succeeded.

This last point highlights the extent to which PEA has been useful for invalidating a whole series of empirically ill-founded theoretical propositions. It is, for

We thank Mario Diani, Erik Neveu, Chris Rootes, and Dieter Rucht for their insightful comments on earlier drafts of this chapter. We also thank the other contributors to this volume for the information they have provided.

example, thanks to the work of Charles Tilly and others that the theories of relative deprivation and social disintegration have been invalidated (Rule and Tilly 1972; Snyder and Tilly 1972; Tilly, Tilly, and Tilly 1975). Applied to urban rioting, other studies, most notably those of Clark McPhail, contradict the notion that the most disadvantaged communities were also those most susceptible to social disintegration (Lieberson and Silverman 1965; Wanderer 1969; Eisinger 1973; Spilerman 1976; McPhail and Wohlstein 1983). PEA has also enabled the questioning of the common idea that there has been a radical transformation in the modalities of political engagement in France (Fillieule 1997, 1999). Finally, the relative simplicity and standardization of procedures have enabled enormous progress in the area of comparative analysis, allowing us to establish cross-national comparisons.

One might then conclude with an unreservedly glowing report, all the more justified since for more than a decade PEA has become increasingly professionalized, with sustained attention to procedures and biases accruing to its methods.[2] However, several issues have received less attention: on the one hand, the issue of choice of sources and biases related thereto; on the other hand, the question of definition and hence construction of the object of study. It is these two issues in turn that interest us here as we explain the reasons for the choices we have made as well as the limitations and advantages imposed by these choices.

Research on social movements based on PEA has been massively reliant on the use of the press as its sole source. As Koopmans (1995: 253) points out, 'this popularity is mainly the result of a negative choice'. Several strategies have been used. Some research has analysed indexes of the national press (e.g. McAdam 1982, Spilerman 1970, and Etzioni 1970 who all used the *New York Times* index). Others increased their range of print sources, combining local and national press, or specialized national periodical and national press (e.g. Kriesi 1981; Rucht and Ohlemacher 1992; Kousis 1999). More recently, some researchers have adopted sampling strategies (Rucht and Ohlemacher 1992; Kriesi et al. 1995). In the late 1990s researchers have turned to CD-ROM versions of newspapers, and others have preferred to make use of data available from wire services and on electronic databases (Bond et al. 1997; Imig and Tarrow 1999). Finally, several researchers have turned to police archives (Fillieule 1997, 1999; Hocke 1999, 2000; McCarthy, McPhail, and Smith 1999; Wisler 1999).

WHY NEWSPAPER SOURCES?

We opted for the printed press. This was justified in the context of comparative research covering seven countries and the Spanish Basque country. The accessibility of agency dispatches and police sources is variable and generally very limited in Europe, and we wanted to employ sources that were as comparable as possible. The growing globalization of news stories and the ways in which they are constructed has, for several decades, subjected journalistic activity to increasingly universal pressures that lead to the erosion of national differences in professional rationales and practices.[3] By contrast, European police forces have retained strong cultural specificities that make their records comparatively idiosyncratic (della Porta and Reiter 1998; della Porta, Fillieule, and Reiter 1998).

In selecting the newspapers to be used as sources, we tried to combine objectives of quality and quantity. Newspapers should provide a reliable source of information about environmental protest events (EPEs) that have taken place in each country; they should, that is, be stable over time and uniform across territory. Hence, daily national quality newspapers published regularly during the decade 1988–97 were considered to meet these requirements best. Wherever possible, other things being equal, we favoured newspapers that had been more sensitive to environmental issues and social movements.

Taking into account these criteria, we confronted the reality of the daily press markets in the seven countries. While the choice was narrowed down to one candidate in the case of *El País* (Spain) or *La Repubblica* (Italy), the selection of *Le Monde* (France), *The Guardian* (Britain), *die tageszeitung* (Germany), *Eleftherotypia* (Greece), or *EGIN* (Basque Country) was made from among a few possible alternatives. The selection of *El País* was a negative choice. Although its limited interest in environmental information[4] is typical of the Spanish national press, the plausible alternatives did not meet our criteria in terms of quality, either because of lack of continuity or due to their clear regional focus, or because they were judged less sensitive to protest activities and environmental issues. Similarly, the fragmented Italian press market left *La Repubblica* as the best choice in terms of national coverage.

In the British case, *The Guardian* met the quality requirements and was the least selective in its reporting of environmental actions. *Eleftherotypia*'s circulation is amongst the highest in Greece and, in contrast to other dailies, it consistently concentrates on political and social issues, is not affiliated with particular political parties, and hosts a wide range of political views from a liberal perspective, and it has covered environmental issues more closely than any of the other major quality newspapers (Kousis 1999). Comparative analysis of German newspapers has shown that the number of reported EPEs in various newspapers does not vary significantly (Eilders 2001). However, among other alternatives, *die tageszeitung*, a left-alternative national newspaper, was thought to provide more information, given its greater attention to social movements and environmental issues. The quality criterion was clearly not met in the case of *EGIN*, a partisan newspaper linked to the extreme nationalist Basque party, Batasuna, and its terrorist branch ETA. However, here the choice was justified by the research focus on the links between environmental protests and nationalism. The possible alternatives do not cover Navarra or the French Basque Country. In the case of France, the decision to use *Le Monde* was grounded on a comparison between different kinds of newspapers presented in analyses by Pierre Lascoumes (1994) and the Professionnal Association of Environmental Journalists (JNE) (Vadrot and Dejouet 1998). If *L'Humanité* and

Libération are the newspapers which devote most space to the environment, other circumstances point to *Le Monde* as a better choice: *L'Humanité* is close to the Communist Party and very hostile to ecologists on topics such as nuclear power; in the case of *Libération*, the creation, then the suppression a few years later, of the *Cahier terre* would have introduced too many disparities in the data collected over the 10 years.

Usually, the analysis of EPEs is based on the national editions of the chosen newspaper, but to reflect adequately the decentralized character of Italy, reports from local editions of *La Repubblica* were also analysed. In Sweden, a local newspaper was also scanned.[5] Table A.1 synthesises the main features of the selected newspapers.

IDENTIFYING BIASES

The proliferation of PEAs based on press sources has been accompanied by a noticeable increase in the attention given to bias due to journalistic sources. This is the result, in particular, of research based on police sources which for the first time offered an opportunity to measure bias by comparison with control databases (Fillieule 1996; Hocke 1996; Barranco and Wisler 1999; McCarthy, McPhail, and Smith 1999; Wisler 1999).

The issue revolves around three questions. First, what is *the degree of selectivity* of the sources used? In other words, what are the chances of any given event being reported in the press? This question contains two others: first, what proportion of protest events are actually covered by the press; next, what are the criteria governing the events that are covered? Second, are the events covered faithfully? It is *description biases* one is interested in here, generally based on a distinction between 'hard' and 'soft' news. Third, what is *the degree of systematicity* of these biases, or, to put it more clearly, do the rationales of media selection vary over time and in relation to contexts (the crucial question for comparative research) and if so, why and how?

Selectivity and the Nature of Bias

The selectivity issue has received a lot of attention. We know that the press covers only a very small proportion of events (variously estimated at between 2 and 10 per cent) and that the rationales that govern this strong selectivity relate systematically to the size of the event, the degree of novelty of modes of action employed, the occurrence of violence, and geographical location (local and/or regional events being always less well covered than those taking place in the capitals or main towns) (Dantzger 1975; Snyder and Kelly 1977; Franzosi 1987; Olzack 1989; Rucht and Ohelmacher 1992; Koopmans 1995; Fillieule 1997; Mueller 1997; McCarthy, McPhail, and Smith 1999).

TABLE A.1. *The main features of the selected newspapers*

Country	Newspaper	Quality and political orientation	Selectivity (interest in environment, human/social issues versus political focus)	Territorial bias (in terms of resources across the national territory)	Other bias (thematic, partisan bias) affecting coverage of environment/ protests
France	*Le Monde*	National quality newspaper centre–left orientation	MEDIUM (environment section, institutional bias)	MEDIUM (focus on Paris region)	Nature, transportation issues
Germany	*die tageszeitung*	National quality newspaper (although not in classical way), left–alternative orientation	HIGH (environment section, attention to	MEDIUM–LOW (focus on Berlin) social movements)	Energy issues
Britain	*The Guardian*	National quality newspaper, left–liberal orientation	MEDIUM–HIGH (environment section; human interest style)	LOW	
Greece	*Eleftherotypia*	National quality newspaper centre–left orientation	MEDIUM–HIGH (environment section; attention to social movement activity)	MEDIUM–LOW (focus more on Athens)	
Italy	*La Repubblica*	National quality newspaper centre–left orientation	MEDIUM (environment section)	MEDIUM–LOW (focus on northern Italy)	
Spain	*El País*	National quality newspaper centre–left orientation	LOW (no environment section, political focus)	MEDIUM (differences across regions)	Bias toward PSOE (Socialist Party)
Sweden	*Dagens Nyheter*	National	MEDIUM–HIGH (environment section)	LOW	
Basque Country	*EGIN*	Nationalist/partisan newspapers linked to ETA	HIGH (though through nationalist prism)	LOW	Nationalist issues

Our research is the first of its kind to focus upon environmental protests. It was therefore important to verify that the generally established rules of selectivity apply in the same manner in this area, all the more so as the literature on relations between media and environmental groups is quite sparse.

The strategy adopted here was to compare data gathered from the national press with other, more exhaustive sources. Within the limits of available resources, we used comparisons with the local press, police sources, agency dispatches, and interviews with specialist journalists. It is not possible, in the limited space of this chapter, to cite these multiple comparisons. We confine ourselves here to illustrating our procedures based on the two strategies adopted: the multiplication of control sources mainly in the case of France, and a strategy centred on comparison between national and local sources in Germany, Sweden, Italy, and Spain.

Multiple Control Sources

Given the availability of multiple sources in the case of France, we sought to establish the determinants of selectivity by means of a limited comparison of our data with police sources, Agence France Press (AFP) dispatches, and interviews with specialist journalists (Fillieule and Ferrier 1999).

First we compared our data with events that fitted our definition of an EPE and were reported in AFP bulletins over 6 months distributed over the decade. The comparison shows that AFP covered a greater number of events than *Le Monde* (about 50 per cent higher for the whole period) and that *Le Monde* strongly underrepresented local, district, and regional events. This result underlines the extent to which one of the biases of *Le Monde* is with respect to geographical location of events. Finally, another bias concerns *Le Monde's* institutional rationale since the events covered were three times more often organized or supported by political parties than those reported by AFP. It is thus clear that voluntary groups were less well treated by *Le Monde* than by AFP, partly as an effect of biases concerning geographical location. To get a more precise picture, we went on to compare the data from *Le Monde* with that from police sources at the Prefecture of Paris.[6] The results are eloquent. First, only 5 per cent of the events recorded by the police were covered by *Le Monde*. As previous research covering protests of all kinds showed that *Le Monde* reported only 2 per cent of the events recorded by the police (Fillieule 1996), it appears that environmental protests were about as badly covered as the ensemble of protest events. The comparison also shows that selectivity related to the number of demonstrators and, more interestingly, to the systematic exclusion of certain topics.

The interviews we conducted with environmental journalists in each country[7] allow us to extend the strategy of multiple control sources. These interviews allow us to be more precise about two common biases: the importance of 'something new' to the likelihood of an event getting coverage, and the difference in treatment relating to the geographic location of events.

The question of newness relates to the notion of *media or issue attention cycles*, introduced by Downs (1972: 59).[8] According to this model, as protests become too repetitive, media attention swiftly moves on to other issues.[9] This is a particularly crucial problem in research that aims to measure the extent of emergence of new modes of action. If one hypothesizes that the media gives good coverage to new forms of political activism, then it becomes all the more tricky to relate them to the number of more conventional events. The way the press functions precludes us from doing so and we might reasonably be reproached for relying on a source that, by its very nature, can only reinforce our initial hypotheses. As it happens, our results show a great stability in the modes of action used in environmental mobilizations during the 10 years. Acknowledgement of media biases thus does not undermine but, rather, strongly reinforces the credibility of our results.

However, one should also bear in mind that environmental movements are composed of reflexive actors who adapt their repertoire of action to the media's requirement of novelty. This is because most of them base their strategies on mobilizing public opinion through the media, continuously assessing their level of coverage, and procuring personal/direct contact with environmental journalists. Hence, at least in the case of forms of protest, we might expect that 'news' will not only reflect novel forms of action, ignoring old ones, but also a 'real' process of change in strategy and repertoire. According to a Spanish journalist:

the coverage of legal complaints made by environmental groups has decreased significantly in recent years, except for the informational pressure of Greenpeace. Most environmental groups have modified their role of denouncing incidents as catastrophic events. Hence, in some ways this decrease in their informative pressure is changing the informational landscape and hence there is no longer the same sense of catastrophe. (Elcacho 1998: 61)

In this sense, the stability in the modes of action suggested by our results should also be interpreted as a mechanical effect due to the fact that we did not consider those forms of action through which protesters gain media attention and coverage (from the press conference to the boycott of international organizations' conferences) but instead coded other actions that were included in the same report (complaints, petitions, etc.), and that might not have been reported had not other actions first caught the attention of the media.

Concerning location bias, interviews with journalists are very useful since they highlight the role of local correspondents. Local correspondents are supposed to keep columnists or staff reporters informed about events that have happened or are about to happen in their locality/region. They are also journalists and, in many of the countries studied, write articles that they try to get published in the newspaper. Sometimes the columnist contacts them directly for more information about an event he has heard about and, occasionally, to commission an article. One might imagine then that bias linked to the geographic location of events is thereby avoided.[10] In fact that is not always the case because local correspondents are generally freelance, so it is in their (economic) interest not to cover events that they think will not appeal to the columnist and, *a fortiori*, the editorial department. One might also hypothesize that some of them are simply hostile to environmental associations, especially since most of their income comes from employment on local newspapers.[11]

Local Newspapers and National Newspapers

In the absence of access to varied sources allowing one to approach the selectivity of data, one can still make a limited comparison with the local press, following the suggestions of Snyder and Kelly (1977: 118), Franzosi (1987), and the Prodat project. This type of comparison is all the more valuable in our case in that relatively few researchers have focused on the question of how environmental coverage by regional and national media differs. However, the little data that is available suggests that environmental groups tend to enjoy qualitatively greater access to local media, at least for some issues (Molotch and Lester 1975; Sandman et al. 1987; Spears, van der Plight, and Reiser 1987; Singh, Dubey, and Pandney 1989; Cottle 1993; Anderson 1997). A simple comparison of the frequencies of EPEs reported in national and local newspapers/pages in Germany, Sweden, Italy, and Spain allows us to identify some components of the nature of the selection bias of national newspapers.

First, the comparison confirms bias due to the number of participants. In Germany and Spain, the size of the mobilization increased the chances of an event being reported in national pages. Second, our results are congruent with the common finding that protests adopting non-conventional forms of action, and among them those that happen to be violent, are proportionately more often reported in national pages/newspapers. Table A.2 shows the distribution of EPEs according to the forms of action adopted. In each of the four selected countries, the first column shows the difference between the relative weight of a particular form in national and local media; the second column indicates the frequency with which each form of protest was reported, taking data from both local and national pages together.

The results clearly illustrate that national coverage of 'procedural complaints' and 'appeals' was proportionately less than that of unconventional forms of participation. This was especially true for *El País* and the Swedish newspapers. On the other hand, as the positive numbers in columns (1) indicate, confrontational and violent forms of protest were always relatively more frequently reported in national editions. The same was also true of demonstrative actions, except in Germany. The fact that demonstrative actions were, in relative terms, less frequent in the national pages of *die tageszeitung* than in their local sections might be explained by the highly unconventional repertoire of protest in Germany.

The nature of selection bias is not only influenced by the form of the protest but also by the type of claims put forward by the protesters. What is interesting here is that, even if Table A.3 shows some similarities among the four countries, national specificities seem to remain very important. If one takes industrial waste,

TABLE A.2. *Protest repertoires reported in national and local pages in Germany, Sweden, Italy, and Spain (1988–97) (proportional distribution*[a]*)*

	Germany		Sweden		Italy		Spain	
	(1)	(2)	(1)	(2)	(1)	(2)	(1)	(2)
Procedural	0.1	10.0	−7.6	4.8	−8.0	11.5	−8.3	16.2
Appeals	−2.7	18.1	−13.0	34.7	−1.2	38.4	−0.7	31.8
Demonstrative	−14.5	36.0	9.1	29.3	4.2	34.1	0.9	25.8
Confrontational	10.7	22.1	5.3	11.1	3.0	11.4	5.8	16.7
Attacks on property	10.6	13.0	2.8	4.8	1.5	1.5	0.3	1.7
Violence	1.4	2.5	1.6	3.2	1.5	2.8	2.2	2.3
Other	0.4	4.4	1.6	12.1	−1.0	0.3	−0.1	5.6
Total		100		100		100		100

Note:
[a] More than one form of action could be recorded per protest (percentages refers to number of cases).
(1) National minus local (% EPFs in national minus % EPFs in local).
(2) Total (distribution).

TABLE A.3. *Environmental claims in national and local pages in Germany, Sweden, Italy, and Spain (1988–97)*

	Germany		Sweden		Italy		Spain	
	(1)	(2)	(1)	(2)	(1)	(2)	(1)	(2)
Nuclear power	10.7	15.3	3.6	3.6	0.9	0.9	4.3	5.2
Nuclear waste	25.2	29.6	1.8	2.1	0.0	0.0	2.1	3.1
Non-nuclear waste	1.4	4.4	1.5	1.8	-2.9	3.7	-0.7	6.6
Domestic waste	-1.4	2.4	-1.3	0.6	0.5	9.7	-1.8	5.2
Ocean pollution	2.2	2.5	4.4	4.7	-3.0	3.6	1.4	2.7
Lake/river pollution	-0.1	1.3	0.0	0.9	3.6	4.9	-0.6	2.1
Air pollution	-1.6	2.7	2.3	3.3	-1.3	10.6	0.8	2.4
Environmentally friendly R&T	5.4	5.4	1.6	1.5	0.1	0.1	0.0	0.0
Environmental effects weapon/military	-0.6	2.9	0.9	0.9	3.9	4.6	1.3	1.7
Roads	-11.1	3.5	-5.7	8.9	-0.8	0.7	3.5	6.3
Car traffic	-16.0	3.1	-5.2	3.3	4.2	7.5	-2.8	0.1
Countryside protection	-2.3	1.9	-6.5	4.2	-2.3	3.0	-5.2	16.7
Animal welfare	-3.4	1.6	10.7	9.8	4.3	7.3	-1.2	0.8
Protecting hunting animals	0.4	0.4	2.9	3.6	6.8	8.1	0.6	1.2
Environmental education	-0.1	0.1	1.3	5.6	0.4	1.1	0.0	0.0

Note:

(1) National minus local (% EPEs in national minus % EPEs in local).
(2) Total (distribution).

for example, one can see that protests over that issue attracted more national media interest in Germany and Sweden, while tending to be relegated to local pages in Italy and Spain. National newspapers were more selective in the two southern countries, for numerous reasons including, in the case of Spain, the degree of waste policy development, the incapacity of protesters to generalize their claims and to transcend the local level of conflict, and their inability to retain media coverage and access when the problem of industrial waste was treated by the national press.

Also dissimilar was the coverage of transport issues. Protests against road construction in Spain and against traffic in Italy were more often reported nationally than were protests on such issues in Germany and Sweden. The greater relative weight of PEs concerning roads construction in the national edition of *El País* compared with the local pages can be attributed to the intervention of the terrorist organization ETA in one road conflict in Navarra in the early 1990s, a conflict that would otherwise have been ignored by *El País*. The national prominence in Italy of protests concerning car traffic reflects the increasing interest of the Environment Ministry in tackling the problem of urban pollution, as exemplified by the introduction of 'ecological weekends'. While urban pollution was a local issue in other countries, it became a national issue in Italy.

On the whole, thinking about the selectivity of our sources leads us to conclude that biases are of a similar nature in the several countries and that they are similar, too, to those already studied in the literature on relations between social movements and media. The patterns of claims demonstrate the importance of nationally contingent elements that influence the media to report environmental protests. We do not consider this an obstacle to crossnational comparison. On the contrary, recognition of the existence of nation-specific issues and their identification is a necessary condition for fruitful comparative work. But environmental claims, like other political claims, change over time; their visibility and relevance in political and informational agenda is far from guaranteed. The temporal instability of environmental issues highlights the problem of the unsystematic nature of the selection biases in our data.

Systematicity

Systematicity refers to the persistence of biases over time, in relation to the variation in contexts. In the literature, the systematicity of bias remains problematic, both in terms of methodological problems (availability of control databases) and because of a certain naiveté in approaching the issue.[12] However, the stakes are considerable. It is no less than a matter of knowing whether variations in volume and characteristics of EPEs over time can be considered as a manifestation of the phenomenon itself or, on the contrary, whether they are artefacts of media practices. To date, the means used to explore the impact of media practices have relied on statistical comparison between different types of sources. The originality of our approach is to have taken this further, by drawing on purely qualitative methods which alone enable understanding and reconstruction of the rules that govern the selection of news items and how they are reported. To achieve this, we have drawn on interviews with specialist journalists.

First, we know from the sociology of journalism that the way environmental issues are dealt with by the media must be related to the positions the journalists specializing in environmental matters occupy within media enterprises. We also know that public and political interest in environmental issues is relatively novel and has followed different rhythms in each European country. This raises questions about the implications of the changing status of environmental journalists since the beginning of the 1980s and, amongst other things, changes in their relationships with activist environmental associations and/or green parties.

Second, research on the decision-making process and organizational hierarchy of media enables us to understand how journalists work and how much effective scope for manoeuvre they have. Such observational work should be supplemented by consideration of financial and economic aspects of media. The changing structure of capital of media enterprises and, since the beginning of the 1980s, their frequently dependent links with big industrial groups might influence reporting of certain environmental subjects.[13] Moreover, the developments in the journalism profession—increasing insecurity of employment, and the proliferation of freelancers who lack both the protection of employment rights and adequate resources fully to research their reports—inevitably play a role in how events were and are covered.

On the basis of interviews conducted in the several countries, we have identified three sets of factors that raise the issue of the systematicity of selection biases.

The first factor concerns the *development of the political agenda in general*. Some researchers have focused on that type of unsystematic bias (Fillieule 1997; Barranco and Wisler 1999). Fillieule (1997: 228–43), for example, has established that critical elections provoke a decrease in protest activity, and the British experience in 1997 appears to confirm this. At least in the cases of Spain and France, we know that protest groups from the left—among them environmental groups—switched their resources to the anti-war campaign, hence reducing the resources devoted to specifically environmental issues (Fillieule 1996; Jiménez 1999*a*). The peaceful revolution in East Germany and the subsequent German unification are thought to have had a broad impact on the nature of coverage of EPEs in Germany, but not necessarily or invariably simply by reducing their share of media space. Interest in environmental problems shifted to problems in the East and problems connected to the transition. In general, due to the defensive nature of many environmental protests, economic crises are associated with decreasing protest activity. However, it is difficult to know to what extent such declines are due to the media marginalizing environmental issues in favour of traditional economic issues or, alternatively, to a decrease in potential conflicts associated with the pressures of economic activity.

The second factor relates more specifically to the *development, in each country, of environmentally relevant current events*. Given that the space allocated to environmental issues in newspapers is not infinitely extendible, the occurrence of major events affects the coverage of protest activities. These may generate increased coverage of EPEs, or make them almost disappear. Events with international impact such as the Chernobyl accident (1986) or the Rio Summit (1992) had the effect of making ecological mobilizations unrelated to nuclear issues or climate change less newsworthy (cf. Anderson 1997). The fact that a major event has international impact does not guarantee that the variation in rates of coverage operates in the same manner in all countries. Indeed, as the previous chapters have shown, in western Europe in the 1990s it clearly did not. On the other hand, when current events in a given country focus attention on a particular problem, the decrease or increase in the rate of coverage only affects that country. In this sense, the relatively decreasing level of EPEs registered in *El País* in 1991–2 might well be explained as a consequence of a focusing of environmental agenda on forest fires and drought, two environmental issues that at the time had not provoked any EPEs. More systematically, it seems that in most cases the increase in environmental coverage followed the development of ecological politics. For example in Italy, interest in environmental issues became substantial for the first time in the mid-1980s due to the Chernobyl accident and, in 1987, to the three referenda won by anti-nuclear campaigners. But interest remained steady in subsequent years mainly due to the attention paid to political parties and institutional politics by Italian media aroused by the initial good electoral results of the greens and the prominence of green MPs.

The third set of factors relates to the turnover of journalists in charge of environmental issues, the organizational transformations of newspapers, and changes in the sources employed by journalists. Our interviews suggest that the field of environmental journalism has undergone a real generational change. In the 1970s, the environment did not constitute a special field and those who covered environmental issues were either journalists close to the movement or generalists who, having no particular interest in the environment, only rarely dealt with such issues, most often from an institutional perspective. In the 1980s, the 'pioneers' of the 1970s were replaced by journalists who clearly opted for professionalism over militant activism. 'This transformation (which is part of the more general development of specialized journalism e.g. health, education, lifestyle, etc.) contributed to the development of a stance of "critical expertise", a combination of rejection of committed journalism and claims to critical judgement in the name of their technical knowledge of the topics ...'(Neveu 1999: 124).

Another major change in the profession in the early 1980s is that environmental journalists for the most part moved from staff to freelance status. At the same time, their incomes improved in recognition of their specialization. These two points underline, on the one hand, the recognition of a hitherto marginalized specialization and, on the other, increasing job insecurity which is not specific to this particular specialization but which reduces journalists' freedom and autonomy in relation to their employers. This economic aspect of the situation is crucial, particularly in a context of high unemployment among journalists and a drastic reduction in fixed costs in press enterprises. It seems that many of the newspapers from which we drew our data to a lesser or greater degree sacrificed the environment sector, considering it less important than others. Thus, for example, although in 1989 *Dagens Nyheter* employed a dozen permanent journalists working on the environment, by 1999 it had only one part-time environmental journalist on the payroll. That example is certainly extreme but it emphasizes why one must be attentive to such considerations when setting out to make international comparisons.

The departure of old or arrival of new journalists responsible for environmental coverage also constitutes a non-systematic bias that must be taken into account. In the cases of *Eleftherotypia* and *Le Monde*, the environment was left to the relative discretion of an officially designated journalist who, over several years, remained the undisputed specialist in his area. This specialization and relative scope for manoeuvre may have several consequences in terms of coverage. The relative freedom of judgement journalists enjoy can only reinforce the discretionary aspect of their work, and this relates back to the difficulty in establishing continuity in our data when those responsible for specific areas change in the course of time. We have been particularly attentive to these changes in the various newspapers analysed, knowing that, for several of them, stability in this respect has been considerable over the period under consideration.

In the same way, one must again relate the issue of systematicity to possible changes of format in the newspapers studied: increase or decrease in the number of pages, changes to the columns, and so on. Rates of coverage may be increased or decreased quite artificially by changes in the constraints of the column. At *Dagens Nyheter*, for example, a regular 'Environment, health and science' section was created in 1990, became more irregular from 1995 onwards, and then was finally dropped altogether. The environment section in *Eleftherotypia*, created in the mid-1980s, was dropped in the 1990s. At *Le Monde*, a regional page was created in 1995, designed to cover, amongst other topics, environmental issues, whereas a regional page in *Eleftherotypia* appeared and then disappeared during the decade.

In addition, the network of local correspondents has generally changed over time according to financial constraints, editorial policy, and the availability of interested journalists in the different regions. For example, in the case of *Le Monde*, coverage seems to have improved particularly in the regions after 1995, due to a major organizational reform. However, if a newspaper's territorial expansion involves decentralization in the form of new local editions/sections, as in the cases of *El País* or *La Repubblica* in the 1990s, it can lead to a reduction in the presence of events in the national news sections. So each time it was clearly identifiable, we have been careful to relate the variations in the trends of reported EPEs to organizational changes at the newspapers that are the sources of our data in order to avoid falsely interpreting variations that were artefacts of changes in the character of the newspapers.

Finally, the issue of the systematicity of bias must be raised from the perspective of sources used by journalists. According to our interviews, it seems that while in the 1970s journalists' sources were essentially located among militant activists, things began to change slowly during the 1980s, the institutionalization of the environment involving the proliferation of press offices belonging to both the public administration and the private sector. Because they are 'free' information and can be used directly, the documents supplied by regional authorities and businesses are an increasingly important source of information for journalists.

This loss of centrality of activist sources by comparison with official and/or expert sources must obviously be considered in relation to the 'despecification' of the environmental issue. As the environment has become a legitimate object in the eyes of the press, various newspaper sections have incorporated it, whether into political, science and health, daily life, or economics sections. As a result, demonstrations about the environment appear to have been of decreasing interest by comparison with other kinds of actors and other modes of public expression. This is a source of bias for anyone wanting to observe trends over the medium term, but it is not a major problem in terms of systematicity. In effect, once again, the discernible developments are broadly similar from one newspaper to another; the European press has undergone similar processes which tends to universalize the modes of news production and the ways in which narratives are constructed.

DEFINITION AND CONSTRUCTION OF THE OBJECT

Wide or Narrow Definition?

In their introduction to *Acts of Dissent*, Rucht, Koopmans, and Neidhart stress that 'from an analytical standpoint, we should not equate the study of protest with the study of social movements. Social movements tend to protest but not all protests are conducted by social movements' (1999: 9). However, by the same token, the repertoire of social movements, and in particular of environmental movements, does not consist exclusively of protest, and the question arises whether conventional actions such as presentation of reports and lobbying by social movement organizations should be included in our investigations.

Such a widening of the definition of protest might appear especially necessary in the case of the environmental sector, which, since the 1980s, has undergone processes of institutionalization and acquisition of expertise. Environmental movements are in this respect part of the class of citizen movements[14] that question the science and expert knowledge of the powerful by recourse to the very weapons of their adversaries, such as expert reports, press conferences and press releases, the taking of samples and measures, laboratory testing, and educational programmes. However, many of these activities are not carried out in public and/or are not considered newsworthy, and so they are not often, reliably or regularly reported by newspapers. It is accordingly impossible for PEA to give an adequate account of such activities and their incidence over time. Accordingly, we have not attempted to enumerate these other less public or non-protest activities of environmentalists.

Protest event analysis relies on a particular conception of the place of the event in relation to structural phenomena, and this must be clarified. On the one hand, the choice made here not to focus attention on memorable events but on the ensemble of environmental actions happening in a given place and over a given period means that our corpus of data is largely composed of 'routine' actions. We distance ourselves then from the definition, sometimes encountered, of the event as a rupture with habitual channels of causality, in other words, of structure.[15] We have thus made no discrimination among the types of events enumerated, each action being taken here as a concentrate of structure. On the other hand, since we intend to argue in terms of process, we must constitute *continuous series*, the concepts of repertoires of action and waves of mobilization suggesting that it is from the accumulation of routine events that possible structural modifications can be read. However, because we have not included an *a priori* definition of 'key events' does not mean that we always give the same weight to the events that comprise our series. Certainly, all events are not of equal weight, but it is only the observation of an entire class of events over a given period that allows one to say which protest actions effectively signal a change in the routine course of events. This point demonstrates the importance of thinking in terms of waves of mobilization and adaptation of repertoires.

Based on this ambition to cover all forms of protest beyond merely verbal and quasi-routinized forms of dissent, and including relatively small and unspectacular protests, the unit of analysis EPE can be defined as *a collective, public action regarding issues in which explicit concerns about the environment are expressed as a central dimension, organized by non-state instigators with the explicit purpose of critique or dissent together with societal and/or political demands.*[16]

Several criteria serve to define an EPE.

First, the protest must have the *character of an action* or, at least, of calling others to action (e.g. resolution, public letter). In most cases, purely verbal protests were excluded. Protest incidents that were primarily of a verbal nature but went beyond mere expressions of displeasure were coded when, because of the character of the activists or the particular forms of activism, they exceeded the ordinary repertoire of the participants.

Second, the activity must be or be able to be connected with *societal and/or political demands*. This occurred as a rule in a negative form (e.g. by the naming of a concrete dissatisfaction through criticism or protest) but it also occurred in a positive form (e.g. by the presentation of an alternative suggestion for action). Legal complaints were tested according to whether the plaintiff's concern was only resistance to individual disadvantages or the attainment of individual advantages (in such cases, the event was not coded) or also, or primarily, a societal or political matter. Theatrical performances and other cultural events, as well as panel discussions and informational events, were not coded as EPEs as long as they were not linked with any political or societal matter, even when they took place within the framework of a broader protest campaign. If, however, the concrete event was characterized by a slogan (e.g. such as 'Ban whaling'), it was coded.

Third, the protest must have a *public character*, that is, it must either have occurred in public space or at least have been directed towards a public effect or a person or institution of public interest.

Fourth, the instigators of the incident must be *collective and non-state activists*. A collective group of instigators exists when the incident is carried out by a minimum of three persons.

Fifth, the *protest event* is determined by the association of place, time or period, form of the incident, demand, and instigating group. An EPE can link in one place or in one time period several interests/claims, several activists, and several forms of incidents. The duration of an EPE is variable and may last from a few minutes to several weeks (e.g. a hunger strike). Only in exceptional cases were protests in different places so linked together by a demonstrable symbolism that they counted as *one* EPE (e.g. a protest march into a big city with groups converging from different starting points or a long human chain linking two cities). Simultaneous protests with identical interests/claims but in different places and by different instigating groups constitute in each instance separate EPEs. Likewise, simultaneous actions by the same organization (e.g. a federal group) in different places constitute in each case separate EPEs. The classification as *one* EPE is dependent on the actual or at least symbolic continuity of the incident. Successive EPEs are separated from each other by intervals. An interval which ends an EPE is indicated when an EPE is implicitly or explicitly concluded (e.g. departure of the activists, conclusion by the organizers) or when the central concern of the protest changes. If the same form of incident for the sake of the same concern by the same activist at the same place is resumed after a temporary conclusion, 24 hours must have elapsed in order for two separate EPEs to be identified. Consequently, regularly recurring EPEs (e.g. on certain feast or seasonal days) were coded as separate EPEs.

Making Sense of the Data

The research procedure used and the sources canvassed impose a number of constraints on the definition of the object. Not all questions can be posed, and only certain aspects of environmental protest activity can be covered (cf. Mueller 1997).

First, given the rationales of media selection, it is probable that some of the more conventional forms of action recorded do not make good copy. The bias raised here operates all the more subtly in that such forms of action are sometimes covered, thus potentially giving the false impression of a balanced coverage of the repertoire effectively exploited by the groups.

Second, if one takes Schlesinger's critique (1990) of mediacentric analyses seriously, one must also bear in mind two phenomena. First, there is the 'professionalization of sources'. For example, Anderson (1997) points out the growth of social movement actors' *savoir-faire* in managing the media and anticipation of the criteria of newsworthiness. This phenomenon is especially patent in the environmental sector which, as we have seen, has long been undergoing a process of professionalization and growing expertise.[17] What is important here is *the unevenness* of this professionalization, which means that groups such as Greenpeace, for example, are capable of 'formatting' events and producing dossiers designed to draw journalists' attention, whereas many others do not have the means to do so. Under these conditions, PEA may sometimes offer not so much indicators of effective levels of activity as a barometer of the degree of professionalization of the groups' media strategies. Moreover, we know from Hilgartner and Bosk's work (1988) that the sufferers of social problems fight to get their claims for reform onto the political agenda. Now, this struggle may be located in different 'institutional arena' which include sites of mediatization (press, elections) or of the management (judiciary, administrative, legislative) of public problems. Each arena operates according to its own rationales and, depending on the resources at their disposal, movements may prefer to apply pressure to one or another. It follows then that not all movements necessarily seek to act in the public arena; indeed they sometimes try to avoid any media coverage. In other words, a rupture in the trends established using PEA may well also be the sign of a development in the activity of movements rather than of a change in their media strategy. Another implication of this assessment raises the question of the success or failure of movements. In effect, one must systematically avoid interpreting the intensity of media coverage as an indicator of success in so far as such visibility can also, if not primarily, be a sign of a co-option by the state or corporate elites.

Third, one must learn from the corroborating results of those who have set out to measure the selectivity of press sources. Events with relatively fewer participants are less likely to be the object of media coverage. As Mueller points out, 'the implications are considerable for the theoretical models of protest based on these data. Namely, theories based on this data will systematically fail to consider the role of protest events that are resource-poor in terms of participants' (Mueller 1997: 182). The arguments invoked in the literature to minimize the implications of this are not convincing. They rely on the notion that only events mentioned in the press would make an impact on public opinion and that, similarly, only those events would attract the attention of the authorities (e.g. see Rucht, Koopmans, and Neidhart 1998: 21).

These arguments are problematic in several respects. First, the authorities do not receive their information solely from reading the press. One of the contributions of the sociology of law and order has been to demonstrate the complexity of the governing authorities' information channels (della Porta, Fillieule, and Reiter 1998). Moreover, it is quite paradoxical that practitioners of PEA should suggest that only demonstrations that arouse public opinion are of interest for analysis because we know that only a small (but nationally highly variable) proportion of Europeans read newspapers, and particularly the quality press used for PEA. Furthermore, despite decades of investigation into media effects, there is little consensus among researchers about the impact of, for example, televised violence upon real life aggression, or of political campaigns on voting behaviour (McQuail 1991: 251). Finally, and above all, the *de facto* exclusion of events of small impact obviously makes it problematic to work with precision on the issue of cycles and waves of mobilization given that the emergence and decline phases of those cycles and waves are largely absent from the published record.

CONCLUSIONS

In the above discussion we have addressed the main methodological questions related to the construction of our object of study, and the selection of our sources. In explaining the rationale for our choices we have identified some of the problems and limitations imposed by these choices. There are limits to what PEA can do and to what we have been able to do with it, but we hope that by acknowledging these limitations we might encourage better understanding of our subject.

Concerning the selectivity of our sources we have concluded that the nature of the selection bias follows comparable patterns across countries, and presents a set of features similar to those identified by the media event analysis literature. In this sense, we consider that the issue of selectivity is not an insurmountable obstacle as far as international comparison is concerned, provided one bears in mind a number of important considerations:

- our data allow us to capture only a small proportion of the ensemble of protest events and overrepresents demonstrations involving larger numbers of demonstrators;
- our data places strong emphasis on non-routine demonstrations, whether they be violent demonstrations or demonstrations which are original in their modes of action (novelty is a context-related concept, a consideration that also affects the coverage given to different types of demand);
- in our data, some demands are less well covered than others. The rationales governing this selection may vary from country to country;
- generally, our data cover local and regional events less well. Local and regional events are more or less well covered depending on rationales which vary from one country to another.

Furthermore, we have considered the problem of the systematicity of this bias. Interviews with environmental journalists working on the selected newspapers proved to be a useful source to address this issue qualitatively. While explaining temporal variations in our data, we have been attentive to alternative interpretations derived from four series of factors which lay behind the (un)systematicity of our sources:

- the evolution of national political agenda and major political events in general;
- the evolution of environmental policy agenda and major environmental events;
- specific newspapers' organizational transformation, growth, personnel turnover, editorial, or style variations;
- the evolution of the environment as 'news', including changes in the notion of novelty, in the status of the environmental journalist, and in the range of sources.

In the course of three decades, PEA has slowly gained significance and recognition. If the first generations of research did not pay much attention to methodological questions and/or to establishing well-documented rules and procedures, things have changed dramatically with the development of critical studies dedicated to biases and the expansion of ambitious crossnationally comparative projects. The TEA project is one such project, and we have tried to show here how far a critical approach that addresses all the problems encountered can be fruitful and can enable us to take a new step forward in the field.

If protest event methodology must always be adapted to the case studied and can not simply be replicated without first thinking about the construction of the object, it nevertheless seems that some fundamental mechanisms are always at work. For example, our analysis of the definition of the event, of coding procedures and of selectivity bias is congruent with other results in the field. This is very encouraging for those of us who would make comparisons.

More importantly, our results speak loudly in favour of the necessity of turning to analyses mixing quantitative and qualitative methods, which alone enable understanding and reconstruction of the rationales which govern the selection of news items and how they are reported. To put it sharply, it is no longer possible to work seriously on systematicity biases without taking into account the now long and rich tradition of journalism studies.

The introduction of qualitative data into PEA has consequences that go further than a simple new refinement of methodological complexity. On the one hand, it intends to stop a tendency, after more than 30 years of empirically grounded case studies, towards armchair theorizing. Far from contenting ourselves with counting and cross-tabulating data, our methodological devices contribute to putting flesh on those statistical bones by linking data collection to the comprehension of data production by means of interviews with journalists. On the other hand, it shows that PEA is not only a useful tool for the construction of structural models but also for answering those new questions that have been put on agenda of social movement research by the cultural turn. In that respect, our analysis of systematicity biases in EPEs sheds empirical light on the way environmental issues are dealt with in general, in particular through journalists' choice of which subjects to cover and the reporting formats preferred. The identification and measurement of biases over time not only aim at validating or invalidating our data; in themselves they tell us a very important story about public perceptions and, consequently, about the results of social movements' framing activities. It is not the least surprising result of our research that, by means of PEA, we contribute to a better understanding of framing by addressing the question of if and how messages are received.

Finally, it should be stressed that the PEA that has been presented in this book is only the first part of a wider research project. The most original trait of the TEA project, compared with other comparative projects in the field, is that the PEA is only the beginning.

NOTES

1. This growing institutionalization of PEA can be clearly seen in the two international colloquia organized by the Wissenschaftszentrum Berlin (WZB), each of which resulted in a publication: Rucht, Koopmans, and Neidhart (1999); Rucht and Koopmans (1999).
2. Proof of this can be clearly seen in the appearance and subsequent growth in volume of appendices in publications devoted to methods of data collection, but also the development of a critical literature, which it should be noted is most often produced by researchers who have themselves undertaken this type of analysis (Fillieule 1996, 1997; Hocke 1996; Mueller 1997; Simon and Wisler 1998; Barranco and Wisler 1999; McCarthy, McPhail, and Smith 1999; Wisler 1999).
3. Space precludes further arguments to justify this assessment. One could, however, mention the increased importance of 'commercial pressures' and of 'journalistic deontology' in journalists' self-image, the general professionalization of the job particularly given the influence of the boom in journalism courses (see Neveu 1999).
4. Only around 2% of its stories deal with the environment.
5. A test conducted over a nine-month sample was carried out at an early stage of the coding process in order to estimate the number of EPEs as well as to identify those sections, where EPEs appear most regularly. When available, local pages were also analysed, making possible national–local comparisons, as well as helping to identify issue attention cycles at the national level. Besides the Italian case, reports have been analysed from the Berlin pages of *die tageszeitung* and several regional editions of *El País*.
6. Using *Parismanif*, a database that covers Parisian demonstrations between 1968 and 1998 (Fillieule 1996, 1997). For the purposes of this comparison, the years corresponding to the TEA database were extracted from *Parismanif* and only those events in the TEA database that met the criteria of definition of a protest event in *Parismanif* were retained.
7. In all, seventeen journalists were interviewed.
8. In the same vein, we know that protests may be under-reported at an early stage when journalists do not know much about the issue and its potential significance (critical mass effect), and that journalists' interest may decline even when, and precisely because, protests go on and on (ceiling effect) (Funkhouser 1973; Dantzger 1975: 582).

9. See Downs (1972: 49) and Lacey and Longman (1993: 210–11) on coverage of environmental and development issues in the British print media.

10. The geographical bias depends on the structure of the newspaper (the level of decentralization in regional/local sections) and the distribution of resources (local correspondents). *die tageszeitung* and *Le Monde* appear to privilege protests taking place in Berlin and Paris, respectively. *The Guardian* is based in London but was originally from Manchester and now publishes in both cities, and is therefore more likely to give nationally balanced coverage than any of the other papers published in London. However, newspaper decentralization may also involve unequal territorial coverage. This seems to be the case of *El País*, where the quality of relations between the environmental editor in Madrid and regional editors varies.

11. In effect, depending on the particular circumstance, the links of dependency can be particularly strong *vis-à-vis* local economic or political interests in this area of the press (Neveu 2002).

12. Many researchers feel authorized to affirm that selection biases (and their respective weights) are stable over time, without really taking on board that by a kind of conjuring trick, they have, along the way, moved from synchronic account to diachronic speculation. More seriously, some researchers base their hopes on choosing a newspaper which is known to have had an editorial policy that has remained consistent over time (Rucht and Ohlemacher 1992; Koopmans 1995), adding that for crossnational studies, one should use 'similar', that is, for example, 'elite' newspapers. Even if this rule were necessary, it would still be quite inadequate, as we shall see in the rest of this section.

13. For examples of research focused upon ownership and control of the media, see Halloran, Elliott, and Murdock (1970), Underwood (1993), McManus (1994), and Klinenberg (2000).

14. Of which anti-AIDS campaigns are another example (see Epstein 1996; Fillieule and Duyvendak 1999).

15. See Tarrow (1999), who develops a rich critique of this conception of the event.

16. This definition and the codebook (Rucht 1999) we used draw to some extent on the Prodat project codebook (Rucht and Ohlemacher 1992). For a comprehensive approach to the question of media events, see Réseaux (1996).

17. Environmental activists are more than proportionately drawn from the upper middle classes and have been exposed, more often than the average, to the social sciences, to more or less academic forms of sociology of the media, or indeed have themselves worked professionally in media-related professions.

Appendix B

The TEA (Transformation of Environmental Activism) Project

This project, funded by the European Commission (DG XII—Research contract no.: ENV4-CT97-0514), commenced in March 1998. Data collection was completed in September 2001. The partners in the project were:

- University of Kent at Canterbury—Christopher Rootes (coordinator)
- Science Centre for Social Research, Berlin (WZB)—Dieter Rucht
- University of Aalborg—Andrew Jamison
- Juan March Institute, Madrid—Manuel Jiménez
- University of the Basque Country, Bilbao—Iñaki Barcena and Pedro Ibarra
- National Foundation of Political Sciences (CEVIPOF), Paris—Olivier Fillieule
- University of Crete—Maria Kousis
- University of Florence—Donatella della Porta
- University of Strathclyde—Mario Diani

The project aims to examine the various forms of environmental activism, changes in their relative incidence during the 1990s and from one EU member state to another, and changes in environmental movement organizations (EMOs) and their relationships with other actors within and outside the wider environmental movement. It also aims to advance explanations for the patterns of variation, and to examine their implications for policy-making at the European level.

The project has involved systematic comparison of the incidence and forms of environmental activism and its relationship with EMOs in Germany, Britain, Italy, France, Spain, Greece, Sweden, and the Basque Country as well as at the level of the European Union itself.

The investigation embraces three complementary strategies:

(1) the quantitative and qualitative study of protest events about environmental issues by means of the analysis of reports published in mass media and environmental movement publications;
(2) examinations, based on literature, documents, and interviews, of EMOs and their relations with other actors;

(3) observation and interviews at local level of current/recent cases of environmental contention, and exploration, principally by means of analysis of local media reports and informant interviews, of the incidence and forms of environmental action in selected localities, urban and rural.

Further information on the project is posted at: www.kent.ac.uk/sspssr/TEA.html.

References

AAVV (1991). 'Algunas reflexiones sobre la campaña vivir sin nucleares', *Mientras Tanto*, 46: 23–50.

——(1995). 'Situación y perspectiva del movimiento ecologista: su relación con los sindicatos', in AAVV *Sindicalismo y medio ambiente*. Madrid: CCOO, 83–95.

Acheimastos, M. and M. Komninou (1998). 'Setting the Agenda: Press and Television in Greece', in R. Panagiotopoulou, C. Rigopoulou, M. Rigou, and S. Notaris (eds.), *The 'Construction' of Reality and the Mass Media*. Athens: Alexandreia (in Greek).

Adell, R. (1997). 'Manifestations et transition démocratique en Espagne', *Les Cahiers de la sécurité intérieure*, 27: 203–22.

Aguilar, P. (1996). 'Political Amnesty in the Spanish Transition to Democracy, 1975–1978: Collective Memory and the Pressures from below'. Paper presented to the HFG conference, Chinchón, 25–29 June.

Alazard, E. (1990). *L'Environnement dans la presse quotidienne française*. Master's dissertation in Geography, Université de Paris VII.

Alexandropoulos, S. and N. Sertedakis (2000). 'Greek Environmentalism: From the Status Nascendi of a Movement to its Integration'. Paper presented at the ECPR Joint Sessions (workshop on Environmental Movements in Comparative Perspective), Copenhagen.

Amery, C. (1976). *Natur als Politik. Die ökologische Chance des Menschen.* Reinbek: Rowohlt.

Anderson, A. (1997). *Media, Culture and the Environment*. London: UCL Press.

Armenakis, A., T. Gotsopoulos, N. Demertzis, R. Panagiotopoulou, and D. Haralambis (1996). 'Nationalism in the Greek Press: The Macedonian Issue during the Period December 1991–April 1993', *Greek Review of Social Research*, 89–90: 188–231 (in Greek).

Bagnasco, A. (1977). *Tre Italie: La problematica territoriale dello sviluppo Italiano*. Bologna: il Mulino.

Baisnée, O. (1998). 'Polémiques autour de la Hague: Construire un problème public en matière de nucléaire'. Master's dissertation, Université de Rennes.

Barcena, I., P. Ibarra, and M. Zubiaga (1995). *Nacionalismo y ecología: Conflicto e institucionalización en el movimiento ecologista vasco*. Madrid: Los Libros de la Catarata.

————(1997). 'The Evolution of the Relationship between Ecologism and Nationalism', in M. Redclift and G. Woodgate (eds.), *The International Handbook of Environmental Sociology*. Cheltenham: Edward Elgar, 300–18.

————(1998). 'Movimientos sociales y democracia en Euskadi. Insumision y ecologismo', in P. Ibarra and B. Tejerina (eds.), *Movimientos sociales, transformaciones politicas y cambio cultural*. Madrid: Trotta, 43–68.

Barranco J. and D. Wisler (1999). 'Validity and Systematicity of Newspaper Data in Event Analysis', *European Review of Sociology*, 15(3): 301–22.

Baukloh, A. and J. Roose (2001). 'The Environmental Movement and Environmental Concern in Contemporary Germany', in A. Goodbody (ed.), *The Culture of German Environmentalism* Oxford: Berghahn, 81–101.

Beaumont, M. J., J. L. Beaumont, P. Arrojo, and E. Bernal (1997). *El embalse de Itoiz: la razón o el poder.* Bilbao: Bakeaz-COAGRET.

Bergstedt, J. (1998). *Agenda, Expo, Sponsering. Recherchen im Naturschutzfilz. Bd. 1: Daten, Fakten, historische Hintergründe.* Frankfurt/M.: Verlag für Interkulturelle Kommunikation.

Biorcio, R. (1998). 'Ambientalismo e politica', in G. Guidorossi (ed.), *Nuovi attori per un pianeta verde.* Milan: Angeli, 63–91.

——(2002). 'Italy', in F. Müller-Rommel and T. Poguntke (eds.), *Greens in National Governments.* London: Frank Cass, 39–62 [also published as a special issue of *Environmental Politics*, 11(1)].

Blühdorn, I. (1995). 'Campaigning for Nature: Environmental Pressure Groups in Germany and Generational Change in the Ecology Movement', in I. Blühdorn, F. Krause, and T. Scharf (eds.), *The Green Agenda: Environmental Politics and Policy in Germany.* Keele, Staffordshire: Keele University Press, 167–220.

Bonacich, P. (1972). 'Factoring and Weighting Approaches to Status Scores and Clique Identification', *Journal of Mathematical Sociology*, 22: 113–20.

Bond J., C. J. Jenkins, C. L. Taylor, and K. Schock (1997). 'Mapping Mass Political Conflict and Civil Society', *Journal of Conflict Resolution,* 41 (4): 553–79.

Borgatti, S. P., M. G. Everett, and L. C. Freeman (1999). *Ucinet 5 for Windows: Software for Social Network Analysis.* Natick: Analytic Technologies.

Bosso, C. (2000). 'Environmental Groups and the New Political Landscape', in N. J. Vig and M. E. Kraft (eds.), *Environmental Policy*, 4th edn. Washington DC: CQ Press, 55–76.

Boström, M. (2001). '*Miljörörelsens mångfald: Organisation, politik och kognitivt handlande'* (The diversity of the environmental movement: Organisation, politics, and cognitive action). Ph.D. dissertation, Stockholm University, Department of Sociology.

Botetzagias, I. (2001). '*The Environmental Movement in Greece, 1973 to the present: An illusory social movement in a semi-peripheral country'.* Ph.D. thesis, SPIRE, Keele University.

Bovin, K. and S. Magnusson (1997). *49 Local Initiatives for Sustainable Development.* Stockholm: Swedish Society for Nature Conservation.

Boy, D., V. Jacques le Seigneur, and A. Roche (1995). *L'Ecologie au pouvoir.* Paris: Presses de Sciences Po.

Brand, K. W. (1993). 'Strukturveränderungen des Umweltdiskurses in Deutschland', *Forschungsjournal Neue Soziale Bewegungen,* 6 (1): 16–24.

——(1999). 'Dialectics of Institutionalization: The Transformation of the Environmental Movement in Germany', *Environmental Politics*, 8 (1): 35–58. Reprinted in Rootes (1999*a*).

Broadbent, J. (1998). *Environmental Politics in Japan: Networks of Power and Protest.* Cambridge: Cambridge University Press.

Bromley, C., J. Curtice, and B. Seyd (2001). 'Political Engagement, Trust and Constitutional Reform', in A. Park, J. Curtice, K. Thomson, L. Jarvis, and C. Bromley (eds.), *British Social Attitudes: The 18th Report.* London: Sage, 199–225.

Brown, P. and F. McDonald (2000). 'Have we "had enough of all that eco-bollox"?', in J. Smith (ed.), *The Daily Globe: Environmental Change, the Public and the Media*. London: Earthscan, 64–78.

Camps, F. (1997). *Iniciativa Legislativa Popular*. Barcelona: Editorial Mediterània.

Carmin, J. (1999). 'Local Activism, National Organizations and the Environmental Movement in the United States', *Environmental Politics*, 8 (1): 101–21. Reprinted in Rootes (1999a).

Casado da Rocha, A. and J. A. Perez (1996). *ITOIZ. Del deber de la Desobediencia Civil al Ecosabotaje*. Pamplona: Pamiela.

Castañer, X. (1998). 'La política industrial. ajustes, nuevas políticas horizontales y privatización', in R. Gomà and J. Subirats (eds.), *Políticas públicas en España*. Barcelona: Editorial Ariel, 79–112.

CEIA (1999). '*A New Model of Environmental Communication for Europe: From Consumption to Use of Information*'. Expert Corner Report, European Environmental Agency.

Charvolin, F. (1993). '*L'invention de l'environnement, 1950–1970*'. Unpublished dissertation, Université de Grenoble.

Chibre, R. P. (1991). '*Les associations écologiques en France et en Allemagne: une analyse culturelle de la mobilization collective*'. Dissertation, Université de Paris II.

Christie, I. and L. Jarvis (2001). 'How Green are our Values?', in A. Park, J. Curtice, K. Thomson, L. Jarvis, and C. Bromley (eds.), *British Social Attitudes: The 18th Report*. London: Sage, 131–57.

Chulia, E. (1995). 'La conciencia ambiental de los Españoles en los noventa'. *ASP Research Paper* 12(a).

CIS (1999). *Barómetro de Marzo*. Estudio 2322.

Clementi, M. (1997). 'I conflitti politici e sociali in Italia nel 1996: un'analisi e alcuni elementi di comparazione', *Quaderni Di Scienza Politica*, 4: 379–427.

Close, D. (1998). 'Environmental NGOs in Greece: The Achelöos campaign as a case study of their influence', *Environmental Politics*, 7 (2): 55–77.

——(1999). 'Environmental Crisis and Recent Challenges to Centralized State authority', *Journal of Modern Greek Studies*, 17 (2): 325–52.

Commission of the European Communities (1992). 'Europeans and the Environment in 1992'. Survey conducted in the context of Euro-barometer 37.0 by INRA (Europe).

——(1996). '*On the implementation of the European Community Programme of Policy and Action in Relation to the Environment and Sustainable Development: "Towards sustainability"*'. Progress report from the Commission, COM(95) 624.

Connelly, J. and G. Smith (1999). *Politics and the Environment*. London and New York: Routledge.

Converse, P. (1990). 'Popular Representation and the Distribution of Information', in J. H. Kuklinski and J. A. Ferejohn (eds.), *Information and Democratic Processes*. Urbana and Chicago: University of Illinois Press.

Cornelsen, D. (1991). *Anwälte der Natur. Umweltschutzverbände in Deutschland*. München: Beck.

Cottle, S. (1993). *TV News, Urban Conflict and the Inner City*. Leicester: Leicester University Press.

Cowell, R. and P. Jehlicka (1995). 'Backyard and Biosphere: The Spatial Distribution of Support for English and Welsh Environmental Organizations', *Area*, 27 (2): 110–17.

Coxall, B. (2001). *Pressure Groups in British Politics*. Harlow: Pearson.

Curtice, J. and R. Jowell (1995). 'The Sceptical Electorate', in R. Jowell et al. (eds.), *British Social Attitudes: The 12th Report*. Aldershot: Dartmouth, 141–72.

Dalton, R. J. (1994). *The Green Rainbow: Environmental Groups in Western Europe*. New Haven and London: Yale University Press.

——(2002). *Citizen Politics: Public Opinion and Political Parties in Advanced Industrial Democracies*, 3rd edn. New York: Chatham House.

——and R. Rohrschneider (1998). 'The Greening of Europe', in R. Jowell et al. (eds.), *British Social Attitudes: The 15th Report*. Aldershot: Ashgate, 101–21.

————(1999). 'Transnational Environmentalism: Cooperation Among Environmental NGOs'. Paper for the ECPR Joint Sessions of Workshops, Mannheim.

Dantzger, H. R. (1975). 'Validating Conflict Data', *American Sociological Review*, 40: 570–84.

Deacon, D. (1996). 'The Voluntary Sector: Changing Communication Environment', *European Journal of Communication*, 11 (2): 173–99.

Dekker, K., M. Diani, A. Jamison, and L. Kvande (1998). 'Representing the Public: New Roles for Environmental Organizations', in A. Jamison (ed.), *Technology Policy Meets the Public. PESTO Papers 2*. Aalborg: Aalborg University Press, 49–79.

della Porta, D. (1996). *Movimenti Politici e Sistema Politico In Italia*. Rome/Bari: Laterza.

——and M. Andretta (2000). 'National Environmental Organizations in the Italian Political System'. Paper presented at the ECPR Joint Sessions (workshop Environmental Organizations in Comparative Perspective), Copenhagen.

————(2002). 'Representing Urban Ecology: Citizens' Committees in Florence', *International Journal of Urban and Regional Research*, 26 (2): 244–65.

——and H. Reiter (eds.) (1998). *Policing Protest: The Control of Mass Demonstrations in Western Democracies*. Minneapolis: University of Minnesota Press.

——O. Fillieule, and H. Reiter (1998). 'Policing Protest in France and Italy: From Intimidation to Cooperation?' in S. Tarrow and D. Meyer (eds.), *The Social Movement Society. Contentious Politics for a New Century*. Boulder: Rowman and Littlefield, 111–30.

Demertzis, N. (1995). 'Greece: Greens at the Periphery', in D. Richardson and C. Rootes (eds.), *The Green Challenge: The Development of Green Parties in Europe*. London and New York: Routledge, 193–207.

Derville, G. (1997). 'Le combat singulier Greenpeace-SIRPA', *Revue française de science politique*, 47 (5): 589–629.

Diani, M. (1990). 'The Italian Ecology Movement: From Radicalism to Moderation', in W. Rüdig (ed.), *Green Politics One*. Edinburgh: Edinburgh University Press, 153–76.

——(1992). 'The Concept of Social Movement', *Sociological Review*, 40 (1): 1–25.

——(1994). 'The Conflict Over Nuclear Energy in Italy', in H. Flam (ed.), *States and Anti-Nuclear Movements*. Edinburgh: Edinburgh University Press, 201–31.

——(1995). *Green Networks: A Structural Analysis of the Italian Environmental Movement*. Edinburgh: Edinburgh University Press.

——(1997). 'Social Movements and Social Capital: A Network Perspective on Movement Outcomes', *Mobilization*, 2 (2): 129–47.

——(2003). 'Networks and Social Movements: A Research Programme', in M. Diani and D. McAdam (eds.), *Social Movements and Networks: Relational Approaches to Collective Action*. Oxford and New York: Oxford University Press, 299–319.

——and P. Donati (1999). 'Organisational Change in Western European Environmental Groups: A Framework for Analysis', *Environmental Politics*, 8 (1): 13–34. Reprinted in

C. Rootes (ed.), *Environmental Movements: Local, National and Global*. London: Frank Cass, 13–34.

Doherty, B. (1999a). 'Paving the Way: The Rise of Direct Action Against Road-building and the Changing Character of British Environmentalism', *Political Studies*, 47 (2): 275–91.

——(1999b). 'Manufactured Vulnerability: Eco-activist Tactics in Britain', *Mobilization*, 4 (1): 75–89.

Donati, P. R. (1996). 'Building a Unified Movement: Resource Mobilization, Media Work, and Organizational Transformation in the Italian Environmentalist Movement', *Research in Social Movements, Conflict and Change*, 19: 125–57.

Dowie, M. (1995). *Losing Ground: American Environmentalism at the Close of the Twentieth Century*. Cambridge, MA: MIT Press.

Downs, A. (1972). 'Up and Down with Ecology: The "Issue Attention Cycle"', *The Public Interest*, 28: 38–50.

Dryzek, J., C. Hunold, and D. Schlosberg, with D. Downes and H.-K. Hernes (2002). 'Environmental Transformations of the State: The USA, Norway, Germany and the UK', *Political Studies*, 50: 659–82.

——D. Downes, C. Hunold, and D. Schlosberg, with H.-K. Hernes (2003). *Green States and Social Movements: Environmentalism in the United States, United Kingdom, Germany, and Norway*. Oxford: Oxford University Press.

Duyvendak, J. (1994). *Le poids du politique, les nouveaux mouvements sociaux en France*. Paris: L'Harmattan.

—— (1995). *The Power of Politics: New Social Movements in France*. Boulder, CO: Westview.

Eder, K. (1996). 'The Institutionalization of Environmentalism: Ecological Discourse and the Second Transformation of the Public Sphere', in S. Lash, B. Szerszynski, and B. Wynne (eds.), *Risk, Environment and Modernity: Towards a New Ecology*. London: Sage, 203–23.

——and M. Kousis (2001). 'Is there a Mediterranean Syndrome?', in K. Eder and M. Kousis (eds.), *Environmental Politics in Southern Europe: Actors, Institutions and Discourses in a Europeanizing Society*. Dordrecht: Kluwer, 393–406.

Ehmke, W. (1998). 'Transformationen der Ökologiebewegung', *Forschungsjournal Neue Soziale Bewegungen*, 11 (1): 142–54.

Eilders, C. (2001). 'Die Darstellung von Protesten in ausgewählten deutschen Tageszeitungen', in D. Rucht (ed.), *Analysen politischen Protests in der Bundesrepublik*. Frankfurt/M.: Campus, 275–311.

Eisinger, P. K. (1973). 'The Conditions of Protest Behavior in American Cities', *American Political Science Review*, 67: 11–28.

Elcacho, J. (1998). 'El periodismo ambiental: bajo el signo de la catástrofe', in AA.VV *Ponencias del II Congreso de Periodismo Ambiental. Madrid, Noviembre 1997*. Madrid: APIA, 59–61.

Elzinga, A., A. Jamison, and C. Mithander (1998). 'Swedish Grandeur: Contending Reformulations of the Great-power Project', in M. Hård and A. Jamison (eds.), *The Intellectual Appropriation of Technology. Discourses on Modernity 1900–1939*. Cambridge, MA: MIT Press.

ENRESA (1998). *Actitudes de los Españoles hacia el medio ambiente (1997–1998)*. Madrid: ENRESA.

Epstein, S. (1996). *Impure Science. AIDS, Activism and the Politics of Knowledge.* Berkeley and Los Angeles: University of California Press.

Escobar, G. (1994). 'Evaluación de impacto ambiental en España: resultados prácticos', *CyTET*, 11 (102): 585–95.

Estevan, A. and A. Sanz (1996). *Hacia la reconversión ecológica del transporte en España.* Bilbao: Bakeaz/Madrid: CCOO. Secretaría de Salud Laboral y Medio Ambiente/Madrid: Los Libros de la Catarata.

Etzioni, A. (1970). *Demonstration Democracy.* New York: Gordon and Breach.

Eyerman, R. and A. Jamison (1991). *Social Movements: A Cognitive Approach.* Cambridge: Polity.

Farro, A. (1991). *La lente verde.* Milan: Angeli.

Faucher, F. (1999). *Les habits verts de la politique.* Paris: Presses de Sciences Po.

Fernández, J. (1995). *Periodismo ambiental en España.* Madrid: MOPTMA.

Festing, S. (1997). 'Friends of the Earth and the Direct Action Movement'. Paper presented at the conference on Direct Action and British Environmentalism, Keele University, 25 October.

Fiddes, N. (1997). 'The March of the Earth Dragon: A New Radical Challenge to Traditional Land Rights in Britain', in P. Milbourne (ed.), *Revealing Rural 'Others'.* London: Cassell, 35–54.

Fidelis-Nogueira, T. (1996). 'Grassroots Environmental Action and Sustainable Development in Portugal', in M. Kousis, S. Aguilar, and T. Fidelis Nogueira, *Grassroots Environmental Action and Sustainable Development in Southern European Union.* Final Report to European Commission, DGXII, Contract No. EV5V-CT94-0393, 5.1–5.53.

Fillieule, O. (1995). 'Methodological Issues in the Collection of Data on Protest Events: Police Records and National Press in France'. Paper presented to conference on Protest Event Analysis, WZB, Berlin.

——— (1996). 'Police Records and the National Press in France: Issues in the Methodology of Data-collections from Newspapers', *EUI Working Papers*, RSC No. 96/25. San Domenico di Fiesole: European University Institute.

——— (1997). *Stratégies de la rue: les manifestations en France.* Paris: Presses de Sciences Po.

Fillieule, O. (1998). 'Plus ça change, moins ça change: Demonstrations in France during the 1980s', in D. Rucht, R. Koopmans, and F. Neidhart (eds.), *Acts of Dissent: New Developments in the Study of Protest.* Berlin: Sigma, 200–26.

——— (1999). 'Plus ça change, moins ça change: Demonstrations in France during the 1980s', in D. Rucht, R. Koopmans, and F. Neidhart (eds.), *Acts of Dissent: New Developments in the Study of Protest.* Lanham, MD: Rowman and Littlefield, 200–26.

——— (2000). 'Dynamics of Commitment in the Sector known as "Solidarity": Methodological Reflections Based on the Case of France', in M. Giugni and F. Passy (eds.), *Political Altruism? The Solidarity Movement in International Perspective.* Lanham, MD: Rowman and Littlefield, 51–66.

——— and J. W. Duyvendak (1999). 'Gay and Lesbian Activism in France: Between Integration and Community-oriented Movements', in B. Adam, J. W. Duyvendak, and A. Krouwel (eds.), *The Global Emergence of Gay and Lesbian Politics.* Philadelphia: Temple University Press, 184–213.

Fillieule, O. and F. Ferrier (1999). 'Some Notes on Methodology: Selection Bias in the French Database on "Environmental Events"'. Paper presented at ECPR Joint Sessions, Mannheim.

——(2000). 'Between the Market and the State: French Environmental Organizations'. Paper presented at ECPR Joint Sessions, Copenhagen.

Flam, H. (ed.) (1994). *States and Anti-nuclear Movements*. Edinburgh: Edinburgh University Press.

Flieger, W. (1992). *Die taz. Vom Alternativblatt zur linken Tageszeitung*. München: Ölschläger.

Flynn, A. and P. Lowe (1992). 'The Greening of the Tories: The Conservative Party and the Environment', in W. Rüdig (ed.), *Green Politics Two*. Edinburgh: Edinburgh University Press, 9–36.

Font, N. (2001). 'La Europeización de la política ambiental: desafíos e inercias', in C. Closa (ed.), *La Europeización del sistema político estatal*. Madrid: Istmo, 380–99.

Forno, F. (forthcoming). '*Protest in Italy 1988–1997*'. Ph.D. Dissertation, University of Strathclyde, Glasgow.

Frankland, E. G. (1990). 'Does Green Politics have a Future in Britain?' in W. Rüdig (ed.), *Green Politics One*. Edinburgh: Edinburgh University Press, 7–28.

——(1995). 'Germany: The Rise, Fall and Recovery of Die Grünen', in D. Richardson and C. Rootes (eds.), *The Green Challenge: The Development of Green Parties in Europe*. London and New York: Routledge, 23–44.

Franzosi, R. (1987). 'The Press as a Source of Socio-historical Data', *Historical Methods*, 20: 12–4.

Freeman, L. C. (1979). 'Centrality in Social Networks: Conceptual Clarification', *Social Networks*, 1: 215–39.

Fuchs, D. and D. Rucht (1994). 'Support for New Social Movements in Five Western European Countries', in C. Rootes and H. Davis (eds.), *A New Europe? Social Change and Political Transformation*. London: UCL Press, 86–111.

Funkhouser, G. R. (1973). 'The Issues of the Sixties: An Exploratory Study in the Dynamics of Public Opinion', *Public Opinion Quarterly*, 37 (1): 62–75.

Gallet, G. (2000). '*L'activisme environnemental: l'exemple de Greenpeace France*'. Unpublished research report for TEA project.

Gamson, W. (1990). *The Strategy of Social Protest*, 2nd edn. Belmont, CA: Wadsworth.

—— and D. S. Meyer (1996). 'Framing Political Opportunity', in D. McAdam, J. D. McCarthy, and M. Zald (eds.), *Comparative Perspectives on Social Movements: Political Opportunities, Mobilizing Structures, and Cultural Framings*. Cambridge: Cambridge University Press, 275–90.

Garavan, M. (2002). 'Patterns of Irish Environmental Activism'. Unpublished paper, Environmental Change Institute, NUI Galway.

Garner, R. (2000). *Environmental Politics: Britain, Europe and the Global Environment*, 2nd edn. Basingstoke: Macmillan and New York: St Martin's.

Gerlach, L. and V. Hine (1970). *People, Power and Change*. Indianapolis: Bobbs-Merrill.

Gil Nave, J. (2000). '*Environmental politics in Portugal*'. Ph.D. thesis, European University Institute, Department of Political and Social Sciences, Florence.

Gitlin, T. (1980). *The Whole World is Watching: The Mass Media in the Making and Unmaking of the New Left*. Berkeley and London: University of California Press.

Giugni, M. (1995). 'The Outcomes of the New Social Movements', in R. Koopmans, J. W. Duyvendak, and M. Giugni, *New Social Movements in Western Europe: A Comparative Analysis*. Minneapolis: University of Minnesota Press; London: UCL Press, 207–37.

—— (1999). 'Le mobilitazioni su pace, ambiente e nucleare: il caso Italiano in prospettiva comparata', *Quaderni di Sociologia*, 43 (21): 45–67.

Gómez, C. and A. Paniagua (1996). 'Caracterización sociodemográfica de la sensibilidad ambiental en España', *ICE*, 751: 128–47.

—— F. J. Noya, and A. Paniagua (1999). *Actitudes y comportamientos hacia el medio ambiente en España*. Madrid: CIS.

Gould, K. A., A. Schnaiberg, and A. S. Weinberg (1996). *Local Environmental Struggles: Citizen Activism in the Treadmill of Production*. Cambridge: Cambridge University Press.

—— A. S. Weinberg, and A. Schnaiberg (1993). 'Legitimating Impotence: Pyrrhic Victories of the Modern Environmental Movement', *Qualitative Sociology*, 16 (3): 207–46.

Grove-White, R. (1992). 'Environmental Debate and Society—The Role of NGOs', *ECOS*, 13 (1): 10–14.

Gundle, S. and S. Parker (eds.) (1996). *The New Italian Republic: From the Fall of the Berlin Wall to Berlusconi*. London and New York: Routledge.

Gunther, R., J. R. Montero, and J. I. Wert (1999). 'The Media and Politics in Spain: From Dictatorship to Democracy'. *ICPS Working Papers*, 176.

Halloran, J. D., P. Elliott, and G. Murdock (1970). *Demonstrations and Communication: a Case Study*. Harmondsworth: Penguin.

Hansen, A. (ed.) (1993). *The Mass Media and Environmental Issues*. Leicester: Leicester University Press.

Hayes, G. (2000). 'Exeunt Chased by Bear: Structure, Action and the Environmental Opposition to the Somport Tunnel', *Environmental Politics*, 9 (2): 126–48.

—— (2002). *Environmental Protest and Policymaking in France*. Basingstoke and New York: Palgrave Macmillan.

Hellmann, K. U. and A. Klein (1994). 'Editorial', *Forschungsjournal Neue Soziale Bewegungen*, 7 (4): 2–9.

Hengsbach, F., R. Bammerlin, C. Dringer, B. Emunds, and M. Möhring-Hesse (1996). *Die Rolle der Umweltverbände in den demokratischen und umweltethischen Lernprozessen der Gesellschaft*. Stuttgart: Metzler-Poeschel.

Hilgartner, S. and C. L. Bosk (1988). 'The Rise and Fall of Social Problems: a Public Arenas Model', *American Journal of Sociology*, 94 (1): 53–78.

Hocke, P. (1996). 'Mass Media and Local Protest: A Case Study of the Selectivity of Print Media', *Forschungsjournal Neue Soziale Bewegungen*, 9 (1): 91–4.

—— (1998). 'Determining the Selection Bias in Local and National Newspaper Reports on Protest Events', in D. Rucht, R. Koopmans, and F. Neidhardt (eds.), *Acts of Dissent*. Berlin: Sigma, 131–63.

—— (1999). 'Determining the Selection Bias in Local and National Newspaper Reports on Protests Events', in D. Rucht, R. Koopmans, and F. Neidhardt (eds.), *Acts of Dissent*. Lanham, MD: Rowman and Littlefield, 131–63.

—— (2002). *'Massenmedien und lokaler Protest. Eine Fallstudie zur Selektivität von Printmedien'*. Wiesbaden: Westdeutscher Verlag.

Hofrichter, J. and K. Reif (1990). 'Evolution of Environmental attitudes in the European Community', *Scandinavian Political Studies*, 13 (2): 119–46.

Hug, S. and D. Wisler (1998). 'Correcting for Selection Bias in Social Movement Research', *Mobilization*, 3 (2): 141–61.

Ibarra, P. and A. Rivas (1996). 'Environmental Public Discourse in the Basque Country: The Conflict of the Leizaran Motorway', *Comparative Social Research*, 2: 139–51.

Imig, D. and S. Tarrow (1999). 'The Europeanization of Movements?', in D. della Porta, H. Kriesi, and D. Rucht (eds.), *Social Movements in a Globalizing World*. London: Macmillan, 112–33.

―――(2001). 'Mapping the Europeanization of Contention', in D. Imig and S. Tarrow (eds.), *Contentious Europeans: Protest and Politics in an Emerging Polity*. Lanham, MD: Rowman and Littlefield, 27–49.

IREF [Istituto di Ricerche Educative e Formative] (1998). *La società civile in Italia: VI rapporto sull'associazionismo sociale*. Rome: Edizioni Lavoro.

Jahn, T. and P. Wehling (1991). *Ökologie von rechts. Nationalismus und Umweltschutz bei den Neuen Rechten und 'Republikanern'*. Frankfurt/M.: Campus.

Jamison, A. (1996). 'The Shaping of the Global Environmental Agenda: The Role of Non-governmental Organizations', in S. Lash, B. Szerszynski, and B. Wynne (eds.), *Risk, Environment and Modernity: Towards a New Ecology*. London: Sage, 224–45.

―――(2001). *The Making of Green Knowledge: Environmental Politics and Cultural Transformation*. Cambridge and New York: Cambridge University Press.

―――and E. Baark (1999). 'National Shades of Green: Comparing the Swedish and Danish Styles in Ecological Modernisation', *Environmental Values*, 8: 199–218.

―――R. Eyerman, J. Cramer with J. Laessoe (1990). *The Making of the New Environmental Consciousness: A Comparative Study of the Environmental Movements in Sweden, Denmark and the Netherlands*. Edinburgh: Edinburgh University Press.

Jänicke, M., P. Kunig, and M. Stifzel (1999). *Lern- und Arbeitsbuch Umweltpolitik*. Bonn: Dietz.

Jehlicka, P. (1994). 'Environmentalism in Europe: An East–West comparison', in C. Rootes and H. Davis (eds.), *Social Change and Political Transformation: A New Europe?* London: UCL Press, 112–31.

Jenkins-Smith, H. C. and P. A. Sabatier (1993). 'The study of public policy processes', in H. C. Jenkins-Smith and P. A. Sabatier (eds.), *Policy Change and Learning: An Advocacy Coalition Approach*. Boulder: Westview Press, 1–9.

Jiménez, M. (1999*a*). 'Consolidation Through Institutionalisation? Dilemmas of the Spanish Environmental Movement in the 1990s', *Environmental Politics*, 8 (1): 149–71. Reprinted in C. Rootes (ed.), *Environmental Movements: Local, National, and Global*. London: Frank Cass.

―――(1999*b*) 'Struggling for the Environment: A Profile of Recent Environmental Protests in Spain'. *Estudio/Working Paper 143*, November. Instituto Juan March de Estudios e Investigaciones.

―――(2000). 'Organising the Defence of the Environment: Spanish Ecologist Groups in the 1990s'. Paper presented at the ECPR Joint Sessions, Copenhagen.

―――(2001). 'Sustainable Development and the Participation of Environmental NGOs in Spanish Environmental Policy: The Case of Industrial Waste Policy', in K. Eder and

M. Kousis (eds.), *Environmental Politics in Southern Europe: Actors, Institutions and Discourses in a Europeanizing Society*. Dordrecht: Kluwer Academic Publishers, 225–53.

——(2002). *Protesta social y políticas públicas: un estudio de la relación entre el movimiento ecologista y la política ambiental en España*. Colección de Tesis Doctorales, No. 34. Madrid: Instituto Juan March.

JNE (1998). (C. M. Vadrot and M. Déjouet). *La place de l'environnement dans les médias*. Paris: Victoires Editions.

Johnston, M. and R. Jowell (1999). 'Social Capital and the Social Fabric', in R. Jowell, J. Curtice, A. Park, K. Thompson, with L. Jarvis, C. Bromley, and N. Stratford (eds.), *British Social Attitudes: The 16th Report*. Aldershot: Ashgate, 179–200.

Joly-Sibuet, S. and P. Lascoumes (1987). *Conflits d'environnement et intérêts protégés par les associations de défense: Aquitaine, Alsace, Bretagne, Rhône-Alpes*. Paris: SRETIE.

Jordan, G. (2001). *Shell, Greenpeace and the Brent Spar*. Basingstoke: Palgrave.

——and W. Maloney (1997). *The Protest Business? Mobilizing Campaign Groups*. Manchester and New York: Manchester University Press.

Jowell, R., J. Curtice, A. Park, L. Brook, K. Thompson, and C. Bryson (eds.), (1997). *British Social Attitudes: The 14th Report*. Aldershot: Ashgate.

—————— and K. Thompson, with L. Jarvis, C. Bromley, and N. Stratford (eds.) (1999). *British Social Attitudes: The 16th Report*. Aldershot: Ashgate.

Jowers, P., J. Dürrschmidt, D. Purdue, and R. O'Doherty (1996). 'DIY Culture in Southwest England'. Paper presented at the Second European Conference on Social Movements, Vitoria-Gasteiz.

Kamieniecki, S. and R. O. Koleman (1995). 'The Effectiveness of Radical Environmentalists', in B. R. Taylor (ed.), *Ecological Resistance Movements*. Albany, NY: State of New York University Press, 315–33.

Karamichas, J. (2001). 'Political Ecology in Southern Europe: A Comparison of Green Party Formation and Development in Greece and Spain'. Paper presented at the First ECPR General Conference, University of Kent at Canterbury.

Kazakos, P. (1999). 'The "Europeanization" of Public Policy: The Impact of European Integration on Greek Environmental Policy', *European Integration*, 21: 369–91.

Kitschelt, H. (1986). 'Political Opportunity Structures and Political Protest: Anti-nuclear Movements in Four Democracies', *British Journal of Political Science*, 16: 57–85.

——(1989). *The Logics of Party Formation: Ecological Politics in Belgium and West Germany*. Ithaca, NY: Cornell University Press.

Klinenberg, E. (2000). 'Information et production numérique', *Actes de la Recherche en Sciences Sociales*, 23: 66–75.

Kolb, F. (1997). 'Der Castor-Konflikt: Das Comeback der Anti-AKW-Bewegung', *Forschungsjournal Neue Soziale Bewegungen*, 10 (3): 16–29.

Kontinen, E., T. Litmanen, M. Nieminen, and M. Ylönen (1999). *All Shades of Green: The Environmentalization of Finnish Society*. SoPhi, University of Jyväskylä.

Koopmans, R. (1993). 'The Dynamics of Protest Waves: West Germany, 1965–1989'. *American Sociological Review*, 58: 637–58.

——(1995). 'Appendix: The Newspaper Data', in H. Kriesi, R. Koopmans, J. W. Duyvendak, and M. Giugni (eds.), *New Social Movements in Western Europe*. Minneapolis: University of Minnesota Press, 253–74.

——(1996). 'New Social Movements and Changes in Political Participation in Western Europe', *West European Politics*, 19 (1): 28–50.

Koopmans, R. and J. W. Duyvendak (1995). 'The Political Construction of the Nuclear Energy Issue and its Impact on the Mobilization of Anti-nuclear Movements in Western Europe', *Social Problems*, 42 (2): 235–51.

Kousis, M. (1997*a*). 'Unraveling Environmental Claim-making at the Roots: Evidence from a Southern European County', *Humanity and Society*, 23 (1): 257–83.

——(1997*b*). 'Grassroots Environmental Movements in Rural Greece: Effectiveness, Success and the Quest for Sustainable Development', in S. Baker, M. Kousis, D. Richardson, and S. Young (eds.), *The Politics of Sustainable Development: Theory, Policy and Practice within the European Union*. London and New York: Routledge, 237–58.

——(1998). 'Ecological Marginalization: Actors, Impacts, Responses', *Sociologia Ruralis*, 38 (1): 86–108.

——(1999). 'Sustaining Local Environmental Mobilisations: Groups, Actions and Claims in Southern Europe', *Environmental Politics*, 8 (1): 172–98. Reprinted in C. Rootes (ed.), *Environmental Movements: Local, National, and Global*. London: Frank Cass.

——(2000). 'Tourism and the Environment: A Social Movements Perspective', *Annals of Tourism Research*, 27 (2): 468–89.

——(2001). 'Competing claims in local environmental conflicts in southern Europe', in K. Eder and M. Kousis (eds.), *Environmental Politics in Southern Europe: Actors, Institutions and Discourses in a Europeanizing Society*. Dordrecht: Kluwer, 129–50.

——(2002). 'Economic Opportunities and Threats in Environmental Contentious Politics: A View from the European South'. Paper presented at the International Conference in honour of Charles Tilly, 'Contentious Politics and the Economic Opportunity Structure', Department of Sociology, University of Crete, Rethimno, October 17–18.

——Dimopoulou, L. (2000). 'Environmental Movement Organizations in Greece: A Comparative Perspective'. Paper presented at the ECPR Joint Sessions (workshop on Environmental Movements in Comparative Perspective), Copenhagen.

——and Eder, K. (2001). 'EU Policy Making, Local Action and the Emergence of Institutions of Collective Action: A Theoretical Perspective on Southern Europe', in K. Eder and M. Kousis (eds.), *Environmental Politics in Southern Europe: Actors, Institutions and Discourses in a Europeanizing Society*. Dordrecht: Kluwer, 3–24.

——and K. Lenaki (1999). 'Protest Events and Environmental Claims in Greece (1988–97): Exploring the Effects of the External Environment'. Paper presented at the ECPR joint sessions (Environmental Protest in Comparative Perspective), Mannheim.

————(2000). 'Major Issues and Socio-political Events in Nea Oikologia, 1988–97'. TEA internal report.

—— S. Aguilar, and T. Fidelis-Nogueira (1996). *Grassroots Environmental Action and Sustainable Development in Southern European Union*. Final report to European Commission, DGXII, Contract No. EV5V-CT94-0393.

——D. della Porta, and M. Jimenez (2001). 'Southern European Environmental Activism: Challenging the "Laggards" Label'. Paper presented at the panel on 'Environmental Politics in Southern Europe', First ECPR General Conference, University of Kent at Canterbury, September 6–8.

—— K. Lenaki, and K. Vlasaki (2000). 'A Systematic Examination of Annual Reviews by *Kathimerini* and when missing by *Eleftherotypia*, 1988–97'. TEA internal report.

Kriesi, H. (1981). *Politische Aktievierung in der Schweiz, 1945–1978*. Diessenhofen: Rüegger.

—— (1993). *Political Mobilization and Social Change. The Dutch Case In Comparative Perspective*. Aldershot: Avebury.

—— R. Koopmans, J. W. Duyvendak, and M. Giugni (1995). *New Social Movements in Western Europe: A Comparative Analysis*. Minneapolis: University of Minnesota Press; London: UCL Press.

Lacey, C. and D. Longman (1993). 'The Press and Public Access to the Environment and Development Debate', *Sociological Review*, 41 (2): 207–43.

Lafferty, W. M. (ed.) (1999). *Implementing LA21 in Europe: New Initiatives for Sustainable Communities*. Oslo: ProSus.

Lahusen, C. (1998). 'Der Dritte Sektor als Lobby. Umweltverbände im Räderwerk der nationalen Politik', in R. von Strachwitz (ed.), *Dritter Sektor, Dritte Kraft. Versuch einer Standortbestimmung*. Düsseldorf: Raabe, 411–36.

Lancaster, T. D. (1989). *Policy Stability and Democratic Change: Energy in Spain's Transition*. University Park, PA and London: Pennsylvania State University Press.

Lascoumes, P. (1985). 'Une sensibilization anecdotique: l'analyse de la presse locale', in *Administrer les pollutions et nuisances, analyse des pratiques sur deux terrains régionaux*. Paris: SRETIE.

—— (1994). *L'eco-pouvoir: environnement et politiques*. Paris: La Découverte.

—— with C. Boulègue and C. Fournier (1993). *L'environnement entre nature et politique: un patchwork mal cousu. Les images de l'environnement et ses politiques dans la presse*. GAPP, CNRS.

Lash, S., B. Szerszynski, and B. Wynne (eds.) (1996). *Risk, Environment and Modernity. Towards a New Ecology*. London: Sage.

Lavdas, K. (1996). 'The Political Economy of Privatisation in Southern Europe', in D. Braddon and D. Foster (eds.), *Privatization*. Aldershot: Dartmouth, 233–60.

Leonhard, M. (1986). *Umweltverbände. Zur Organisation von Umweltschutz interessen in der Bundesrepublik Deutschland*. Opladen: Westdeutscher Verlag.

Lewanski, R. (1997). *Governare l'Ambiente*. Bologna: il Mulino.

Lidskog, R. and I. Elander (2000). 'After Rio: Environmental Policies and Urban Planning in Sweden', in N. Low, R. Lidskog, and I. Elander (eds.), *Consuming Cities*. London: Routledge.

Lieberson, S. and A. R. Silverman (1965). 'The Precipitants and Underlying Conditions of Race Riots', *American Sociological Review*, 30: 343–53.

Linden, A. (1997). 'Man, Culture and Environment'. Paper presented at the ISA & SISWO conference on 'Sociological Theory and the Environment', Woudschoten, The Netherlands, March 20–23.

Linton, M. (2000). *Veganerna—en bok om dom som stör*. Stockholm: ATLAS.

Lofland, J. (1996). *Social Movement Organizations: Guide to Research on Insurgent Realities*. New York: Aldine de Gruyter.

Lowe, P. and S. Ward (1998). 'Britain in Europe: Themes and Issues in National Environmental Policy', in P. Lowe and S. Ward (eds.), *British Environmental Policy and Europe*. London: Routledge, 3–30.

Lundqvist, L. (1996). 'Sweden', in P. Christiansen (ed.), *Governing the Environment. Politics, Policy and Organization in the Nordic Countries*. Copenhagen: Nordic Council of Ministers.

Maresca, B. and O. Zentay (1997). 'Dossier de recherche concernant l'espace régional bas-normand'. Unpublished research report, Paris: CREDOC.

Markovits, A. and P. Gorski (1993). *The German Left: Red, Green and Beyond.* Cambridge: Polity.

Marks, G. and D. McAdam (1999). 'On the Relationship of Political Opportunities to the Form of Collective Action: The Case of the European Union', in D. della Porta, H. Kriesi, and D. Rucht (eds.), *Social Movements in a Globalizing World.* London: Macmillan, 97–111.

Martin, S. and J. Garcia (1996). 'El plan nacional de regadios', *GAIA*, 10: 36–9.

Martínez, J. (1997). *La nueva cultura del agua.* Bilbao: Bakeaz.

Mattout, P. and E. Metayer (1987). *Incidence des médias sur la perception des problèmes d'environnement.* Montréal: GESTE.

McAdam, D. (1982). *Political Process and the Development of Black Insurgency, 1930–1970.* Chicago: University of Chicago Press.

——J. D. McCarthy, and M. N. Zald (eds.) (1996). *Comparative Perspectives on Social Movements: Political Opportunities, Mobilizing Structures and Cultural Framings.* Cambridge: Cambridge University Press.

McCarthy, J. D. and M. Zald (1987). *Social Movements in an Organizational Society.* New Brunswick, NJ: Transaction Books.

——C. McPhail, and J. Smith (1999). 'Media bias in the Coverage of Washington, D.C. Demonstrations', *American Sociological Review*, 61: 478–99.

McCormick, J. (1991). *British Politics and the Environment.* London: Earthscan.

McManus, J. (1994). *Market-driven Journalism: 'Let the Citizen Beware'.* Sage: London.

McNeish, W. (2000a). '*The Anti-roads Protests in Nineties Britain: A Sociological Interpretation'.* Ph.D. thesis, University of Glasgow, Department of Sociology.

——(2000b). 'The Vitality of Local Protest: Alarm UK and the British Anti-roads Protest Movement', in B. Seel, M. Paterson, and B. Doherty (eds.), *Direct Action in British Environmentalism.* London: Routledge, 183–98.

McPhail, C. and R. T. Wohlstein (1983). 'Individual and Collective Behavior Within Gatherings, Demonstrations and Riots', *Annual Review of Sociology*, 9: 579–600.

McQuail, D. (1991). 'Mass Media in the Public Interest: Towards a Framework of Norms for Media Performance', in J. Curran and M. Gurevitch (eds.), *Mass Media and Society.* London: Edward Arnold, 68–81.

Milbrath, L. (1984). *Environmentalists: Vanguard for a New Society.* Albany, NY: State University of New York Press.

Molotch, H. and M. Lester (1975). 'Accidental News: The Great Oil Spill as Local Occurrence and National Event', *American Journal of Sociology*, 81 (2): 235–60.

Mueller, C. (1997). 'Media Measurement Models of Protest Event Data', *Mobilization*, 2 (2): 165–84.

Neidhart, F. and D. Rucht (1992). 'Towards a Movement Society? On the Possibilities of Institutionalizing Social Movements'. Paper presented at the First European Conference on Social Movements and Societies in Transition, Berlin.

Neveu, E. (1999). 'Médias, mouvements sociaux, espaces publics', *Réseaux*, 17 (98): 17–85.

——(2000). 'The Local Press and Farmers' Protests in Brittany: Proximity and Distance in the Local Newspaper Coverage of a Social Movement', *Journalism Studies* 1: 53–67.

North, P. (1998). '"Save our Solsbury!" The Anatomy of an Anti-roads Protest', *Environmental Politics*, 7 (3): 1–25.

Ollitrault, S. (1996). *Action collective et construction identitaire: le cas du militantisme écologiste en France.* Dissertation, Université de Rennes I.

Olzack, S. (1989). 'Analysis of Events in the Study of Collective Action', *Annual Review of Sociology,* 15: 119–41.

Opp, K. D. (1996). 'Aufstieg und Niedergang der Ökologiebewegung in der Bundesrepublik', in A. Diekmann and C. Jaeger (eds.), *Umweltsoziologie* (Special issue 36 of KZfSS). Opladen: Westdeutscher Verlag, 350–79.

Osti, G. (1998). *La natura, gli altri, la societa : il terzo settore per l'ambiente in Italia.* Milan: Angeli.

Parry, G., G. Moyser, and N. Day (1992). *Political Participation in Britain.* Cambridge: Cambridge University Press.

Paterson, M. (2000). 'Swampy Fever: Media Constructions and Direct Action Politics', in B. Seel, M. Paterson, and B. Doherty (eds.), *Direct Action in British Environmentalism.* London and New York: Routledge, 151–66.

Perrow, C. (1997). 'Organizing for Environmental Destruction', *Organization and the Environment,* 10 (1): 66–72.

Plows, A. (1997). 'Roads Protest/Earth First! and "Multi-issue" New Social Movements: Beyond the Dualisms of the "Red/Green" Debate', in C. Barker and M. Tyldesley (eds.), *Alternative Futures and Popular Protest 3*, Conference Proceedings Vol. II, Manchester Metropolitan University.

Poggio, A. (1996). *Ambientalismo.* Milan: Editrice Bibliografica.

Prendiville, B. (1994). *Environmental Politics in France.* Boulder, San Francisco, and Oxford: Westview.

Preston, P. W. (1997). *Political Cultural Identity.* London: Sage.

Pridham, G. (2001). 'Tourism Policy and Sustainability in Italy, Spain and Greece', in K. Eder and M. Kousis (eds.), *Environmental Politics in Southern Europe: Actors, Institutions and Discourses in a Europeanizing Society.* Dordrecht: Kluwer, 365–92.

Pronier, R. and V. Jacques le Seigneur (1992). *Génération verte: les écologistes en politique.* Paris: Presses de la renaissance.

Putnam, R. D. (1993). *Making Democracy Work: Civic Traditions in Modern Italy.* Princeton, NJ: Princeton University Press.

Radtke, I. (1997). 'Old and New Forms of Environmental Protest Within the EU: The New Anti-roads Movement'. Paper prepared for the workshop on 'Environmental Movements', European Consortium for Political Research Joint Sessions, Bern.

Rawcliffe, P. (1998). *Environmental Pressure Groups in Transition.* Manchester: Manchester University Press.

Reising, U. (1999). 'United in Opposition? A Cross-national Time-series Analysis of European Protest in Three Selected Countries, 1980–1995', *Journal of Conflict Resolution,* 43 (3): 317–42.

Réseaux (1996). 'Le temps de l'évènement' (I et II), 75–76.

Ribeiro, T. and V. Rodrigues (1997). 'The Evolution of Sustainable Development Policy in Portugal', *Environmental Politics,* 6 (1): 108–30.

Rink, D. (with assistance of S. Gerber) (2001). 'Institutionalization in lieu of mobilization: The Environmental Movement on Eastern Germany', in H. Flam (ed.), *Pink, Purple and Green: Women's, Religious, Environmental and Gay/Lesbian Movements in Central Europe Today.* Eastern European Monographs.

Rivasi, M. and H. Crié (1998). *Ce nucléaire qu'on nous cache*. Paris: Albin Michel.

Robinson, N. (2000). 'The Politics of the Car: The Limits of Actor-centred Models of Agenda Setting', in B. Seel, M. Paterson, and B. Doherty (eds.), *Direct Action in British Environmentalism*. London: Routledge, 119–217.

Roose, J. (1999). 'Is the European Court of Justice a Political Opportunity for the German Environmental Movement?'. Paper presented at the 4th European Sociological Association Conference, Amsterdam, August 18–21.

Rootes, C. (1992). 'The New Politics and the New Social Movements: Accounting for British Exceptionalism', *European Journal of Political Research*, 22 (2): 171–91.

——(1995a) 'Britain: Greens in a Cold Climate', in D. Richardson and C. Rootes (eds.), *The Green Challenge: The Development of Green Parties in Europe*. London and New York: Routledge, 66–90.

——(1995b). 'Environmental Consciousness, Institutional Structures and Political Competition in the Formation and Development of Green Parties', in D. Richardson and C. Rootes (eds.), *The Green Challenge: The Development of Green Parties in Europe*. London and New York: Routledge, 232–52.

——(1997a). 'Shaping Collective Action: Structure, Contingency and Knowledge', in R. Edmondson (ed.), *The Political Context of Collective Action*. London and New York: Routledge, 81–104.

——(1997b). 'Environmental Movements and Green Parties in Western and Eastern Europe', in M. Redclift and G. Woodgate (eds.), *International Handbook of Environmental Sociology*. Cheltenham and Northampton, MA: Edward Elgar, 319–48.

——(1997c). 'From Resistance to Empowerment: The Struggle Over Waste Management and its Implications for Environmental Education', in N. Russell et al. (eds.), *Technology, The Environment and Us*. London: IRNES/Graduate School of the Environment, Imperial College, 30–39.

——(ed.) (1999a). *Environmental Movements: Local, National and Global*. London and Portland, OR: Frank Cass.

——(1999b). 'The Transformation of Environmental Activism: Activists, Organisations and Policy-making', *Innovation: The European Journal of Social Sciences*, 12 (2): 153–73.

——(1999c). 'Political Opportunity Structures: Promise, Problems and Prospects', *La Lettre de la Maison Française d'Oxford*, 10: 75–97.

——(1999d). 'Acting Locally, Thinking Globally?' *Environmental Politics*, 8 (1): 290–310. Reprinted in C. Rootes (ed.), *Environmental Movements: Local, National and Global*. London: Frank Cass, 290–310.

——(2000). 'Environmental Protest in Britain, 1988–1997', in B. Seel, M. Paterson and B. Doherty (eds.), *Direct Action in British Environmentalism*. London and New York: Routledge, 25–61.

——(2001). 'Discourse, Opportunity or Structure? The Development and Outcomes of Local Mobilisations Against Waste Incinerators in England'. Paper presented at European Consortium for Political Research Joint Sessions, Grenoble. http://www.essex.ac.uk/ecpr/jointsessions/grenoble/papers/ws10/rootes2.pdf.

——(2002a). 'The Europeanisation of Environmentalism', in R. Balme, D. Chabanet, and V. Wright (eds.), *Action Collective en Europe*. Paris: Presses de Sciences Po, 377–404.

——(2003a). 'The Resurgence of Protest and the Revitalisation of British Democracy', in P. Ibarra (ed.), *Social Movements and Democracy*. New York: Palgrave Macmillan, 137–68.

—— (2003*b*). 'Environmental Movements', in D. Snow, S. Soule, and H. Kriesi (eds.), *Blackwell Companion to Social Movements*. Oxford and Malden, MA: Blackwell.

—— (2004). 'Is there a European Environmental Movement?', in B. Baxter, J. Barry, and R. Dunphy (eds.), *Europe, Globalisation, and the Challenge of Sustainability*. London and New York: Routledge.

—— and A. Miller (2000). 'The British Environmental Movement: Organisational Field and Network of Organisations'. Paper presented at European Consortium for Political Research Joint Sessions, Copenhagen. http://www.essex.ac.uk/ecpr/jointsessions/Copenhagen/papers/ws5/rootes_miller.pdf.

—— D. Adams, and C. Saunders (2001). 'Local Environmental Politics in England: Environmental Activism in South-east London and East Kent Compared'. Paper presented at European Consortium for Political Research Joint Sessions, Grenoble. http://www.essex.ac.uk/ecpr/jointsessions/grenoble/papers/ws10/rootes1.pdf.

Roth, R. (1994). *Demokratie von unten. Neue soziale Bewegungen auf dem Wege zur politischen Institution*. Köln: Bund.

—— and D. Murphy (1998). 'From Competing Factions to the Rise of the Realos', in M. Mayer and J. Ely (eds.), *The German Greens: Paradox Between Movement and Party*. Philadelphia: Temple Press, 49–71.

Rothenberg, D. (1995). 'Have a Friend for Lunch: Norwegian Radical Ecology Versus Tradition', in B. Taylor (ed.), *Ecological Resistance Movements. The Global Emergence of Radical and Popular Environmentalism*. Albany, NY: State University of New York Press, 201–18.

Rucht, D. (1989). 'Environmental Movement Organizations in West Germany and France: Structure and Interorganizational Relations', in B. Klandermans (ed.), *Organizing for Change: Social Movement Organizations Across Cultures*. Greenwich, CT: JAI Press, 61–94.

—— (1991). 'Von der Bewegung zu Institution? Organisationsstrukturen der Ökologiebewegung', in R. Roth and D. Rucht (eds.), *Neue soziale Bewegungen in der Bundesrepublik Deutschland*. Frankfurt/M.: Campus, 334–58.

—— (1993). ' "Think Globally, Act Locally"? Needs, Forms and Problems of Cross-national Environmental Groups', in J. Liefferink, P. Lowe, and A. Mol (eds.), *European Integration and Environmental Policy*. London: Belhaven, 75–95.

—— (1994). 'The Anti-nuclear Power Movement and the State in France', in H. Flam (ed.), *States and Anti-nuclear Movements*. Edinburgh: Edinburgh University Press, 129–62.

—— (1997). 'Limits to Mobilization: Environmental Policy for the European Union', in J. Smith, C. Chatfield, and R. Pagnucco (eds.), *Transnational Social Movements and Global Politics: Solidarity Beyond the State*. Syracuse, NY: Syracuse University Press, 195–213.

—— (1999). *Transformation of Environmental Activism—Workpackage 1: Environmental Protests—Codebook and Practical Guide*. Canterbury: Centre for the Study of Social and Political Movements, University of Kent at Canterbury.

—— (2001). 'Lobbying or Protest? Strategies to Influence EU Environmental Policies', in D. Imig and S. Tarrow (eds.), *Contentious Europeans: Protest and Politics in an Emerging Polity*. Lanham, MD: Rowman and Littlefield, 125–42.

—— and R. Koopmans (eds.) (1999). 'Special Issue on Protest Event Analysis', *Mobilization*, 4 (2): 123–256.

Rucht, D. and F. Neidhardt (1999). 'Methodological Issues in Collecting Protest Event Data: Units of Analysis, Sources and Sampling, Coding Problems', in D. Rucht, R. Koopmans, and F. Neidhardt (eds.), *Acts of Dissent: New Developments in the Study of Protest*. Lanham, MD: Rowman and Littlefield, 65–89.

—— and Ohlemacher T. (1992). 'Protest Event Data: Collection, Uses and Perspectives', in R. Eyerman and M. Diani (eds.), *Issues in Contemporary Social Movement Research*. Beverly Hills: Sage, 76–106.

—— and Roose, J. (1999). 'The German Environmental Movement at a Crossroads?' *Environmental Politics*, 8 (1): 59–80. Reprinted in Rootes (1999*a*).

—————(2001*a*). 'Neither Decline nor Sclerosis: The Organisational Structure of the German Environmental Movement', *West European Politics*, 24 (4): 55–81.

—————(2001*b*). 'The Transformation of Environmental Activism in Berlin'. Paper presented at the ECPR Joint Sessions, Grenoble.

—— B. Blattert, and D. Rink (1997). *Soziale Bewegungen auf dem Weg zur Institutionalisierung: Zum Strukturwandel alternativer Gruppen in beiden Teilen Deutschlands*. Frankfurt/M.: Campus.

—— R. Koopmans and F. Neidhardt (eds.) (1998). *Acts of Dissent: New Developments in the study of Protest*. Berlin: Sigma.

——————(eds.) (1999). *Acts of Dissent: New Developments in the Study of Protest*. Lanham, MD: Rowman and Littlefield.

Rüdig, W. (1995). 'Between Moderation and Marginalization: Environmental Radicalism in Britain', in B. Taylor (ed.), *Ecological Resistance Movements*. Albany, NY: State University of New York Press, 219–40.

—— P. Lowe (1986). 'The Withered "Greening" of British Politics', *Political Studies*, 34 (2): 262–84.

—— L. Bennie, and M. Franklin (1991). *Green Party Members: A Profile*. Glasgow: Delta.

Rule, J. and C. Tilly (1972). '1830 and the Unnatural History of Revolution', *Journal of Social Issues*, 28 (1): 49–76.

Ruzza, C. (1996). 'Inter-organizational Negotiations in Political Decision-making: Brussels' EC Bureaucrats and the Environment', in C. Samson and N. South (eds.), *The Social Construction of Social Policy*. Basingstoke: Macmillan; New York: St Martin's Press, 210–23.

Sainteny, G. (1992). '*La constitution de l'écologisme comme enjeu politique en France: mobilization des ressources et stratégies des acteurs'*. Dissertation, Université de Paris I.

—— (2000). *L'introuvable écologisme français?* Paris: PUF.

Sandman, P. M., D. B. Sachsman, M. R. Greenberg, M. Gochfeld, and S. Dundwoody (1987). *Environmental Risk and the Press: An Exploratory Assessment*. New Brunswick, NJ: Transaction Books.

Santamarta, J. (1998). 'Turismo y medio ambiente', *GAIA*, 14: 48–51.

Schlesinger, A. (1990). 'Rethinking the Sociology of Journalism: Sources Strategies and the Limits of Media Centrism', in M. Ferguson (ed.), *Public Communication: The New Imperatives*. London: Sage, 61–83.

Schlosberg, D. (1999). 'Networks and Mobile Arrangements: Organisational Innovation in the U.S. Environmental Justice Movement', *Environmental Politics*, 8 (1): 122–48. Reprinted in Rootes (1999*a*).

Schnaiberg, A. (1994). 'The Political Economy of Environmental Problems and Policies: Consciousness, Conflict, and Control Capacity', *Advances in Human Ecology*, 3: 23–64.

Seel, B. (1997a). 'Strategies of Resistance at the Pollok Free State Road Protest Camp', *Environmental Politics*, 6 (3): 108–39.

——(1997b). ' "If Not You, Then Who?" Earth First! in the UK', *Environmental Politics*, 6 (3): 172–79.

Simon, H. and D. Wisler (1998). 'How to Correct Media Bias?', *Mobilization*, 3 (2): 141–61.

Singh, R. P. N, V. K. Dubey, and K. N. Pandney (1989). 'Mass Media and the Environmental Issues—A Case of India'. Paper presented to the conference of the International Association for Mass Communications Research.

Sklair, L. (1995). 'Social Movements and Global Capitalism', *Sociology*, 29: 495–512.

Smyth, J. (1998). 'Nacionalismo, globalizacion y movimientos sociales', in P. Ibarra and B. Tejerina (eds.) *Movimientos sociales, transformaciones politicas y cambio cultural*. Madrid: Trotta, 321–36.

Snow, D. A. and R. D. Benford (1992). 'Master Frames and Cycles of Protest', in A. D. Morris and C. M. Mueller (eds.), *Frontiers in Social Movements Theory*. New Haven and London: Yale University Press, 133–55.

Snyder, D. and W. R. Kelly (1977). 'Conflict Intensity, Media Sensitivity and the Validity of Newspaper Data', *American Sociological Review*, 42: 105–23.

——and C. Tilly (1972). 'Hardship and Collective Violence in France, 1830–1960', *American Sociological Review*, 37: 520–32.

Spanou, C. (1991). *Fonctionnaires et militants, l'administration et les nouveaux mouvements sociaux*. Paris: L'Harmattan.

Spears, R., J. van der Plight, and R. Reiser (1987). 'Sources of Evaluation of Nuclear and Renewable Energy Contained in the Local Press', *Journal of Environmental Psychology*, 7: 31–43.

Spilerman, S. (1970). 'The Causes of Racial Disturbances: A Comparison of Alternatives Explications', *American Sociological Review*, 35: 627–49.

——(1976). 'Structural Characteristics of Cities and the Severity of Racial Disorders', *American Sociological Review*, 41(5): 771–93.

Statham, P. (1997). 'Telling Tales: Constructing and Using Political Opportunities Through Media Discourse'. Paper presented at the workshop on 'Environmental Movements', European Consortium for Political Research Joint Sessions, Bern.

Subirats, J. and R. Gomà (1998). 'Democratización, dimensiones de conflicto y políticas públicas en España', in R. Gomà and J. Subirats (eds.), *Politicas Públicas en España*. Barcelona: Editorial Ariel, 13–20.

Szasz, A. (1994). *Ecopopulism: Toxic Waste and the Movement of Environmental Justice*. Minneapolis: University of Minnesota Press.

Tarrow, S. (1989). *Democracy and Disorder: Protest and Politics in Italy 1965–1975*. Oxford: Clarendon Press.

——(1994). *Power in Movement: Social Movements, Collective Action and Politics*. Cambridge, New York, and Melbourne: Cambridge University Press.

——(1995). 'The Europeanization of Conflict: Reflections from a Social Movement Perspective', *West European Politics*, 18 (2): 223–51.

Tarrow, S. (1999). 'Studying Contentious Politics: From Event-full History to Cycles of Collective Action', in D. Rucht, R. Koopmans, and F. Neidhart (eds.), *Acts of Dissent: New Developments in the Study of Protest*. Lanham, MD: Rowman and Littlefield, 33–64.

Thomson, K. and N. Robins (1994). 'On the Path to Sustainable Development? The Post-Rio Environment Agenda', *ECOS*, 15 (1): 3–11.

Tilly, C. (1994). 'Social Movements as Historically Specific Clusters of Political Performances', *Berkeley Journal of Sociology*, 38: 1–30.

——(1995). 'Contentious Repertoires in Great Britain, 1758–1834', in M. Traugott (ed.), *Repertoires and Cycles of Collective Action*. Durham, NC and London: Duke University Press.

——(2002). 'Event Catalogs as Theories', *Sociological Theory*, 20 (2): 248–54.

——L. Tilly, and R. Tilly (1975). *The Rebellious Century, 1830–1930*. Cambridge, MA: Harvard University Press.

Tsakiris, K. and K. Sakellaropoulos (1998). 'The Social Profile, Policies and Action of Non-governmental Nature and Environmental Organizations in Greece'. Paper presented at the international conference on 'Environmental Movements, Discourses, and Policies in Southern Europe', Department of Sociology, University of Crete.

Underwood, D. (1993). *When MBAs Rule the Newsroom*. New York: Columbia University Press.

Vadrot, C. M. and M. Dejouet (1998). *La place de l'environnement dans les médias*. Paris: Victoires Éditions.

van der Heijden, H. A. (1997). 'Political Opportunity Structure and the Institutionalisation of the Environmental Movement', *Environmental Politics*, 6 (4): 25–50.

——R. Koopmans, and M. Giugni (1992). 'The West European Environmental Movement', *Research in Social Movements, Conflicts and Change* (Supp. 2): 1–40.

Vega, P. (1993). 'El plan director de infraestructuras: un impedimento para la movilidad sostenible', *Ciudad y Territorio*, 97: 375–84.

Villalba, B. (1995). *De l'identité des Verts: essai sur la constitution d'un nouvel acteur politique*. Dissertation, Université de Lille II.

Vonkemann, G. (2000). 'Transformation of Environmental Activism: A Dutch Contribution'. Brussels: Institute for European Environmental Policy.

Wall, D. (1999a). *Earth First! and the Origins of the Anti-roads Movement*. London and New York: Routledge.

——(1999b). 'Mobilising Earth First! in Britain', *Environmental Politics*, 8 (1): 81–100. Reprinted in Rootes (1999a).

——B. Doherty, and A. Plows (2002). 'Capacity Building in the British Direct Action Environmental Movement'. Paper for the workshop on 'Direct action at local level', Manchester, June 25. Keele: SPIRE, Keele University.

Wanderer, J. J. (1969). 'An Index of Riot Severity and Some Correlates', *American Journal of Sociology*, 74: 500–05.

Ward, S. and P. Lowe (1998). 'National Environmental Groups and Europeanisation: A Survey of the British Environmental Lobby', *Environmental Politics*, 7 (4): 155–65.

Weatherford, M. S. (1992). 'Measuring Political Legitimacy', *American Political Science Review*, 86 (1): 149–65.

Weidner, H. (1995). '25 Years of Modern Environmental Policy in Germany: Treading a Well-worn Path to the Top of the International Field'. Discussion Paper FS II 95–301. Berlin: Wissenschaftszentrum Berlin.

Welsh, I. (2000). *Mobilising Modernity: The Nuclear Moment.* London and New York: Routledge.

Wey, K. G. (1982). *Umweltpolitik in Deutschland. Kurze Geschichte des Umweltschutzes in Deutschland seit 1900.* Opladen: Westdeutscher Verlag.

Wisler, D. (1999). 'La couverture médiatique de l'action protestataire: étude à partir du cas Suisse', *Revue Française de Sociologie* 40: 121–38.

Wissenschaftlicher Beirat der Bundesregierung Globale Umweltveränderungen (1995). *Welt im Wandel: Wege zur Lösung globaler Umweltprobleme.* Heidelberg: Springer.

Wörndl, B. and G. Fréchet (1994). 'Institutionalization Tendencies in Ecological Movements', in S. Langlois with T. Caplow, H. Mendras, and W. Glatzer (eds.), *Convergence and Divergence? Comparing Recent Social Trends in Industrial Societies.* Frankfurt/M.: Campus; Montreal: McGill-Queen's University Press, 247–68.

Index